CHAUCER

AND THE

LATE MEDIEVAL WORLD

Lillian M. Bisson

St. Martin's Press

CHAUCER AND THE LATE MEDIEVAL WORLD
Copyright © Lillian M. Bisson, 1998

ISBN 0-312-22466-4

Library of Congress Cataloging-in-Publication Data
Bisson, Lillian M., 1941-
    Chaucer and the late medieval world / Lillian M. Bisson.
        p.   cm.
    Includes bibliographical references and index.
    ISBN 0-312-10667-X (cloth)   ISBN 0-312-22466-4 (paper)
    1. Chaucer, Geoffrey, d. 1400—Political and social views.
    2. Chaucer, Geoffrey, d. 1400—Contemporary England.
    3. Civilizations, Medieval, in literature. 4. England—Social
    conditions—1066-1485. 5. Social history—Medieval, 500-1500.
    6. Fourteenth century. I. Title.
    PR1933.S59B57 1998
    821'.1—dc21   98-5802
                                                                   CIP

Design by Orit Mardkha-Tenzer

First edition: May, 1998
First paperback edition: December, 1999
10 9 8 7 6 5 4 3 2 1

For Art,

Oh my beloved,
I live in the fleeting shadow of your wings.

—"A Gust,"
Rachel Hadas

Contents

Acknowledgments

I would like to express my appreciation to the National Endowment for the Humanities, which funded the two institutes that were the seedbed for this book and to the enthusiastic and tireless teachers who participated in the institutes. Special thanks go to Jo Ann Hoeppner Moran-Cruz of Georgetown University, who provided historical expertise at the institutes and who read this manuscript in its early stages. Much of the credit goes to her for historical insights and nuances; the errors that remain are entirely my own.

I am also indebted to Marymount University for the support it provided during a sabbatical semester and to my family and friends for their ongoing interest and encouragement. Finally, I owe gratitude to the entire body of Chaucer scholarship within which I have been navigating for many years.

Preface

Sometimes in reading Chaucer's *Canterbury Tales* and other medieval texts we experience a comfortingly familiar glimpse into our own origins; at others we sense a disturbing otherness as invisible barriers undercut our attempts at gaining insight. For the late medieval world can provide a contemporary audience the "shock of recognition" suggested by Barbara Tuchman's concept of that era as "a distant mirror" of our world. But it can also appear as Stephen Medcalf's "half-alien culture" (*The Later Middle Ages* 1), which unpredictably closes the door on our understanding, leaving us with the impression that we are missing something without being sure what it is.

The recent explosion of scholarly interest in medieval studies compounds the difficulty, especially since new and often revisionist insights constantly emerge. In its first phase twentieth-century medieval scholarship challenged some of the negative stereotypes about the period. But it tended to concentrate on official literate culture and to portray the era as univocal and hegemonic, communicating only the single voice of a dominating Church, a voice echoed by undifferentiated masses sharing a common faith. In this view Christianity achieves equilibrium in the thirteenth century, when it brings together into a harmonious whole all the elements of its complex belief system—what is known as "the Gothic synthesis." Supreme examples of that synthesis are Thomas Aquinas's comprehensive theology/philosophy as expressed in the *Summa Theologica*, Dante's *The Divine Comedy*, and the Gothic cathedral itself.

Many contemporary scholars now pay increased attention to unofficial culture and look at previously neglected sources for their insights: at the traces of oral culture, at the marginalia on manuscripts, at overlooked court and church records, at the underside of misericords. Their work has yielded a more complicated and nuanced understanding of the era: they increasingly recognize how long the Christianization process took and how thinly Christianity penetrated the consciousness of the average person who—particularly in rural areas—continued to cling to age-old folk beliefs and practices long after Christianity had nominally established itself as the dominant religion. From this revisionist perspective the medieval period reveals itself as a messier, more contentious time than the earlier model suggests.

Both the traditional and the revisionist views of medieval culture agree in seeing the fourteenth century, Chaucer's Late Gothic world, as a time when profoundly unsettling changes—major paradigm shifts—were under way. The former sees decline and increasing crackle on a formerly smooth canvas; the latter argue that the canvas was never smooth in the first place. In any case, it was a time when—depending on one's angle of vision—one can see the fading of a thousand-year-old culture or the sprouting seeds of a new one. In sum, by that time whatever synthesis had held Christian culture together became increasingly precarious as the medieval world yielded to the early modern one. For this period was a turning point in Western culture, a time when old assumptions were collapsing and new ones struggling to form. The period witnessed increasing assaults on the teachings and structures of orthodox religion, threats to the existing socio-political order, doubts about the validity of old ideals, and fundamental questions about the meaning of human existence.

Chaucer's work affords an excellent window on the era because he straddled the external world of business and politics and the inner world of philosophic and poetic insight. His life intersected with major historical turning points: the ravages of the Black Death, the Avignon papacy and the Great Schism, the Hundred Years' War, the Peasants' Revolt, the growth of a money economy, the rise of the Wycliffite heresy, anxiety about gender roles and stereotypes, and the shift to an increasingly literate culture. Much twentieth-century criticism has portrayed him as ironically detached from the issues these changes sparked in his world. But the surge of interest in historical criticism has focused more attention on his overall social and political attitudes, and scholars have recognized that his apparent detachment is deceptive. As John Ganim observes,

> current studies, some very conservative and some methodologically radical in their approach, have given us a Chaucer much more deeply implicated in fourteenth-century controversy, particularly the crises of schism, rebellion and authority that plagued fourteenth century England. This is a position which Chaucer studies had avoided for a very long time. . . . The presumption of a Chaucer, or a Chaucerian text, serenely removed from crisis and disruption is one rarely held now. ("Chaucer and the Noise of the People" 303)

Traveling widely on the Continent, Chaucer absorbed a variety of cultural influences. He spent busy days in the world of affairs, but he also retreated into a mental world filled with ancient authorities and contemporary poets. His own poetry was a way of exploring—and inviting his audience to explore—the conflicting realities he confronted in his world. The questions he asked himself were not new, but they asserted themselves with special urgency in his era: What constitutes true nobility? How can society best be governed? To what extent are people able to control their own destinies? What is the value of human love? How should men and women relate to each other? What can a person really know? What kind of life assures one's salvation? How does one balance authority against one's lived experience?

No consensus has emerged, however, about just how Chaucer answered these questions and just where his loyalties lay. The interpretive challenges his work, especially *The Canterbury Tales,* poses are formidable. Foremost among these is that the *Tales* is clearly unfinished—very much a work-in-progress at the time of his death in 1400. Furthermore, no existing manuscript dates back to his own time; the earliest ones—from the fifteenth century—reveal considerable disarray and uncertainty even about the intended order of the tales. Also, Chaucer included in this story collection some pieces he had written prior to his plan for writing the *Tales* and which he modified very little or not at all, others that he adapted for inclusion into the collection, and still others that he wrote specifically for the context in which they appear. Other problems abound: the work consists of a series of very diverse tales—representing an encyclopedic array of medieval genres—each demanding to be seen through a variety of lenses: the expectations created by its genre, its degree of connection to the character who tells it, its treatment of repeated themes or motifs, and its place in the overall work, especially in light of the apocalyptic—or moralistic—implications of the pilgrimage framework and the concluding "Parson's Tale." Finally, Chaucer provides few clear-cut intratextual clues about his intended meaning: his narrator pointedly assumes the role of a detached reporter, a not-too-bright observer who faithfully records what he sees and what others say without attempting to assess or pass judgment.

Chaucer explores the questions that intrigued him through the multiple narrative frames of *The Canterbury Tales* in the form of themes that appear, reappear in a new context, and fold back on themselves from yet another perspective. John Leyerle compares the *Tales's* thematic pattern to the interlaces found in medieval art ("Thematic Interlaces in *The Canterbury Tales*" 108-9). In the decorative arts of the early medieval period linear patterns twist and curve and turn back upon themselves until they fill every available space. Similarly, Chaucer creates a complex pattern by interweaving materials and motifs from a broad spectrum of medieval culture. His choice of a pilgrimage as the framing device for the *Tales* brilliantly captures the complexities of his world, allowing him to juxtapose the voices and worldviews of characters across a broad social spectrum. Only a framework that recognizes multiple, conflicting voices could do justice to his complex vision. As Peter Brown and Andrew Butcher suggest in *The Age of Saturn,*

> Chaucer had an unusually assimilative, syncretic and integrative imagination, but he lived at a time of disintegrating social and religious forms and values. He is not a poet who chose to "rise above" such circumstances; rather he wrote works which articulate and analyze, sometimes in coded form, the specific problems which he and his society faced. His tendency was not to offer easy solutions, but to provoke, air and sustain debate, often by adopting the point of view of a Christian radical. (9-10)

The close connection between audience and poet in Chaucer's milieu afforded him the opportunity to directly engage his auditors and readers with the issues with which he was grappling. His poetry was part of an ongoing cultural conversation; it was, as Craig Berry comments, "a form of negotiation with the world of negotiations represented in it" ("The King's Business" 239). Late twentieth century readers who attempt to enter into that conversation often find themselves lacking the underpinnings that would render it meaningful.

This book has its roots in two exhausting, exhilarating National Endowment for the Humanities institutes for secondary-school teachers. The institutes sought to provide a rich cultural context for approaching *The Canterbury Tales* by juxtaposing historical topics against relevant aspects of Chaucer's life and work. Similarly, this book seeks to foster understanding of the societal contexts Chaucer is exploring; it aims to help readers better understand the overall framework for the major issues that underlie his work. After an introductory section that explores the nature of the intellectual world Chaucer inherited and his conception of his task as a poet, the book falls into three main sections—religion, class and commerce, and gender and sexuality— all areas of medieval life that were experiencing significant paradigmatic shifts in the late medieval world. Each chapter is essentially funnel shaped, starting from a discussion of the topic in its seminal phase, usually the early Christian period. A broad-ranging historical overview follows, leading to a consideration of the topic in a late medieval context and, more specifically, in the context of Chaucer's immediate milieu and of his works. Though I have not tried to disguise my own interpretive leanings, I have sought more to provide a framework for discussion than to argue for particular readings. This book's governing conviction, however, is that Chaucer used his poetry—for both himself and for his audience—as a way of trying to make sense of and to bring order to the confusing, conflicted world in which he lived. *The Canterbury Tales*—with its multiple voices, its short circuits between announced intentions and realized outcomes, its incomplete journey—suggests that his effort was only partially successful.

I.

THE POET AND HIS WORLD

CHAPTER ONE

Double Vision:
The Gothic Mind's Eye

*T*his chapter explores the medieval era's conceptual framework—its centripetal elements, those articulated by its official
representatives and tending to pull the belief system into balance. We
are pursuing an understanding of the intellectual world Chaucer inherited, his era's underlying and unifying mythology: those shared beliefs that a society holds in common, its often unspoken assumptions
that do not need to be fully articulated because they become so thoroughly ingrained in people's thinking. For what characterizes the medieval period—and distinguishes it from our own—is the extent to
which people across educational levels and social classes shared core
beliefs. As Russell Peck observes, "Medieval society enjoyed a common mythology. . . . What is so striking about medieval literature is the
uniformity of its depersonalized dream" ("Public Dreams and Private
Myths" 462). The changes taking place in the late medieval world,
however, were undermining that common mythology.

To gain insight into the culture's shared beliefs, we shall consider
two separate—but frequently interconnected—literate and Latinate
traditions: the philosophical/scientific strand deriving mostly from
Greco-Roman sources and the religious/theological strand rooted in
Hebraic and Early Christian sources. The mindset that results from
the interweavings of these multiple strands forms the conceptual matrix which Chaucer shared with his contemporaries. Though his poetry was "notable for the hospitality it offers the unofficial cultures"
(Brewer, *Tradition and Innovation in Chaucer* 122), Chaucer, as an educated man, had certainly absorbed and understood the intricacies of
the dominant worldview and frequently drew on it in his work.

A constant dual awareness characterizes the medieval mindset:
spiritual reality is a given, a persistent presence behind every physical entity. Wylie Sypher speaks of the era's "double vision of reality,

presenting both the concrete fact and the conceptual form" (*Four Stages of Renaissance Style* 38). As Otto von Simson explains, "At the basis of all medieval thought is the concept of analogy. All things have been created according to the law of analogy . . . they are, in various degrees, manifestations of God, images, vestiges, or shadows of the Creator" (*The Gothic Cathedral* 54). The late medieval period—having moved away from Platonic exemplars of eternal forms to Aristotelian essences—placed more emphasis on the individual and the particular than did earlier centuries. But every particular still evoked an intangible yet supremely real backdrop. Modern readers of medieval texts—verbal, visual, musical—must remain mindful that an unseen reality impinges on their meaning.

Though Christianity's roots rested in the soil of Judaism, which defined itself through its sacred writings, and in the highly literate classical culture, its own origins lay in the oral tradition: the sayings of Jesus and the "good news" of salvation that form the earliest Christian message spread first by word of mouth. Furthermore, the new religion defined itself by its freedom from rigid adherence to written behavior guides. Jesus reserves his harshest chastisements for the Pharisees and their excessively literal approach to Mosaic law, and Paul teaches that the letter kills, but the spirit gives life (2 Cor. 3:7). This distinction between letter and spirit became central to Christianity's self-definition. Nevertheless it quickly evolved toward literacy and textualiy, collecting and canonizing its own body of sacred writings (Stock, *Listening for the Text* 3-5).

Though Christianity faced the problem of defining its identity, that self-definition took place in the context of both its Judaic and Greco-Roman matrices. Faced with either rejecting or absorbing and adapting these traditions, after a significant internal struggle it decisively adopted a syncretistic or assimilative stance toward both. First it needed to define its relationship to its Hebraic ancestry: among the earliest questions it faced was whether Christians must obey Mosaic law. The previously mentioned distinction between letter and spirit helped formulate a consensus that answered negatively: Christians saw themselves as freed from dietary minutiae and other restrictions while simultaneously being held to the law of love's exacting requirements. Equally important, Christianity incorporated the Hebrew people's covenant relationship with their God into its own understanding of the divine plan for salvation. While absorbing into its central heritage the major body of Hebrew sacred texts, it simultaneously staked out its own identity by labeling them "the Old Testament." Frank Kermode characterizes this approach as "an extraordinary transformation" because "a whole literature produced over many centuries and forming the basis of a highly developed religion and culture, is now said to have value only insofar as it complies with the foreunderstanding of later interpreters" (*The Genesis of Secrecy* 18).

While accepting the historicity of events and personages recorded in Hebrew texts, Christians saw them as prefiguring later historical realities: their true significance appears only when other events—those in the New Testament, Christianity's own sacred texts—complete them. For instance, the Exodus, Moses's leading his people out of slavery in Egypt, does not simply mark a defining moment in Yahweh's special care for the chosen people. It prefigures Jesus's role in leading humanity out of sin's bondage, and Moses is both himself and Jesus's type or "figura." The event functions on two levels: it is historically embedded in its own context, but its full meaning is not manifest until placed within a Christian framework. This *typological* approach contributes to the medieval tendency to obliterate temporal distinctions by treating events as related in a timeless symbolic context rather than in a sequenced historical one.

Christianity took longer—and struggled more profoundly—about relating to the vast achievements of classical culture. In the third century Tertullian's famous question—"What has Athens to do with Jerusalem?"—invited a negative response. But his was not the prevailing view. Once Christianity began to appeal to the educated, it could not ignore classical culture's achievements. Augustine of Hippo (354-430) advanced an argument that proved very useful: drawing on the Book of Exodus, he maintained that Christians should seize what is valuable in the classical world and make it serve their purposes (*On Christian Doctrine* 75). Ultimately, medieval thinkers absorbed the ancient world's achievements by seeing themselves as its beneficiaries—a concept rendered visually by depicting a medieval man sitting upon the shoulders of a much larger classical one. The former sees further because he has the advantage of perching higher. By the late medieval period Christianity had absorbed significant portions of classical culture (Seznec, *The Survival of the Pagan Gods* 18).

The philosophical tradition that Christianity found most compatible was the Platonic: its distinction between changing sense appearances and unchanging, immaterial "Forms" known through the intellect complemented Christianity's otherworldly orientation. Though most of Plato's writings were not directly available during the medieval period, the *Timaeus*, his last dialogue, did exert a profound influence on the way the era conceived of the universe's nature and structure. "Plato shows human life, both physical and moral, to be a microcosm of the macrocosmic order," Robert Jordan points out. "The human head, for example, is spherical in imitation of the heavenly exemplar, the spherical cosmos; since the latter contains the revolutions of the world-soul, it is fitting that the organ which contains the revolutions of the human soul should have the same shape" (*Chaucer and the Shape of Creation* 15). The *Timaeus* presents a rational, harmonious cosmology that complements Christian doctrine, and it uses the deductive and quantitative approach that became central in the medieval understanding of nature (Jordan 15).

Although Plato never developed a comprehensive philosophical system, his later followers—known as Neoplatonists—worked the threads of his thinking into a fully articulated pattern that shaped Christian philosophy for over a thousand years. A significant example is Plato's concept of the Form of the Good, to which, in a single passage, he ascribes a primary position. Developing that suggestion, Neoplatonists posit a hierarchy of being rooted in a totally immaterial and unknowable entity called both the Good and the One. From this entity—which caps a stable, ordered range of beings from the angelic to the inanimate—emanate increasingly material realities, ranging from Divine Mind or Spirit to Soul to Matter, the last the furthest removed from the divine reality (Knowles, *The Evolution of Medieval Thought* 8-27). This perspective—which sees the created world as conceptually complete—differs from the evolutionary perspective that our world takes for granted: "The world does not move toward better things that as yet do not exist: it exists as a hierarchy, with perfection at the top. This hierarchy of being is fixed eternally; it unites in a chain of relationship all parts of the created universe" (Reeves and Medcalf, "The Ideal, the Real, and the Quest for Perfection" 57). This hierarchy includes several levels of incorporeal beings who are less perfect than God but more perfect, because of their incorporeality, than humans (Erickson, *The Medieval Vision* 12).

In the Neoplatonic view, love—which emanates from and returns to the One—becomes the universe's binding force: like a fountain whose waters spill over into a series of extending basins before pulling back into the center to once again be recirculated, the One is both the source and goal of all that exists. The One creates in its overflowing goodness; it attracts as that which is beloved, pulling all toward itself. The Neoplatonic One who binds together the entire universe through love—though lacking Christianity's transcendent but personal deity—came to evoke the New Testament's God of Love. Thus the Neoplatonic concept of the One coincided with the Judaeo-Christian belief in a Creator God who providentially sustains all that exists.

Neoplatonism—which explains the ascent to the divine as a series of steps that moves one gradually away from the material to the spiritual—underpins most medieval mystical theology (Cook and Herzman, *The Medieval World View* 31). Neoplatonists hold that being incorporated into the material realm—though not in itself evil—makes a person fall into a state of exile and forget existence's true goal: reunion with the divine. Thus the human condition leaves people longing for their spiritual home but frequently confused or misguided about how to find it. Boethius compares this condition to that of a drunken man unsuccessfully struggling to find his way home (*The Consolation of Philosophy* 80). In contrast, the mystic's discipline creates the path that leads to reunion with the divine.

Throughout the medieval era Neoplatonism exerted a pervasive and lasting impact that Carolly Erickson maintains was central to the era's belief in a vast realm of unseen beings and in the possibility of using magic to control the natural world, "triggering by secret methods the life principle that united all things" (13). Thus the medieval period's double vision, its pervasive sense of an unseen, spiritual level of existence—which is more real and more permanent than the visible material world—had its roots, at least partially, in the Neoplatonic philosophical framework.

That framework merged successfully with the Ptolemaic geocentric model of the universe to provide an overarching paradigm that lasted until the Copernican revolution in the sixteenth century. This model pictures a universe consisting of ten concentric circles with the earth lying at its center (Lewis, *The Discarded Image* 96). Unlike our current image of a vast cosmic darkness and coldness, the medieval person saw a universe bathed in a pervasive luminosity. Light—because it is the least material of all substances—had a special significance: it revealed "an insight into the perfection of the cosmos, and a divination of the Creator" (Von Simson 51). Building on Neoplatonic ideas and on the Gospel of John's identification of Christ as the creative light by which all things were made, pseudo-Dionysius the Areopagite, an early Christian philosopher/ mystic who wrote *On Celestial Hierarchy* and *On the Ecclesiastical Hierarchy,* developed a theology that was to become very influential in later centuries. For him, "God is light. Every creature stems from that initial, uncreated, creative light. Every creature receives and transmits the divine illumination according to its capacity, that is, according to its rank in the scale of beings, according to the level at which God's intentions situated it hierarchically" (Duby, *The Age of the Cathedrals* 100). Faced with having to capture the beatific vision's ineffability,

Dante draws on this deeply ingrained Neoplatonic tradition, rendering God in images of light as he approaches his journey's goal (*Paradiso* XXX, ll. 55-66; 100-6). The metaphysical significance attributed to light underpins the Gothic striving to dissolve the fortresslike walls of Romanesque architecture into an intricate framework for the play of light on stained glass, the evoker of divine presence. "In the physical light that illuminated the sanctuary, that mystical reality seemed to become palpable to the senses," Von Simson observes (55). Indeed the cathedral itself functions as an image of heaven and exists in a typological relationship with the Temple of Solomon, which also prefigures the Heavenly Jerusalem (Von Simson 8-11).

The medieval universe was also conceived as rotating in constant and perfectly circular motion, each sphere contributing to the overall harmony and moved by its governing Intelligence in response to divine love's attractive power: as the still and unchanging center of all existence, God moves "as an object of desire moves those who desire it" (Lewis, *The Discarded Image* 111-13). This model draws upon the Aristotelian concept of the Prime Mover, the hierarchy of being's pinnacle: though motionless, the Prime Mover is "the cause of all movement, development and change within the cosmos. . . . the whole machinery of the world is set and kept in motion by the love and desire that all being, consciously or unconsciously, has for God" (Knowles 14).

Belief in the universe's comprehensive harmony was closely associated with the conviction that its structure is rooted in laws of mathematical proportion ultimately derived from Pythagoras, whose ideas Plato incorporated into the *Timaeus*. Arithmetical ratios assume a metaphysical dimension, capable of revealing divine structural principles. Certain ratios—1:1, 1:2, 2:3, and 3:4—became "audible echoes of metaphysical perfection" (Von Simson 21). Thus for medieval thinkers, as Jesse Gellrich points out, "The concordia of the heavenly rotations, the even proportion of nature's four elements and the orderliness of diurnal and seasonal succession constituted a compelling example of the harmony of the physical universe" (*The Idea of the Book in the Middle Ages* 81). Gothic architects strove to design and build cathedrals according to the same mathematical principles that God had used in creating the universe, trying, in effect, to create a microcosmic version of God's macrocosm (Jordan, *Chaucer and the Shape of Creation* 44-45).

Belief that the universe's harmony rests on numerical proportion led to belief in the almost magical power of numbers to reveal meaning (Mâle, *The Gothic Image* 10). Thus certain numbers have special importance: one captures the unity of God; three reveals the mystery of the Trinity; four is associated with the earthly, human realm; seven combines the earthly and the divine; nine—as the square of three—is doubly sacred, while ten (nine plus one) signifies both the unity and the trinity of the Godhead. Explaining the significance of the number twelve, Emile Mâle provides a fascinating summary of how medieval tradition, drawing on Augustine, attributes divine significance to numbers:

> From St. Augustine onwards all theologians interpreted the meaning of the number twelve after the same fashion. Twelve is the number of the universal Church, and it was for profound reasons that Jesus willed the number of his apostles should be twelve. Now twelve is the product of three by four. Three, which is the number of the Trinity and by consequence of the soul made in the image of the Trinity, connotes all spiritual things. Four—the number of the elements—is the symbol of material things—the body and the world—which result from the combinations of the four elements. To multiply three by four is in the mystic sense to infuse matter with spirit, to proclaim the truths of the faith to the world, to establish the universal Church of which the apostles are the symbol. (11)

While Dante draws heavily on number symbolism to integrate the structure and meaning of his work, Chaucer usually undercuts such implications.

Just as the universe is bathed in light and structured according to numerical proportion, so too does it resonate with sound. The harmonious relationships of the spheres moving in perfect rotations produce a heavenly sound called the music of the spheres. Chaucer alludes to this heavenly music in *The Book of the Duchess* when the narrator awakes to the joyful sound of birds singing (ll. 301-8). Belief in this unheard music of the spheres connects the era's music theory with medieval number theory. Just as visual beauty results from harmoniously related parts, so too does beautiful sound depend on numerical relationships between sounds. This principle of harmony extends to the theological and moral realms, so that, for instance, "the Trinity is musical because it is a perfect numerical proportion of one in three and three in one" (Gellrich 83) and human virtue creates moral music—the "new song" of Christian charity. Conversely, sin is associated with chaos and noise, which in turn evoke the underworld (Gellrich 87-89). Thus noise is not simply a psychic annoyance: it reveals underlying moral disorder. In medieval drama, for instance, virtuous characters behave with measured calm, while sinful or satanic figures make raucous noise. According to this line of thought, Chaucer's Miller's boisterous bagpipe music reveals his flawed moral character.

All of these images—the numerical, the visual, and the auditory—have Neoplatonic origins. J. D. North's *Chaucer's Universe* reveals that the poet was well acquainted with the minute details of the medieval cosmological scheme; *A Treatise on the Astrolabe,* Chaucer's foray into technical writing, shows the extent and depth of his knowledge, though he wrote it around 1393 after the bulk of his creative work was completed. But North finds cosmological references from *The Book of the Duchess* through *The Canterbury Tales* (8). For instance, in *The Parliament of Fowls* Chaucer—drawing from Macrobius's commentary on Cicero's "Dream of Scipio"—directly refers to the medieval macrocosm when—in a dream—Scipio Africanus sets the whole universe before his grandson:

> And after shewede he hym the nyne speres;
> And after that the melodye herde he
> That cometh of thilke speres thryes thre,
> That welle is of musik and melodye
> In this world here, and cause of armonye. (ll. 59-63)

The model appears more fully in "The Knight's Tale," where Theseus's lengthy philosophical speech—delivered several years after the ill-fated tournament that leads to Arcite's death—attempts to place that unhappy event into a broader perspective: (ll. 2987-93; 3041-43). Whether Theseus's speech reflects his deep philosophical insight or thinly disguises his political opportunism, it underscores Chaucer's ability to draw upon the medieval macrocosmic model for his poetic purposes.

In keeping with Neoplatonism's distinction between matter and spirit, this model sees everything that lies beneath the sphere of the moon—everything material that is associated with the earth—as drawn inexorably downward; it is subject to time, change, and decay. All that exists above the moon is spirit, eternal and unchangeable, moving inevitably upward toward the divine source of all being. These "physical facts" assume moral/theological dimensions through the belief that humans participate in both realms of being: their bodies belong to the changing material world, their souls to the timeless realm of spirit. Thus the medieval person faces the constant challenge of giving priority to the spirit's claims while recognizing that the material world's illusory attractiveness constitutes a powerful downward pull.

Chaucer humorously treats these ideas in *The House of Fame* when the loquacious and unabashedly didactic eagle—who has seized the narrator in his talons for an unexpected aerial journey—undertakes to teach his passenger about gravity. Explaining that everything that exists has a natural place to which it is drawn, the eagle follows up with a number of examples to support his point:

> As thus: loo, thou maist alday se
> That any thing that hevy be,
> As stoon, or led, or thyng of wighte,
> And bere hyt never so hye on highte,
> Lat goo thyn hand, hit falleth doun.
> Ryght so seye I be fyr or soun,
> Or smoke or other thynges lyghte;
> Alwey they seke upward on highte,
> While ech of hem is at his large:
> Lyght thing upward, and dounward charge. (ll. 737-46)

This passage casts a retrospective light on the eagle's earlier complaint about the narrator's being a heavy burden, "noyous for to carye!" (l. 574), thereby suggesting that his passenger's substantial materiality drags him down toward earth and makes the heavenly journey on which he is engaged particularly difficult to execute. For the aerial voyage in effect affords the narrator a spiritual perspective that radically shifts his view of earthly affairs:

> But thus sone in a while he
> Was flowen fro the ground so hye
> That al the world, as to myn yë,
> No more semed than a prikke. (ll. 904-7)

In *The Parliament of Fowls* a similar lesson emerges when Affrican offers his grandson a view from above the earth, which enables him to recognize its smallness and insignificance; he thereby emphasizes the folly of delighting in the world and supports ascetic devotion to duty and to the "commune profit" (l. 75):

> Than bad he hym, syn erthe was so lyte,
> And dissevable and ful of harde grace,
> That he ne shulde hym in the world delyte. (64-66)

The same motif appears again in the epilogue of *Troilus and Criseyde*, when Troilus—having enjoyed love's joys and then suffered its bitterest disappointments—looks down from the eighth sphere and laughs at all his earthly sufferings (V: ll. 1814-22). The epilogue makes explicit the less fully articulated implications of the eagle's teachings in *The House of Fame* and of Affrican in *The Parliament of Fowls*. As Troilus—like a protoastronaut—looks down on the earth beneath him, it shrinks to insignificance. He thus physically achieves the God's-eye view that affords him a basis for a spiritual perspective, what medieval thinkers refer to as seeing *sub specie aeternitatis*—under the aspect of eternity.

This Ptolemaic macrocosmic model (which Dante adopts for structuring his *Paradiso*) provided the human imagination with a satisfying harmony and completeness. Unlike our current paradigm, the older model situates humanity in a universe in which its place is central and in a space whose dimensions the human imagination can conceive (Lewis, *The Discarded Image* 99). This paradigm also made it easier for people to see their ethical choices against a universal perspective, as Russell Peck points out:

> Earth is not the center of Ptolemy's mathematical construct—man is. The universe confirms his roundness and his oneness. Its order and rhythms teach him rhythm and order. But although creation revolves around his perspective, the effect is not solipsistic. Moral and ethical questions require him to maintain a discrete perspective both close and far, small and large, on what surrounds him. His inner and outer selves are understood through reciprocation between himself, the rest of creation, and the Creator. ("Public Dreams and Private Myths" 464)

One of Neoplatonism's chief conduits to the medieval world was Boethius's *The Consolaton of Philosophy*. This sixth century work—composed when the author had experienced a dramatic reversal in his life, having lost his power and prestige and facing imminent execution—involves a searching exploration of why the innocent suffer. Through an ongoing dialogue with Lady Philosophy, the despairing narrator learns that all the goods he complained about losing—wealth, fame, status, political power—belong under Fortune's rule and thus are inevitably subject to change. When people complain about her fickleness, Fortune says in self-defense:

> Inconstancy is my very essence; it is the game I never cease to play as I turn my wheel in its ever changing circle, filled with joy as I bring

the top to the bottom and the bottom to the top. Yes, rise up on my wheel if you like, but don't count it an injury when by the same token you begin to fall, as the rules of the game will require. (57)

This passage provides the medieval period with one of its favorite images: that of a woman, frequently blindfolded, turning a wheel on which several figures perch; one sits comfortably crowned on the top, while others hang on precariously to the wheel's upward curve or fall off its downward curve.

Philosophy teaches—and Boethius must learn—that the gifts of Fortune cannot satisfy the quest for true and lasting happiness that is humanity's goal. Complete happiness can come only from returning to its true home, the unchanging and totally satisfying good that is God, the *summum bonum* or highest good: "But we have agreed that perfect good is true happiness; so that it follows that true happiness is to be found in the supreme God" (100). Having absorbed this important lesson, the narrator moves on to explore another vexing question about human existence: the relationship between God's foreknowledge and human free will. If God providentially orders and governs the universe—the narrator wonders—how can people exercise any freedom of action? Philosophy's response distinguishes between the human experience of time as a sequence of past, present, and future and the divine experience of time as an all-encompassing present that is eternity (164-66). She concludes that divine foreknowledge does not negate free will: "it simply sees things present to it exactly as they will happen at some time as future events" (166).

Boethius's high-minded but nontechnical philosophizing appealed to many medieval thinkers, including Chaucer, who translated the *Consolation* and continued to reflect its influence throughout his life. No text—except the Bible—is more frequently and more intricately interwoven into the entire spectrum of his poetry. Its presence is particularly evident in *Troilus and Criseyde*. John P. McCall, for instance, argues that the poem's five-book structure—rather than the nine sections found in its source, Boccaccio's *Filostrato*—parallels the structure of Boethius's work ("The Five-Book Structure in Chaucer's *Troilus*" 297). Further, the Boethian structure reflects the state of Troilus's fortunes: Books One and Two—which portray Troilus moving from despair to hope—represent the upward sweep of Fortune's wheel; Book Three—with the lovers fulfilling all their desires—conveys that point of rest at the top of the wheel; and Books Four and Five—as the lovers' relationship sours—suggest the wheel's downward turn.

In addition, characters throughout the poem unconsciously echo Boethian sentiments. Pandarus, for instance, functions as an inverted Lady Philosophy. When Troilus—lamenting the hopelessness of his love for Criseyde—complains that Fortune is against him, Pandarus advises him not to give up hope, since Fortune is ever-changing: if she is frowning on him now, she will certainly smile later. Lady Philosophy argues precisely the opposite: since Fortune changes, one should not place one's hope for happiness on any good that comes under her sway (Gaylord, "Uncle Pandarus as Lady Philosophy" 572-73). In Book Four, when Troilus struggles to understand the turn of events that will take Criseyde away from him, he engages in a lengthy reflection on fate and free will, finally concluding that people have little control over their destinies. Unaided by the guidance of Lady Philosophy, he arrives at an essentially deterministic position, one that she would disapprove.

Boethian references are prevalent in "The Knight's Tale" as well. The weeping women who interrupt Theseus's victorious homecoming by seeking his assistance in avenging their husbands' deaths remind him that though they have once been duchesses and queens, now they are sunk in misery, "thanked be Fortune and hire false wheel" (1. 925)—a not-so-subtle reminder that their roles could easily be reversed. Palamon in prison and Arcite in exile mirror the two states that portray human life in Boethian terms. Philosophy's task is to provide the mind with "wings on which to lift itself" (*The Consolation of Philosophy* 117) to enable a person to rise above adversity, but the two pagan lovers struggle on without her intervention. On his deathbed Arcite raises fundamental questions about the meaning of human life: "What is this world? What asketh men to have?" (1. 2777), but the narrator eschews taking any position on what happens after death: "His spirit changed hous and wente ther/As I cam nevere, I kan not tellen wher" (ll. 2809-10). In short, this tale—in which, as some critics have argued, Chaucer restricts himself to an essentially pre-Christian framework—raises a number of philosophical issues that appear in Boethius's work, but it refrains from advancing the answers that Philosophy confidently provides in the *Consolation*. Throughout his life Chaucer found in that work a rich repository of images and motifs that evoke Neoplatonic/Christian otherworldliness, but his treatment remains open-ended.

In addition to this Neoplatonic philosophical framework, the medieval mind absorbed a complex body of Christian doctrine, one that provides an overarching account of salvation history from creation to apocalypse. No thinker was more influential in shaping that doctrine than Augustine, whose conversion to Christianity in the fourth century permanently shaped the direction of its theology. Drawing on Paul's teachings, Augustine fully developed the doctrine of original sin, which distinguishes between a prelapsarian and a postlapsarian state. This doctrine holds that the Creator endowed human beings with two distinguishing features: reason, which made it possible for them to understand their place in the divine plan, and free will, which allowed them to freely choose to fulfill it. Though free will permitted rejecting that plan, humans initially were able to remain free from sin.

But Adam and Eve, the prototypical humans, rebelled against the divine plan by a proudly disobedient act. By this original sin they introduced a radical change in human nature: now reason is clouded, free will is weak, and humans are born with an innate predisposition to sin, which Augustine called concupiscence. The weakened human condition in the postlapsarian state introduces a chasm between God and humanity, one that only the Incarnation—God's becoming human, suffering, and dying to redeem humanity—could bridge. Christianity's central teachings thus relate to Jesus's role in repairing the damage caused by original sin, which—because of the gulf between God and humanity—closes off the path to salvation. As Augustine teaches in *On Christian Doctrine,* "We used our immortality so badly as to incur the penalty of death; Christ used his mortality so well as to restore us to life" (I: 14).

Redemption comes not just from the God-man's assuming human form but from his willingness to suffer and die to free humanity from sin's bondage. His resurrection announces a victory over death for all faithful believers. Not everyone is saved, however: those who continue to lead sinful lives, remaining more attached to earthly than spiritual goods, suffer eternal damnation. The Church—the mystical body of Christ, or alternately, his beloved spouse—functions as God's intermediary on earth, having the power to forgive sins—or to deny forgiveness; it thus holds the key to salvation or damnation. Initially Christians focused on the Last Judgment as the moment that would determine their eternal fate. All of history moves toward this second coming of Christ—the apocalypse—the final reckoning on all aspects of human experience and a permanent sorting of the good from the bad, the sheep from the goats. In *The Golden Legend,* Jacobus de Voragine's famous collection of saints' lives, the author gives the following account of that final rendering:

> The Judge will be inexorably severe. He will not be influenced by fear, since He is all-powerful, nor by bribes, since He is Abundance

itself, nor by hate, since He is Benevolence itself, nor by love, since He is Justice itself, nor by error, since He is Wisdom itself. Against His wisdom neither the pleading of advocates nor the sophisms of the philosophers nor the discourses of orators nor the tricks of hypocrites will prevail. (qtd. in Miller, *Chaucer: Sources and Backgrounds* 482)

Indeed the Last Judgment loomed large in the medieval imagination: Christ the Judge sternly presiding over the final disposition of souls frequently greeted believers as they entered through the west portals of their churches. By the late medieval period, people were also concerned with the particular judgment, the moment right after death that seals the soul's destiny. An illumination by the Rohan Master in the fourteenth century graphically portrays the moment: as the emaciated corpse lies in rigor mortis, the soul—rendered visually by a small, childlike figure—is caught by a fiend who, in turn, is about to be smitten by a sword-wielding angel. An aged and bearded God the Father—holding the sword of justice—looks on with concern, perhaps with compassion. But if the Judge is often severe and the pangs of the damned excruciating, the joy of the blessed is delectable. The final section of "The Parson's Tale," the sermonlike tract that concludes *The Canterbury Tales,* describes heavenly bliss as total fulfillment (ll. 1076-80).

Over the centuries the Church developed a doctrine that modified the stark opposition between salvation and damnation. Since few people could expect to die in the state of spiritual perfection required for admittance to eternal bliss, and since most clung to the hope that their failings did not merit eternal torment, the doctrine of purgatory—which advanced the possibility of severe but temporary punishment—gained increasing acceptance, until it was officially incorporated into Christian teaching in 1274 at the Second Council of Lyons (Le Goff, *The Birth of Purgatory* 237). In its fully developed form the doctrine holds that Purgatory cleanses the soul of all its minor—or venial—sins and of all the impurities from the mortal sins that, though forgiven in confession, leave a residue on the soul. Belief that through prayer and good deeds the living can shorten the painful purification process substantially influenced both official and popular religion in the late medieval period (Le Goff, *The Birth of Purgatory* 4-14).

To live virtuously and thereby attain salvation, individuals must follow reason, God's imprint or image in humanity; when they give themselves over to passion rather than exercising rational control, they mar the divine likeness and become less than fully human (Robertson, "Chaucer and Christian Tradition" 3). The ongoing challenge of human life after the fall is that of controlling the natural tendency to love so that it seeks the proper goal, the only one that will completely satisfy its nature: God. Human beings must love, but they have the reason and free will to control what they love. Unfortunately, they tend to love out of proportion—to love creatures rather than the Creator—and thus perversely to work against their own long-range happiness. In *On Christian Doctrine* Augustine clearly articulates the distinction between the two kinds of love:

> I mean by charity [caritas] that affection of the mind which aims at the enjoyment of God for His own sake, and the enjoyment of one's self and one's neighbor in subordination to God; by lust [cupiditas] I mean that affection of the mind which aims at enjoying one's self and one's neighbor, and other corporeal things, without reference to God. (III: 10, 16)

This distinction carries over into Augustine's social and political analysis, where he distinguishes between the city of God and the city of man, the former associated with Jerusalem, the latter with Babylon:

> We see then that the two cities were created by two kinds of love: the earthly city was created by self-love reaching the point of contempt for God, the Heavenly City by the love of God carried as far as contempt of self. In fact, the earthly city glories in itself, the Heavenly City glories in the Lord. (*The City of God* 593; Bk 14: ch 28)

Augustine maintains that, though the two cities are inextricably intertwined on earth, those who make the love of God their priority are true pilgrims heading for the Heavenly Jerusalem (*The City of God 842*).

Because original sin clouded the human mind, it can no longer apprehend truth unaided. But rather than abandoning humanity to its own devices, God bolsters it with sacred scripture to enlighten the mind and with grace to strengthen the weakened will in its attempts to avoid sin. Divinely inspired scripture becomes the instrument by which God reveals the mysterious plan of redemption. Properly understanding scripture thus becomes the center of intellectual endeavor:

> Interpretation of Holy Scriptures was the primary labor of medieval learning . . . The symbolic interpretation of the Bible was a

rational process which proceeded logically from premise to conclusion. . . . But the truth of premises could be determined only
from the sacred books of the Church. . . . The articles of faith provide the basis for certitude. (Jordan, *Chaucer and the Shape of Creation* 26-27).

As a result, scripture becomes the touchstone against which to test all
knowledge: it provides a basis for certainty, thereby fostering "intellectual absolutism" (Jordan, *Chaucer and the Shape of Creation* 27). As
Jesse Gellrich points out, medieval thinkers saw the Bible as "the
book that revealed or made present God's transcendent and absolute
will, law, and wisdom, a container of the divine plan and itself a sign
of the totality of that plan in the world" (32). Biblical references are
an ubiquitous part of the medieval vocabulary, and Chaucer makes
extensive use of them. But because he rarely uses them straightfor-
wardly, he challenges the reader to puzzle their significance.

Besides the book of scripture—medieval people believed—God
has provided the book of nature to point to divine truth: the perceptible world functions as a vast symbol of divine reality. This view appears in the teachings of Hugh of St. Victor, a twelfth-century
Neoplatonist theologian: "This entire perceptible world is as a book
written by the finger of God, that is, created by divine power, and individual creatures are as figures within it, not invented by human will
(placito) but instituted by divine authority (arbitrio) to make manifest the wisdom of the invisible things of God" (qtd. in Jordan,
Chaucer and the Shape of Creation 28; *Eruditionis didiscaliae* VII: cap. 4;
PL, vol. 176, col. 814). Acting on this belief, Gothic architects incorporated all aspects of the natural world into their structures: plants,
animals, seasons, stars, zodiacal signs, all resonate with meaning that,
as with sacred scripture, requires the spiritual insight of the adept
(Mâle 29). So, for instance, the perceptive viewer like Adam of St.
Victor looks at a nut and sees Jesus: "The green and fleshy sheath is
His flesh, His humanity. The wood of the shell is the wood of the
Cross on which that flesh suffered. But the kernel of the nut from
which men gain nourishment is His hidden divinity" (qtd. in Mâle
30). Peter of Mora associates roses with martyrs, while Hugh of St.
Victor links the dove with the Church: "The dove has two wings even
as the Christian has two ways of life, the active and the contemplative. The blue feathers of the wings are thoughts of heaven; the uncertain shades of the body, the changing colours that recall an
unquiet sea, symbolize the ocean of human passions in which the
Church is sailing" (qtd. in Mâle 30).

Medieval geographical conceptions also reflect theological principles. The most well-known type of medieval map was the T-and-O
map, which places Jerusalem at the earth's center; of these, the one
produced at Hereford Cathedral in the early fourteenth century and
housed there ever since is the most famous. This map serves more
ideological than practical purposes (Lewis, *The Discarded Image* 144).
Such maps depict the earth as a flat disc surrounded by an ocean; the
top half of the disc—pointing east rather than north—shows Asia,
while the bottom half is divided in two with Europe in one quadrant
and Africa in the other. Separating the continents is the Mediterranean in the shape of a large T. On this map recounting salvation
history is as important as locating geographical features in space; indeed the mapmaker at Hereford thinks of his work as an "estoire" or
story and sees his function as "explaining the world as well as drawing
it" (Moir, *The World Map in Hereford Cathedral* 7-8). The map places
Christ sitting in judgment in the pinnacle that lies outside the circle
of the earth. Below him is the earthly paradise—where humanity's
journey began—set on a circular island, permanently cut off from the
rest of earth. Jerusalem sits at the center, the site of humanity's redemption on Calvary and thus "the focal point of human history"
(Moir 13) and the symbolic goal of all medieval pilgrimages (see
Chapter Five). Other biblical narratives portrayed are Noah and the
ark, the exodus from Egypt, the incarnation, and the crucifixion—all
central events in Christian salvation history (Moir 28).

Theological factors dominate medieval temporal perceptions as
well. The Jewish notion of a covenant relationship with a transcendent God who nevertheless works in and through history yields an
implicitly linear notion of time as it moves from creation to apocalypse. The typological thinking discussed earlier tends to blur temporal distinctions by establishing connections between historical
entities in a way that ignores the widely differing time frames that
separate them. In this perspective what matters is not so much how
people and events are embedded in a historical matrix as how they
are linked in the Boethian overarching eternal present that establishes their meaning. Russell Peck summarizes medieval temporal
conceptions as follows:

> A cosmology of concentric circles yields a chronology of concentric
> times. Combined with a Christian sense of linear time progressing
> from creation to apocalypse, it evokes a triple time sense. Man lives
> in the moment. He also lives within the span of history, a history
> that defines itself by repeating its own plots. And, ultimately, man

> lives in eternity. His problem is to coordinate these three time
> senses in his psyche synchronically. ("Public Dreams and Private
> Myths" 466)

Both medieval art and medieval drama provide good examples of
this kind of thinking (Peck 466). For example, crucifixion scenes are
set against a timeless gold background, portraying either an impas-
sive and triumphant Jesus or a visibly anguished and suffering one;
figures at the foot of the cross may include Mary and the apostle
John—mentioned as present in the gospel narratives—as well as
other saints from several different eras; in the Late Middle Ages a
contemporary donor—whose hope for salvation depends upon Jesus's redemptive activity and the saints' participation in that activity—may also figure as a prominent part of the scene. On a
companion panel the primal fall of Adam and Eve—which the suffering and death of Jesus remedies—often appears.

The medieval drama that flourished from the thirteenth to the
fifteenth centuries also functioned in a dual time frame: in the mystery cycles the players reenacted the central events of sacred history,
but their words often had a contemporary resonance, providing a
means for indirect social commentary. In "The Second Shepherd's
Play," for instance, the Wakefield Master situates most of the action
among suffering and complaining contemporary shepherds. But after their merciful gesture toward Mak, their sheep-stealing fellow,
they inhabit the sacred time of Jesus's nativity in the closing scene.
Lawrence Ross underscores the fact that "the play reenacts the central event of Christian history. . . . the Incarnation is indeed an eternally recurrent mystery—and needs to be" (209). What matters is
sacred reality rather than historical or contemporary authenticity.

Gaining an encompassing and right-minded understanding of all
these dimensions of reality has an importance that transcends
merely satisfying intellectual curiosity: salvation itself is at stake. For
the medieval thinker identifies the Truth with God: "Truth is not
only 'what is true,' but God himself. . . . The nature of salvation was
thought to depend on getting the truth about the universe, and
about oneself" (Brewer 131-32). Throughout the medieval period—
and culminating in the thirteenth century—intellectual endeavor
centered on attempting to encompass all the cultural elements that
Christianity had assimilated and all aspects of the world, into one
overarching framework: the Gothic mind strove "to gather all
strands of learning together into an enormous Text, an encyclopedia or *summa*, that would mirror the historical and transcendental

orders just as the Book of God's Word (the Bible) was a *speculum* [mirror] of the Book of his Work (nature)" (Gellrich 18). This assimilative, integrative impulse asserted itself most notably in Dante's *The Divine Comedy,* in thirteenth-century scholasticism, especially in Aquinas's *Summa Theologica,* and in the Gothic cathedral.

In Chaucer's work this Gothic impulse toward inclusivity manifests itself in the broad social and moral spectrum his pilgrims represent and in the wide variety of genres he includes in his story collection. Helen Cooper's *The Structure of the Canterbury Tales* maintains that the work is a *summa,* an encyclopedia of genres, each tale vying for supremacy of its kind:

> There are romances, of five distinct kinds; there are fabliaux, again of several varieties; there are moral tales of the kind that lie on the border between romance and saint's life; there is a saint's life proper, and a miracle of the Virgin; there are beast fables, a sermon, a moral prose tract, a penitential tract, the Monk's story— collection of tragedies, and, in the General Prologue, an estates satire. It is quite difficult to think of any literary kind available to him that Chaucer has omitted. (52-53)

Chaucer's art also manifests its Gothic quality in its structure—the arrangement of episodes similar to the mystery plays strung out on wagons (Sypher 51)—and in what Jordan characterizes as "inorganic form"; he compares the structure of *The Canterbury Tales* to the succession of bays in a Gothic cathedral, stressing its additive rather than organic aspect and makes an explicit link between their purposes and Chaucer's (*Chaucer and the Shape of Creation* xi-xii, 46).

Finally, Chaucer's vision is Gothic in its pervasive duality—its tension between the human and the divine—revealing "the inherent strain of living in the double world of gothic art and thought: the world of abstract system, and the actual, immediate world of human experience" (Sypher 37). A constant challenge in responding to Chaucer's poetry is determining, in any given instance, how much value he ascribes to each realm. Just as all Chaucer's pilgrims respond to two voices, though in significantly varying proportions (Hoffman, "Chaucer's Prologue to Pilgrimage" 30-45), so too does the poet himself constantly modulate between the sacred/spiritual and the secular/physical. Like his contemporaries, his eyes see double, his ears hear two voices: nothing is simply itself, a particular entity existing in time and space; everything resonates with a spiritual significance. Much that is comic in Chaucer's art results from his ability to juxtapose and exploit the incongruities between these two perspectives. Though he tests official culture's limits, in his most serious moments—in the epilogue to *Troilus and Criseyde* and in his "Retractions"—he moves back within its framework. As Derek Brewer observes: "Chaucer's own advances in naturalistic realism are huge, and deserve recognition, but they are still set against a conceptual abstract view of reality" (135).

Still, the tightly fitted, comprehensive conceptual model so well articulated in the overarching structure of Dante's *The Divine Comedy*—with its carefully worked number symbolism, its pilgrimage from error to mystic insight, its structural and thematic symmetries—was dissolving rapidly in Chaucer's world. In the succeeding chapters I will explore several areas in which long-established certainties were yielding to new realities. Though Chaucer adopts one of the era's most familiar paradigms, the pilgrimage, for framing his work, he responds to the shifting sands of his intellectual and social universe by incorporating into his treatment of that frame elements that radically reorient its significance.

CHAPTER TWO

The Role of the Poet: Minstrel, Maker—or More?

*I*f Chaucer inhabited a world that had double vision, he also led a double life—as civil servant and as court poet: on the one hand, he bustled in the world of affairs—of custom houses, diplomatic missions, and public works; on the other, he pursued his scholarly and literary interests to amuse and edify the court. The medieval period, however, did not see literature as a self-justifying activity. Indeed Christian culture had a deep-rooted and persistent tendency to question all poetic activity. In that problematic context Chaucer frequently—and perhaps ultimately unsuccessfully—struggled to understand and define his role as a poet. For, as Lee Patterson explains, "He is the originator of a national literature in a culture that lacks both the concept of literature and a social identity for those who produce it" ("'What Man Artow'?" 135). Though Chaucer did not develop a full-blown literary theory, questions about the nature of poetry and about the poet's role were important to him (Jordan, *Chaucer's Poetics* 6). Among the questions he asked himself are the following: What is the poet's proper role in his community? How can the poet achieve the best balance between entertainment and instruction? How should the poet relate to the literary tradition that precedes him? Can the poet hope to capture and communicate truth? In this chapter I will explore the evolving view of the poet's role to gain insight into how Chaucer may have conceptualized the task of responding to and communicating with his world.

Chaucer's attempts at defining his role reflect the contemporary distinction between "vernacular versifying and learned humanist composition" (Olson, "Making and Poetry" 273). The former, referred to as "making," was socially contextualized and focused on technical skill. Producing poetry, on the other hand, implied having a serious moral purpose and an affinity with divine creativity. Typically, Chaucer refers to himself as "makyng," indicating that he sees himself as a craftsman responding to social expectations. He reserves the term "poet"—which seems to imply for him special authority and a moral stance as well as an excellence that transcends social exigencies—for writers from classical antiquity and for two Italian poets: Dante and Petrarch. But his role underwent a transformation over the course of his lifetime: he is a "maker" who became a "poet" (Olson, "Making and Poetry" 274-88). Then, perhaps, he pulled back from the implications of that transformation.

Chaucer's literary career began at court, where writing verse for oral delivery to divert a social elite was an expected skill for a promising courtier. He functioned in a fluid social environment in which aristocratic patrons and their retainers periodically reassessed their ties. In addition to court patrons like John of Gaunt, for whom Chaucer probably composed *The Book of the Duchess*, we can best understand Chaucer's initial audience as consisting of his social peers at court, though his specific audience varied from one decade to another and from one composition to the next (Strohm, *Social Chaucer* 36-51). In the large, mobile late medieval court, literary activity was just one of many recreational pursuits like chess, cards, skittles, dancing, and singing (Green, *Poets and Princepleasers* 56-58). By the fourteenth century the storytelling minstrel who had performed in the courts of the High Middle Ages was yielding to a court poet who composed and recited love poems and recounted stories of knightly romance and adventure. Contemporary French poetry, which Chaucer translated and performed for his audience in the early phases of his career, introduced him to a wealth of materials and genres that continued to influence him throughout his life. Romantic love was the late medieval poet's chief subject, and he had to assume the stance either of a fellow lover or of someone who stands apart but sympathizes with the lovers. The poet's auditors considered themselves—at least potentially—as fellow artists. Because of the aristocracy's new role in shaping literary tastes and in actually producing their own literary works, the poet-performer lost much of his mystique (112-25). No doubt, at least part of what critics perceive as Chaucer's ironically detached, self-mocking stance has roots in the social matrix in which he spent his formative years.

In this environment the poet-performer and his audience were closely linked. The fifteenth-century frontispiece to the Corpus Christi manuscript of *Troilus and Criseyde* helps us to visualize the circumstances in which Chaucer presented his compositions. Slightly off-center in the lower-right section the bearded poet stands reading to elegantly attired men and women who manifest varying degrees of attentiveness. The upper section—partially separated from the poet and his audience by a dark triangular mass—depicts a central scene from the text: the climactic moment of Criseyde's departure from a medievalized Troy to join her father in the Greek camp. The illumination captures the intimate moment when the artist, the audience, and the text come together.

Besides being entertaining the late medieval composer of literary texts also was expected to produce morally edifying works that would educate the audience (David, *The Strumpet Muse* 5). Public poetry during Richard II's reign articulated the era's common values: "worldly felicity and peaceful, harmonious communal existence. . . .bourgeois moderation" (Middleton, "The Idea of Public Poetry" 95). This poetry avoids both totaling schemes and introspective excesses, serving instead a "mediating" role (Middleton 95-101). The ironic, detached stance of late medieval poets encouraged a shift from "a literature of performance" to "a literature of participation" (Green, *Poet and Princepleasers* 111) that draws the audience into conversation about issues raised in the poem. The open-endedness of many Chaucerian works and his tendency to leave his audience with a question like the one at the end of "The Franklin's Tale" reflect this shift and highlight the involvement that a medieval poet expected from his audience. This highly interactive relationship between the poet-performer and his attending audience supports the recent critical emphasis on a community of readers'/auditors' role in creating a text's meaning. Thus in addition to diverting his auditors, the poet engaged his audience in a process of forming and sharing common values. Judson Allen's study of late medieval poetics, for instance, insists upon its essentially ethical basis (289).

If, early in his career, Chaucer's contact with French court poetry introduced him to a variety of literary genres and motifs and fostered his self-image as a "maker" who seeks to divert and edify his audience, his two journeys to Italy during the 1370s enlarged the scope of his materials and his vision of the poet's function. Being a court entertainer and a moral counselor must have seemed limited and inadequate to him after his encounter with the exalted vision of the poet found in the early humanism of contemporary Italians like Dante, Petrarch, and Boccaccio. Interestingly, that humanistic concept developed as Christianity's counter to its long-standing suspicion against all poetic activity, especially that of classical antiquity.

As late as the fourteenth-century Christian rigorists still attacked poetic fictions, maintaining that only religious or moral writings are justified and that rhetorical embellishment detracts from serious and elevating writing like sermons and moral tracts. Petrarch—who devoted so much energy to reviving classical knowledge and to producing his own poems—had to defend poetry to his brother Gherardo, a Carthusian monk. Anticipating the latter's objection to the poem included with his letter, Petrarch argues that "poetry is not at all inimical to theology" (qtd. in Minnis, *Medieval Theory of Authorship* 413). His defensiveness highlights Christianity's continuing unease about poetic endeavor. Boccaccio manifested that malaise when, in response to a monk's dream that foretold Boccaccio's damnation if he did not give up his literary activities, he was sufficiently unnerved to seek advice from Petrarch about how to respond (Petrarch, *Letters* 225). Chaucer's Parson adheres to the rigorist view: when in "The Parson's Prologue" Harry Bailly calls on him to participate in the tale-telling contest, he refuses to tell a fiction, opting instead to deliver a lengthy sermon on the seven deadly sins, thereby effectively ending the *Tales:*

> Thou getest fable noon ytoold for me,
> For Paul, that writeth unto Thymothee,
> Repreveth hem that weyven soothfastnesse
> And tellen fables and swich wrecchednesse.
> Why sholde I sowen draf out of my fest,
> Whan I may sowen whete, if that me lest?
> For which I seye, if that yow list to heere
> Moralitee and vertuous mateere,
> And thanne that ye wol yeve me audience,
> I wol ful fayn, at Cristes reverence,
> Do yow plesaunce leefful, as I kan. . . .
> I wol yow telle a myrie tale in prose
> To knytte up al this feeste and make an ende.
> (ll. 31-41; 46-47)

As some critics have pointed out, the Parson's intolerance about poetic fictions would have short-circuited the whole tale-telling enterprise if he had taken center stage after the Man of Law's performance when Harry Bailly first called on him. Indeed some have argued that Chaucer's decision to use prose for both "The Parson's Tale" and "The Tale of Melibee" and his comments at a couple of crucial points, where he appears to be speaking in his own voice—passages that Robert Jordan identifies as "ground zero" (*Chaucer's Poetics* 114)—reflect his own doubts about poetry's validity. In the epilogue to *Troilus and Criseyde* he questions his own poetic enterprise by repudiating the kind of love to which his poet/narrator has devoted the entire poem. And in the "Retractions" to *The Canterbury Tales* he begs forgiveness for "my translacions and enditynges of worldly vanitees," including most of his work prior to the *Tales,* for those tales in the Canterbury collection "that sownen into synne," and for "many another book, if they were in my remembrance, and many a song and many a leccherous lay" (328).

The negative attitude toward poetry is derived from Plato, who attacks poets as liars and objects to their stimulating the emotions and passions rather than appealing to reason. Some Christian apologists adopted a similar position, rejecting classical poetry as seductive and misleading. Boethius follows their lead in the opening scene of *The Consolation of Philosophy,* when Lady Philosophy banishes the Muses by the narrator's bedside, accusing them of worsening his condition. Augustine also shares in this tradition's negativism toward poetry. Obtaining a classical education in rhetoric by studying the Latin poets was his avenue to achieving worldly success. Though he quickly became an adept scholar who loved his literary studies, after his conversion he considered them dangerously misleading, as his comments about the *Aeneid*'s poetic beauties illustrate:

> I loved Latin, not the elementary lessons but those which I studied later under teachers of literature. . . . But in the later lessons I was obliged to memorize the wanderings of a hero named Aeneas, while in the meantime I failed to remember my own erratic ways. . . . It is true that curtains are hung over the entrances to the schools where literature is taught, but they are not so much symbols in honour of mystery as veils concealing error. (*Confessions* 33-34)

Nine hundred years later Boccaccio, defending poetry in his *Genealogiae deorum gentiles,* sums up the arguments of its detractors as follows:

> They say, besides, that their poems are false, obscure, lewd, and replete with absurd and silly tales of pagan gods. . . . Again and again they cry out that poets are seducers of the mind, prompters of crimes, and . . . they say they are philosophers' apes, that it is a heinous crime to read or possess the books of poets; and then, without making any distinction, they prop themselves up, as they say, with Plato's authority to the effect that poets ought to be turned out-of-doors, nay, out of town. . . . (*Boccaccio on Poetry,* Bk 14: Ch. 5, 35-36)

The charges against poetry for its paganism, superficiality, and seductiveness have a familiar resonance for those acquainted with medieval misogynist literature. The objections that clerical culture leveled against poets closely parallel those raised against women (Bloch, *Medieval Misogyny and the Invention of Western Romantic Love* 46).

Despite this persistent negativism Christian apologists could not shut the door on all poetic fictions. Though Boethius's Lady Philosophy begins by banishing the Muses, she herself alternates poetry with prose in her educational process. And elsewhere in the *Confessions* Augustine recognizes that the poets' stories—which he never accepted as literally true—pose less moral danger than the philosophers' and religious leaders' false teachings (62). Perhaps the most compelling factor preventing Christians from rejecting poetic fictions outright was scripture's extensive dependence on figures of speech and parables. The Bible's authority was beyond debate—but its meaning was by no means clear-cut: many passages were ambiguous, and some were contradictory. In reconciling them all into a single, unified truth the distinction between the letter and the spirit served a crucial function. Augustine's response to Ambrose's teaching that biblical texts do not have to be read literally was an important step for his conversion and ultimately for medieval literary theory:

> I was pleased to hear that in his sermons Ambrose often repeated the text: "The written law inflicts death, whereas the spiritual law brings life," as though this were a rule upon which he wished to insist most carefully. And when he lifted the veil of mystery and disclosed the spiritual meaning of texts which, taken literally, appeared to contain the most unlikely doctrines, I was not aggrieved by what he said, although I did not yet know whether it was true. (*Confessions* 115-16)

Christianity, then, has texts that, though considered divinely inspired, make extensive use of parable and figurative language. Jesus himself, when asked why he speaks in parables, defends them as a means of preserving faith's mysteries for those worthy to hear them (Mark 4: 10-12). In *On Christian Doctrine* Augustine develops further justifications for textual obscurity, arguing that it chastens intellectual pride and curbs the human tendency to undervalue that which is too easily accessible (Bk. II: Ch. 6, 7). He also observes that the human mind takes greater pleasure in confronting a truth cloaked in figurative language than one baldly expressed. Citing the Song of Songs, which compares the beloved's teeth to a flock of sheep, he says: "Nevertheless, in a strange way, I contemplate the saints more pleasantly when I envisage them as the teeth of the Church cutting off men from their errors and transferring them to her body after their hardness has been softened as if by being bitten and chewed" (Bk. II: Ch. 6, 7).

But the thrust of Augustine's justification for figurative language rests on its didactic utility: the spiritually mature person casts aside the external shell to reach the nutritious kernel within. Yet scriptural obscurity necessitates authoritative guidance lest the uninitiated fall into error. To that end a long line of biblical commentary, or *exegesis,* stretching back to the Church Fathers provided sanctioned glosses that established interpretive parameters for sacred texts. Biblical exegetes distinguished between a text's *sense*—its surface or literal level—and its *sentence,* its underlying moral or spiritual meaning. A jealously guarded clerical prerogative, exegesis favors spiritual over literal—or carnal—readings. Especially with regard to the Old Testament, the exegetes relied upon the typological principle discussed in Chapter One: figures and events have a factual historicity in their own context and a further significance when they are fulfilled in the Christian dispensation (Auerbach, *Mimesis* 64).

Because biblical motifs and typological thinking were so deeply ingrained in medieval culture, poets—by drawing on a reservoir of shared beliefs, images, and key words—could count on their audience's grasp of connections that explanatory notes must spell out for us. Indeed a well-established line of critics, with D. W. Robertson, Jr., at their head, has stressed the centrality of exegetics for a sound grasp of medieval poetry. David Jeffrey observes in the introduction to *Chaucer and the Scriptural Tradition:* "Most critics of medieval poetry now agree that at least some understanding of medieval exegetical method is indispensable for an historical understanding of the language of medieval poetry" (xiv). Simply put, this branch of criticism applies exegesis to all texts produced in the medieval Christian tradition; these critics argue that medieval texts all have a didactic message: the importance of *caritas* (the selfless love of God) over *cupiditas* (the excessive love of any worldly good). Though often illuminating, the exegetical method can be excessively restrictive, as Judson Allen points out: "In the Robertsonian tradition . . . there has been what amounts to a platonist or twelfth century reductionist approach to particulars, under which they do not merely relate to the normative, but disappear into it" (*The Ethical Poetic of the Late Middle Ages* 99). Most recent criticism finds this approach too one-sided, arguing that the clerical establishment could not control patterns of

signification throughout medieval society. Jeffrey, for instance, notes
that Chaucer does not fit into the rigid interpretive matrix that some
exegetical critics strive to impose on all medieval texts (xiv). Nevertheless, exegetical criticism has heightened awareness of historical
context. A thorough grounding in scripture and in exegesis usually
adds resonance to our understanding of medieval texts. Critics who
recognize the validity of exegetical principles without applying them
single-mindedly often find that "doctrinal nuance constitutes not a
fruit which is the essence of a tale, but a *fruity flavour* enriching a
tale's bouquet," as Alcuin Blamires pithily observes (*The Canterbury
Tales: An Introduction to the Variety of Criticism* 25).

Typology and exegesis affect the structuring and imagery of much
medieval poetry. Dante, for example, builds the entire *Divine Comedy*
on a typological foundation: the Exodus becomes the underlying pattern for the pilgrim's journey from the dark wood of error to the beatific vision (Demaray, *Dante and the Book of the Cosmos* 17). Chaucer too
frequently makes typological associations. He draws on scriptural tradition and makes extensive use of biblical parallels and echoes (Wood,
"Artistic Intention 36; Reiss, "Biblical Parody" 48), but he frequently
inverts the prototypes. When the Miller promises to tell a "legende" of
a "carpenter and his wyf," he inevitably calls to mind the chaste marriage of Joseph and Mary, just the opposite of that between John and
Alisoun. "The Miller's Tale" also uses the story of Noah as a central
motif: its plot pivots on old John's foolish willingness to see himself as
a new Noah singled out for divine protection from a second flood,
which the biblical text promises will never occur. And while the original flood, according to medieval belief, punishes lechery, the flood
Nicholas predicts facilitates his adultery with Alisoun; while Noah responds in faith to a divine command, old John responds out of foolish
lustfulness. Depending on our point of view, we can see Chaucer using
typological parallels either to underscore human sinfulness or to poke
fun at the clerical enterprise of exegetical interpretation, as Sandra
Prior points out: "The parody in the Miller's Tale is large and complex
and covers three related areas: biblical figures and events, the contemporary religious drama in which they were represented, and finally,
the technique of exegesis" ("Parodying Typology" 57).

If spiritual readings and typological parallels constituted the
bases for Christians' approach to sacred texts, how were they to react
to the classical texts that underlay their education? Augustine provides the basic argument for accommodation, maintaining that
Christians can put the classical world's riches to better uses than did
their classical counterparts. His distinction between *use* and *enjoy-*

ment helps to clarify his position: "to enjoy something is to cling to it with love for its own sake. To use something, however, is to employ it in obtaining that which you love, provided that it is worthy of love" (*On Christian Doctrine* Bk. I: Ch. 4, 4); God is the only proper object of enjoyment (Bk. I: Ch. 5, 5); everything else should serve to bring humanity closer to the divine, "so that by means of corporal and temporal things we may comprehend the eternal and spiritual" (Bk. I: Ch. 4, 4). In Augustine's thinking things are neither good nor evil in themselves; what matters is the use to which they are put. Thus Christians should use whatever means are at hand—including those from non-Christian sources—to help them reach their goal: "But we should not think that we ought not to learn literature because Mercury is said to be its inventor. . . . Rather, every good and true Christian should understand that wherever he may find truth, it is his Lord's" (Bk. II: Ch. 18, 28) Rabanus Maurus (ca. 780-856), in his *Clerical Institute,* stresses that Christians should prune and reshape for their purposes what they find in secular literature:

> If we wish to read the poems and books of the gentiles because of their flowers of eloquence, we must take as our type the captive woman in Deuteronomy. . . . If an Israelite should want her as a wife, he should shave her head, cut off her nails, and pluck her eyebrows. When she has been made clean, he can then embrace her as a husband. By the same token, we customarily do this when a book of secular learning comes into our hands. (qtd. in Hardison, "Medieval Literary Criticism" 265)

A major justification for classical poetry was that it provides rhetorical models for effective expression, a pattern already established in the ancient world (Hardison 270). Augustine clearly recognizes the power inherent in classical rhetoric and the folly of ceding that power to Christianity's opponents: "For since by means of the art of rhetoric both truth and falsehood are urged, who would dare to say that truth should stand in the person of its defenders unarmed against lying, so that they who wish to urge falsehoods may know how to make their listeners benevolent, or attentive, or docile in their presentation, while the defenders of truth are ignorant of that art?" (*On Christian Doctrine* Bk 4: Ch. 2, 3). Accordingly, medieval students studied classical poetry to familiarize themselves with engaging ways of presenting Christian doctrine.

But perhaps the most important justification for studying the classical poets was to seek moral guidance. The previously discussed distinction between the Bible's surface and inner levels of meaning set the stage for Christianity to establish a primarily didactic justification for reading classical texts: they provide "useful doctrina (general knowledge) and, above all, moral instruction through examples" (Hardison 274). For if the inspired biblical writer could cloak his truths behind a veil, so too might a classical writer's fictitious surfaces conceal truths. Whereas Christianity used typology to absorb Hebrew texts, it assimilated classical ones by resorting to allegory, an approach that some classical thinkers had already used to account for the mythic and fabulous elements in their own literature (Seznec 84-87). Allegorical interpretation provided the most compelling argument for accepting classical poetry: on the surface level, the poets' fables and figurative expressions are lies, but that surface covers hidden truth. Christian commentators saw studying classical secular literature as a desirable—indeed necessary—preliminary step to the more rigorous and challenging study of sacred scripture (Minnis 33). Thus began a long tradition that links poetry with moral philosophy or ethics by allegorically interpreting classical literature (Hardison 279). In the medieval view "a poem is not a thing, rather it is both an example of and the result of behaviour" (Allen, *Ethical Poetic* 86).

Eventually a number of classical Roman authors found their way into the medieval curriculum. Virgil achieved a special place, in part because his Fourth Eclogue was read as prophetic of Jesus's birth. Also, the *Aeneid* was easy to interpret allegorically. Aeneas—voyaging throughout the Mediterranean world trying to fulfill his destined mission of leading the defeated Trojans to their new home in Rome—became the Christian soul, wandering through life searching for its true heavenly destination. A long commentary tradition culminating in Bernardus Silvestris, a twelfth century Neoplatonist, treated Aeneas's journey as that of "the soul seeking wisdom" (Cook and Herzman 40). The special esteem that medieval culture had for Virgil reaches its zenith when Dante chooses him as his revered guide through hell and purgatory, greeting him enthusiastically as "quella fonte/che spandi di parlar si largo fiume" (*Inferno* I: l. 79) [that fountain which pours forth so rich a stream of speech] and as the "delli altri poeti onore e lume" (l. 82) ["glory and light of other poets"].

Other Roman writers were highly valued—Cicero, for instance. His "Dream of Scipio"—preserved in Macrobius's commentary—advances an asceticism that was very compatible with the Christian outlook. In the opening section of *The Parliament of Fowls* Chaucer draws on this work, summarizing how Affrican instructs his grandson about the importance of "commune profyt" (l. 47): Affrican promises that the person who strives for it "shulde into a blysful place wende/There as joye is that last withouten ende" (ll. 48-49). When his grandson inquires about an afterlife, Affrican responds that "oure present worldes lyves space/ Nis but a maner deth, what wey we trace;/ And rightful folk shul gon, after they dye,/ To hevene;" (ll. 54-57). This stress on earthly life's insignificance and on the heavenly reward awaiting the virtuous had a familiar ring to Christian ears. Furthermore, Macrobius's use of a dream vision using an authoritative allegorical figure appealed to medieval sensibilities (Hardison 279). Even the much more sensual and irreverent Ovid was welcomed: though his *Metamorphoses* recount the exploits—frequently sexual—of the ancient gods, the allegorical method provided a means of transmuting that seeming dross of pagan sensuality into the gold of Christian moral edification.

Medieval culture ultimately appropriated a significant body of Roman classical literature; in addition to the writers discussed above, others like Statius, Horace, Cato, Juvenal, Lucan, and Terence gained admittance to the curriculum (Curtius, *European Literature and the Latin Middle Ages* 48-54), thereby gaining the status of "auctours":

> The term "auctour" may profitably be regarded as an accolade bestowed upon a popular writer by those later scholars and writers who used extracts from his works as sententious statements or "auctoritates," gave lectures on his works in the form of textual commentaries, or employed them as literary models. Two criteria for the award of this accolade were tacitly applied: "intrinsic worth" and "authenticity." (Minnis 10)

The auctour's task was to pass on ancient stories that derived from other established authors and preserved old truths (Blamires, *The Canterbury Tales* 51). Ultimately both Christian and classical authors were commingled (Curtius 48-49). The latter could be invoked alongside patristic or other ecclesiastical figures, and both achieved authoritative status (Minnis 37). However, classical writers, according to Christian apologists, could not achieve the same measure of truth as the inspired biblical writers; rather, through limited human reason classical poets could reach valid, though incomplete, insights. Dante's treatment of his beloved Virgil and of the other poets— Ovid, Horace, Lucan, Homer—who inhabit the first circle of hell is instructive: they live in the light—that of human reason—but a vast darkness surrounds them because they are forever cut off from God, light's true source.

But what of writers functioning within the Christian dispensation? Because scripture was seen as divinely inspired, those who wrote sacred texts were considered God's instruments and authoritative sources rather than creators for their own purposes. In discussing the author of the Book of Job, Gregory the Great (ca. 540-94) forcefully articulates this position by comparing the human author to a pen:

> If we were reading the epistle of some great man with his Epistle in our hand, yet were to enquire by what pen they were written, doubtless it would be an absurdity, to know the Author of the Epistle and to understand his meaning, and notwithstanding to be curious to know with what sort of pen the words were marked upon the page. When then we understand the matter, and are persuaded that the Holy Spirit was its author, in stirring a question about the author what else do we than in reading a letter enquire about the pen? (*Morals on the Book of Job* I: 15)

In this view, the author functions as a scribe, simply taking down what God dictates; his purposes and personality matter not at all, and the truth he conveys is all-important (Minnis 21).

But the High Middle Ages paid greater attention to the human author. The twelfth-century humanistic movement recognized Christian poets as having an active role first in grasping the cosmic divine order and then in recreating that order through their work (Mazzotta, *Dante's Vision and the Circle of Knowledge* 7). The poet's creative work was compared to the divine: just as God had written the "book" of nature and had inspired biblical writers to convey truth in the Bible—sometimes under cover of parable—so too does the Christian writer produce books, transmitting—through the often allegorical cover of his fictions—instructive truths for his readers. Thus from an essentially passive conduit of divinely inspired truths, the poet becomes a more active creator whose own mind functions as a shaping instrument. In the early thirteenth century Geoffrey of Vinsauf's *Poetria nova*, whose very title suggests new directions, conveys this idea in a famous passage that compares the poet to an architect:

> If a man has a house to build, his impetuous hand does not rush into action. The measuring line of his mind first lays out the work, and he mentally outlines the successive steps in a definite order. The mind's hand shapes the entire house before the body's hand builds it. Its mode of being is archetypal before it is actual. Poetic

art may see in this analogy the law to be given to poets: let the poet's hand not be swift to take up the pen, nor his tongue be impatient to speak; trust neither hand nor tongue to the guidance of fortune. . . . Let the mind's interior compass first circle the whole extent of the material. (16-17)

The shift from pen to architect links *homo artifex*—the human artist as maker—to the contemporary image of *Deus artifex*—God the Maker—laying out the dimensions of the universe with a compass. Commenting on the *Poetria nova*, O. B. Hardison observes: "Its novelty is its philosophy of art: the artist as creator, the superiority of mind to the materials of poetry, and ornament as the objectification of inner radiance" (291). But Vinsauf restricted himself to compositional guidelines without providing a comprehensive theoretical framework for late medieval poets (Jordan, *Chaucer's Poetics* 13).

Chaucer knew the *Poetria nova* well and drew on it in his work. In "The Miller's Tale," to highlight Alisoun's physical desirability, he shapes his memorable detailing of her charms by subtly modulating the earlier Geoffrey's instructions for describing a beautiful woman (Brown, *Chaucer at Work* 81-84). In "The Nun's Priest's Tale," when the fox abducts Chaunticleer on a Friday, the narrator spoofs Vinsauf's exemplary lament on the death of Richard I:

> O Gaufred, deere maister soverayn,
> That whan thy worthy kyng Richard was slayn
> With shot, compleynedest his deeth so soore,
> Why ne hadde I now thy sentence and thy loore,
> The Friday for to chide, as diden ye? (ll. 3347-51)

Most interestingly, at the end of Book I in *Troilus and Criseyde* Chaucer applies Vinsauf's architect image not to the narrator's poetic activity but to Pandarus's role as orchestrator of the lovers' affair, thereby linking the two functions:

> For everi wight that hath an hous to founde
> Ne renneth naught the werk for to bygynne
> With rakel hond, but he wol bide a stounde,
> And sende his hertes line out fro withinne
> Aldirfirst his purpos for to wynne.
> Al this Pandare in his herte thoughte,
> And caste his werk ful wisely or he wroughte. (ll. 1065-71)

Stress on the poet's creative capacity led to greater emphasis on poetry's link to philosophy and theology and to seeing the poet as prophet: one divinely charged to convey moral or spiritual truths through his fictions. The Neoplatonist Proclus (410-85) maintains that poetry can express truths that transcend reason; indeed their transcendence helps to explain why the poet uses language that, though beautiful, often remains obscure; he sees "poetry as revelation, the poet as inspired seer, the poetic faculty as supra-rational, allegory as a veil or as an accommodation, and ethical teaching as an important but subsidiary poetic function" (Hardison 277-78). In the twelfth century Neoplatonic revival at Chartres these ideas appear in the work of Bernard Silvestris and Alan of Lille (Hardison 277-81). The latter—in the *Anticlaudianus,* an allegorical poem about the creation of a new primal man—believes that his poem can reveal the divine and sees himself functioning as a prophet (Dronke, *Dante and Medieval Latin Traditions* 9). For Alan, "the divine nature . . . is a poetic one: it conceives the world in poetic form. . . . And insofar as we can glimpse the divine, it will also be by way of images, poetically rather than rationally" (Dronke 12).

The fourteenth-century Italian humanist movement gave renewed vigor to the poet's prophetic role and extended the range of poetry's reach toward the ineffable. Dante clearly saw himself as a prophet: the entire arduous journey the narrator undertakes in the *Comedy* prepares him for that role. The process culminates in his encounter with his ancestor Cacciaguida, who vigorously commissions his great-grandson to speak the truth as he sees it whatever the consequences (*Paradiso* XVII: ll. 127-35). Guiseppe Mazzotta argues that Dante makes a "radical claim about poetry as nothing less than the foundation of all possible knowledge" (3). It transcends even theology, the queen of the medieval sciences, the capstone of the curriculum, the discipline for which all other intellectual endeavor is but a preparation (13). The essence of Dante's argument is that divine truth exceeds the capacity of human reason to grasp and human language to express; thus the rational attempts to attain it through the ordered disciplines of philosophy and theology must inevitably fail. Poetry, however, especially in its image-making, creates a bridge between the material world and that of the spirit; though it too can never fully capture the divine mind, it allows brief but genuine glimpses into the sacred mysteries (135-73). In the following generation early humanists more fully justified poetry's role in a Christian society and more explicitly linked poetry and theology. They argued that Christian poets—because they have access to a revealed truth not available to classical poets—actually share in the truth of sacred scripture:

> Poetry, whether pagan or Christian, reveals truth beneath
> a veil of fiction; Scripture reveals truth beneath a veil of
> truth, though the writers of Scripture sometimes used the
> locutions of the poets. But Christian poetry shares the
> truth of Scripture, though it employs the fictions of pa-
> gan poetry. (Green, "Dante's Allegory" 125)

The tradition we have traced derives from Latin literature and culminates in the Italian fourteenth-century humanism that paved the way for the Renaissance: it justifies poetry through its truth-capturing and didactic functions. Boccaccio's theories about poetry bridge medieval and Renaissance views and practices by applying to secular poetry ideas that had developed in the context of sacred writings (Spearing, *Medieval to Renaissance in English Poetry* 7).

Medieval culture also recognized pleasure as a desirable goal for literary activity. A well-known passage from the Roman poet Horace's *Ars poetica* considerably influenced medieval literary theory: "aut prodesse volunt aut delectare poetae, aut simul et incunda et idonea dicere vitae" (ll. 333-34) ["Poets wish either to benefit, or to delight, or to say things that are simultaneously pleasing and applicable to life"]. As we have seen, poetry's ability to please was associated with its surface textual beauties, while its instructive function was linked with the text's inner meaning (Olson, *Literature as Recreation* 22). Other theories argued for poetry's therapeutic role, its capacity to contribute to both bodily and mental health. Medical treatises like the *Tacuinum* recognize that a cheerful, temperate frame of mind supports good health. The enjoyment derived from reading or listening to poetic fictions promotes that frame of mind. These treatises saw refreshing conversation—including serious and humorous storytelling—as supporting overall well-being and as inducing the relaxation that leads to healthful sleep. In *The Book of the Duchess* Chaucer reflects these beliefs in his narrator's turning to Ovid's stories to combat his life-threatening insomnia; serendipitously, he finds references to a god of sleep and achieves the desired result (Olson, *Literature as Recreation* 39-89).

Medieval culture even acknowledged the value of purely recreational activity, thereby providing a basis for admitting that goal in literary pursuits. After the thirteenth century's Aristotelian revival the *Nicomachean Ethics* lent its authority to a more tolerant attitude toward recreational pleasure. Concessions to human frailty after the fall—even in a monastic environment—allowed temperate recreation to balance against physical labor and contemplation's spiritually rigorous leisure. Both Petrarch and Boccaccio argued in favor of literature's recreational value, maintaining that it brings refreshment to solitary hours and restoration to spirits worn out by stress (Olson, *Literature as Recreation* 90-132). Paradoxically enough, attempts to combat the plague may have fostered new ways of thinking about literature's function as a source of pleasure rather than only of edification and instruction. Glending Olson's study of medieval plague tracts has shown that the advice medical experts provided about the kind of behavior most likely to stave off disease has much in common with the way Boccaccio's storytellers in the *Decameron* planned their activities during their escape into the countryside. They put themselves in a pleasing and relaxing environment, eat and drink moderately, avoid exertion and excessive emotions, and keep their thoughts away from the morbid and depressing. Their storytelling—which Pampinea proposes as a way to pass the time during the hottest part of the day—becomes part of an overall hygienic regime designed to keep the young people healthy while the plague rages in the Florence they have temporarily left behind. The storytelling, in effect, functions as a kind of play that has a serious underlying purpose: to foster a healthful frame of mind that will prevent people's succumbing to disease. This view bridges the traditional medieval position that literature is suspect unless it directly or indirectly teaches moral or spiritual truths and the later view that literature constitutes its own justification, its main purpose being to give pleasure. In the *Decameron* literature serves its useful function precisely because it gives pleasure. As Mazzotta suggests in his discussion of the relation between plague and play,

> Their [Boccacccio's storytellers] playing is, in a way, an imitation of the philosopher, who in his schole, literally in his leisure, seeks wisdom as its own aesthetic end; it is an instance of a deliberate shirking of work and duties, a truancy, which, while it relieves from the anxieties of the plague, asserts the players' freedom and mastery, by the imagination, of the space they occupy in the midst of the world's dereliction. (*The World at Play in Boccaccio's Decameron* 42)

Indeed the *Decameron* occupies a pivotal place in the shift toward recognizing literature's recreational function. It takes a crucial step, what Donald Howard calls "the birth of fiction" (*Chaucer: His Life, His Works, His World* 283). In spite of critical efforts to find allegorical meanings, Howard argues, most stories in the collection exist purely for entertainment: "the message is that there is no message" (*Chaucer* 296). The stories provide a temporary escape from the horrors of a plague-ridden world and celebrate, without didacticism, the values that lead to worldly success: tolerance, shrewdness, good humor. By allowing brief excursions into other lives and temporary escapes from overwhelming pain, they afford the opportunity for a new perspective and for a mind refreshed to return to mundane existence (Howard, *Chaucer* 291-96).

As Chaucer matured as an artist, he came under the influence of all these traditions: classical Latin poetry, vernacular court poetry, and early Italian humanistic poetry. Out of these he struggled to carve out his own poetic identity, always functioning within the constraints of a politically charged environment. As suggested earlier, his contact with the heady atmosphere of early humanism during his two Italian journeys in the 1370s were pivotal in his development. The unfinished *House of Fame* records his bewildered reaction to the poetic riches he found there. This poem reveals him self-consciously exploring his role as poet and his doubts about language's capacity to capture truth (Jordan, *Chaucer's Poetics* 24). In *Troilus and Criseyde*—which many consider Chaucer's masterpiece—the poet reflects upon and synthesizes the motifs and materials to which his Italian experiences had introduced him. He produces a work of profound philosophical reflection that simultaneously captivates and diverts its audience through vividly realized characters and an engrossing plot. Olson argues that, because it had classical subject matter and explored philosophical issues, Chaucer recognizes the possibility of calling this work "poesye" ("Making and Poetry" 289-90). Citing the following lines from one of the poem's last stanzas,

> Go, litel bok, go, litel myn tragedye,
> Ther God thi makere yet, er that he dye,
> So sende myght to make in som comedye!
> But litel book, no makyng thow n'envie,
> But subgit be to alle poesye;
> And kis the steppes where as thow seest pace
> Virgil, Ovide, Omer, Lucan, and Stace. (ll. 1786-92)

Olson concludes: "The delicacy of those lines, which intimate but do not specify its proper category, reflects something of the complex situation of the late medieval vernacular writer and his relation to "poesye" ("Making and Poetry" 290).

But though Chaucer's conception of his role as a poet evolved over his lifetime, he, unlike Dante, never completely assumed the prophetic stance. Nor does he seem to have believed that poetry can approach divine truth. Through the Wife of Bath's comments about the significance of point of view, Chaucer reveals his awareness of the subjective dimension in all knowledge (Blamires 52). As Lisa Kiser points out, "Chaucer's narrative poetry consistently exposes the limitations of human knowledge and calls into question the accessibility of 'truth'"(*Truth and Textuality in Chaucer's Poetry* 1). But though diffident about speaking out with prophetic authority, the mature Chaucer certainly saw himself as more than a court entertainer: his concept of his audience expands to include the unseen readers who turn the pages of his manuscript, and he worries about the text's susceptibility to scribal error, indicating that he has an eye on how posterity will respond to and understand his work.

If in *Troilus and Criseyde* Chaucer came within inches of placing himself among the poets, in *The Canterbury Tales* he leaves the issue of the poet's role and of poetry's function, though extensively explored, very much unresolved. As he begins the *Tales*, he foregrounds his concern about the relationship between moral edification and entertainment when Harry Bailly announces that the pilgrim who tells the tale of "best sentence and moost solaas" (GP, l.798) will win the contest, thereby implicitly suggesting that a balance between the two is most desirable. The tales that follow provide a wide range, from almost total diversion—like "The Miller's Tale"—to almost exclusive didacticism—like "The Parson's Tale."

The juxtaposition of the entertaining and the didactic appears in graphic contrast in the two tales the Chaucer pilgrim tells in Fragment VII, which, according to Alan Gaylord, "comes the closest of anything we have from Chaucer to providing his literary aesthetic" ("'Sentence' and Solaas'" 227). Ann Astell, drawing on Gaylord's designation of that fragment as "the literature group" (227), argues that "the tales of Thopas and Melibee provide a key that unlocks the whole structure of the fragment. . . . 'To teach and to delight' is, of course, the classical definition of the causa finalis [final cause or purpose] of poetry, a formulation that applies to the contrastive tales of Chaucer the pilgrim" ("Chaucer's 'Literature Group'" 270). Harry Bailly establishes parameters and creates expectations when, in the "Prologue to Sir Thopas," he calls on the pilgrim for "a tale of myrthe" (l. 706) and tells the others, "now shul we heere/Som deyntee thyng, me thynketh by his cheere" (ll. 710-11). In response, the pilgrim, the only one to actually tell two tales, begins with an airy account of chivalric adventure with no sign of didactic intent. C. David Benson comments, "The achievement of 'Sir Thopas' is its style and wit. . . . It is pure fun without the slightest desire to edify or improve"

("Their Telling Difference" 66). But the pilgrim has no more than warmed up to his topic when Harry, apparently missing the parody, abruptly interrupts him, complaining that "Thy drasty rymyng is nat worth a toord!" (l. 930). Harry commands another performance, perhaps one in prose, since the pilgrim cannot seem to manage rhyme, and a tale that offers either mirth or doctrine:

> Sire, at o word, thou shalt no lenger ryme.
> Lat se wher thou kanst tellen aught in geeste,
> Or telle in prose somwhat, at the leeste,
> In which ther be som murthe or som doctryne.
>   (ll. 932-35)

Overlooking the insults, the pilgrim acquiesces, expressing his willingness to tell "a moral tale vertuous" (l. 940). Then, drawing an analogy with the four gospels, which "alle acorden as in hire sentence/Al be ther in hir tellyng difference" (ll. 947-48), he asks his audience's indulgence for the variations he may introduce into his tale because those variations will not change the moral:

> And though I nat the same wordes seye
> As ye han herd, yet to yow alle I preye
> Blameth me nat, for, as in my sentence,
> Shul ye nowher fynden difference
> Fro the sentence of this tretys lyte
> After the which this murye tale I write. (ll. 959-64)

The pilgrim proceeds with the prose "Tale of Melibee," in which Melibee hears, at great length, the advice of his wife, Prudence, about not seeking revenge on the enemies who have injured their daughter, Sophie.

Clearly, Chaucer uses these two tales in a contrastive way to explore the role of the poet and the relationship between poetry's and prose's truth-telling capacity. As Benson observes, "The tales Chaucer assigns to himself are a microcosm of the *Canterbury Tales* as a whole; they . . . explore the responsibilities of Christian art" ("Their Telling Difference" 71). But critical opinion remains divided on what he intends by the juxtaposition. Some see him parodying in "Sir Thopas" the popular chivalric romances that were staple courtly entertainment and repudiating the role of courtly entertainer. A negative reading of "Sir Thopas" often yields a more positive assessment of "Melibee," in spite of what many contemporary readers see as its tedious didacticism. As

Richard Firth Green comments: "his [Chaucer's] position as court entertainer, successor to generations of professional minstrels, is belittled in the self-mockery of 'Sir Thopas,' but as the adviser to kings the author of 'Melibee' writes essentially without irony" (*Poets and Princepleasers* 143). Lee Patterson reverses this judgment, maintaining that Chaucer was no more comfortable with the role of court counselor ("'What Man Artow?'"139). Indeed he goes on to argue that "Chaucer is disowning not the childish frivolity of 'Sir Thopas' but the pragmatic didacticism of 'Melibee'" (123). Modern discomfort with the latter tale's didacticism, in Patterson's view, is more than a failure of historical imagination; rather, it points to the irony of a moral tale whose lessons fail to have the intended effect either on Melibee within the tale or on Harry Bailly outside of it (157-58). Prudence's barrage of proverbial wisdom undercuts its own aim of encouraging internalized thoughtfulness: "the meditative self-reflectiveness that is the goal of Prudence's pedagogy is foreclosed by the very means with which it is sought" (158).

In Fragment VII Harry makes abundantly clear that a moral story that bores its audience to inattention fails to accomplish its goal: when the Monk has told a series of repetitiously structured tales— with a promise of more to come—all on the theme of falling from prosperity to disaster, Harry joins the Knight's protest, stressing the uselessness of even the most edifying discourse that puts its audience to sleep:

> Youre tale anoyeth al this compaignye.
> Swich talkyng is nat worth a boterflye,
> For therinne is ther no desport ne game. . . .
> I pray yow hertely telle us somwhat elles;
> For sikerly, nere clynkyng of youre belles
> That on youre bridel hange on every syde,
> By hevene kyng that for us alle dyde,
> I sholde er this han fallen doun for sleep,
> Although the slough had never been so deep;
> Thanne hadde your tale al be toold in veyn.
> For certeinly, as that thise clerkes seyn,
> Whereas a man may have noon audience,
> Noght helpeth it to tellen his sentence. (ll. 2789-801)

When the Monk refuses the opportunity for a second start, Harry turns to the Nun's Priest—the elusive pilgrim whom some, like Dolores Frese, see as a Chaucerian alter ego ("'The Nun's Priest's

Tale'" 330-43)—to "telle us swich a thyng as may oure hertes glade"
(l. 2811). Indeed "The Nun's Priest's Tale" has seemed to many
readers to balance the demands for "sentence" and "solaas" and
thus to deserve the prize-winning supper at the Tabard Inn. The
Nun's Priest's choice of a fable about a cock who almost gets eaten
by a fox approaches truth-telling and moral teaching in the poetic
mode, "under a veil" (Astell, "Chaucer's 'Literature Group'" 279).
In the tale's concluding lines the narrator, a member of the clerical
establishment, specifically evokes the exegetical tradition, directing
the audience to look beyond the tale's delightful surface to the lesson that it teaches:

> But ye that holden this tale a folye,
> As of a fox, or of a cok and hen,
> Taketh the moralite, goode men.
> For Seint Paul seith that al that writen is,
> To oure doctrine it is ywrite, ywis;
> Taketh the fruyt, and lat the chaf be stille. (ll. 3438-43)

But distinguishing "the fruyt" from "the chaf" is no easy matter. As
Piero Boitani points out, some time earlier when reporting Chaunticleer's mistranslation of a crucial text, the Nun's Priest abdicates his
role as exegete in favor of his heroic cock ("'My Tale Is of a Cock'"
33). The tale's elaborately rhetorical expansion of a beast fable delights its audience as it mocks several medieval literary genres: epic,
romance, exemplum. But its *sentence* proves to be permanently elusive: it advances so many morals, some of them contradictory, that no
amount of critical commentary has succeeded in pinning it down.

Summing up Chaucer's exploration of literature in Fragment VII,
Astell comments on the contradictory claims to which he would have
responded:

> Chaucer explores the multiple causality of art and the contradic-
> tory claims it makes upon the poet who must be a mechanically
> competent versifier and an inspired, spontaneous oracle; inge-
> nious in sophistic ornamentation and, at the same time, artlessly
> ingenuous; absolutely true to his sources but equally creative with
> them; an instructor who teaches indirectly and thus has little guar-
> antee that his true intent will be realized by his audience; an enter-
> tainer whose success in delighting endangers his didactic purpose
> as much as or more than does his failure to please. ("Chaucer's
> 'Literature Group'" 283-84)

Perhaps we might conclude that Chaucer achieves the balance between edification and entertainment precisely in his fusion of a storytelling contest in a pilgrimage framework. But in the concluding segments of the Canterbury collection, he seems ever more radically to call into question the possibility that language can capture or even approximate the reality it attempts to signify. The collection concludes with a series of withdrawals, from fiction, from discourse, from earthly life into a prayer for forgiveness and salvation (Jordan, *Chaucer's Poetics* 149). "The Manciple's Tale," the shortest of them all, is "a simpler example [than "The Nun's Priest's Tale] . . . of the fundamentally ambiguous condition of language" (151). Here Chaucer tells of a truth-telling crow who loses both beauty and voice because he unguardedly uses language. The simple plot is embedded in rhetorically circuitous digressions that often seem not only irrelevant but also subversive of the points that they purport to exemplify. The tale concludes with a lengthy passage in which the narrator repeats his mother's advice to embrace silence:

> My sone, be war, and be noon auctour newe
> Of tidynges, wheither they been false or trewe.
> Whereso thou come, amonges hye or lowe,
> Kepe wel thy tonge and thenk upon the crowe.
> (ll. 359-62)

As Blamires observes: "The crow is a storyteller who cannot control interpretation of his tale. A poet who wants to eliminate these risks of authorship can easily do so. It is just a matter of 'breaking his minstrelsy,' depriving his various voices of their tongue, and ceasing to write at all" (56). Michaela Paasche Grudin, on the other hand, argues that the tale supports what she terms "the poetics of guile" (329). Linking the tale to a repressive political environment in which unguarded speech could lead to dire consequences, she sees it as posturing between the crow's tactless blurting of the truth in the tale and the Manciple's cautious withdrawal from speech in the "Prologue" (339).

Finally, Chaucer does take leave of all his writing, but not before adding the longest piece in the collection, in prose. In the concluding segment, "The Parson's Prologue and Tale," Chaucer places his pilgrimage in an eschatalogical framework by evoking the Heavenly Jerusalem and, for the second time in *The Canterbury Tales*, resorts to prose for his treatise on penance and the seven deadly sins. Then in the "Retraction," which at one extreme critics see as a purely mechanical concession to conventional piety and at the other as a deeply felt expression of religious remorse, he pulls himself into the penitential frame by seeking forgiveness for his works whose frivolity or licentiousness may have led others to sin. Does the "Retraction" reflect the scrupulous angst of a dying man or the deliberative results of a lifetime's meditative reflection, or perhaps something in between? As with so much in Chaucer's work, no definitive answer is possible. Robert Jordan aptly captures the poet's elusiveness: "For an artist whose metier is artifice and the accommodation of disjunct materials, Chaucer appears to have achieved the ultimate disjunction. But it is difficult to assess conclusively Chaucer's last words on the subject of his art; no doubt the master of obliquity would not have it otherwise" (*Chaucer's Poetics* 149).

Still, we must remember that in *The Canterbury Tales* Chaucer does give literature's element of play a central role: the work pivots on the interconnection between *sentence* and *solaas*, between *ernest* and *game*. Perhaps the recurrent cycles of plague that Chaucer's world endured both highlighted human life's fragility and unpredictability and made it appear more precious and more to be savored. The balancing act between an essentially spiritual versus an essentially earthly orientation that characterized European Christian culture at least since the twelfth century tipped firmly in the direction of the earthly—at the point at which it was most threatened. The pleasure of storytelling encourages Chaucer's pilgrims, like Boccaccio's *brigata*, to enjoy the interlude—the journey itself—to linger along the way, temporarily distracting them from the apocalyptic implications of attaining their pilgrimage's goal.

II.

RELIGION

CHAPTER THREE

The Church in Turmoil:
The Hierarchy and Heresy

*T*he stereotype of the medieval period as an age of faith dominated in all aspects by a single-minded, hegemonic Church has
persisted in many people's minds. To be sure, in the fourteenth century a still-undivided Christendom enjoyed a core of shared beliefs
and assumptions difficult for us to imagine in our highly fragmented
era. But the medieval Church was not, nor had it ever been in actual-
ity rather than in theory, a monolith single-mindedly advancing its interests. Rather, it was a collection of competing factions with often
contradictory agendas (Knapp, *Chaucer and the Social Contest* 46). In
the fourteenth century the Church experienced particularly unsettling turmoil: its helplessness in the face of the plague's onslaughts
contributed substantially to the laity's declining trust in its mediatory
power with an inscrutably angry deity; furthermore, its internal strife
and clerical abuses left people as spiritually ravaged as plague left
them physically ravaged.

The repeated epidemics of plague that Christian Europe experienced in the Late Middle Ages did much to weaken the Church by
highlighting the clergy's impotence in the face of a formidable adversary. The virulence of the disease made traditional deathbed and
burial rites impossible, as Boccaccio observes in the opening section
of the *Decameron* (55-57). Even when the clergy did engage in typical
devotional practices to appease an angry deity, all of its prayers,
masses, and processions proved fruitless, as people could see: the
clergy's mortality matched or exceeded that of the general population (Ziegler, *The Black Death* 128). Furthermore, though many clergymen, recognizing the Church as the institution to which people
turned in troubled times, did attempt to meet their spiritual responsibilities to the people, the clergy's overall performance fell short of
expectations. In addition to being fundamentally helpless, some

clergymen were also cowardly. Hoping to escape infection, they abandoned their posts and left their people to fend for themselves, as Jean de Venette records: "In many towns timid priests withdrew, leaving the exercise of their ministry to such as were more daring" (qtd. in Bowsky, *The Black Death* 16). The clergy's inability to provide useful relief from the plague's suffering did not turn most people away from religion and God, but it did call into question the efficacy of the Church's traditional measures and left people looking for ways to exercise greater control over their own spiritual destinies, radically altering their perception of the extent to which they could entrust their hope for salvation to a professional clerical class whose weaknesses had become all too apparent.

Though the clergy's weaknesses and failings often led to bitingly satiric attacks, anticlericalism could coexist comfortably with deep religious faith in the medieval period. Like many of his contemporaries, Chaucer shows his acute awareness of shortcomings in those who exercise spiritual authority, while at the same time apparently reverencing the ideals associated with their offices. He devotes more time to figures representing the Church than to any other group on the Canterbury pilgrimage, and *The Canterbury Tales* makes us acutely aware of their overt and covert tensions. While in the following chapter I will focus on the religious orders that bound themselves to special rules, in this chapter I deal with the Church's hierarchy, ranging from the pope to the bishop and the parish priest—what is known as the secular clergy—and with Chaucer's treatment of the Church through his portrayal of such pilgrims as the Pardoner, the Summoner, and the Parson. This chapter also reveals the extent to which Chaucer's work may reflect his own inner dialogue with England's first heretical movement: John Wyclif and his Lollard followers' critique of the Church's wealth, its representatives' shortcomings, and its role in governmental affairs. For though scholars have traditionally seen Chaucer as theologically and politically conservative, many clerical abuses he points to echo Lollard concerns. The difficulty of drawing a line between orthodoxy and heresy and the gradualness with which that line was drawn in Chaucer's England increase the complexity of ascertaining his views.

In attempting to understand the medieval Church we must consider it both as a spiritual entity and as a socio-political institution with a strong hierarchical structure. Most broadly conceived, the Church is the people of God or the communion of saints—all those, both dead and alive, united by their love of God. As we have seen in Chapter One, Augustine's *The City of God* distinguishes between two cities: "the earthly city . . . created by self-love [and] . . . the Heavenly City by the love of God" (593; Bk 14: ch 28). Jerusalem was associated with the heavenly city, while Babylon was its symbolic antithesis. Johannes van Oort, citing the work of William Kamlah, argues that in the final analysis Augustine links the City of God with *ecclesia* or church: "The historical congregation (or Church) is the city of God on earth, at present in exile, in the end at home in the heavenly Jerusalem" (*Jerusalem and Babylon* 127). But some question arises about just what Augustine meant by *ecclesia* (124). By the twelfth century, however, the link between the city of God and the institutional church was well established. Otto of Freising clearly equates them: "the City of God, which is the Church" (*The Two Cities* 251). Elsewhere he maintains that God "bestowed upon it the greatest temporal power possessed by any realm. . . . He exalted His kingdom, which is the Church, to the highest dignity" (281). Otto's comment highlights the Church's immersion in the earthly sphere, where the intermingling of religious and secular affairs becomes a constant source of tension, controversy, and potential abuse.

By administering its sacraments and spreading its teachings, the Church serves as a mediator of God's grace and fulfills its spiritual function: to draw people toward their heavenly goal. Its mission underpins a central binary opposition in the medieval period: that between the clergy and the laity. Those who received ordination became an elite who had special duties and privileges related to humanity's ultimate destiny: through their prayers and the exercise of their sacramental powers they eased the way to salvation. Gradually the priestly class developed into a highly complex, hierarchical structure whose evolution tended to marginalize the laity by downplaying the concept of the Church as a communion of believers and increasingly identifying it with the hierarchy (Southern, *Western Society and the Church* 37-38). The pope, as the vicar of Christ—a title which was first used by Innocent III (1198-1216)—occupies the topmost position; though the papacy's centrality and importance evolved slowly, it ultimately achieved high visibility and power. At the local level is the bishop, claiming descent from the apostles, who has extensive powers in his diocese and delegates his authority to the parish priest, through whom the faithful, especially in the medieval period, had their most frequent, often their only, contact with the Church. But this hierarchical structure, with established parish boundaries, was not in place until the thirteenth century, when the movements toward centralization, standardization, and reform sought to have the Church permeate all layers of society and most aspects of life.

After the earliest Christians stopped expecting an imminent apocalypse and settled into establishing a workable organization for this world, the bishop emerged as the spiritual leader of local Christian communities. From the first Christian centuries, the bishop of Rome had special significance because he was seen as Peter's successor, but the implications of his position took centuries to develop (Schimmelpfennig, *The Papacy* 6-14). In the early Christian era the power ecclesiastical leaders wielded was exclusively spiritual. But the Church's move to preferential status after Constantine's conversion radically and permanently altered its relationship to secular authority. From being marginalized and sometimes persecuted, it achieved power in its own right, at times acting in conjunction with secular authority, at others actively opposing it. Conflict between the two powers dominated much of the political history of the medieval period.

In the fifth century Gelasius I (492-96) articulated a policy that outlined the parameters of the dispute. Challenging what had been prior practice, he maintained that bishops, rather than secular authorities, had responsibility for administering the Church; he also maintained that two powers rule the world: "the sacred authority of bishops" and the "royal power," arguing that the former has primacy because the spiritual life overweighs the material one (Barraclough, *The Medieval Papacy* 28). The theory of the two powers proved to be very influential. Papal apologists, most fully developing this theory, likened the relationship between pope and emperor to that between the sun and the moon: just as the moon reflects only the light it receives from the sun, so too does the emperor's authority derive from the pope, God's appointed vicar on earth. But this view was by no means universally accepted; those supporting the imperial side argued that secular rulers do not derive their authority from the clergy, but rather receive it directly from God. Dante's *De Monarchia*, for instance, forcefully rejects the validity of the sun/moon analogy (60).

Throughout the medieval period papal and imperial apologists jockeyed for advantage, their fortunes dependent on political circumstances and on the strength of the papal and imperial incumbents. The fourteenth century marks a particularly troubled era for the papacy. It experienced a series of traumas—some externally imposed, others self-generated—which were but harbingers of greater challenges to come. The century began with Boniface VIII's disastrous reign (1295-1303), which culminated in the Pope's capture by French forces at Anagni in 1303, a move so disturbing that it earned him the sympathy of Dante, one of his severest critics. It closed with the Great Schism, which saw the Church governed by two—and at one point by three—rival claimants to the papal throne. Bridging these two crises was the Avignon papacy (1309-78), labeled "the Babylonian Captivity" by hostile contemporaries, who thereby likened it to the Hebrews' period of exile from their homeland. Though the papacy survived these challenges, the issues they raised in people's minds and the forces they set in motion proved difficult to contain and continued to reverberate for centuries thereafter.

The papacy of Boniface VIII foreshadowed many of the evils, both external and internal, that the Church had to contend with throughout the century. In his encyclical *Unam Sanctam* he made a sweeping claim concerning the papacy's centrality: "We declare, state, define and pronounce that it is altogether necessary for salvation for every human creature to be subject to the Roman Pontiff" (qtd. in Holmes and Bickers 101). But in spite of such ringing assertions of papal authority, his personal weaknesses, corrupt practices, and inability to accurately assess his situation left the Church very debilitated by the end of his papacy (Holmes and Bickers, *A Short History of the Catholic Church* 102). Boniface's capture by Philip the Fair's forces signaled the French monarchy's increasingly aggressive intervention in Church affairs, contributing greatly to the disrepute the papacy suffered during this period. When Clement V (1305-14) was elected pope, he recognized the threat Philip posed and chose to conciliate rather than to confront him. Clement, a Frenchman, initially planned to move to Rome after his election, but he allowed himself to be crowned in Lyons and subsequently took up a supposedly temporary residency in Avignon. Because moving the papal seat to Avignon took the papacy out of Rome's political turmoil and provided a more centralized location for conducting the Church's business, it had some logic (Southern 133). But the move caused much discomfort among Christians because of Rome's symbolic and historic associations as Peter's see.

Furthermore, during the years when popes resided in Avignon, the French crown exerted much control over the Church, leading to a general impression that political considerations dominated Church policy (Holmes and Bickers 102-3). Thus, though the Avignon popes exhibited a wide range of abilities and personal qualities, the contemporary perception of the papacy was generally negative. Accentuating the negativism was a pervasive sense that the papal court's lifestyle was inordinately luxurious and corrupt. John XXII's condemnation of the well-regarded Spiritual Franciscans as heretics in 1323 reinforced the perception that the hierarchy was most intent on protecting its prerogatives to live in affluent comfort.

When Benedict XII (1335-42) decided to build a papal palace in Avignon, people interpreted that move as strong testimony of his intention not to return to Rome (Holmes and Bickers 106); furthermore, the papal palace itself—a large fortresslike structure—visually symbolized the Church's wealth and isolation

The reign of the Clement VI (1342-52) firmly sealed in the popular mind the image of Avignon as wasteful and corrupt. Maintaining that his predecessors "did not know how to be popes" (qtd. in Barraclough 153), Clement—an aristocrat determined to live like an earthly lord—reinforced the widespread belief in the papal court's dedication to high living (Barraclough 153-54). In the *Liber sine nomine* Petrarch, who spent considerable time in Avignon, compares the city to a labyrinth and to the new Babylon: "This part of the world has its own Babylon. For where, I ask, may the 'city of confusion' (Gen. 11: 9) be more appropriately located than in the west? . . . Here is the dreadful prison, the aimless wandering in the dwelling place of shadows. . . . There is only one hope of salvation here, gold. . . . Christ is sold for gold" (71-73).

As the century progressed, the Avignon popes experienced increasing pressure to return to Rome. Prophetic women saints like Catherine of Siena and Brigetta of Sweden helped to create a climate for return that was difficult to ignore. In a letter to Gregory XI (1371-78), for instance, Catherine urged:

> If up to now you have not been very strong, I beg and beseech you that for the time that remains you act courageously and follow Christ whose vicar you are. . . . Go forward and accomplish with holy zeal the good resolutions undertaken; return to Rome and start the holy crusade. (qtd. in Coogan, *Babylon on the Rhône* 106-7)

By 1377 Gregory XI returned to Rome, where he died the following year. His death set in motion a series of events that shook Christendom to its core and had grave repercussions for the Church's future: the election of two popes by the same group of cardinals within a few months—what is known as the Great Schism.

Before the election that followed Gregory's death the Roman people made clear to the cardinals that they wanted a Roman pope; indeed a delegation of magistrates warned the cardinals that failing to meet the people's expectations could be dangerous. The cardinals elected, and reaffirmed the election on the following day, the archbishop of Bari—an Italian, not a Roman—and he assumed office as Urban VI (1378-89). Once installed, Urban began to act in ways that caused the cardinals consternation. Having grown accustomed to a consultative approach to Church governance and to a prominent role in decision-making during the Avignon era, the cardinals regretted their choice when Urban reverted to autocratic rule, proceeding unilaterally to achieve reforms that he believed to be necessary, though they impinged on the cardinals' prerogatives (Holmes and Bickers 108). Particularly distressing was the fact that Urban was unpredictable and irascible, breaking into raging tirades when he was displeased and alienating secular rulers as well as the princes of the Church (Ullman, *The Origins of the Great Schism* 45-49). Indeed he was probably mentally unbalanced (Swanson, *Universities, Academics, and the Great Schism* 7).

Lacking any mechanism for removing a pope, the cardinals withdrew from Rome to Anagni and began to call Urban's election into question because it had taken place under threat of harm from the Roman populace. They then proceeded to elect a new pope, a Frenchman who took the name Clement VII (1378-94) and installed himself in Avignon. Once again the strong voice of Catherine of Siena denounced the ills the Church was undergoing. In a letter to three Italian cardinals she excoriates their unprincipled behavior:

> You know and understand the truth that Pope Urban VI is truly the Pope, the highest Pontiff, chosen in an orderly election uninfluenced by fear. . . . You wish to corrupt this truth and show us the opposite by saying that you elected Pope Urban because of fear. This is not the case. And—speaking now irreverently because you no longer merit reverence—whoever says so lies right to the crown of his head. (qtd. in Coogan 119)

As a result of the cardinals' actions, Christian Europe faced the scandal of having two rival popes, each claiming to be Peter's legitimate heir. Supporters lined up on both sides, their loyalties reflecting their political interests: because of its ongoing war with the French, for instance, England gave its allegiance to Urban in Rome.

The Schism that began in 1378 lasted throughout the rest of the century and into the next, scandalizing the faithful and seriously undermining the Church's claim to spiritual authority. As the contemporary Henry of Langenstein observed: "One Pope excommunicates a man and the other declares him unloosed from it. One condemns a man justly, another unjustly justifies him on appeal; so justice is injured, the keys of the Church are debased, and the sword of Peter loses its terror" (qtd. in Jordan, *The Inner History of the Great Schism* 32).

The fact that popes during the Schism tended to have worse moral characters than secular leaders intensified the problem. Also, the efficacy of the sacraments came into question: if papal authority was in doubt, how could Christians trust the validity of powers which derived from it? All in all, the Schism encouraged a spirit of cynicism and fostered heresy (Jordan, *The Inner History of the Great Schism* 26-43).

By the 1390s Christian Europe began to explore three major avenues to resolve the impasse: council, cession, and withdrawing obedience. Each potential solution foundered. Authorities could not find a basis in canon law for a council called by anyone other than the pope; neither pope was willing to voluntarily give up office; and the effort to force resignation through withdrawing allegiance left too much power to the rival claimant (Jordan, *Inner History of the Great Schism* 111). Thus a resolution did not emerge until well into the fifteenth century—and then not until the situation had been further complicated by having three claimants to the papacy. When the problem finally did get resolved, the settlement reflected a pragmatic need to address political realities. Though the papacy and the curia were saved, the hard work of reform did not occur (Holmes and Bickers 116-17).

Chaucer was on his second major Italian journey in 1378 when the Schism first erupted. He could not have avoided knowing and forming an opinion about it. Yet not a word of his reaction to the whole sorry situation finds its way into his work. The contemporary papacy is a great absence—a black hole—in his portrayal of the Church, but that absence speaks eloquently in its silence. Earlier in the fourteenth century Dante had vigorously denounced the corrupt practices of contemporary papal incumbents: for instance, in *Inferno* XIX he places Clement V among the simoniacs, those guilty of selling spiritual goods, and he anticipates the damnation of Boniface VIII, excoriating them both for their greed, and in *Paradiso* XXIV Saint Peter laments that, in the truest sense, his seat is vacant (ll. 21-25). While Dante speaks with the exiled prophet's unrestrained voice, Chaucer renders his judgments more cautiously. We are left to assess the significance of the pope's appearing in *The Canterbury Tales* only in the saintly figure of Urban I. In "The Second Nun's Tale" an earlier Pope Urban lives among the poor on the outskirts of Rome, always under threat of persecution, as Cecile's brother-in-law, Tiburce, makes clear when he hesitates about going to Urban for instruction in the faith:

> "Ne menestow nat Urban," quod he tho,
> "That is so ofte dampned to be deed,

And woneth in halkes alwey to and fro,
And dar nat ones putte forth his heed?
Men sholde hym brennen in a fyr so reed
If he were founde, or that men myghte hym spye,
And we also, to ber hym compaignye." (ll. 309-14)

Chaucer may have intended a quiet critique of the contemporary Urban through the stark contrast between the two men's lifestyles. "The Man of Law's Tale," also set in Christianity's distant past, makes a couple of brief references to the pope, as does "The Clerk's Tale." Most telling is the fact that Chaucer links the contemporary papacy only with the morally bankrupt Pardoner, who comes directly from Rome with his pardons: "His walet, biforn hym in his lappe,/Bretful of pardoun comen from Rome al hoot" (GP, ll. 686-87).

Discontent with the Church's wealth and abuses led to the unfolding of England's first heresy during Chaucer's prime and indeed in his very circle. John Wyclif, a doctor of theology at Oxford, was unusual in being an academician who spawned a popular dissenting movement against the Church (Lambert, *Medieval Heresy* 227), but surprisingly he escaped official condemnation during his lifetime (Aston, "Wyclif and the Vernacular" 285). Early in Wyclif's academic career his excursions from orthodoxy fell within the range of normal academic discourse. Convinced that the Bible is the key to Christian spirituality, he was the first Oxford professor to teach a course on the entire Bible, devoting himself to familiarizing future clergymen with it. Besides insisting on its divine authority, he stressed the need for both a proper mindset and upright moral character in approaching scriptural study and in carrying on Christian ministry (Jeffrey, *The Law of Love* 30-35). He began to attack the clergy's wealth and to question the Church's right to collect taxes, and he undermined the hierarchy's authority by holding that when Church leaders become sinful, the faithful no longer need to heed them. Indeed Wyclif came to conceive of the Church as existing from eternity and as distinct from the visible Church, which he eventually equated with the Antichrist (Lambert 232). Pressing for the Church's return to simplicity, Wyclif saw the responsibility for achieving that goal as falling to secular government (Hall, *The Perilous Vision of John Wyclif* 82).

Such views, predictably, involved him in politics early in his career (1371-72), when his thinking was still taking shape (Lambert 230). Since Wyclif's theories justified resisting taxes imposed by a papacy seen as sympathetic to France, he attracted the civil authorities' attention. In 1374 they sent him to Bruges to argue against Gregory

XI's attempt to collect taxes supposedly owed from the beginning of the century. Also, John of Gaunt—seeing a potential ally in his struggle with the bishop of London—called Wyclif to London, where the two developed a mutually supportive relationship. The latter argued, for instance, that the state has the right to compel the Church to turn its wealth over to the poor (Hall, *Perilous Vision* 83-92).

Between 1379 and 1381 Wyclif moved irrevocably beyond criticizing Church practices toward challenging Church doctrines, specifically transubstantiation, which the Fourth Lateran Council had affirmed in 1215. His move to heresy in his eucharistic teachings caused a rift among his supporters, including John of Gaunt (Aston, "Wyclif and the Vernacular" 291). The doctrine of transubstantiation relies on the scholastic distinction between *substance*—an entity's essence—and *accident*—that which can change without affecting a substance's inherent nature; it holds that at consecration, through the miracle that the priest's words effect, bread and wine, while retaining their accidents, become in substance Christ's body and blood. Wyclif, however, maintained that consecration does not change the bread and wine and that the Mass consists primarily of the individual's spiritual union with Christ (Keen, "Wyclif, the Bible, and Transubstantiation" 6-15). Though the eucharistic debate was highly academic, it was closely linked to clerical prerogatives (Knapp, *Chaucer and the Social Contest* 69).

Wyclif's most revolutionary effect lay in his stress on the Bible as the sole source of Christian authority. Though traditionally he has received credit for first translating the Bible into English, recent scholarship has questioned whether he actually did any translating himself. But Anne Hudson argues that "if not the immediate cause, Wyclif was the ultimate effective cause of the versions that have come to be known as the Wycliffite Bible" ("Wyclif and the English Language" 85). For him and his followers, using the vernacular was a conscious decision to assault an entrenched intellectual system (Hudson, "Wyclif and the English Language" 90). Without the barricade created by a clerical language, the laity was able to explore faith issues and to make decisions about them on their own. Thus Wyclif's views attacked the heart of the clerical establishment. John of Gaunt's protection and later Wyclif's retirement to his home parish because of ill health allowed him a peaceful death and Christian burial (Knapp, *Chaucer and the Social Contest* 66-71). But in 1415 the Council of Constance formally denounced his views as heretical—on 260 issues. In 1427 his bones were dug up and burned (Hall, *Perilous Vision* 260-61).

Several factors fostered the spread of Wyclif's views. After his death in 1384 his followers—known as "Lollards," originally a derogatory term meaning "mumblers" and applied to heretics— took advantage of the laity's increasing literacy and intense devotion by using preaching, religious tracts, and vernacular biblical texts to spread their views. Also important in spreading Lollardy was the lower clergy, who often did not identify with the hierarchy and who lacked the educational background to follow the academic attacks on Wyclif's teachings. Because one of the movement's central tenets was parity between clergy and laity, lay people also disseminated Lollard doctrines. Among those was a group known as the Lollard knights, who were close to the English court in the early 1380s (Lambert 249-56). In responding to Lollardy the English establishment initially received help from Archbishop Courtenay's vigorous attack on Wyclif and from the coincidence of the Peasants' Revolt, for which—though Wyclif opposed it—the Lollards received some blame. But many bishops failed to respond quickly, moderating their response and avoiding torture. Widespread lay sympathy also curtailed repression (Lambert 260-62).

The extent of Chaucer's sympathy for and involvement with Wyclif and his supporters remains tantalizingly elusive. Whether or not the poet attended Oxford, he could scarcely have avoided contact with him and his ideas: both moved in John of Gaunt's milieu, and they shared some friends. Furthermore, Chaucer's thinking parallels Wyclif's in a number of key areas: his negative attitude toward the mendicants, his stress on the vernacular, his beliefs about authority, and his conviction about the importance of the reader's intention in interpreting a text (Jeffrey, "Chaucer and Wyclif" in *Chaucer and the Scriptural Tradition* 109-14). Scholars like Anne Hudson and Alcuin Blamires have also explored more thoroughly how Lollard language and motifs find their way into Chaucer's poetry. We must keep in mind that in most of the poet's lifetime the line between orthodoxy and heresy was much more loosely drawn than it was in the fifteenth century (Pearsall, *The Life of Geoffrey Chaucer* 182; Hudson, *The Premature Reformation* 393). Still, Wyclif's teachings about Church and State relationships "stirred up a hornet's nest" (Blamires, "The Wife of Bath and Lollardy" 225); most of Chaucer's professional and literary careers played themselves out in the midst of that hornet's nest. Traces of his reflections about the issues raised appear in *The Canterbury Tales*, as we shall see.

Several of the pilgrims—the Pardoner, the Summoner, and the Parson—are linked to the secular clergy and evoke contemporary controversies about the Church's role in society. The Pardoner introduces a particularly problematic dimension of papal authority. For in the late medieval period the way in which papal power most directly touched the individual Christian relates to the doctrine on confession and to the closely related doctrine on indulgences. Private confession to a priest developed slowly in the Church, with the requirement for yearly confession not imposed until the Fourth Lateran Council in 1215. Initially, penitents sought forgiveness directly from God, open confession was voluntary, and penance for serious sins was public—and rigorous—the proverbial sackcloth and ashes (Lea, *A History of Auricular Confession* I: 21-22). Gradually a doctrine developed about the desirability and then the necessity of confessing one's sins, whenever possible, to obtain forgiveness. The doctrine rested on "the power of the keys," derived from several biblical passages, like Matt. 16:19: "And I will give to thee [Peter] the keys of the kingdom of heaven; and whatsoever you shalt bind on earth, it shall be bound also in heaven: and whatsoever you shalt loose on earth it shall be loosed also in heaven." Such passages became the basis for the evolving belief that God had given the Church power to forgive sins (Lea I: 107). Bishops claimed the power of the keys, and the ability to bind and loose was conferred through ordination (Lea I: 121). The Fourth Lateran Council's requirement for yearly confession introduced a major shift in Christian life: instead of coming from within the sinner, confession became an externally imposed requirement, one that the faithful frequently resisted. In effect, the Church imposed on all its members a practice initially intended as a monastic discipline (Milis, *Angelic Monks and Earthly Men* 82) and wielded "a mighty instrument . . . for giving to the Church control over the conscience of every man and establishing its authority on an impregnable basis" (Lea I: 228).

Closely related to the doctrine on confession was that on indulgences. In the developing theology concerning sacramental penance, the Church came to rely on a distinction between *culpa*, which relates to the *guilt* resulting from one's sin, and *poena*, which refers to the *punishment* deserved because of one's sin (Lea I: 143). This distinction became central to the teaching on how pardon for sin comes about. The Church holds that confession and repentance wipe away sin but that a residue—the temporal punishment due to sin—remains; this temporal punishment, along with one's less serious sins, one expiates in purgatory. But the Church's treasury of grace—derived from the superabundant merit earned by Christ's death—can be tapped for the individual's benefit. As Christ's vicar on earth, the pope exercises authority over this treasury and can grant indulgences to the faithful upon their performing certain acts of devotion—initially almost entirely linked to supporting the Crusades—either directly by becoming a crusader or indirectly by making a financial contribution for the crusading effort (Shaffern, "Learned Discussion of Indulgences" 367-68). In 1343 Clement VI clearly articulated the papal theory of indulgences:

> One drop of Christ's blood would have sufficed for the redemption of the whole human race. Out of the abundant superfluity of Christ's sacrifice there has come a treasure which is not to be hidden in a napkin or buried in a field, but to be used. This treasure has been committed by God to his vicars on earth, to St. Peter and his successors, to be used for the full or partial remission of the temporal punishments of the sins of the faithful who have repented and confessed. (qtd. in Southern 139)

As the preceding passage suggests, indulgences can be either *partial* or *plenary*, removing either part or all of the punishment merited by sin. The latter promise that a properly confessed and repentant person who dies after obtaining one would go directly to heaven. Bishops grant partial indulgences for such activities as visiting shrines, saying certain prayers, or making contributions to worthy causes, such as constructing churches or other religious facilities. Only the pope grants plenary indulgences, usually in special circumstances, such as jubilee years. Properly understood, indulgences do *not* substitute for confession and true repentance, nor do they promise absolution. To be effective, indulgences require that a person be in the state of grace, that is, free of serious sin (Shaffern 368).

Though the doctrine of indulgences mitigated the harsh juxtaposition of salvation versus damnation by affording the faithful a means of influencing the afterlife's punitive system, it had troubling consequences: it placed increased power in papal hands; it was easily subject to abuse; and it was overly complicated (Southern 142-43). At first issued only in exceptional circumstances or for extraordinary service to the Church, indulgences—or pardons as they were known—rapidly underwent an inflationary cycle that led to their debasement and to multiple abuses related to their sale for monetary gain (Lea II: 282). The potential for abuse was particularly great with the establishment of pardoners, the means by which indulgences reached the faithful. Pardoners had the right to dispense indulgences, usually with the acceptance of a fee. Already in the thirteenth century the prohibitions issued by the councils of Paris, Lateran, and Mainz provide good insight into the abuses pardoners perpetrated: they used relics to make false promises of pardon; they assaulted other members of the clergy; they defied the Church's interdicts; they claimed special privileges for themselves and refused to obey the law; they frequented taverns; they falsified documents to establish their authority; they used their ill-gotten gains in drunkenness, gambling, and lechery (Lea II: 284-87).

Chaucer's Pardoner highlights the extent to which the office could be exploited for personal gain. He remains one of the most controversial and elusive figures in the assemblage, the one whom Kittredge characterizes as the pilgrimage's "most abandoned character" (*Chaucer and His Poetry* 211) because he so blatantly flaunts his corrupt practices. The "General Prologue" outlines a picture for which the "Prologue" to his tale—one of the lengthiest in the collection—fills in the details. One striking aspect of the Pardoner's portrait is that it suggests his sexual anomaly:

> A voys he hadde as smal as hath a goot.
> Ne berd hadde he, ne nevere sholde have.
> As smoothe it was as it were late shave.
> I trowe he were a geldyng or a mare. (ll. 688-91)

Extensive critical debate has centered on the precise nature of his dysfunction and its relationship to his spiritual condition, but no real consensus has emerged. Some, like Monica McAlpine, have maintained that he is homosexual; others have characterized him as hermaphroditic; still others have linked him to the tradition of spiritual eunuchry. C. David Benson ("Chaucer's Pardoner: His Sexuality and Modern Critics" 337-49) and Richard Firth Green, on the other hand, have argued that the Pardoner is best understood as a profligate heterosexual, engaging in behavior stereotypically associated with his office in the era's satiric literature ("The Pardoner's Pants" 144-45).

The concluding section of the "General Prologue" portrait makes clear that the Pardoner's main focus is on his own financial gain, which clearly comes at the expense of the country clergy in whose parishes he preaches. A polished rhetorician, he places all his skill at the service of his greed, drawing his audiences in by his word web. The "Prologue" to his tale functions as a confessional self-revelation, in which he demonstrates for his audience of fellow pilgrims his successful techniques in exploiting simple parish folk, making clear that

he cares only about lining his own pockets and not about the state of
their souls:

> For myn entente is nat but for to wynne,
> And nothyng for correccioun of synne.
> I rekke nevere, whan that they been beryed,
> Though that hir soules goon a-blakeberyed. (ll. 402-6)

The danger he poses is not that he will dupe his victims into parting
with their meager funds but that he will lull them into believing that,
by purchasing his pardons, they do not need true repentance,
thereby jeopardizing their salvation.

"The Pardoner's Tale" exemplifies the sermons the Pardoner delivers to convince his audiences to contribute to his purse, and, to
spur them into action, it includes an extended story to show the
sorry consequences of greed. For as the Pardoner brags, he preaches
always on the same theme—*radix malorum est cupiditas* ("avarice is the
root of all evil")—attacking the very sin of which he is guilty. A stark
parable that functions as a central mechanism in the Pardoner's con
game, the tale reveals his tendency to conflate physical and spiritual
death, thereby revealing at the same time the teller's lack of genuine
spiritual insight. But the Pardoner is considerably more complex
than the classic con man, a hypocrite of heroic proportions. Taken
together, his prologue, tale, and epilogue confront us with one of
the major interpretive cruxes of *The Canterbury Tales*. Criticism has
presented a broad range of analyses, from the psychological to the
theological, to account for the drastic shifts in his behavior: the brag-
gadocio of his self-revelatory prologue, the moralism of his tale, the
apparent lapse into religious sincerity in the epilogue, followed
rapidly by his puzzling attempt to obtain contributions from his fellow pilgrims, to whom he has previously exposed his charlatanism.

Recently, Lee Patterson has placed the Pardoner's performance
within the context of the late medieval debate over confession and
contrition. At issue was the extent to which sacramental confession
itself—as opposed to the penitent's true interior disposition—could
erase sin. The sacramentalists, though never denying the necessity of
sorrow for one's sins, stressed the sacrament's efficacy and maintained that with it a lower level of sorrow, called attrition, would produce the desired results. The contritionists, on the other hand, held
that nothing less than full and deep sorrow for one's sins could lead
to forgiveness. Both positions had pitfalls: the sacramentalist view
could reduce forgiveness to mere external form, while the contri-

tionist perspective, by placing the burden so highly on the penitent's interior state of mind, could foster oversensitive and despairing consciences (*Chaucer and the Subject of History* 374-84). Patterson focuses on the Pardoner as "a man in despair whose discourse is best understood in confessional terms," reflecting "a spiritual condition familiar to penitential theology" (384). Donald Howard also argues that the Augustinian analysis of guilt that produces despair provides a basis for understanding the Pardoner's spiritual condition (*The Idea of The Canterbury Tales* 356).

While Patterson and Howard discuss the Pardoner's performance in light of penitential theology, Alan Fletcher theorizes that through his treatment of the Pardoner Chaucer was cautiously injecting himself into the Lollard controversy. He analyses the Pardoner's hypocrisy in moral rather than psychological terms, pointing out that in contemporary polemic hypocrisy and heresy were frequently linked: the argument was that false teachers hide behind a veil of seeming sanctity to lead others astray. Thus in making the Pardoner his chief hypocrite rather than creating a false Lollard or making the Friar his only hypocrite, Chaucer was reflecting the era's debates without clearly taking sides, for the portrayal of the Pardoner challenges the orthodox to address abuses without specifically attacking the doctrine on indulgences ("The Topical Hypocrisy of Chaucer's Pardoner" 117-20).

Peter Brown and Andrew Butcher also see the Pardoner and his tale as closely linked to contemporary issues. They treat his prologue and tale as Chaucer's response to both the late medieval Church's failings in general and more specifically to the jockeying for advantage between the English Church and crown during the 1370s, a situation they believe provides the central kernel out of which the Pardoner's performance evolved over twenty years. The Treaty of Bruges, at which John Wyclif, before his views took him into heresy, functioned as the crown's envoy, attempted to resolve the controversy over papal taxes on the one hand and ecclesiastical privileges on the other (114-48). Referring to Wyclif's role in those negotiations, they argue that the reference to "Stilboun"—perhaps evoking the sterility of being stillborn—in the tale's denunciation of gambling (l. 603) criticizes Wyclif, whose rigid principles caused him to opt out of the political rough-and-tumble and thus to fail in his mission. Brown and Butcher see Chaucer as expressing his distaste for the behavior of both parties through "The Pardoner's Tale," which becomes "a picture of a betrayed kingdom in which church and court have been consumed by corruption and avarice" (114). The sins of the tale's three revelers—drunkenness, gaming, and avarice—function metaphorically as "the intoxications of power," "the gamblings of policy-making," and "the demands of papal taxation" (148).

Whatever the state of the Pardoner's own spiritual condition— and the argument that he despairs is attractive—his bold admission about his avaricious manipulations of the faithful calls into question the authenticity of the Church's claim to bind and release from sin. Indeed Howard treats "The Pardoner's Prologue and Tale" as part of a "floating fragment" whose cynical hypocrisy haunts the work as a whole, threatening to undermine the penitential enterprise of pilgrimage that engages the characters (*The Idea of the Canterbury Tales* 139-42). We can see it as a threatening presence, hovering and lurking in the background like the skeletal death figures in medieval paintings and illuminations. Indeed "The Pardoner's Tale" is specifically linked with the plague, thereby suggesting a connection between the disease that ravaged the population and the moral blight spread by pardoners. Thus in the Pardoner's character and performance Chaucer embodies both the corruption rampant in the Church and the paralyzing despair it engendered in the faithful.

If the Pardoner represents the reach of papal authority into the lives of ordinary Christians, another unsavory character, the Summoner, portrays ecclesiastical authority at the diocesan level. Dioceses, overseen by bishops, are the Church's main administrative units, responsible for upholding orthodox belief and proper religious practices among both clergy and laity. Though theoretically the cathedral clergy elected bishops, by the mid fourteenth century in England the papacy regularly intervened, often at the king's instigation. Clement VI (1342-52) reportedly commented that he would consent to making an ass a bishop if the king so requested (Pantin, *The English Church in the Fourteenth Century* 56). The resulting close ties between secular and religious authorities had a substantial impact on Church courts, which had evolved for trying sinners guilty of offenses ranging from fornication to usury to heresy (Olson, *The Canterbury Tales and the Good Society* 192). For though the reforms of the twelfth and thirteenth centuries stressed the importance of interior contrition, the impulse toward public penance and shaming sinners had by no means disappeared, as Mary Mansfield's recent study of thirteenth-century French practices has shown. The scope of offenses the ecclesiastical courts prosecuted was extensive, but contemporary records support Chaucer's implication that lechery received particular attention (Hahn and Kaeuper, "Text and Context: Chaucer's Friar's Tale" 74-75).

Both bishops' courts and archdeacons' courts tried cases, the most serious offenses being directed to the former. Summoners functioned like bailiffs in secular courts, issuing citations that required the accused to appear in court. These citations could proceed from written requests of officials like the parish priest, but summoners also had the authority to issue spoken rather than written charges and to require the accused to make an immediate court appearance without time for preparing a defense (Olson, *The Canterbury Tales and the Good Society* 193). Corporal punishment was the usual fate of those who were convicted; they could be flogged around the marketplace or around the church, for instance (Hahn and Kaeuper 77).

The ultimate weapon these courts could employ on the unrepentant was excommunication, a spiritual penalty that left their salvation in serious jeopardy by cutting them off from the communion of the faithful and by denying them access to the sacraments, the channels of God's grace. However, when the sinner was judged unrepentant, the ecclesiastical courts could turn to the secular courts to issue a writ that brought them under the latter courts' jurisdiction. People became subject to these writs not for their sins but for remaining unrepentant and thus in effect for not properly respecting the ecclesiastical court's authority (Logan, *Excommunication and the Secular Arm in Medieval England* 43-45). The right to issue these writs was limited to those bishops who actually resided in England and to persons subject to their jurisdiction (Logan 25). In such cases the King's Chancery conducted no independent investigation but contacted local authorities to imprison the excommunicate until proper satisfaction occurred. The automatic nature of the royal courts' response meant that, though theoretically the Church exercised power only in the spiritual sphere, in effect its reach extended into the secular arena, where the accused were subject to penalties that directly attacked their persons or property (Olson, *The Canterbury Tales and the Good Society* 195-96). The famous case of Joan of Arc's trial highlights the problems that resulted from the collusion between secular and ecclesiastical courts: the Church later found itself in the position of canonizing a person whom it had condemned as a heretic.

As with the office of pardoner, that of summoner lent itself to major abuses. The courts could be very profitable; in fact Henry II once complained that archdeacons had better incomes than he did. Church synods tried to curtail court costs by such measures as prohibiting summoners from going about on horseback. They also legislated, mostly in vain, against summoners' issuing false citations and accepting gifts (Hahn and Kaeuper 80-82). Because the courts had the power to submit the accused to fines, public humiliation, physical pain, and ultimately to the loss of property and life, the potential for extortion was also great. As Chaucer's portrayal of the corrupt summoner in "The Friar's Tale" suggests, "Even the innocent could be made by a corrupt summoner to pay simply to avoid the inconvenience, danger, and embarrassment of prosecution" (Hahn and Kaeuper 81). As a result, popular resentment against summoners ran very high: in some instances they were subject to beating, kidnapping, harassment, and even death (Hahn and Kaeuper 86). Brian Woodcock observes, "To the subjects of the archbishop they [summoners] were the ubiquitous symbols of ecclesiastical jurisdiction and their conduct and behavior were no doubt largely responsible for the ill favour with which that jurisdiction came to be so frequently regarded" (*Medieval Ecclesiastical Courts in the Diocese of Canterbury* 49).

Chaucer presents his pilgrim Summoner as both physically and spiritually repugnant. He suffers from a skin disease resistant to the harshest medicines, thereby suggesting "inner corruption" (Cooper 57), and he is guilty of tolerating and profiting from the very sins, especially those of a sexual nature, that the courts were supposed to discourage (Cooper 56). As with the Pardoner, his failings reflect systemic rather than individual flaws. "Although the Summoner is described as a despicable person individually," Peggy Knapp comments, "his social role is enacted in a much larger system of corruption, collusion, mismanagement, and betrayal of the people's interests and religious ideals" (*Chaucer and the Social Contest* 54). Chaucer links the portraits of the Pardoner and the Summoner in the "General Prologue," suggesting a relationship between the two that many read as evidence that they are lovers. Rejecting that suggestion, Howard focuses on the practical alliance that allowed both to abuse their offices for financial gain (*The Idea of the Canterbury Tales* 344-45).

In "The Friar's Tale" Chaucer extends his treatment of corrupt summoners by portraying one in action and by consigning him to damnation. He merges the summoner within the tale with the pilgrim summoner, revealing him to be the devil's ally. To show off his skill to the devil who is his companion, the summoner attempts to extort money, and a new pan, from a poor widow whom he accuses of fornicating with a friar or a priest. Protesting her innocence, the widow curses: "The devel so fecche hym er he deye,/And panne and al, but he wol hym repente!" (ll. 1628-29). When the devil who accompanies the summoner ascertains that she clearly intends her words to be effective and that the summoner remains obdurate, he makes his rightful claim:

> Thy body and this panne been myne by ryght.
> Thou shalt with me to helle yet tonyght. . . .
> And with that word this foule feend hym hente;
> Body and soule he with the devel wente
> Where as that somonours han hir heritage. (ll. 1635-41)

Olson links "The Friar's Tale" with the story of Judas, characterizing it as "the familiar Biblical story of the apostle who betrayed an innocent person, cursed himself, and found himself taken off to hell by a familiar devil" (*The Canterbury Tales and the Good Society* 191).

Counterbalancing the ecclesiastical corruption evident in the Pardoner and the Summoner is the country Parson whose lifestyle mirrors that of his impoverished parishioners; his entire energies serve their spiritual well-being. Criticism frequently juxtaposes the Parson and the Pardoner, the latter a fraudulent counterfeit, the former a somewhat stern but true exemplar of virtue's narrow path. As Frank Cespedes notes,

> In the General Prologue the portraits of the Parson and the Pardoner stand opposed, and an important foundation for this opposition is the *res et verba* [thing and word] distinction of Paul and Augustine. The thrust of the Parson's portrait is that, in this man at least, word and deed are not hypocritically disjoint; the Parson's strength as a preacher is ethical persuasion. ("Chaucer's Pardoner and Preaching" 7)

The Parson's portrait in the "General Prologue" strikes no sour notes: he is both intellectually and morally suited for his role as pastor of a far-flung parish. Conscious of his exemplary role among his parishioners, he lives simply, does his duty, and plays no favorites. The very fact that he has chosen to stay in his parish, rather than going off to more glamorous places like Saint Paul's in London and hiring another to take his place, testifies to his commitment to the apostolic life. With the Good Shepherd as his model, he operates on the principle that practicing what he preaches constitutes the most effective way of guiding his flock: "if gold ruste, what shal iren do?" (GP, l. 500).

No doubt there were virtuous, dedicated, and theologically well-versed parsons like the one Chaucer portrays, but they may well have been more the exception than the rule. For the preparation of the clergy during this period was by no means uniform; no equivalent to today's system of seminary training existed. Though some priests did have the opportunity to spend time in a university and even to obtain a degree, their doing so was by no means required; those who excelled at the university were, for that very reason, likely to be siphoned away from the parishes (Pantin 29). Furthermore, as mentioned earlier, though contemporary evidence suggests that the beneficed clergy probably experienced much the same mortality rate as the laity during the repeated appearances of the plague throughout the latter half of the fourteenth century (Ziegler 128), the clergy's inability to offer effective help during the crises did much to undermine the laity's trust. After the onslaughts of plague the quality of the local clergy fell considerably, partly because the epidemics had taken such a huge toll on the clergy that, to meet its needs, the Church recruited and speedily ordained candidates whose suitability was questionable (262). Significantly, Chaucer presents much of what is admirable in the Parson's portrait in the negative rather than in the positive, thereby suggesting frequent abuses among ordinary practioners. As Jill Mann observes, "The account of the Parson's virtues inevitably suggests the sins of the average priest, and his portrait thus becomes representative of the estate in both its good and its bad aspects" (*Chaucer and Medieval Estates Satire* 56).

As the pilgrims approach the saint's shrine, the Parson offers his fellows an opportunity for serious reflection on their own sinfulness. Howard characterizes "The Parson's Tale" as "a book on sin sandwiched into a book on penitence, and its text is about the good way or the true pilgrimage" (*The Idea of the Canterbury Tales* 380). Whatever the role of the Parson's tale within Chaucer's artistic scheme, it reflects the Parson's mandated role as the auditor of his parishioners' yearly confession. In response to Harry Bailly's request that he take his turn in the tale-telling, the Parson makes clear that he will comply—but only on his own terms. Instead of a fiction, even a moral one, he proceeds to deliver a treatise on penitence that includes a detailed review of the seven deadly sins, what amounts to the basis for the thorough examination of conscience that should precede contrition and confession (Delasanta "Penance and Poetry in the *Canterbury Tales*" 242). Thus the humble parish Parson becomes the most authentic exemplar of the Good Shepherd, the pastoral leader whose concern for the spiritual needs of those in his charge transcends human avarice and selfishness.

Intriguingly, the Parson is the only pilgrim Chaucer specifically links to Lollardy: in the epilogue to "The Man of Law's Tale" the Parson's objection to Harry Bailly's using the expression "by Goddes dignitee" causes Harry to exclaim:

> "I smelle a Lollere in the wynd," quod he.
> "Now! goode men," quod oure Hoste, "herkeneth me;
> Abydeth, for Goddes digne passioun,
> For we schal han a prediccacioun;
> This Lollere heer wil prechen us somwhat." (ll. 1173-77)

Also, the Parson's objection to fables in the prologue to his tale may reflect a Lollard perspective, though its implications remain ambiguous (Pearsall, *The Life of Geoffrey Chaucer* 183).

At the same time, the Parson's presence on the pilgrimage and his delivery of what amounts to a penitential sermon counterbalance his association with Lollardy. For the Host's accusation masks the fact that a true Lollard would probably not have gone on a pilgrimage. The Man of Law's epilogue's authenticity, moreover, is questionable, since it appears in neither of the most reliable manuscripts (Blamires, "Wife of Bath and Lollardy" 224). Still, the Parson's portrait resonates with the issues of the reform movement in which Lollardy was a significant player (Pearsall, *The Life of Geoffrey Chaucer* 183). In discussing the widespread desire for ecclesiastical reform even within an orthodox framework, Lambert comments on the Parson's portrayal:

> Chaucer, when he described the Parson in the General Prologue to the *Canterbury Tales*, making him so like Wyclif's blueprint and omitting (perhaps fortuitously, perhaps not) any mention of saying mass or hearing confessions and drawing so black a picture of the monk, the friar, and other ecclesiastical personalities, witnesses not so much his own positive Lollardy as the degree to which Lollard ideas in the years after the founder's death ran parallel to some widespread concerns about Church life. (258)

Truly the fourteenth century was a period of special turmoil for the Church—partly for reasons out of its control, partly for its own weakness and corruption. The clergy's helplessness in providing protection from the plague's onslaughts raised doubts about its efficacy as a intermediary with the divine, while the move to Avignon—with its luxurious living and political collusion—followed by the scandal of the Schism undermined people's faith in the Church's health and, for some, its legitimacy. For most people the hierarchical Church remained a powerful and pervasive presence in their lives. But the emergence of heresies specifically related to the clergy's role in interpreting sacred texts and in paving the way to salvation reflected not only repugnance at the clergy's perceived failings, it also revealed the laity's longing for greater involvement in its own spiritual life, resulting from the era's increased literacy and heightened inferiority. Though strong anticlericalism could go hand in hand with doctrinal orthodoxy, it also frequently provided a starting point for heretical challenges to the Church's mediatory role.

Chaucer's treatment of the hierarchy in *The Canterbury Tales* reveals the explorations of an educated and insightful layman. Though he uses satiric irony rather than prophetic invective, he, like Dante before him, seems to have been deeply disturbed by the abuses of religious power he saw in his world. In fact, he appears to be perched between orthodoxy and heresy. Paul Olson, for instance, sees the poet as moving selectively in Wyclif's intellectual universe, engaging in "a Wycliffite analysis of the problems of the institutions connecting Church and state without accepting Wycliffite solutions to those problems" (129). While maintaining a judicious caution, Chaucer explores the issues in his milieu relating to the need for Church reform and involves his audience in the societal dialogue about the nature of that reform and about the proper relationship between the clergy and the laity. Though nothing in Chaucer's work unequivocally identifies him as a Lollard, some aspects of his creative approach suggest that "in appropriating the energies of popular discourses and languages to the uses of his fiction he also incorporates some destabilizing and dissident attitudes, if only in quotation" (Ganim, *Chaucerian Theatricality* 44). Perhaps he goes even further in identifying himself with heretical postures: "However playfully," John Ganim observes, "Chaucer regards the making of poetry or at least his own poetic development as akin to heresy" (44).

CHAPTER FOUR

The Quest for Perfection:
The Regular Clergy

*T*he Church's hierarchy—the secular clergy discussed in the preceding chapter—undertook its ongoing pastoral care and administrative work. But from the earliest Christian centuries some believers sought to achieve spiritual perfection by holding themselves to the highest religious standards. At first the intensely devout could signal their commitment by openly refusing to bow to Roman secular authorities and accepting martyrdom as a consequence. But when the persecutions stopped, monasticism—which grew alongside but somewhat independent of the Church's hierarchical structure—offered the chief arena for achieving spiritual heights (Lawrence, *Medieval Monasticism* 3-4). The monastic orders—called the regular clergy because they followed the rule, or *regula*, of their founders—seek to perfect themselves through prayer and self-discipline. Monks testify to humanity's heavenly destiny by separating themselves from worldly pursuits; they parallel the angelic choir, devoted to praising God, and anticipate on earth the heavenly life to which humans aspire (Leclerq, *The Love of Learning* 56-58).

During Christianity's spread throughout Europe monastic ideals set the tone for the dominant culture: for the relationship between monasticism and Christian society is one of "exemplary microcosm to macrocosm" (Verdon, *Monasticism and the Arts* 8). But the movement's high ideals meant that inevitably its adherents would fall short of meeting them. Its history throughout the medieval period repeatedly sounds the note of reform, attempting to recapture the founding era's spiritual energy. By the High Middle Ages the impulse toward reform veered in a new direction: the emerging mendicant orders sought to perfect themselves not by withdrawing from the world but by teaching and by serving the laity, especially the poor. Rather than living an angelic life, they saw themselves as modeling the life of Jesus and the apostles. The divergent visions of spiritual perfection within the monastic orders, as well as clashes with the secular clergy, intensified dissension within the Church at a time of spiritual awakening among the laity. An overview of the regular clergy's origins and functions will provide a context for understanding Chaucer's portrayal of its representatives and for understanding his era's grappling to come to terms with how an intensely committed Christian could best model Christ, serve the world, and achieve salvation.

In the Late Classical/Early Christian world's ascetic climate, transcending bodily imperfections and limitations through self-mortification was a powerful goal. Monastic asceticism had both classical and biblical roots: Stoic and Neoplatonic philosophy and the Judaic Essene movement (Lawrence 2). New Testament sayings like Jesus's counsels to perfection—"If you would be perfect, go, sell what you possess and give to the poor, and you will have treasure in heaven; and come, follow me" (Matt. 19:21)—were also influential. More directly, monasticism emerged in third-century Egyptian Christianity by modifying practices engaged in by the hermits who sought the desert's rigors—harsh living conditions, food and sleep deprivation, extended prayer, and self-mortification (Verdon 7). A central figure in early monasticism was Anthony, a third-fourth century saint who sparked the imagination of succeeding generations. His conversion and retreat into the desert to engage in a focused, solitary struggle against evil and in a quest for spiritual perfection through self-denial, prayer, and meditation on scripture set the basic pattern for monasticism's future development (Holmes and Bickers 42).

Central to the monks' self-image was belief in their living the angelic life. In his *Comparison Between a King and a Monk* John Chrysostom (d. 407) tells us that if we were to be present at night, "we should see the monk adorned with the worship of God and with prayers, singing much earlier than the birds, living with the angels, conversing with God, enjoying the goods of heaven" (72). Belief in an angelic existence undergirded the stress on monastic celibacy: angels do not procreate or seek sexual pleasure; neither should monks. Another central image for the monk was that of the *miles Christi*, or soldier of Christ, battling against the forces of evil by cultivating virtues through self-discipline and renunciation. The monks' efforts to defeat evil supernatural powers were considered central to society's well-being (Southern 224).

During monasticism's formative phase the hierarchy looked upon it uneasily because monks, who owed their primary allegiance to their abbot rather than to the local bishop, did not function within the normal chain of command (Lawrence 16). John Cassian's remark that "the monk ought to flee women and bishops" (qtd. in Lawrence 16) underscores mutual distrust. But ultimately monasticism closely allied itself with the hierarchy: the papacy promoted it and relied on monks for evangelization. Like the Church as a whole, monasticism moved from society's outer margins to its core (Verdon 19). This shift inevitably influenced its sense of identity and mission.

The ascetic lifestyle attracted women as well as men; monasteries for women, called convents or nunneries, reach back into the Early Christian era. In the fourth century, for instance, Marcella and Paula, two wealthy Roman widows influenced by reading *The Life of Saint Anthony,* played a central role in helping Jerome found communal establishments: Marcella turned her substantial Roman property into a common dwelling, and Paula followed Jerome to the Holy Land and financed both a monastery and a convent there (Lawrence 13). In northern Gaul and in Anglo-Saxon England double monasteries housed both men and women in separate facilities but often with a shared liturgical space. Usually an abbess headed such institutions; they were essentially female communities that included some males responsible for heavy manual labor and for the liturgical functions denied to women. Often such abbesses had noble blood; they led their convents with easy confidence, often wielding influence in the world of affairs (Lawrence 51-61).

The person who most influenced Western monasticism was Benedict of Nursia, a sixth century saint whose *Rule* established precise, and relatively moderate, guidelines for monastic living. Remarkable for its flexibility and adaptability, his *Rule* sets rigorous standards, but it treats human nature with sympathetic understanding (Southern 219-20). It prescribes an austere lifestyle but avoids rigorous self-denial. For instance, it forbids the flesh of four-footed animals but allows two, possibly three, cooked dishes at a meal, a pound of bread a day, and a sparing measure of wine—as long as the monks do not grumble if wine is unavailable (*The Rule of St. Benedict* 206-9).

Obedience to spiritual superiors assumes a central role among monastic virtues; through it the monk renounces pride and cultivates humility, making spiritual growth possible: "The first degree of humility is obedience without delay" (*Rule* 109). Closely allied with humility is silence, which recalls desert austerities while also preserving social harmony in an enclosed environment (Milis 138). Monks, especially in the Benedictine tradition, also vow to practice stability by remaining in the monasteries that provided their spiritual formation. Stressing stability reinforces humility and obedience, the strict hierarchical control on which monastic life centers. The eleventh-century monk Peter Damian (1007-72) underlines stability's importance: "Whoever, therefore, as a monk hastens to attain the height of perfection, let him confine himself within the walls of his cloister, let him love spiritual quiet, let him have a horror of running about in the world, as he would of immersing himself in a pool of blood" (qtd. in Ross and McLaughlin, *The Portable Medieval Reader* 51). The ideal of stability makes problematic even such religiously inspired journeying as pilgrimages; monastics should make spiritual, not physical, journeys. Some scholars, for instance, point to Chaucer's Monk's and Prioress's presence on the Canterbury pilgrimage as signaling their lukewarm adherence to the *Rule*. Monks also subscribe to voluntary poverty: they are to own nothing individually, though the monastery can, and usually does, own substantial communal property (*Rule* 196).

Cultivating all these virtues serves a monk's most important labor: the inner struggle to tame the passions, achieve spiritual tranquillity, and attain the ultimate goal of mystic union with God. The monastery becomes the soul's workshop, in which shaping the monk's life toward spiritual perfection becomes an artistic process (Verdon 2): "Behold these are the tools of the spiritual craft. . . . But the workshop wherein we must work all this out is the enclosure of the monastery and stability in the community" (*Rule* 106). In the medieval period monastic life centered on communal prayer and work: the monk's day organized itself around periods of chanted prayer— the eight canonical hours—beginning in early morning and recurring regularly throughout the day. Alternating with prayer were times of work, both manual and intellectual. Initially all monks were supposed to do manual labor, but gradually as monks had to devote more time to chanting and saying Masses for their benefactors, manual labor decreased significantly (Lawrence 80, 115). Sacred reading, and meditation upon it, was the starting point for mystic contemplation and union with God, the goal of monastic life (Ozment, *The Age of Reform* 82).

Monasticism emphasized personal salvation for those who turned away from the world's superficial allures and nurtured their souls to attain spiritual perfection (Le Goff, *Medieval Callings* 45). But monasteries were inevitably deeply entangled with worldly institutions: the monks' ascetic practices and hard work led to increasing worldly prosperity and involvement in secular affairs (Lesnick, *Preaching in Medieval Florence* 36). Another force drawing monks into worldly affairs was that in a culture moving from orality to literacy aristocratic courts became increasingly dependent on writing, and the nobility had to rely on literate monks to handle bureaucratic functions. As an educated elite, monks occupied central positions at court, functioning as advisors, as secretaries, as emissaries. Also, belief in the monks' direct access to divine wisdom through mystic contemplation provided a rationale for their special role as advisors in temporal matters (Olson, *The Canterbury Tales and the Good Society* 131).

Further entanglements arose precisely from the social function that medieval society ascribed to the monks: to pray for the community's spiritual well-being. Because of their mystique of sanctity, monasteries received considerable material support—as offerings, endowments, bequests—from the laity. They developed special ties with the nobility and with ruling monarchs: throughout the medieval period rulers founded and supported monasteries to secure salvation for themselves and a heavenly safeguard for their reigns (Le Goff, *Medieval Callings* 46-54). In 909, for instance, William III of Aquitaine made the bequest that founded Cluny, one of monasticism's greatest centers: "And this is my trust . . . that although I myself am unable to despise all things, nevertheless by receiving those who do despise the world, whom I believe to be righteous, I may receive the reward of the righteous" (qtd. in Lawrence 71). Monasticism's ties to the nobility were further strengthened because aristocratic families used monasteries to forestall splitting their holdings among multiple offspring: they sent them their younger sons and unmarriageable daughters (Lucas, *Women in the Middle Ages* 51). Using monasteries as outlets for surplus children meant that some monastic aspirants had the religious life unwillingly thrust upon them. Indeed until the twelfth century, when canon law forbade the practice, families sent to the monks children as young as seven, a custom known as "oblation."

In the tenth and eleventh centuries monasticism reached a high point in the achievements of the Cluniac order. Located in central France, Cluny strove to reinvigorate Benedictine monasticism after a period of decline. From its inception it had a special relationship with the papacy, lending its support to the latter's attempts to free the Church from secular leaders' undue influence in its affairs, especially in filling ecclesiastical offices (Lawrence 86-93). Cluny's success derived from the order's ably executing what contemporary society perceived as monasticism's central function: awe-inspiring liturgical celebration (Knowles, *Christian Monasticism* 52). Even the ascetic Peter Damian paid homage to its accomplishments: "When I recall the strict and full daily life of your abbey, I recognize that it is the Holy Spirit that guides you" (qtd. in Knowles, *Christian Monasticism* 53).

But the Cluniac approach to monasticism drew critics as well; its elaborate liturgical settings and practices, which in its view testified to God's power and glory, from another perspective appeared overly worldly and luxurious. Beginning in the twelfth century major reform efforts sought to return monasticism to its original simplicity. One that had a long-lasting, though not widespread, success was that of the Carthusians, who sought to bring the desert's solitary rigors into the monastery's communal environment. At the Grande Chartreuse in the French Alps and at Carthusian charterhouses monks lived mostly in individual cells and on small attached plots of land. They ate most of their meals in solitude, their frugal repasts being passed into their cells through small doors. Unlike the Benedictines, they gathered for communal prayer only twice a day, performing the other religious offices individually. They followed the rule of silence, speaking among themselves only after Mass on Sundays and on major feast days (Lawrence 160). The Carthusians' exacting lifestyle limited the order's appeal, but it did attract a steady supply of zealous candidates. The order was "unique in having successfully domesticated the ideal of the desert in the form of a distinctive pattern of life" (Lawrence 161).

Another twelfth-century reform movement, the Cistercians, attracted greater numbers and had a wider impact on monasticism and on medieval society as a whole. Bernard of Clairvaux, its most outstanding member, became a vocal critic of Cluny's elaborate rituals and ornate structures. For the Cistercians also sought to return monasticism to its founding moment's simplicity, to eliminate "corporate wealth, worldly involvements, and surfeited liturgical ritualism" (Lawrence 174). Drawing their inspiration from Egyptian desert monasticism as well as from the Benedictine tradition, the Cistercians, like the Carthusians, sought "to combine the life of the hermit and the cenobite" (Knowles, *Christian Monasticism* 66). Because the Cistercians rigorously adhered to the *Rule,* they claimed greater perfection than those who took a less ascetic approach. From their inception the Cistercians—known as White Monks because their habits were made of coarse undyed wool—rejected protracted liturgical services, imposed a return to manual labor, refused feudal obligations, and required a year-long trial period before permitting entry into the order, no longer accepting child oblates (Knowles, *Christian Monasticism* 72-73).

Cistercianism introduced a number of new practices to the monastic movement. It gave individual monasteries equal participation by requiring that abbots, or their representatives, from all its monasteries gather for a yearly chapter meeting to review their adherence to their *Rule* and to make needed changes. The Fourth Lateran Council (1215) recognized their approach as exemplary (Lawrence 192). The Cistercians thus became "an international order with a cosmopolitan and partly representative legislature" (Lawrence 191). The Cistercian practice of seeking and cultivating remote, unclaimed lands led to another important innovation. Though committed to having their members perform manual work, they soon found that, without the peasant labor used in the traditional manorial system, they needed additional help. Furthermore, sometimes they acquired properties distant from the motherhouse, but they were determined not to dilute discipline by dispersing their monks. They therefore began to accept lay brothers, or *conversi*, from the peasantry. As illiterates, the *conversi* did not participate in chanting the liturgy, their task being to provide the necessary agricultural labor (Lawrence 149).

By accepting lay brothers, the Cistercians opened the monastic vocation to many people previously denied the opportunity to pursue Christian perfection. For monasteries reflected secular society's class divisions: although they were theoretically open to all and although the Church expressly forbade requiring dowries, only those whose families could provide financial support usually gained admittance (Lawrence 35-38). But the *conversi* were not admitted on the same basis as full-fledged monks; their second-class status revealed itself in the material conditions of their lives: they received less food; their clothing was coarser; they were excluded from voting for an abbot; and they were denied frequent communion. In withholding the order's full privileges, the Cistercians introduced a two-tier system that fostered resentment. The resulting frustrations sometimes erupted into violence, especially since the brothers' tools could easily become weapons (Sayers, "Violence in the Medieval Cloister" 539). One incident highlights how smoldering anger could undermine monastic peace: "In 1209, deprived of their beer, the *conversi* of Margam revolted against the abbot, threw the cellarer from his horse, attacked and then pursued the fleeing abbot for some miles and finally barricaded themselves in their dormitory, refusing to provide the monks any sustenance" (Sayers 539). Unfortunately, the *Rule* had no mechanism for dealing with the lay brothers' complaints.

Lacking feudal obligations, the Cistercians kept their labor's profits; consequently they too achieved significant prosperity (Knowles, *Christian Monasticism* 89). In England they were particularly successful in sheep farming and in the wool trade (Burton, *Monastic and*

Religious Orders in Britain 236). As their bequests and endowments mounted, the Cistercians became feudal overlords, often exacting ones. Walter Map, the thirteenth-century critic of monasticism, makes some strong accusations against the Cistercians' practices in consolidating land: "they raze villages, overthrow churches and turn out parishioners, not scrupling to cast down altars and level all before the ploughshare" (qtd. in Coleman, "Nasty Habits: Satire and the Medieval Monk" 38). As with their predecessors, their properties inevitably brought entanglements with the world they sought to leave behind (Bolton, *The Medieval Reformation* 48).

During these reform movements women too sought a more intense spirituality by establishing themselves in new monastic communities. Though both the Cluniac and the Cistercian movements oriented themselves toward men, establishments for women followed. The Cistercians, at least in the early phase, decidedly rejected women's participation. But the order could not prevent spiritually oriented women from founding communities and following its rule; however, the monks were enjoined against assuming any responsibility for their spiritual direction and against any visitation. But ultimately the nuns' claims could not be ignored (Thompson, *Women Religious* 94-95). Janet Burton comments, "The admission of the existence of Cistercian nuns was a triumph of female persistence" (101).

Whatever their level of formal incorporation, convents could not function totally independently of men, for the bar against women's ordination meant that nuns had to depend on priests to perform sacerdotal functions such as saying Mass, receiving their vows, and hearing confessions (Shahar, *The Fourth Estate* 31). Still, the abbess had substantial, though carefully circumscribed, power: she was the one to whom the nuns owed obedience. She provided spiritual direction to her sisters, enforced compliance with the rule, and dispensed punishments. The abbess also exercised authority over the male and female servants in the house and over the male religious who served the convent (Shahar 38). Such is the relationship between Chaucer's Prioress and the appropriately labeled Nun's Priest. Though technically the Prioress's superior as a male cleric, he serves her convent's needs and takes direction from her. In telling his tale he reveals his ambiguous position by slipping into, and then retreating from, conventional misogynist arguments when he explains how his rooster hero has courted disaster by heeding his favorite hen's advice:

> But for I noot to whom it myght displese,
> If I conseil of wommen wolde blame,

Passe over, for I seyde it in my game.
Rede auctours, where they trete of swich mateere,
And what they seyn of wommen ye may heere.
Thise been the cokkes wordes, and nat myne;
I kan noon harm of no womman divyne. (ll. 3260-66)

Women who headed well-endowed religious houses also exercised real power in the secular sphere (Shahar 37). Abbesses who held the rank of baroness oversaw their properties and incomes, found knights to fulfill military obligations, presided at debtors' court, and sometimes, in England, had a seat in Parliament (Lucas 46). In some instances they could preside over criminal cases, establish punishments, select champions for fighting in duels, rule on land sales and transfers, and authorize fairs and markets. Abbesses could also wield influence in ecclesiastical arenas by calling synods, enforcing tithes from churches that belonged to the nunnery, and approving clerical appointments (Shahar 37). In rare instances, an abbess—like the mystic Hildegard of Bingen, a twelfth-century German leader dedicated to monastic reform—adopted a prophetic stance and spoke with authority, earning respect at the highest levels of both sacred and secular government (Newman, *Sister of Wisdom* 11).

In Chaucer's England monks continued to wield political and economic power: they occupied numerous seats in the House of Lords and owned considerable land that could not legally be taken away from them (Knapp, *Chaucer and the Social Contest* 46). In their landowning capacity they could be hard taskmasters, as their being major targets during the Peasants' Revolt makes evident (47). Monastic involvement in the political world, however, was becoming controversial. Both Edward III and the Black Prince employed monks in high-level bureaucratic positions. But John of Gaunt was opposed to the practice, drawing support from Wycliff's attacks on clerical involvement in secular affairs. Uthred of Boldon, on the other hand, strongly supported having monks serve earthly rulers (Pantin 170).

Monasticism held the ideological high ground throughout the medieval period. But in the twelfth and thirteenth centuries the quest for spiritual perfection took a new turn with the appearance of the mendicant movement, which originated in the nascent spiritual restlessness associated with the growth of urban centers where the laity was becoming increasingly literate (Lawrence 194). The rural, inward-looking monasteries were ill-suited to respond to these changes, whereas the new mendicant orders, the most important of which were the Franciscans and the Dominicans, defined their missions as apostolic service in these environments. The conversion of Francesco Bernardone, an Umbrian cloth merchant's charismatic son—"a figure unique in the history of the Church" and one who "transformed medieval spirituality" (Cook and Herzman 296)—began a widespread international movement. Rejecting his merchant-class patrimony, Francis made poverty the keystone for the apostolic life—and ultimately its most controversial and divisive feature. Citing the Biblical counsel, "if you would be perfect, go, sell all you have, and give to the poor" (Matt. 19:21), Francis embraced poverty and identified with society's outcasts, such as the lepers he had previously shunned. He believed that he should own nothing, trusting that God would provide all he needed through the free gifts others would make in response to spiritual services rendered, for "the laborer is worthy of his food" (Matt. 10:10). For Francis, using the Gospels as his guide, living in poverty meant imitating Jesus's life with his apostles on earth (Lawrence 199). His adopted lifestyle and the rule he developed for his rapidly increasing following implicitly criticized a Church hierarchy long aligned with the aristocracy and richly endowed with material possessions. But whereas others who criticized the Church's wealth had aroused the hierarchy's ire, Francis—because he always maintained a deferential attitude toward Church authorities—succeeded both in bringing a breath of fresh air into the institution and in responding to some of the faithful's unmet spiritual needs. When he and some followers visited Rome in 1210, he gained Innocent III's approval for his rule. This episode signals the special relationship that developed between the papacy and the mendicants, who became important in consolidating papal power.

Francis's order increased rapidly during his lifetime and already had strong roots when he died in 1226. But though he was a charismatic leader, he was ill-equipped to address the order's practical problems. Conflicts about just how strictly to apply the rule of poverty arose even during his lifetime. Providing for the material necessities of a rapidly expanding following, known as the Order of Friars Minor, caused acute problems. Francis's initial rule of 1221 strictly interpreted the requirement for poverty, but two years later, when Honorius III approved the official rule, it allowed the order "use" of property technically owned by the papacy. Francis's final testament, however, went back to the first rule's ideals (Olson, *The Canterbury Tales and the Good Society* 218-19). "The friars must be very careful not to accept churches or poor dwellings for themselves, or anything else built for them, unless they are in harmony with the poverty which we have promised in the Rule; and they should occupy those places only as strangers and pilgrims," (qtd. in Cook and Herzman 302-3) Francis warns his followers.

Francis's intense spirituality also attracted women. Among his earliest recruits was Clare, a young noblewoman from Assisi. Fired by the same zeal for the apostolic life as Francis, she founded the Poor Clares and initially intended to pursue a mendicant lifestyle (Lawrence 264). Contemporary evidence suggests that Francis too planned to have the sisters working closely in his ministry. But medieval society could not tolerate women roaming city streets and country byways. Enclosure was the price exacted for the order's gaining papal recognition (Bolton, *The Medieval Reformation* 90-91). The Clares ultimately assumed the features of a more traditional monastic order, whose members were strictly enclosed but who followed more rigorous guidelines on poverty than most (Lawrence 264). "The ideal of voluntary poverty was not a male monopoly," Lawrence observes, "but female mendicancy seemed unthinkable" (264).

However, Clare did get for her order the *privilegium paupertas* ["the privilege of poverty"]: unlike traditional orders, it did not need to have income-producing property as its financial base (Bolton, *The Medieval Reformation* 91). Furthermore, Clare's conception of the religious life showed some independence: it stressed service to the poor, respect for the sisters' individuality, communal decision-making, and physical rigor (Petroff, *Body and Soul* 68-75). This last point was important because, as Elizabeth Petroff observes, "it asserted the belief that women are as strong as men—a very new and rather shocking idea" (75). Thus Clare's commitment to poverty and rigorous asceticism highlighted not just her devotion to gospel values but also her belief that women can be self-sufficient (Petroff 75).

After Francis's death in 1226 the poverty issue continued to cause dissension. Though Gregory IX (1227-41) held that Francis's testament was not binding, the order remained seriously divided: one segment, known as Spirituals, held that the friars should own nothing and take no care for providing for the morrow, trusting in God to meet their needs; the mainstream group, known as Conventuals, based themselves on the 1223 rule and held that the friars could own nothing as individuals but could have communal goods. Corporately owning the material resources necessary for carrying out their mission, though not revenue-producing property like the monastic orders, was permissible.

An extremist group among the Spirituals, the Fraticelli, was eventually declared heretical; some were actually put to death. In part, their problems stemmed from their radical critique not only of their fellow Franciscans' departure from their founder's vision but especially of the hierarchy's wealth and corruption. They maintained that Christ and his apostles had not owned property, that the whole Church was in apostasy, and that the pope was the Antichrist (Christie-Murray, *A History of Heresy* 111). Equally problematical for Church authorities was their adapting Joachim of Fiore's (1132-1202) apocalyptic scheme for their own purposes. Using Joachim's ideas about how history is subdivided, John of Parma, a Franciscan Spiritual, held that Christianity had failed and that a new religion that dispensed with church structures and sacraments would take its place and introduce a perfect age (Christie-Murray 111).

By the early fourteenth century, when the papacy moved to Avignon, the long-standing quarrel among the Franciscans became especially intense because the Spirituals had a strong presence in Provence. In 1317 John XXII attempted to enforce obedience on them concerning their attire and storing emergency supplies; he also refused to hold the order's property, thus eliminating the technicality that had allowed the order to consider itself poor (Schimmelpfennig 214). Finally, in 1322 John declared heretical the Spirituals' contention that Christ and the apostles had owned nothing. His rigid posture made compromise difficult, and the moderates' hopes that establishing a new order within the Church would resolve the conflict quickly faded (Hamilton, *The Medieval Inquisition* 88-91).

Contemporaneous with the Franciscan movement was that of the Dominicans. The former had its roots in a lay environment: Francis himself was never fully ordained, though he did become a deacon; many of his early followers were laymen, but subsequently, in keeping with the Church's commitment to a professional clergy, the order became increasingly clericalized (Lawrence 250). The Dominicans, however, arose in ecclesiastical circles among those engaged in combating the Cathar heresy in southern France. Dominic, a Spanish priest, understood that adopting the apostolic life of preaching and poverty would undermine a heretical group whose leaders were noted for their asceticism (203-4). He and his followers devoted themselves to attacking heresy through exemplary living, but even more through convincingly demolishing the heretics' arguments. In its origins and mission, then, the Dominican movement had both a clerical and an intellectual thrust. The Dominicans, known as the Order of Preachers, modified the existing rule of Augustine. Their rule, which eliminated manual labor and downplayed the observance of the divine office, focused on the friars' mission as preachers.

The mendicant orders established themselves quickly and firmly in the growing urban centers of the thirteenth and fourteenth centuries. They undertook a preaching and teaching mission to a laity increasingly intent on becoming involved in its own spiritual development. They met a need to which the often poorly educated secular clergy was ill-prepared to respond (208) and from which the monastic orders were often too detached. Indeed the mendicants' success was probably due to their lay appeal: "they pioneered the idea of the devout life for the laity; a Christian life, that is, not modeled upon the life of monks or dependent upon the vicarious merits acquired by professional ascetics, but one lived fully in the world. They offered a new theology of the secular life" (208-9).

Another important aspect of the mendicants' apostolate was serving as confessors in the areas they serviced. Influenced by a new approach to moral theology, they placed more emphasis on the context in which a sin occurred and on the penitent's intentions or state of mind when sinning; this approach allowed more flexibility than relying on the penitential manuals, which established set, and severe, penalties for each type of sin. Thus the more sophisticated laity in both aristocratic milieus and urban centers sought out friars as confessors (209). Their role was problematic, however, because the Fourth Lateran Council required that one should confess annually to one's parish priest; even after the mendicants had secured papal authorization, penitential manuals questioned whether confessing to anyone else was valid (214). "The Summoner's Tale" raises this issue when Thomas refuses to confess to the visiting friar, insisting that his sins have been forgiven by his parish priest (ll. 2095-98).

Inevitably abuses occurred in the friars' exercise of their role as confessors because their institutionalized mendicancy created a strong temptation to link lenient treatment for sins to generous support for their order (Southern 291). The "General Prologue" portrait ascribes this failing to the Friar who, the narrator ironically observes, takes generous contributions as an external sign of the inner contrition the penitent cannot otherwise manifest (ll. 223-32).

To interact successfully with the increasingly literate laity and to combat heresy through the force of argument, the friars also became deeply involved with education, both to prepare themselves for their mission and to spread their ideas in lay circles. The Dominicans especially immersed themselves in the universities, which at that time were becoming the new centers of intellectual activity. Indeed their preaching style was much influenced by the methodology they learned in the universities. Because intellectual activity was less centrally tied to the

Franciscans' mission, they moved into educational spheres less aggres-sively. Francis had been suspicious of learning, seeing it as an induce-ment to pride. But contemporary needs propelled the Franciscans into the challenging thirteenth century educational arena (Lawrence 211). The Franciscan instructional approach, however, reinforced Francis-can spirituality's central aspect: it leaned more heavily toward the affec-tive than toward the rational, stressing religion's experiential aspects and urging the faithful to identify with Jesus (Lesnick 94, 134-71).

Developing in roughly the same context, though having different roots, the mendicant orders cross-pollinated each other: the Francis-cans adopted the Dominicans' organizational structure and their pursuit of knowledge in the universities; the Dominicans, for their part, followed the Franciscan lead on poverty, thereby increasing their credibility in urban centers (Southern 284). The mendicant or-ders responded to deeply felt societal needs: "They made the road to heaven easier for everyone," Southern comments (284-91). For a laity long resigned to the clergy's remoteness and unwillingness to validate lay experience, the mendicants provided an alternative vi-sion of the religious life. These orders responded, within the Church's framework, to challenges the institution faced from within and without, quickly becoming its cutting edge:

> In less than a hundred years these new orders had also affected drastically the progress of papal centralization, the development of the medieval universities, the theology and practice of confession, the final flowering of Scholasticism, the growth of nominalism, the revival of classical literature, the flourishing of lay piety, the spread of missionary activity as far as the steppes of Asia—and more.
> (Szittya, *The Antifraternal Tradition in Medieval Literature* 4)

But these successes did not come without problems. The mendi-cant orders' tremendous surge in membership and their popularity with the laity led to their currying favor and accumulating wealth. In addition to attracting criticism about their members' failures to live up to their founders' high standards, the mendicants aroused in-tense professional antagonism from other ecclesiastical sectors. Ini-tially the secular clergy welcomed the mendicants, seeing them as useful allies in reaching the faithful. But when the friars started re-ceiving bequests, building their own churches, supplanting the parish clergy as confessors, and collecting burial fees, the seculars perceived them as rivals for the laity's loyalty and limited resources (Lawrence 212). Also, the mendicants' direct authorization from the papacy meant that they could bypass the bishops' authority, thereby further intensifying local ire against them.

Both the monastic and the mendicant orders set high standards for their adherents; inevitably they fell short of meeting them. Sometimes their shortcomings were as egregious as those Peter Abelard describes in his autobiographical *Historia calamitatis*. The twelfth-century philosopher-turned-monk reports his fears for his life when, upon becoming abbot of Saint Gildas in remote Brittany, he attempted to enforce stricter discipline upon some unruly monks who kept concubines and children: "I was certain at any rate that if I tried to bring them back to the life of the rule for which they had taken their vows it would cost me my own life; yet if I did not do my utmost to achieve this, I should be damned" (*The Letters of Abelard and Héloïse* 95). Recalling when Benedict also faced danger from rebellious monks who resisted his discipline, Abelard tells of attempts on his life: "How many times have they tried to poison me—as happened to Saint Benedict! . . . And while I guarded as well as I could against their daily assaults by providing my own food and drink, they tried to destroy me during the very act of sacrament by putting poison in the chalice" (102-3).

Diocesan visitation records provide a prime source of evidence concerning monastic shortcomings (Daichman, *Wayward Nuns in Medieval Literature* 3-4). Some lapses were minor, as exemplified in a thirteenth-century record from Rouen, which notes that "all [the nuns] wear their hair improperly and perfume their veils" (qtd. in Daichman 8-9). But the records also provide evidence of serious failings relating to lapses from chastity. Though liaisons with laypeople occurred, those among the clergy appear to have been more common because they had many opportunities and legitimate reasons for contact. The next sentence in the record which mentions hairstyles and perfumed veils points up just this problem: "Jacqueline came back pregnant from visiting a certain chaplain who was expelled from his house on account of this" (qtd. in Daichman 9).

The visitation records show that bishops issued a variety of injunctions to curtail abuses and punish offenders. They issued rules—not very successfully enforced—about nuns remaining confined within their convents and always being accompanied by a companion. The archbishop of Romsey Abbey, for instance, forbade the nuns in his charge "to hold converse with any man save either in the parlour or in the side of the church next the cloister" (qtd. in Daichman 27). Offending nuns could be subjected to public humiliation, to solitary confinement, to punitive fasts. The most serious punishments, however, were reserved for those who attempted to flee their convents. When threats and pleas failed to convince the runaway, bishops called on the secular arm for assistance in forcing her return (Daichman 10-11).

Monasticism's high ideals coupled with its worldly entanglements made monks and nuns ready targets for strong denunciations and satirical barbs. Chaucer's contemporary and friend, John Gower, for instance, lamented the monks' deviations from their founders' inspiration:

> When their order began, monks' homes were caves; now a grand marble palace sets them off. They used to have no steaming kitchen, and no cook served them delicacies roasted or baked by the fire. . . . Bodily gluttony did not afflict their souls, nor were they inflamed by lust of the flesh to seek out debauchery on the sly. . . . There was no envy or splendor in a monastery then; he who was the greater served as did the lesser. There was no great quantity of silver or chain of gold that could corrupt their holy state then. (qtd. in Miller, *Chaucer: Sources and Backgrounds* 221-24)

Portrayals of monastic failings were a standard feature of the genre known as estates satire: the monk's stereotypical features as depicted in such literature were "a love of good food, luxurious clothing, a love of horses and hunting, contempt for patristic and monastic authority, laziness, a refusal to stay within cloister walls, the temptations of holding various monastic offices" (Mann, *Chaucer and Medieval Estates Satire* 17).

Another weakness commonly attributed to monks was lechery. Gerald of Wales, for instance, notes Hugh of Lincoln's answer to a woman who had sought advice about her husband's impotence: "Let us make him a monk and the power will be immediately restored to him" (qtd. in Coleman 40). The lecherous monk was a stock figure in such genres as the fabliaux. Chaucer's "The Shipman's Tale," for instance, falls within the tradition in which lusty monks either dupe unsuspecting husbands or are duped by clever women. In this case the monk and his merchant friend's wife conspire to make the merchant pay for his own cuckolding. While superficially charming, the monk—immersing himself in business and pleasure-seeking—completely lacks spiritual resonance. By the fourteenth century "wayward nuns" were also stock figures in satiric literature (Daichman 115). The *Decameron* includes a story about an abbess who, rushing out from her chamber to catch one of her nuns with a lover, mistakes her own priest-lover's breeches for her veil; when the accused nun points out the abbess's error, the latter retreats from the moral high ground. Thereafter, all the nuns have her permission to gratify themselves whenever they wish, as long as they manage their affairs discreetly (691).

The mendicants also were subject to virulent satiric attacks. The rivalries between orders and the tensions between the mendicants and the seculars resulted in a body of intensely antifraternal literature that circulated in both ecclesiastical and lay circles. Penn Szittya points to the unique aspects of the attacks on the mendicants: "Other ecclesiastical groups and individual churchmen of all orders had often been attacked for falling into immorality, heterodoxy, or heresy. Some friars were too, but the mendicant orders were attacked primarily as an institution, whose claim to the *vita apostolica* was false and whose legitimacy as religious orders was suspect" (7). The rivalry between the seculars and the mendicants created a major controversy at the University of Paris where professional rivalry fueled the conflict. William of St. Amour, the chief spokesman for the antifraternal position, argued that the diocesan structure, rather than the friars' mendicant lifestyle, was derived from the apostles and had divine sanction. On the other hand, the Franciscan Bonaventure, arguing for the mendicants, strongly affirmed papal prerogatives, maintaining that the pope's authority has primacy and that he has the right to delegate it to whomever he pleases (Lawrence 213).

Though officially condemned, William's work became a mine for many future antimendicant attacks (Szittya 17). Applying a long scriptural tradition of apocalyptic literature to the friars, William linked them to three major groups: the Pharisees, the pseudoapostles, and those foreshadowing the Antichrist's coming. Associating the Pharisees with hypocrisy and pride, William criticizes the friars for wanting the title of "magister" or master, for pressing their unjustified claims to the right to preach, and for insinuating themselves into the homes of the spiritually weak, specifically of widows. He calls the friars false teachers because they claimed to be reviving the apostles' lifestyle. Alluding to the friars' begging, William identifies preaching to obtain material rewards rather than to enhance their auditors' spiritual lives as a sign of false teachers (Szittya 24-52). Finally, William associates the friars with the Antichrist's precursors because they spread rapidly and caused dissension in the Church, leading the faithful away from their proper leaders. Drawing on a verse from the Letter of Timothy—"for of such are they who penetrate into houses and captivate silly women who are laden with sin and led astray by various lusts" (2 Timothy 3:6)—William applies it to the friars both literally and spiritually. As the *penetrante domos,* a phrase that would stereotype the friars for the next two hundred years, they violate both the homes and the consciences of the faithful (Szittya 58).

Though English writers probably had no direct knowledge of William's work, the antifraternal stereotype that emerged in it, with its strong roots in Biblical imagery, carried over into secular spheres and remained remarkably consistent (Szittya 200). That stereotype portrays friars as hypocritical smooth talkers, as predators on the gullibility of women whom they exploit to satisfy both their lechery and their avarice, as crowd-pleasing entertainers rather than stern moralists, and thus as purveyors of an easy religious pabulum (Mann, *Chaucer and Medieval Estates Satire* 37-54). Thus unlike the satiric thrusts directed at the monastics who were often faulted for wallowing in comfort, those aimed at the mendicants' failings focused on their hypocrisy and cunning. As Southern notes, "They were more notorious for sharpness than for sloth" (292). Boccaccio's story of the reprobate who became a Franciscan known as Frate Alberto highlights this aspect of the friars' image. Gaining a reputation for sanctity by his ascetic life, by preaching repentance, and by exhibiting a deep religious feeling, Alberto wins the Venetians' complete confidence. But he overreaches: he convinces Monna Lisetta that the Angel Gabriel has been won by her charms and needs to assume Alberto's body to make love with her. When the lady's relatives learn of the ruse, they expose him to public ridicule. Commenting on Alberto's fate with evident satisfaction, the narrator says:

> Thus it was that this arch-villain, whose wicked deeds went unnoticed because he was held to be good, had the audacity to transform himself into the Angel Gabriel. In the end, however, having been turned from an angel into a savage, he got the punishment he deserved, and repented in vain for the crimes he had committed. May it please God that a similar fate should befall each and every one of his fellows. (353)

Chaucer portrays a wide spectrum of monastic behavior and indirectly explores some of the questions his contemporaries were raising about monasticism's proper societal role. Four pilgrims—the Monk, the Prioress, the Nun's Priest, and the Second Nun—as well as one of the main characters in "The Shipman's Tale" are monastics. The spiritually busy, self-effacing Second Nun provides a model

of monastic perfection; she devotes herself to spiritual study by translating the story of Saint Cecilia, most likely her patron saint. Her
prologue underscores the importance she attaches to avoiding idle-
ness and, some readers believe, indirectly criticizes the lifestyle of
the Prioress, her religious superior:

> And though men dradden nevere for to dye,
> Yet seen men wel by resoun, doutelees,
> That ydelnesse is roten slogardye,
> Of which ther nevere comth no good n'encrees;
> And syn that slouthe hire holdeth in a lees
> Oonly to slepe, and for to ete and drynke,
> And to devouren al that othere swynke. (ll. 15-21)

The Second Nun tells the story of an Early Christian saint whose virginity yields spiritual fruits: she converts those around her to Christianity. Cecile achieves mystic contemplation—the aim of monastic
discipline—as she enjoys visions of her guardian angel; ultimately
she earns the reward of martyrdom, with its promise of immediate
salvation.

Against the Second Nun's portrait of ascetic self-denial and spiritual fruitfulness, the Monk and the Prioress are figures of worldly
self-indulgence. Yet Chaucer is deft rather than heavy-handed in
drawing their portraits. He includes tantalizingly ambiguous details
in the "General Prologue" and deflects into "The Shipman's Tale"
the most standard features of monastic misbehavior. Neither the
Monk nor the Prioress appears to be truly corrupt, but they remain
beginners in ascending the ladder of spiritual perfection because
they love comfort and aristocratic pursuits rather than the hard work
of self-discipline.

The Monk's portrait includes many details from satiric works
such as those discussed above. The Monk is "a manly man" and "a fat
prelaat" who enjoys hunting, wears fine boots and fur-trimmed garments, and loves fat roast swans. Ironically the Monk's worldliness is
probably central to his monastic function, since he must oversee his
house's far-flung properties. Some of the behavior that deviates from
the *Rule* may have been necessary to advance the monastery's business interests, thereby shifting the satiric thrust to the order itself
(Knapp, *Chaucer and the Social Contest* 47). Suggestions of the Monk's
lechery remain veiled: he wears a gold pin wrought in a loveknot,
and he loves the hunt, which the contemporary Gawain-poet links
with seduction. Complementing the "General Prologue's" hints of

the Monk's possible lechery are the Host's comments in "The Prologue to the Monk's Tale": Harry laments that such a fine physical
specimen was consigned to celibacy, telling him that "thou woldest
han been a tredefowel aright" (l. 1944). But the Monk can scarcely
be held responsible for Harry's levity. Finally, the Monk specifically
repudiates, as old-fashioned and useless, the *Rule's* requirements for
staying within the cloister studying and toiling:

> What sholde he studie and make hymselven wood,
> Upon a book in cloystre alwey to poure,
> Or swynken with his handes, and laboure,
> As Austyn bit? How shal the world be served?
> Lat Austyn have his swynk to hym reserved! (ll. 183-88)

The Chaucer pilgrim seemingly approves of his attitudes—"And I
seyde his opinion was good" (GP, l. 183)—thereby complicating attempts to assess the dimensions of Chaucer's satire.

The tale the Monk tells—really a repetitious collection of tales
about the fall of individuals ranging from Adam to the contemporary Pedro the Cruel—has generated critical controversy. Some
readers find the tale, with its rigidly moralistic thrust, an unlikely
one for the worldly Monk to tell. Others argue that the tale reinforces our impression of the Monk's spiritual aridity. What he manifests contrasts with *otium*, the soul's peaceful rest that is the goal of
the monk's spiritual discipline. David Berndt, for instance, argues
that the shortcomings that emerge both in the Monk's portrait and
in his tale suggest spiritual sloth, or *acedia*. In this reading, the
Monk's restlessness, as manifest in his joining the pilgrimage, becomes a sign of his desire to avoid the difficult challenge of spiritual
growth, which for a monk can occur only in his cloister (436-40).
Furthermore, while his tales all point to a proper moral—that the
wheel of Fortune turns, especially for those in high places—they offer an unrelievedly bleak picture of human destiny. The Monk's
many tales envision no transcendent perspective to offer relief from
the wheel's downward rotation and no moral basis from which to assess the victims' fate. Because the Monk fails to distinguish between
those who simply must endure Fortune's changes and those who fall
through their own behavior, Peggy Knapp characterizes his performance as "more pagan than the Knight's" (48). And, as Olson points
out, all of the Monk's examples of falling from power to disaster take
place in a secular framework, suggesting that he fails to recognize
the potential pitfalls his own estate faces (*The Canterbury Tales and the*

Good Society 170-71). The Monk's performance, in its total inattentiveness to his audience's needs, reveals "the discourse of proud feudal monasticism" (Knapp, *Chaucer and the Social Contest* 49), functioning in effect like "The Pardoner's Tale" by preaching against the very sin of which its teller is most guilty: pride (Knapp 8).

In the Prioress Chaucer creates a more elusive figure than the Monk. Critics have long debated the extent to which her portrait is satirical: some see the poet gently tweaking a woman whose imperfections are slight; others see a much more serious rendering of a failed nun whose role as a monastic leader intensifies her shortcomings. The "General Prologue" presents a vacuous, spiritually shallow woman: her attention focuses on mimicking aristocratic manners, and her religious feeling is mired in sentimentality as she lavishes all her charitable impulses on little animals. The Prioress indulges her pets, worries about her table manners, and adorns herself with brightly colored jewelry. Though nothing in her portrait explicitly points to sexual improprieties, many details derive from the courtly romances' characterizations of the beloved lady; in fact the discussion of the Prioress's table manners echoes the advice of La Vieille in the *Roman de la rose* about how to attract a lover, and ultimately derives from Ovid (Daichman 142-43). The concluding details of her coral beads and the brooch with the ambiguous inscription *amor vincit omnia* ("love conquers all") complete Chaucer's finely nuanced treatment of the Prioress, for the beads and the inscription both have sacred and secular—even erotic—connotations (Daichman 157-58).

"The Prioress's Tale" considerably complicates attempts to assess its teller. In the invocation—addressed to the Virgin Mary, the Prioress's model of virginity and humility—she likens herself to a twelve-month infant, perhaps unconsciously revealing her identification with her main character's unthinking piety (ll. 484-87). Her blatantly anti-Semitic tale—with its innocent chorister trying to honor the Virgin by memorizing songs he does not understand and its demonized Jews who kill him without provocation—falls within the popular genre of miracles of the Virgin. Perhaps we shall never determine whether Chaucer shared in its anti-Semitism. But the readings that see the Prioress's spiritual immaturity reflected in the tale's superficial religiosity strike me as convincing. For hers is not the childlikeness that Christians must achieve to attain the kingdom of heaven but the childishness that Paul urges Christians to put aside to reach spiritual maturity. In her self-indulgence the Prioress is blind to her own limitations, barred from growth by her smug satisfaction with her own virtue.

In accounting for her tale's anti-Semitism, Paul Olson advances a related argument: that the Prioress's fault stems from her confused identification of secular and spiritual power. The Jews' extreme punishment—drawing, quartering, and hanging, which takes place without due process and exceeds the requirements of the law—highlights her naive assumption of moral superiority, even as she avoids the difficult task of spiritual growth: "Clearly, Eglantyne is an ironic 'Innocent' who does not will death or spiritual suffering for herself, but for others. Her side has all the power, the miracle, and the glory. What need of discipline?" (Olson, *The Canterbury Tales and the Good Society* 143-44). By contrast, the Second Nun recognizes that when the two powers remain separate true wisdom may occur (144). Cecile's confrontation with Almachius establishes that the power he wields is limited indeed: he can only take life, not give it (ll. 480-83). Drawing on her spiritual wisdom, she speaks with power and authority, questioning head-on the Roman governor's misguided logic and testifying to the superior relevance of transcendent values. Indeed by confronting Almachius with his limitations and reminding him where true power lies, she provides a model of monasticism's proper relationship to secular authority.

While Chaucer's treatment of the monastics includes a range of behaviors, his portrayal of friars sounds a mostly negative note. The suave but avaricious Friar Hubert in the "General Prologue," the altercation that breaks out between the Summoner and the Friar in the midst of "The Wife of Bath's Prologue," the Wife of Bath's sly reference to the dangers friars pose to women's chastity, and the satirical and scatological aspects of "The Summoner's Tale," all paint an unrelievedly negative picture of the friars' role in medieval life. Chaucer seems to have absorbed the basic features of the antifraternal stereotype. As Arnold Williams notes, "Whenever Chaucer had occasion to mention friars, we get the same characterization, of unextenuated hypocritical villainy" (499). Perhaps he had some reason for personal animus against them: the *Chaucer Life-Records* refer to a lost but tantalizing document that mentions his being fined two shillings for fighting with a friar on Fleet Street (12). Or perhaps, as David Lyle Jeffrey suggests, he was influenced by John Wyclif's antifraternalism ("Chaucer and Wyclif" 114, 139). In any case we must see Chaucer's negativism about the friars both in the light of a satiric tradition that points up many friars' failure to live up to their founders' ideals and in that of the professional rivalries that yielded the antifraternal stereotype. As Lawrence comments: "Chaucer's Friar—the confidence trickster who sold easy penances and traded on the credulity of pious women—was a stereotype lampoon derived, by a process of literary descent, from the bitter polemics of thirteenth century Paris" (214).

Though Chaucer does not tie his friars to any specific order, several details in the "General Prologue" portrait suggest an inversion of specifically Franciscan ideals (Howard, *The Idea of The Canterbury Tales* 100). For instance, while Francis was famous for overcoming his aversion to lepers and for ministering to their needs, the Friar avoids lepers and the poor, thinking himself too important to be in their company; instead he cultivates the favor of the rich:

> For unto swich a worthy man as he
> Acorded nat, as by his facultee,
> To have with sike lazars aqueyntaunce,
> It is nat honest; it may nat avaunce,
> For to deelen with no swich poraille,
> But al with riche and selleres of vitaille. (ll. 243-48)

His ability to sing popular ballads and play musical instruments recalls the reputation of Francis's followers as "God's minstrels" (Mann, *Chaucer and Medieval Estates Satire* 45). Other aspects of his portrait are stereotypical as well: his lechery (which is hinted at rather than insisted upon); his cultivating the well-to-do; his ability to smooth-talk poor widows out of their pittance; his overall superficially pleasing personality. Jill Mann argues that, as with the portrait of the Monk, Chaucer's treatment is double-edged, implicating not only the Friar for his failings but the audience whose standards are also called into question:

> It is we (and Chaucer's original audience) who prefer real music to spiritual entertainment, and who set up a notion of respectability which rates innkeepers higher than lepers and beggars. We may suspect that the Friar's portrait is so long and complex because his estate reveals more clearly than any other the gulf between the standards of an ordered society and of Christianity. (*Chaucer and Medieval Estates Satire* 54)

Like the Pardoner's confessional prologue and tale, which provide an extended example of that shyster in action, the Summoner's tale conflates Friar John in the tale with Friar Hubert, the pilgrim— "sanctimonious, greedy, self-indulgent, monstrously hypocritical and fraudulent" (Howard, *The Idea of The Canterbury Tales* 257). However,

Chaucer's portraying the Friar through the jaundiced eyes of his archrival, the Summoner, complicates the problem of rightly assessing him.

The tale depicts a Conventual friar penetrating into the home of Thomas and his wife and attempting to probe Thomas's conscience—and ultimately his buttocks. While paying lip service to asceticism, Friar John ensconces himself in comfort, secures food delicacies, and enjoys an easy familiarity with Thomas's wife, as the kiss he gives her when she enters the room indicates. The Friar's self-serving hypocrisy is evident in his claim to mystic vision. After Thomas's wife tells John—and not before—that their child died within the past two weeks, he pretends to have seen the child's soul ascending into heaven as a result of the friars' prayers (ll. 1854-72). His conveniently remembered "vision" has the self-serving end of convincing Thomas and his wife that the friars have special access to God's secrets and that supporting the friary pays off in proper spiritual rewards. As a prelude to hearing the ailing Thomas's confession and to securing additional contributions for his friary, he delivers an extended sermon—replete with *exempla*—on the sin of anger and then urges Thomas to contribute once again to the friary's building fund. Thomas's scatological response—the fart to be equally divided among the twelve friars—underscores his growing annoyance with Friar John and produces in the latter the very anger against which he has been preaching.

The tale has yielded a number of intriguing interpretations. Paul Olson's analysis focuses on how Chaucer adapts Spiritualist rhetoric to attack a Conventual friar (214-34). Alan Levitan, on the other hand, first suggested that the tale involves Pentecostal parody, with Thomas's "wind" inverting that of the Holy Spirit: "what appears as a merely ribald anecdote is, in fact, a brilliant and satirical reversal of the Holy Ghost at Pentecost" ("The Parody of Pentecost" 236). Expanding on Levitan's argument, Szittya underscores Pentecost's special significance for the Franciscans: their founder associated it with the apostolic life and specified that the order's general chapter would be held at Pentecost every third year. But unlike the apostles to whom the Holy Spirit's descent brings the gift of tongues, Friar John remains speechless after Thomas delivers his "gift" (236-38).

Chaucer's highly allusive handling of the mendicants in *The Canterbury Tales* suggests that he knew both their founding ideals and the satiric attacks against them. As Peggy Knapp sums up: "The treatment of friars throughout this fragment weaves together the antifraternal discourse begun by William, current struggles between the mendicants and parish clergy for the loyalty of congregations, and the coarser, more personal insults of the Summoner" (59).

By the late fourteenth century the religious orders—those who set themselves apart from society to attain a higher level of Christian perfection by imitating either the angels or the apostles—shared in the overall ecclesiastical malaise. The older monastic orders were experiencing an identity crisis: the institution whose origins and ideals involved a radical challenge to materialistic values and a testimony to the spiritual life's transcendent importance had itself become entrenched in comfort and privilege. Past reform movements had called attention to its deficiencies and drawn it back to its founding moment. But the challenges of this era went beyond such traditional reform efforts. Chaucer's monastic leaders, the Prioress and the Monk, highlight the dimensions of the problem: she embodies the superficial spirituality of a person drawn into a way of life for which she has no vocation; he—the only one among the pilgrims to do so—explicitly raises the question of monasticism's contemporary relevance.

Though the Chaucer pilgrim's apparent approval of the Monk's rejecting a life of prayer and study has traditionally been read as ironic, it may also hint at late medieval society's attempt to assess the value of spiritual pursuits undertaken for one's own personal salvation in a world beset with problems that demanded the skills of the most able. The apparently ironic question, "How shal the world be served?" (GP, 1.187)—which fuses the voices of Chaucer's narrator and of the Monk—may mask the era's underlying uncertainty about what constitutes the best model for one's life. For the increasing involvement of lay people in developing their own spiritual lives and the mendicant movement's tremendous growth and popularity provided a challenge to monasticism's underlying and defining assumptions: that withdrawal from the world best leads to salvation and that a spiritual elite can assume responsibility, through its prayers, for the salvation of others. Those basic beliefs were not fully rejected—indeed are not to this day—but their hold on people was weakened: they questioned not just deviations from the ideal but the ideal itself.

The mendicant orders, through their greater involvement with the world and the laity, provided a partial response to monasticism's decline and gave a more earthly orientation to the quest for perfection: a life of apostolic service to others captured the hearts and imaginations of many. But the dissension the mendicants spawned and the abuses they engaged in undercut the expectations they raised. Though lacking Dante's penchant for prophetic invective, Chaucer reveals an intelligent layman's dismay at the way in which a movement rooted in the need to respond to laypeople's spiritual longing often became another avenue for manipulating and exploiting them. Long taught that striving for spiritual perfection was reserved for the clergy, the late medieval laity, responding to its own intense inner longings, questioned clerical models and began to claim the spiritual quest for itself. Like many of his contemporaries, Chaucer wrestled with the problem of what constitutes Christian perfection in a beleaguered world.

CHAPTER FIVE

The Road to Canterbury: Pilgrimage, Saints, and Popular Religion

*T*hough the clergy loomed large in the medieval world's conception, it constituted only a miniscule part of the population. By no means was it able to encompass or totally control the religious life of the vast majority. This chapter will concern itself with some of the era's most central manifestations of popular religion: pilgrimage and the related cult of saints and relics. For when Chaucer decided upon a pilgrimage to Canterbury as the unifying framework for his story collection, he drew upon one of the most deeply ingrained images and social realities in medieval culture. His choice of a pilgrimage as a framing device has profound implications for assessing his overall conception for the work. Some scholars see his choice as nothing more than a plausible and convenient mechanism for bringing together a variety of people from a broad societal spectrum. At the other end are critics who see the pilgrimage motif as governing the entire meaning of the work, by placing all the pilgrims and their tales in an eschatalogical framework. Exploring both the symbolic and the societal aspects of medieval pilgrimages will give us a better basis for understanding the implications of Chaucer's choice.

Pilgrimages stretched back into the first centuries of the Christian era and beyond that into the ancient world. In the Epistle to the Hebrews Peter describes Christians as "pilgrims and strangers on the earth" (11:13), thereby underlining a concept that would become an integral part of how Christians saw themselves: as *viatores,* travelers who willingly dissociate themselves from this world as they journey to their heavenly homeland. Thus pilgrims acquired a special status in medieval society; set apart from their fellows by a distinctive garb, they served as visible reminders of the essentially ascetic, otherworldly thrust of the Christian religion. Not everyone agreed on the desirability of external, physical pilgrimages, however; some stressed that the internal journey to salvation is what really matters (Hamilton, "The Impact of Crusader Jerusalem" 695). Despite such objections, pilgrimages absorbed the energies of the devout from the fourth to the sixteenth centuries when the Reformation, especially in England, led to the destruction of many pilgrimage sites. Indeed pilgrimages have remained an important, though less central, part of Christian devotion well into the twentieth century.

People were drawn to holy places because they believed that the past miracles that had taken place there held out the hope that new miracles would again occur; they saw miraculous events—especially healings—as the reward for the rigors and travails of their successfully completed journey. For Christians, such journeys re-enacted the way of the cross Jesus had undertaken—the necessary, painful steps to death that precede resurrection. Undertaking a pilgrimage at crucial points in one's life became the ordinary Christian's substitute for leading the monastics' life of complete devotion to God as Victor and Edith Turner point out: "While monastic contemplatives and mystics could daily make interior salvific journeys, those in the world had to exteriorize theirs in the infrequent adventure of pilgrimage. For the majority, pilgrimage was the great liminal experience of the religious life" (*Image and Pilgrimage in Christian Culture* 6-7). Thus as early as the second century, the faithful began to externalize their vision of human life as a pilgrimage by undertaking journeys to Christianity's most sacred sites: Jerusalem and Rome. These *prototypical* pilgrimage sites are linked with Christianity's seminal figures and events: Jesus's life and death and the martyrdoms of some important early Christians saints like Peter and Paul (Turner 18).

Jerusalem—thought to be the center of the earth, as is shown in the famous *Mappa Mundi* in Hereford Cathedral (see Chapter One)—was especially important: "in Christian thought, Jerusalem might imply the ordered soul of the faithful, the City of Heaven, or the Church" (Robertson, *A Preface to Chaucer* 293). Margery Kempe, the fifteenth-century laywoman who undertook several pilgrimages after experiencing a religious conversion, captures its symbolic equivalence with the Christian's heavenly destination:

> And when this creature saw Jerusalem . . . she thanked God with all her heart, praying him for his mercy that, just as he had brought her to see this earthly city of Jerusalem, he would grant her grace to see the blissful city of Jerusalem above, the city of heaven. (*The Book of Margery Kempe* 103)

Upon reaching the Holy Land, many pilgrims tried to retrace the major events in Jesus's life by going out into the desert, immersing themselves in the Jordan, and following the route of the passion in Jerusalem (Loxton, *Pilgrimage to Canterbury* 93). Because sacred events had occurred in Jerusalem and Rome, Christians believed these two cities were places where heaven touched earth and thus were places where they could contact the sacred (Brown, *The Cult of the Saints* 10). But Christianity never entirely localized the sacred in one or two special spots (Brown, *The Cult of the Saints* 90).

Closely related to the practice of undertaking pilgrimages was the cult of saints and their relics, an area of religious devotion that was particularly subject to popular enthusiasms and singularly resistant to clerical control. As early as the second and third centuries, Christians started venerating as saints those whose martyrdom or heroically virtuous lives gave them a claim to being especially close to God. As Pamela Sheingorn comments,

> Recalling the words of Jesus to the good thief crucified with him, "Today you shall be with me in Paradise," early Christians concluded that the souls of martyrs ascended directly into the presence of God. From their places near God's throne, these martyr-saints were ideally positioned to intercede on behalf of still-living Christians. (*The Book of Saint Foy* 3)

To honor the saints on the anniversary of their deaths, Christians began to gather at their tombs to celebrate a communal meal; they also collected stories about the saint's last days and transcripts from their trials to keep alive within the community the memory of the saints' affinity with Jesus's sufferings and death (Sheingorn 3).

The cult of saints became one of Western Christianity's characteristic features (Brown, *The Cult of the Saints* 12). Official Christianity carefully distinguished between the proper attitudes toward God and the saints: only the former was due adoration, while the latter received veneration. It also insisted that all miracles were God's work, not the saints', who were merely conduits of divine power (Sheingorn 3). In popular Christianity, however, that distinction often disappeared: people looked directly to their favorite saints for results. Saints' graves and their bodily remains attracted the faithful for religious observances, and the ever-increasing number of saints resulted in a proliferation of sites attractive to pilgrims. Believers saw saints' graves, like the sacred sites associated with the founding of their religion, as intersections between heaven and earth (Brown, *The Cult of the Saints* 3). Saints' bodies could arouse intense religious emotion, as is evident from the comments of Gregory of Nyassa (ca. 335-94): "Those who behold them embrace, as it were, the living body in full flower: they bring eye, mouth, ear, all the senses into play, and then, shedding tears of reverence and passion, they address to the martyr their prayers of intercession as though he were present" (qtd. in Brown, *The Cult of the Saints* 11). Christians had a strong desire to experience closeness with the saints directly, through contact with their bodies or belongings—their relics—which were considered "especially effective channels of communication through which living Christians could direct their prayers and petitions; it was as if some of the saints' power had adhered to their mortal flesh" (Sheingorn 3). Thus the cult of saints and relics became an important propelling force behind the impetus to pilgrimage.

Christians who arrived at the sacred spots where saints were venerated sought to take away something that would keep alive for them the holiness they had touched; wanting some memento or relic to bring back with them, they brought pieces of cloth to touch either the bodies or the tombs of the martyrs. These *brandea* acquired a sacredness of their own, as is evident in Gregory of Tours's (538-94) description of how to capture the sacredness associated with St. Peter's tomb in Rome:

> He who wishes to pray before the tomb opens the barrier that surrounds it and puts his head through a small opening in the shrine. There he prays for all his needs and, so long as his requests are just, his prayers will be granted. Should he wish to bring back a relic from the tomb, he carefully weighs a piece of cloth which he then hangs inside the tomb. Then he prays ardently and, if his faith is sufficient, the cloth, once removed from the tomb, will be found to be so full of divine grace that it will be much heavier than before. Thus will he know that his prayers have been granted. (qtd. in Sumption, *Pilgrimage* 24)

Having a belonging touch the holy tomb did not content some of the faithful; they also wanted their own authentic bodily relics. Their desire to own famous relics overpowered their scruples about moving the relics from their original locations. For though the Church initially resisted disturbing saintly remains, that resistance eroded when, in the eighth and ninth centuries, the bodies of early Christian martyrs in Rome were moved from their initial resting places in the catacombs to other locations; these moves provided a justification for many other such actions in later centuries (Shein-gorn 4). Indeed, because the Germanic tribes responded to the new religion's miraculous aspects, moving relics from Christianity's center in Rome to northern Europe played an important role in the missionaries' efforts at conversion. These removals of sacred remains, called "translations," often took place with great pomp and solemnity and often involved moving the remains to more elaborate surroundings (Finucane, *Miracles and Pilgrims* 22). Much-sought-after saints' bodies were subdivided into myriad components and moved to locations far from their first burial sites. Thus the practice of moving relics from place to place—with all its potential for abuse—was well established before the great age of pilgrimages began in the eleventh century.

Saint James the Apostle's fate provides a good example of the dispersal of saintly remains. According to popular belief, a tenth century discovery made known the presence of his body in northwestern Spain, where he had gone to preach the gospel (Ward, *Miracles and the Medieval Mind* 110, 115). That discovery spurred the development of an already important pilgrimage destination: the Church of Santiago de Compostela. In the twelfth century the saint's head was formally moved from Jerusalem to Compostela. But his hand became the center of devotion at Reading Abbey in England (Ward 115). The new destinations thereby acquired the special powers with which the sacred objects were imbued. Thus sprang up new pilgrimage sites far removed from the original locations associated with Christianity's sacred events.

To encase the venerable remains of saintly individuals and elicit religious awe and devotion from the faithful, medieval artists crafted jeweled reliquaries; initially these were rectangular boxes, but later craftsmen frequently designed reliquaries that graphically suggest the body part they contain (Sheingorn 4). For instance, the arm of Saint Louis, king of France and leader of the Seventh Crusade, now rests in a reliquary of that shape in the small chapel linked to the castle at Castelnaud-Bretenoux in the Dordogne region of France. New York's The Cloisters, as well as many other museums throughout Europe, houses a number of exquisitely detailed enameled and cloisonné foot, arm, and head reliquaries. Perhaps most disturbing to twentieth-century sensibilities was the practice of enclosing whole bodies in glass coffins and incorporating them into a church altar. Popular belief held that the body's intactness was in itself a proof of sanctity; the glass coffin provided evidence that the corpse, though wizened and darkened, was indeed intact. One can still see such coffins in churches like

Santa Chiara in Assisi and San Frediano in Lucca, where the bodies of Saint Clare and Saint Zita await the startled visitor.

The cult of relics received a significant boost when the Council of Nicaea in 787 required, upon threat of excommunication, that all consecrated churches have relics (Hall, *English Medieval Pilgrimage* 8). Also, private individuals became obsessed with building up their own collections. Localities competed with each other to obtain the holiest, most attention-catching objects, because these were most likely to attract pilgrims and thus increase the region's fame. Even highly placed churchmen got swept away by the desire to obtain desirable relics. For instance, while Saint Hugh of Lincoln was visiting France, he viewed the bandaged arm of Mary Magdalen. To the distress of onlooking local monks, he cut off the wrapping and tried to break off a piece of bone; when that attempt failed, he used first his incisors and then his molars to bite off a piece of finger (Hall, *Medieval English Pilgrimage* 11; Sumption 35). Another report reveals that he once pulled out a bone of Saint Nicosius through the eye socket (Finucane 28).

Relics were valued for their miracle-working and protective capacities. But when they did not appear to be fulfilling their function, for example, when people under their protection suffered oppression from their adversaries, there developed in the tenth and eleventh centuries several practices intended to signal the evildoers' failure to properly respect the saint. These practices, referred to as "the humiliation of saints," involved some kind of ritualistic debasement such as placing the saint's relics on the floor, spreading thorns on the saint's tomb, and having the monks prostrate themselves during the liturgy. Another dimension crept into these ceremonies, however, especially when laymen were involved: they sometimes resorted to loud complaints and even to violence to express their hostility at the saint's abandoning their needs, hoping thereby to shame the saint into action (Gurevich, *Medieval Popular Culture* 46). Vestiges of such practices remain in the Hispanic culture of northern New Mexico, where the devout turn their *santos'* faces to the wall when they have failed to perform their expected roles, for instance, helping to find lost objects.

The significance attached to relics made them important commodities. Intense competition for them led to one of medieval culture's most bizarre aspects: the theft of sacred objects, *furta sacra*, from their original sites and transportation to new locations throughout western Europe (Geary, *Furta Sacra* 30). Though thefts were not always condoned, ordinary standards of conduct did not apply when it came to dealing with relics. The translation accounts justified theft by arguing that the relics were being neglected in their original locations or that the health and well-being of the community to which they were being taken required their presence (Geary 114). Also, those who stole and transported relics justified their actions by claiming that the relic's successful theft and transportation signified the saint's approval of the move. Miracles that took place at the new site became further confirmation of the saint's blessing (Geary 33).

The cult of Saint Foy at Conques in southwestern France provides one of the most famous instances of relic theft. The relics of Foy, an early Christian adolescent girl who suffered martyrdom, fostered an active cult at Agen, her hometown. But during the ninth century the long-standing monastic community at Conques was disputing its prerogatives with another community in Figeac, a nearby town. Lacking local relics to enhance its prestige, the Conques community decided upon a long-range plan to acquire some. The monks dispatched a brother named Arinisdus to the community at Agen, where over a period of several years he won its trust; then one day, after offering to guard the relics, he made off with them and brought them to Conques. When three "guileless and worthy" (Sheingorn 272) monks failed in their attempts to move the remains to the new church, they decided upon a reliquary instead:

> It was fashioned with marvelous workmanship and made a great display of gleaming red gold and scintillating gems. The most worthy virgin, sealed beneath it, rests there happily in Christ and there is no doubt that she is constantly visited there by countless people. (Sheingorn 272)

A more famous reliquary houses a piece of Foy's skull: a stylized seated figure with a large head crowned in jewels; the statue is covered with gold, and it too is jewel-studded. Now on display in the abbey's treasury, the statue remains both an object of devotion and a masterpiece of early medieval sculpture.

Once Conques had acquired its relics, reports of Foy's miracles began to attract pilgrims. The most famous of her wonders was restoring not just the sight but the eyeballs of a priest named Guibert, whom a jealous colleague had blinded. One day Guibert had a vision in which Saint Foy appeared to promise a cure if he fulfilled certain conditions. That night the miracle occurred:

> At about midnight it seemed to Guibert that he saw two light-filled globes like berries, scarcely larger than the fruit of the laurel tree,

which were sent from above and driven deeply into the sockets of his excised eyes. The force of the impact disturbed his brain and in a state of bewilderment he fell asleep. . . . Scarcely returned to full consciousness, he recalled his vision, and reaching up with his hands he touched the windows of his reborn light with their perfectly restored pupils. Immediately he summoned witnesses and proclaimed the immeasurable greatness of Christ with boundless praise. (Sheingorn 48-49)

Other wonders *The Book of Sainte Foy's Miracles* records are "How a Mule Was Revived from Death," "The Miracle of the Golden Doves," and "How a Man Was Freed from Hanging on the Gallows through Saint Foy's Aid" (Sheingorn 42-43). Through the presence of Foy's relics Conques, a tiny village, became and remains an important pilgrimage site. On the beautifully preserved Last Judgment scene that graces the tympanum on the church's west portal, Arinisdus, whose theft made it all possible, has his place among the elect: he is a crouching, diminutive figure, but he occupies the same compositional framework as the Virgin Mary, Saint Peter, and Charlemagne.

Besides stealing authentic relics, those involved in the trade faced strong temptations to commit fraud. Once the saintly remains began to be broken up and moved around, the Church found it very difficult to control their authenticity. For instance, two different localities claimed to have Saint John the Baptist's head. Others made even more questionable assertions: "Some Western churches claimed to possess Christ's breath in a bottle, his tears or blood, Mary's milk, even Lucifer's tail" (Finucane 31). Both Boccaccio and Chaucer portray relic hucksters who exploit the credulity of the simple with fake relics such as these. In the *Decameron* Boccaccio's Friar Cipolla promises to show his eager audience the Angel Gabriel's feather:

> Since I know how deeply devoted you all are to the Lord Saint Anthony, I shall show you by way of special favour, a most sacred and beautiful relic, which I myself brought back from a visit I once paid to the Holy Land across the sea; and this is one of the feathers of the Angel Gabriel, which was left behind in the bedchamber of the Virgin Mary when he came to annunciate her in Nazareth. (507)

Chaucer's Pardoner too claims to be well provisioned with authentic relics:

For in his male he hadde a pilwe-beer,
Which that he seyde was Oure Lady veyl;
He seyde he hadde a gobet of the seyl
That Seint Peter hadde, whan that he wente
Upon the see, til Jhesu Crist hym hente. (GP, ll. 694-98)

His false relics are the centerpiece of his con game as he works to dupe the credulous.

Pilgrims who undertook long journeys to venerate saints and their relics enjoyed a special status in medieval society. They wore special attire that evoked deeply rooted biblical images about the human condition as an exile after the expulsion from Eden. In the postlapsarian state Adam and Eve went forth in sheepskins. Desert ascetics first adopted this attire as a way of signifying their status as strangers and exiles on earth. Later, lay pilgrims adopted a similar dress (Holloway, *The Pilgrim and the Book* 3-4). Besides their coarse fleece tunics, or sclaveins, pilgrims carried a long staff with a knob at the top and a spike at the bottom; they also wore crosses on their breasts, leather pouches, or scrips, attached to their waists, broad-brimmed hats, and some emblem linked to the shrine they were honoring: palms for Jerusalem (hence Chaucer's reference to "palmers" in the opening lines of the "General Prologue"), scallop shells for Compostela, and a representation of Becket's head or a vial of his diluted blood for Canterbury. Another distinguishing feature was that male pilgrims usually went unshaven (Holloway, *The Pilgrim and the Book* 43). In the Wilton Diptych, a well-known painting by Chaucer's anonymous contemporary, a bearded John the Baptist dressed in sheepskin—the wilderness dweller in pilgrim's attire—flanks the elegantly dressed Richard II. Saint Roch, a devout fourteenth-century layman who survived the plague and therefore was invoked by those seeking protection from it, is also depicted in traditional pilgrim's garb: in paintings and sculptures like the one in The Cloisters he wears the sclavein and carries a staff; his legs are covered with rough leggings, but one hangs down to reveal a characteristic plague bubo—a sign that he has suffered and recovered from the dreaded disease.

To underscore their spiritual orientation, pilgrims were supposed to make their wills before they left and to give up their worldly wealth. In the eyes of the law they were considered dead: they did not have to pay taxes or tolls nor honor their feudal obligations since, as pilgrims, they owed allegiance only to God and to the saints. They were also expected to pray, to fast, and to give alms to the needy. An especially important requirement was that they remain chaste. As a gesture of penitence and humility, they were supposed to make substantial parts of their journey barefoot. Horses were used on long journeys, but riding horseback the whole way was thought to negate the benefits of the pilgrimage (Holloway, *The Pilgrim and the Book* 8). Chaucer's pilgrims, however, are not dressed as they should be nor doing what they should be doing: they are wearing bright garments like the Wife of Bath's scarlet hose rather than traditional pilgrims' tunics; they are eating and drinking heartily rather than fasting; they are on horseback rather than barefoot; they are engaging in a storytelling contest rather than praying.

People's motives for undertaking a pilgrimage varied greatly. At one end of the spectrum was the purely voluntary religious desire to honor God by placing oneself in proximity to a sacred space where heaven touched earth. A more self-interested motive, and perhaps the most important one, was the desire to receive healing for a physical affliction through the intervention of the saint whom one was honoring. People in the medieval period believed that physical and spiritual health are closely connected, in part because Jesus frequently forgave sins as he worked his healing miracles. Furthermore, by requiring proof of miracles as an essential condition for canonization, the Church encouraged people to undertake a pilgrimage for medical reasons as well as spiritual ones (Theilmann, "Medieval Pilgrimage" 101). Thus belief in the saints' miracle-working capacity provided a strong motivation for undertaking the journey's rigors. Medieval people believed that the saints, through their martyrdom or heroic virtue, had special power as intermediaries between sinful, imperfect humans and a majestically remote God.

Another major motive was penitential: people undertook arduous journeys to holy places to seek forgiveness for their sins, especially in the case of pilgrimages to Rome or Jerusalem. These sites had sufficient claims to holiness on their own terms that pilgrims sought them out without the expectation that miracles would occur there. Rather they came to these locations seeking forgiveness for their sins (Ward, *Miracles and the Medieval Mind* 124). Rocamadour, a hilltop town in southwestern France, was an important penitential destination: pilgrims climbed over two hundred steps on their knees; prisoners did so in chains, which they were permitted to remove once they had reached the top. Confessors were likely to impose going on a pilgrimage as a penance for public sins like murder, sacrilege, or sexual violations by the clergy. In one case an English chaplain had to go on two pilgrimages—one to Hereford and one to

Canterbury—and he had to fulfill the following conditions: "These [the pilgrimages] are to be carried out barefoot before Whitsun, and the chaplain is to obtain certificates from the sacristans at each shrine to prove that he had performed this penance" (qtd. in Finucane 43). Sometimes pilgrimages were undertaken by proxy: sinners who could not or would not subject themselves to the journey's rigors might pay others to take the trip for them; at times people left money in their wills to pay someone to go on pilgrimage for the repose of their souls (Loxton 94-96).

Because pilgrims had such a variety of motives, they could include among their number a curious jumbling of the pious and the profane. Indeed pilgrimages attracted some of the less savory elements of society: thieves, pimps, bawds, and pickpockets found ample opportunities to exercise their talents (Finucane 44). But in spite of their widely varying motivations and status, all pilgrims dressed alike and were supposed to be treated alike in the communities they passed through (Holloway, *The Pilgrim and the Book* 5). For this reason, as Stopford points out, some scholars see pilgrimage as "involving a social transformation by which the hierarchies encountered in daily life were replaced by a universal *communitas* or brotherhood for the duration of the journey" ("Some Approaches to the Archaeology of Christian Pilgrimage" 59). Others disagree, insisting that far from undermining social hierarchies, pilgrimages reinforced them, for example by offering several levels of accommodations in hostels (Stopford 59, 67). But at least symbolically, the uniformity of pilgrims' garb highlights the medieval belief that all people will be held to the same rigorous standard on Judgment Day.

Perhaps the most natural, least religious reason for going on a pilgrimage was simply that of having fun and being free of restraints. Christian Zacher observes that by the fourteenth century "the journey itself, more than the sacred goal, became the object of travel" (*Curiosity and Pilgrimage* 4-5). In a sense pilgrimages were the ancestors of today's tourism and group travel (Theilmann 100). They gave people the chance to make safer journeys, see new sights, meet new people, and enjoy a break from the humdrum. The famous opening lines to *The Canterbury Tales* capture the natural human longing to respond to springtime's renewed vitality with physical as well as spiritual movement. For some pilgrims the physical goad was the strongest. As Ronald Finucane observes, "Casual sexual opportunities were no doubt more likely on pilgrimage, and some may have used the journey to facilitate their adultery. . . . in a poem, an English servant, impregnated by a cleric, coyly mused, 'I shall say to man and page/That I have been on pilgrimage'" (40). On the Canterbury pilgrimage the Wife of Bath may be as intent on finding her sixth husband as on responding to spiritual impulses; other Chaucer pilgrims are drinking heavily, and all are telling and listening to stories, many of which are bawdy.

Paradoxically then, the underlying idea of a straightforward journey focused exclusively on a spiritual goal—the "way" to salvation—was undercut by the temptation to make the journey's pleasures—"wandering by the way"—a major priority. The curiosity about the world that pilgrimages whetted was at odds with the stated purpose of having pilgrimage focus people's attention on the transitoriness and hardship of earthly life and on their spiritual destinies. The pilgrimage experience was inevitably dualistic, focused both on this world and on the next. Scholars have drawn attention to the way some medieval pilgrimage churches captured that doubleness in their architectural framework by juxtaposing the rose windows placed in the church's west façade and the labyrinths built into the nave's pavement (Demaray 9-32). At Chartres, for example, calculations have shown that if one could lower the west end's rose window onto the floor, it would just about cover the pavement's labyrinth. The window, in its glittering harmony, suggests the ordered perfection of the Heavenly Jerusalem; the twistings and turnings of the labyrinth's path, on the other hand, suggest the wanderings and deviations of earthly life (Cowen, *Rose Windows* 98-99). As Painton Cowen observes:

> Labyrinths generally symbolize the path of the soul through life, and medieval pilgrims re-enacted this, following the path of the labyrinth in the cathedral on their knees, symbolizing the journey to Jerusalem. The rose window superimposed on this labyrinth suggests the mandala, the viewfinder of meaning, projected on to life, as a means not only of finding one's way but also of differentiating between the forces of good and evil. (98)

Beginning in the eleventh century a tremendous upsurge in pilgrimages took place. Pilgrimage routes crisscrossed the countryside, becoming one of the chief means of cultural exchange in medieval Europe. In England the most popular shrine quickly became that of Thomas à Becket, both a traditional martyr-saint who could work miracles at his burial site and a culture hero who had defied the still-foreign Norman king, Henry II. Becket's cult developed quickly after his murder. The circumstances of his death—his strong defense

of the Church and the attack by armed knights in a sacred space—
captured the popular imagination, and reports of miracles resulting
from his intercession quickly spread his fame. Within three years he
was officially recognized as a saint, despite some initial resistance
from those who saw the quarrel between Henry and Becket as essentially political (Finucane 122-23). From the very moment when
Becket was killed, his attendants took pains to preserve his bloody
remnants for future use:

> They carried the most holy body and laid it before the high altar,
> and it lay there through the night, surrounded by the monks in
> great sadness and grief. They placed under it a container to catch
> the blood that flowed from it, being not ignorant of the value of
> the most precious blood of the martyr which flowed for the love of
> God and the liberty of the church. (qtd. in Ward, *Miracles and the
> Medieval Mind* 102)

Later the blood was mixed with water, which, as "the water of Saint
Thomas," was believed to have miraculous properties. Within a short
time after his death there were reports such as the following by John
of Salisbury:

> In the place where Thomas suffered . . . the palsied are cured, the
> blind see, the deaf hear, the lepers are cleansed, those possessed of a
> devil are freed, and the sick are made whole from all manner of dis-
> ease, blasphemers taken over by the devil are put to confusion. . . .
> I should not have dreamt of writing such words on any account had
> not my eyes been witness to the certainty of this. (qtd. in Ward, *Mira-
> cles and the Medieval Mind* 100)

In the first decade after Becket's death many miracles were reported,
and high-level dignitaries came to honor the saint. At first those attracted to Becket's cult came from the lower classes, but his popularity grew so rapidly that soon people from all layers of society
honored him as a saint (Ward, *Miracles and the Medieval Mind* 95).
Even Henry had to recognize the power of Becket's appeal. Walking
barefoot from nearby Harbledown, he came to Canterbury to do
public penance for his part in Becket's death by submitting himself
to flogging by the cathedral monks. King Louis VII of France also
came to do the saint homage.

Initially Becket's body was placed in a crypt chapel and surrounded by heavy stone walls; two openings in the stone allowed the

devout to come closer to the saint by touching the coffin (Butler, *The Quest for Becket's Bones* 17). But after a fire seriously damaged the main church, the cathedral monks determined to build a more grandiose shrine to the martyr as part of the overall reconstruction of the cathedral. By 1220, the fiftieth anniversary of Becket's death, the project was complete and the translation took place. The new tomb was elaborate, "a rich gold shrine" (Vance, "Chaucer's Pardoner" 739). The walls around it were filled with magnificent stained-glass windows recounting events from Becket's life and the miraculous deeds attributed to his relics after his death (Vance 739). From 1220, when the Canterbury pilgrimage was at its peak, until the Reformation, pilgrims coming to honor the saint had this tomb as their journey's goal:

> they would first prostrate themselves at the tomb containing the body and the relics, reliving in their minds the story of Becket's martyrdom, considered as an extension of Christ's archetypal sacrifice into local history. . . . the most pious pilgrims could actually insert themselves in one of two holes in the tomb in order to gain proximity to the saint's remains and his relics. Then, before a priest they would kneel and confess their sins, and receive absolution. After making an offering, the pilgrims would depart, often bearing with them ampullae worn as badges to signify the pilgrimage that had been made. (Vance 739)

Today visitors can still find relics of St. Thomas in Canterbury, not in the cathedral, where the shrine was destroyed by order of Henry VIII, but down a side street in the Church of St. Thomas, Martyr: on the altar of a small side chapel dedicated to the English martyrs rests a reliquary containing a piece of Becket's garment and a bit of his bone.

Many miracles attributed to Becket took place away from the shrine itself and were linked to relics that had been transported from the primary site. "The water of Saint Thomas," which pilgrims carried away with them in small leaden ampullae, was the most important of these. One stained-glass window in Canterbury Cathedral portrays such a miracle:

> returning from the shrine, some pilgrims received hospitality from Sir Jordan Fitzeisulf, whose son was dying from the plague. The water of Saint Thomas saved his life, and the grateful father vowed to offer four pieces of silver to the saint. Unfortunately, he failed to keep his promise within the specified time, thereby causing the

death of another son. Only when he kept his promise was the saint's wrath assuaged—but the lost son was not restored. (Ward, *Miracles and the Medieval Mind* 93-94)

This story highlights how cult saints, especially the older ones honored chiefly for their miracle-working capacity, were perceived to be jealous of their prerogatives.

Another relic that caught the popular imagination was Becket's hairy undergarment, which he had worn as a form of self-discipline. Though Becket's popular appeal as a saint was linked to his defense of the Church in its struggle with the king, and though in his earlier life he had acquired a reputation for profligacy, the monks who were responsible for tending his shrine circulated stories designed to increase his reputation for saintly living. One account tells of the monks' finding the hair shirt:

Then the monks removed his clothing, and they found underneath a very harsh hair shirt, and his flesh severely lacerated and full of worms. When the monks saw that the most holy man had secretly borne all the marks of sanctity and religion they rejoiced beyond measure and wonderingly said quietly to each other, "Lo, here is a true monk and ascetic! Lo, here is a martyr indeed, who suffered torments not long in his death but in his life" (qtd. in Ward, *Miracles and the Medieval Mind* 99).

Pilgrims still venerated this hairshirt at Canterbury in Chaucer's time. Some readers hear an ironic reference to this garment at the end of "The Pardoner's Tale" (Knapp, "The Relyk of a Saint" 1-26). When the Pardoner invites his fellow pilgrims to kiss his fake relics and make him a contribution, Harry Bailly explodes in indignation:

Thou woldest make me kisse thyn olde breech,
And swere it were a relyk of a seint,
Though it were with thy fundement depeint!
But, by the croys which that Seint Eleyne fond,
I wolde I hadde thy coillons in myn hond
In stide of relikes or of seintuarie.
Lat kutte hem of, I wol thee helpe hem carie;
They shul be shryned in an hogges toord! (VI, ll. 948-55)

Critics have long argued over the significance of this incident: why does the Pardoner—after revealing his hypocrisy and avariciousness to his fellow pilgrims—have the audacity to invite them all, especially Harry Bailly whom he singles out, to venerate his relics and make him an offering? Equally puzzling is Harry's explosive reaction, one of the bitterest moments in the *Tales*. Both Eugene Vance and William Kamowski see this moment as having the potential to undermine the entire pilgrimage, though for different reasons. Vance comments:

> If the pilgrimage route to Canterbury may be conceived as a route from marginality and abjection to a spiritual center, the Pardoner conspires to make that route as crooked as possible and even to displace the center, setting himself up as a moveable shrine endowed with relics unsurpassed by those of anyone else in England. . . . If the Pardoner seems more threatening than the other scoundrels in the pilgrimage, it is not only because he has subverted man's most spiritual powers, but also because he has challenged the necessity of the pilgrimage itself as a framework and "raison d'être" for their social world. (741)

Vance stresses the Pardoner's attempt to function as a substitute for the authentic experience of pilgrimage and the veneration of relics. Kamowski, on the other hand, comments on the Pardoner's role in bringing into the open doubts about the validity of relics in general, since many official relics had a dubious provenance:

> By offering his relics for veneration, in effect he asks the pilgrims to consider whether they will play along, show reverence to objects that are plainly fraudulent—and not the Pardoner's alone—or reject part of the ritual of pilgrimage that often preceded the granting of indulgence. . . . The Pardoner's assessment of his own relics—as "faire" as any in England—retains a disturbing element of truth: they are as good as many, if not most, in England, and less absurd than some. ("'Coillons,' Relics, Skeptics, and Faith" 6, 8)

Though Becket's shrine continued to attract pilgrims from the twelfth century on, by the late fourteenth century a decline had set in. People seeking to escape the plague or thankful for having survived it still came to the shrine, as did those seeking healing from other afflictions and forgiveness for their sins. But belief in Becket's miracle-working capacity seems to have diminished: in a letter to the archbishop written in 1394 Richard II referred to a recent cure at the shrine as an unusual occurrence (Finucane 193). By 1420 the monks lacked sufficient income to petition the Vatican for special permission to hold a jubilee celebration at the shrine, always a potent mechanism for attracting pilgrims.

The reasons for the declining attractiveness of pilgrimages, especially to traditional miracle-working saints' shrines, are complex. A central factor was the decided shift that took place in the nature of late medieval popular spirituality. People placed much more emphasis on Christianity's two central figures, Jesus and Mary, especially on their suffering, human side. The fourteenth century saw the laity's increasing tendency to identify with Jesus's passion and with Mary's sorrows as she either foresaw or witnessed his agony (Kieckhefer, *Unquiet Souls* 89-94). Also, the late medieval period witnessed a much greater emphasis on religious interiority. Confession and indulgences began to play a more important part in people's spiritual lives as they turned inward to assess the state of their souls (Morris, *The Papal Monarchy* 30). In the first flush of her religious conversion early in the fifteenth century, Margery Kempe went on pilgrimages to Jerusalem, Rome, and Compostela. But her religious experiences focused increasingly upon extended, intense meditations on Jesus's life and passion. Her sense of close union with Jesus and the saints gave her a measure of spiritual autonomy that enabled her to chastise wayward clergymen and to follow her own religious insights, even if they sometimes conflicted with her confessor's directives. An increasing portion of the laity now claimed the inner journey to God through prayer and self-discipline, which the clergy had traditionally monopolized (Vauchez, *The Laity in the Middle Ages* 234).

Another significant factor was that pilgrimages were coming under attack for promoting morally questionable behavior. The Lollard followers of John Wycliff—Chaucer's contemporary and the first notable English heretic (see Chapter Three)—were especially critical of the behavior pilgrims sometimes exhibited. In 1407 William Thorpe, under questioning by Archbishop Arundel for his heretical views, made a sharp distinction between what he called true and false pilgrims. He characterized the former as follows:

> I call them trew pilgremis travelyng toward the blisse of heven which—in the state, degre, or ordre that God calleth them—doo besy them feithfully for to occupie all their wittes, bodely and gostely, to knowe trewly and to keape feithfully the biddinges of God, hatyng and fleyng all the seven dedely synnes and every braunche of hem. (qtd. in Kolve and Olson, *The Canterbury Tales* 259)

But, he argued, this admirable behavior does not always characterize those who undertake actual pilgrimages:

And as I have learnid and also know somwhat by experience of thes same pilgremis tellyng the cause why that many men and women go hither and thither now on pilgrimagis, it is more for the helthe of their bodies than of their soules, more for to have richesse and prosperite of thys worlde than for to be enrychid with vertues in their soules, more to have here worldely and fleschely frendship than for to have frendship of God and of his seintis in heven. . . . I know well that whan diverse men and women will go thus after their own willes, and fynding out one pilgrimage, they will orden with them before to have with them bothe men and women that can wel synge wanton songes; and some other pilgremis will have with them baggepipes, so that every towne that they come throwe—what with the noyse of their syngyng, and with the sounde of their piping, and with the jangelyng of their Canterbery bellis, and with the barkyng out of dogges after them—that they make more noyse than if the kyng came there awaye with all his clarions and many other menstrelles. And of thes men and women be a monethe out in their pilgrimage, many of them shall be, an halfe yeare after, greate jangleres, tale tellers, and lyers. (qtd. in Kolve and Olson 261-62)

In these passages Thorpe clearly establishes that to become a true pilgrim one must look to one's inner state; merely setting out on the pilgrimage way is not sufficient, especially when the way itself offers so many temptations and opportunities to wander astray.

The pilgrimage metaphor, then, embodies the central medieval conviction that life is a one-way journey to a spiritual destination; it suggests that humans are transients or exiles in the world and that they are on the path to their true home. Augustine captures that concept in his *Confessions* when he refers to his parents as "fellow citizens in the eternal Jerusalem," the goal for which "people sigh throughout their pilgrimage, from the time when they set out until the time when they return to you [God]" (205). Imaging life as a pilgrimage has clear implications for the way people conceive of their lives on earth. In the *Morals on the Book of Job* Gregory I (ca.540-604) specifically articulates the attitude true Christian pilgrims should have toward earthly goods:

And they are cheered by temporal support, just as a wayfarer enjoys a bed in a stable; he stops and hurries to be off; he rests still in the body, but is going forward to something else in imagination. But sometimes they even long to meet with afflictions, they shrink

from having all go well in transient things, lest by the delightful-
ness of the journey, they be hindered in arriving at their home; lest
they arrest the step of the heart on the pathway of their pilgrimage, and one day come in view of the heavenly land without a rec-
ompense. . . . And thus the righteous are indifferent to build
themselves up here below, where they know themselves to be but
pilgrims and strangers. (vol. 1: VIII, 54, 92; 491-92)

Thus keeping an eye always firmly placed on the goal of their destination, their true country, pilgrims should be prepared to endure
the journey's hardships and privations, recognizing that these are
but temporary inconveniences that will disappear in the joy of their
homecoming. To settle too comfortably on earth, to enjoy its attrac-
tions, to be distracted by worldly pleasures belies humanity's spiritual
nature and frustrates the divine plan of ultimate reunion with God.

A major function of pilgrimage, then, is to disorient, to remove
the individual from everyday surroundings, to break the pattern of
sin, pain, and despair into which human life too readily falls. The pilgrim literally becomes a stranger, an exile whose external condition
mirrors the spiritual reality of his separation from home. Going on a
pilgrimage is a liminoid or initiatory experience, one that separates
individuals from their society, takes them to the margin of a new reality, and then returns them renewed and on a higher level to the society they have left behind (Turner 2). The structure of Dante's *The
Divine Comedy* highlights this underlying movement. Dante's pilgrim
finds himself isolated in a dark wood; makes an arduous, circuitous
journey down into hell, up the mountain of purgatory, and through
the spheres of paradise; attains the beatific vision—the direct sight
of God, which is the goal of all human life and the reward of all human effort—and returns as a prophet to his society to tell the lessons
of his marvelous experience. The transformation the experience
produces—from being lost in confusion and sin to sharing in God's
life and vision—forms the core of successful pilgrimage: "The anguished path of the thinker starts at the crossroads of doubt and
faith, of earthly temptation and spiritual aspiration. From inner crisis the voyage proceeds until the harbor of the Heavenly Jerusalem
has been reached" (Fiore, "The Medieval Pilgrimage" 5).

The pervasiveness of pilgrimage as an expression of medieval
popular religion and its aptness in capturing the era's conception of
human life make Chaucer's choosing to place his final work in a pilgrimage context deeply significant, though there is no consensus
about what his choice signifies. The pilgrimage frame affords him a

seemingly realistic mechanism for portraying a broad social cross section of his society, though as a realistic device the choice leaves something to be desired: thirty pilgrims on horseback, strung out in single or double file, is not the best situation for storytelling (Owen, *Pilgrimage and Storytelling in The Canterbury Tales* 7). In the past forty years scholars who have sought to interpret the *Tales* as a whole, rather than focusing on single tales or groups of tales, have paid more attention to the significance of pilgrimage as the framing device. Ralph Baldwin's *The Unity of the Canterbury Tales* is an early effort to make the pilgrimage motif the work's thematic core. D. W. Robertson, Jr.'s exegetical approach in *A Preface to Chaucer: Studies in Medieval Perspectives* stresses the importance of reading the *Tales* against an Augustinian backdrop; though Robertson's work does not focus on pilgrimage, he clearly acknowledges its significance:

> Among scriptural concepts which appear in *The Canterbury Tales,* the most important is the idea of pilgrimage. . . . The pilgrimage of the soul was not in itself a journey from place to place, but an inner movement between the two cities so vividly described by St. Augustine, one founded on charity, and the other on cupidity. (373)

In *A Reading of the Canterbury Tales* Bernard Huppe applies exegetical principles to individual tales and notes the significance of the pilgrimage metaphor to his analysis (17-20). Donald Howard's *The Idea of The Canterbury Tales* strongly argues for the centrality of pilgrimage as the work's unifying framework. Drawing on contemporary pilgrimage narratives, he stresses that they usually do not recount the return trip: "We must conclude that medieval pilgrims conceived of and experienced a pilgrimage as a one-way journey; the return was a mere contingency" (30). Thus pilgrimages end at the shrine, emblematic, as they all are, of the Heavenly Jerusalem. Applying that insight to the *Tales,* he maintains that though the work is unfinished, it is conceptually complete: "The pilgrimage, so conceived as a one-way journey, gave *The Canterbury Tales* an overall unity, a 'frame.' It is a work, not works" (30).

Though Chaucer seems clearly aware of the collapsing ideal of pilgrimage, he still places all his pilgrims on the road to Canterbury, symbolically the Heavenly Jerusalem. In spite of their diversities, they share the common human destiny: they all aspire to salvation in the midst of a life filled with tribulation and uncertainty. As pilgrims they lose their distinctions of social class, gender, even moral status; all these are absorbed in their journey to their heavenly goal. The

Parson explicitly evokes the symbolic pilgrimage as he utters a prayer for his fellow pilgrims in the prologue to his tale, the one intended to end the collection:

> And Jhesu, for his grace, wit me sende
> To shewe yow the wey, in this viage,
> Of thilke parfit glorious pilgrimage
> That highte Jerusalem celestial. (ll. 47-50)

But in contrast to Dante's driving thrust to his spiritual goal in *The Divine Comedy,* Chaucer leaves us in a more problematic posture in *The Canterbury Tales.* The Canterbury journey does not end with a grand consummation like the beatific vision that the Dante pilgrim experiences at the end of his journey through the otherworld; it ends with the pilgrims approaching Canterbury, the spires of the cathedral looming in the distance. Like Keats' lover captured in art at the precise moment of anticipation just before obtaining the long-desired kiss of his beloved, Chaucer's pilgrims—himself among them—have their goal within sight but never reached. His choosing a pilgrimage frame affords him a uniquely appropriate way of capturing his sense of both the deep meaningfulness and the rich complexity of human life. For pilgrimages and the associated cult of saints and relics reflect a broad spectrum of medieval religious attitudes, from an intensely spiritual sense of human destiny to a belief in the magical properties of bones and bits of cloth. In *The Canterbury Tales* Chaucer drew upon all those resonances in portraying his pilgrims and the forces that motivate them. Taken together, they reflect both the sublimity and the ridiculousness that characterize the human condition. Though Chaucer, like Dante, provides an eschatological backdrop for the *Tales,* he focuses on the changing, conflictive, problematic world of everyday life. The Canterbury pilgrimage—at least in Harry Bailly's announced plan—is supposed to end in a tavern rather than at the shrine.

III.

CLASS AND COMMERCE

CHAPTER SIX

Aristocratic Ideals:
Conflicting Chivalric Ideologies

*T*he expression "chivalry is dead" is probably the late twentieth century's most familiar truism concerning a value system that dominated European military and aristocratic circles from the tenth through the sixteenth centuries. As Lee Patterson observes: "Chivalry must be understood as the central form of self-definition by means of which the noble class situated itself within medieval society" (*Chaucer and the Subject of History* 178). Furthermore, as medievalists have increasingly recognized, chivalric concepts as conveyed in imaginative texts did not so much reflect social values as play a significant role in shaping them.

Though Johan Huizinga's *The Waning of the Middle Ages* argues that chivalry was in decline by the fourteenth century, more recent scholars like Maurice Keen argue that it remained a vital force in the late medieval world. Indeed chivalric ideals still exercised a powerful grip over people's imaginations in Chaucer's England. Warrior heroes like the Black Prince captivated the nation's affection; people still thrilled to tournaments' color and pageantry; and families took each other to court over the right to heraldic coats-of-arms, as in the Scrope/Grosvenor trial at which Chaucer testified. But chivalry was no simple, one-dimensional code: it encompassed an aggregate of complex, often conflicting, values, so that those attempting to live up to its ideals often found themselves pulled in multiple directions.

Furthermore, as England's fortunes soured in the protracted confrontation with France known as the Hundred Years' War, a profound malaise about the viability of chivalry, its adequacy as a guide to human conduct, and its compatibility with Christianity produced what Patterson has termed "a crisis of chivalric identity" (*Chaucer and the Subject of History* 165), not only among those who looked at it from the outside but also among those at its center. Chaucer's poetry reflects and invites his audience to participate in the reexamination of chivalric values that engaged the aristocratic society which formed his audience for most of his poetic career.

To gain a fuller understanding of the context within which that crisis occurred, we must retrace the broad outlines of chivalry's development from the tenth to the fourteenth centuries. The word "chivalry" has its root in the French *chevalier*, or horseman, thereby highlighting both the central role France played in chivalry's formative phase and the importance of combat on horseback in delineating its original features. In the tenth century horsemen assumed an increasingly important military role: they formed a socially cohesive group that fell between the landowners and the peasantry; in effect, they were relatively low-ranking vassals. But by the eleventh century armed horsemen had risen socially and had begun to claim knightly status (Boulton, *The Knights of the Crown* 6-7).

Chivalry and knighthood clearly had strong roots in a class-based system. But the code's emphasis on action in conformity to its requirements gave the boundaries of access to that class some permeability. Noble behavior, not just noble blood, was a central chivalric requirement: the Hag in Chaucer's "The Wife of Bath's Tale" instructs her knightly husband about this requirement when he complains about her base birth:

> Looke who that is moost vertuous alway,
> Pryvee and apert, and moost entendeth ay
> To do the gentil dedes that he kan;
> Taak hym for the grettest gentil man. (ll. 1113-16)

Indeed one could be formally stripped of knighthood's external trappings for acts of cowardice or treachery. Contrarily, notably gallant acts or extraordinary deeds of service could lead to the reward of knighthood (Allmand, *The Hundred Years' War* 135).

Medieval treatises on chivalry, such as Ramon Lull's *The Book of the Order of Chivalry* (ca. 1276) and Geoffroi de Charny's *The Book of Chivalry* (ca. 1350) reveal chivalry's three main strands: "martial, aristocratic [or courtly], and Christian" (Keen, *Chivalry* 16). Initially it was closely allied to an oral culture and warrior class's heroic code, with its emphasis on martial skills, loyalty to one's leader and companions-in-arms, and concern about performing deeds worthy of having one's name remembered in song. This martial ethic, with its glorying in the violence of warfare, remained at the center of the chivalric code.

The early twelfth-century *Song of Roland*, a *chanson de geste*, or song of deeds, conveys just these martial values. The anonymous poet portrays a male world that focuses on war councils and battlefield confrontations and celebrates Roland's determination to serve Charlemagne—both his uncle and his feudal lord—without regard for personal concerns save those related to his reputation for heroic action. The poet glorifies Roland's prowess in battle, getting caught up in excitement over his hero's display of martial skill and unstinting bravery (ll.1320-23; 1341-44). Roland's strong friendship with Oliver, his companion-in-arms, though somewhat marred by their disagreement concerning the best time to call for reinforcements, remains a model of the male bonding between fellow warriors that is so central to the heroic code. When Oliver dies, Roland laments:

> Sire cumpaign, tant mar fustes hardiz!
> Ensemble avum estet e anz e dis,
> Nem fesis mal ne jo nel te forsfis.
> Quant tu es mor, dulur est que jo vif! (ll. 2027-30)
> [Companion, sir, what a pity, you were so brave!
> We were together for years and days,
> You never did me harm and I did not wrong you.
> Now that you are dead, it is painful for me to live!]

Equally important in motivating Roland's actions is his determination to avoid tarnishing his name through any act of cowardice and, more positively, to assure that he will be remembered for his heroic actions.

These three values—devotion to one's leader, loyalty to one's fighting companions, and determination to perform memorable deeds—remained central to the chivalric code. Indeed there emerged a whole class of heralds, whose task was to observe and record tournament and battlefield heroics for posterity. They focused almost exclusively on external behavior to measure nobility. For instance, the Chandos Herald, who wrote *La vie du Prince Noir*, celebrates his subject primarily for his military exploits and bravery (Clein, *Concepts of Chivalry* 24-28).

While the battlefield provided the prime testing ground for a knight's skill and courage, tournaments, and later jousts, helped knights to develop and perfect their skills, simultaneously affording outlets for their martial energies in peace time. Lull advises: "Knights ought to joust upon their coursers and go to tournaments, to hold open table, to hunt after harts, boars, and other wild beasts, for in doing these things knights exercise themselves for arms, to maintain the order of knighthood" (qtd. in Miller, *Chaucer: Sources and Background* 184). Tournaments developed in chivalry's formative phase, from the late eleventh through the mid-twelfth centuries. In addition to training knights for war, tournaments gave aspiring young men a chance to capture the attention of powerful patrons; tournaments also became ceremonious occasions for conspicuous display and consumption (Keen, *Chivalry* 83-94).

Initially a tournament consisted of a mock battle, called a melee, in which the two opposing sides vied for victory that sometimes entailed ransoms, captured arms and equipment, and prizes for the winner. The stakes were high since there could be heavy casualties. The two sides would arm themselves on opposite ends of the field and then would gallop toward each other with drawn lances. The unhorsed continued to wield swords on foot. Melees were all-day affairs with combat often ranging throughout the countryside (Gies, *The Knight in History* 88). By the early fourteenth century jousts—single combats between two armed knights in a confined space demarcated by fences— became more popular: they offered better opportunities for displays of individual prowess; they could more easily be monitored by heralds whose task was to assess chivalric behavior; they were considerably more manageable and less destructive than large-scale melees; and they provided better viewing opportunities for spectators. Still, chivalric courtesy books suggest that tournaments enjoyed greater prestige (Barker, *The Tournament in England* 13-14; 145-48). Interestingly, in "The Knight's Tale" when Chaucer depicts a tournament involving two hundred knights trying to determine who will win the fair Emelye, he portrays an anachronistic melee rather than single combat, which was more characteristic of his era. Indeed as G.A. Lester points out, what Chaucer presents in this tale is "a strange combination of melee and duel to the death" ("Chaucer's Knight and the Medieval Tournament" 464). Though events foil Theseus's efforts, he attempts to limit the violence in this large-scale tournament by restricting it to the huge amphitheater he has built specifically for the occasion, and he tries to minimize injury by decreeing that no one shall fight to the death. His actions remind us that both religious and secular authorities tried to curb the violence in tournaments.

From tournaments' inception the Church attempted to discourage them, Innocent II decreeing at the Council of Clermont in 1130 that anyone killed in one should be denied Christian burial. The clergy denounced them for creating an environment that encouraged all seven deadly sins, for leading to an unnecessary loss of lives, and even for deflecting crusading energies. Though the Church's intent was clear, the ban's original wording was sufficiently imprecise to allow dedicated tournament fans to argue that it did not refer to their activities. Besides, churchmen often shied away from enforcing the ban: they feared offending powerful patrons and the families of the tournaments' victims often made generous donations to the Church as reparations for their defiant behavior (Barker 70-75). Secular authorities also had their reservations about tournaments, imposing fines on those who sponsored unauthorized events and attempting to regulate the weapons used to minimize deaths and injuries. For the violence spawned at these large gatherings of armed knights could be severely disruptive, providing as they did an excuse for continuing, or even starting, private feuds. Also, insecure rulers like Henry III and Edward II feared that tournaments provided the perfect cover for their political opponents to gather substantial military forces and to foment rebellion (Barker 50-60).

By the thirteenth century tournaments had moved beyond being brutal encounters between armed knights and had become sporting events with a strong communal function. Influenced by courtly romances, a late medieval ruler like Edward III adapted tournaments to his own purposes by making them public festivals at which he could be the center of attention, thereby exploiting their political potential by spreading his name afar (Barker 65-69). Thus in the end neither the Church's prolonged opposition nor secular leaders' anxieties could dampen the chivalric class's enthusiasm for tournaments. Indeed Boulton has characterized them as "perhaps the most important single vehicle for the expression of heroic chivalry" (12). Patterson makes a more acid comment: "It was knighthood itself that continually reinforced its own sense of its own identity through rituals that it staged by and for itself—an early instance of the apparently endless capacity of the military for self-congratulation" (*Chaucer and the Subject of History* 174).

The essentially militaristic ethic that formed the core of the chivalric code needed to be integrated with the Christian religion, the second strand in the chivalric ethic. The connection between the two always remained uneasy because the two value systems had inherent contradictions. Christianity has a strong pacifist element that dominated when the new religion defined itself in opposition to the proudly militaristic Roman Empire. Furthermore, Christianity focuses on a suffering savior whose victory consisted of passively enduring death, and many scriptural passages urge humility, disdain for worldly glory, and love of—rather than triumph over—one's enemies. Indeed the Church initially juxtaposed monks, the soldiers of Christ, with soldiers in the secular world, and early penitential manuals imposed penalties for killing in battle (Keen, *Chivalry* 46).

But several factors tipped the balance in favor of the Church's ultimately condoning—indeed celebrating—military endeavors undertaken for a sanctioned cause. When Christianity aligned itself with the established power structure after Constantine's conversion in the fourth century, military engagements against adversaries became acceptable. For scripture, especially the Old Testament, also portrays a God who succors His people in battle and wreaks havoc on their enemies, while the New Testament provides numerous examples of force disciplining a wrongdoer, an argument Augustine developed in his just war theory (Keen, *Chivalry* 45).

In the ninth and tenth centuries, when northern invaders and Muslims besieged Christians, the clergy's support for military action grew; eventually, in the context of the Crusades, the Church reversed the position articulated in the penitentials by promising salvation for those killed battling against its enemies (Keen, *Chivalry* 45-47). Churchmen developed the argument that using armed force was an act of Christian love when it served God, aided one's fellow Christians, or punished the evil (Riley-Smith, "Crusading as an Act of Love" 177-92). During the First Crusade (1095-1099) the clergy urged Christians to show their love and loyalty to God by evoking the feudal relationship between a vassal and his lord: they equated Christ with an earthly king deprived of his rightful inheritance: the Holy Land controlled by Muslims, whom medieval Christians considered pagans (Riley-Smith 180) or, as in Dante's case, heretics. Innocent III (1198-1216), for instance, maintained that just as an earthly lord would "look on his vassals as unfaithful and traitors against the crown and guilty of *lèse majesté*" (qtd. in Riley-Smith 181), if they failed to fight in his cause, so too would Jesus Christ condemn his followers for ingratitude and infidelity if they did not support attempts to reclaim the Holy Land. Support for one's Christian brothers living in Muslim areas also constituted a rationale for military enterprises in those areas (Riley-Smith 184).

Chansons de gestes like *The Song of Roland* testify to the way in which the First Crusade promoted the alliance of martial and religious values. Roland asserts, "Paien unt tort e chretiens unt dreit" (l. 1015) ["Pagans are in the wrong and Christians are in the right."]); Archbishop Turpin, one of Charlemagne's most stalwart warriors, leads his men into battle after promising that their sins will be forgiven if they fight bravely for their cause (ll. 1133-38). And when Roland, having fought against impossible odds, finally dies on the battlefield, his soul is welcomed into heaven (ll. 2393-96). Such views were still current in the fourteenth century, as is evident in *The Tree of Battles* (1387) by Honoré Bonet, a Benedictine who served France's Charles VI:

> if a knight die in war ordained by the Church, as in the case of unbelievers or the enemies of the Pope or of the Faith, and is not otherwise in mortal sin, his soul goes forthwith to Paradise. . . . if a soldier die in battle in a just war and to maintain a just quarrel, he, similarly, will be saved in Paradise. (qtd. in Miller, *Chaucer: Sources and Background* 190)

Besides fighting for God and against the Church's enemies, chivalry entailed an obligation to succor the oppressed, most specifically widows and orphans. The knight's might had to serve right, and he was obliged to champion those who could not properly defend themselves. Ramon Lull clearly delineates this responsibility: "The office of a knight is to uphold and defend women, widows and orphans, and men who are in distress and not strong" (qtd. in Miller, *Chaucer: Sources and Background* 185). Thus the evolving concept of chivalry combines martial prowess and strength with service to a worthy cause, either to the Church or to helpless victims of oppression.

The dubbing ceremony by which a man was formally admitted to knighthood underscores chivalry's religious overtones while also pointing to its essentially secular nature. The earliest accounts recording a knighting ceremony make no reference to the clergy's presence and focus mostly on a knight's acceptance into a band of warriors through his lord's formally presenting him with arms (Keen, *Chivalry* 64-71). In a tenth-century pontifical the formula for blessing a sword provides early evidence of the dubbing ceremony's religious dimension. However, nothing clearly indicates that this blessing, in its initial form, differed significantly from the Church's blessing of many other daily-used items. The essentially secular delivery of arms appears to have been conflated with the ecclesiastical blessing of the sword, and the Church's role in crowning kings was blended with the secular knighting ceremony. But while the clergy sought to accentuate its role in commissioning knights, it never succeeded in establishing its centrality in this area as it did with coronations. Thus, though the chivalric code had close ties with Christian symbolism and was laced with religious rhetoric, it remained essentially secular (Keen, *Chivalry* 71-77).

Chivalry came to encompass much more than a code for warriors on the battlefield, however: its third strand—the aristocratic or courtly element—included a whole range of behaviors associated with manners at court and with the clerical class's educational system. Maurice

Keen observes: "Without clerical learning in the background, chivalry could scarcely have progressed far beyond a kind of hereditary military professionalism, occasionally heroic but essentially crude" (*Chivalry* 6). Courtly behavior emerged in the tenth-century Ottonian episcopal courts, where the educational system encouraged and rewarded behavior markedly different from that needed on the battlefield (Jaeger, *The Origins of Courtliness* 9). An account by Saxo Grammaticus in the *Gesta Danorum* concerning the knights associated with King Canute the Great highlights the problem that needed to be addressed:

> Many were more weighty of muscle than grave of manner, and though they bore themselves gloriously in war, they had only a dim perception of the ways appropriate to peace. The result was that those distinguished on the field were despised at court. It was rare indeed to find a man of ardent spirits who at the same time had some sense of the honorable conduct of life. Hence many of them, tied to pernicious habits, would bring violence and squabbling into the court itself. (qtd. in Jaeger 138-39)

Such rude manners and coarse language created barriers at court: they reflected badly on the ruler and increased the potential for disorderly conflict. Success in a courtly atmosphere—where postponing gratification and biding one's time were less disruptive than openly displaying anger or disappointment—entailed developing urbane, articulate, witty speech and having a handsome, polished appearance. The successful courtier needed to be able to negotiate by skillfully manipulating language, and he was better served by having a capacity for intrigue than by dexterous swordsmanship (Jaeger 12, 127-76), though the latter skill was still required.

The late-fourteenth-century poet of *Sir Gawain and the Green Knight* makes clear that polished behavior and speech are expected of a knight representing King Arthur's famous court. When the members of Bercilak's entourage learn Gawain's identity, they murmur to each other:

> "Now schal we semely se slyghtes of thewes
> And the techles termes of talkyng noble.
> Wich spede is in speche unspured may we lerne,
> Syn we have fonged that fyne fader of nurture.
> (ll. 916-19)
> [Now displays of deportment shall dazzle our eyes
> And polished pearls of impeccable speech;

The high art of eloquence is ours to pursue
Since the father of fine manners is found in our midst.]

Thus the twelfth century witnessed the gradual fusion of a heroic society's martial ideals with a courtly society's social ideals. The vernacular courtly romances became important educational devices for transmitting the expanded chivalric values, both providing entertainment for the knightly class and heightening its awareness of the demands courtly ideals made upon it. As Jaeger points out:

> One great accomplishment of courtly romance is that it achieved a synthesis of the warrior and the statesman, the knight and the courtly cleric. From the second half of the twelfth century, we encounter a literary hero who represents the harmonizing of those two codes. . . . This new hero magnanimously pardons vanquished enemies. He speaks flowingly as he greets fellow knights and particularly ladies in elaborate formulas. His manners are modest, decorous, polished and restrained. He is in control of himself and knows, or learns, compassion and regard for other human beings. He courts damsels in flowery speeches filled with high sentiments. . . . The knight remains an efficient engine of death and destruction in combat, but at court and in the presence of ladies his soul is strung as finely as a harp. (196)

Awareness of the romances' educational function helps us to put into more balanced perspective the vexing question of the extent to which they reveal social versus purely literary realities. Indeed they provide a fascinating instance of literary reality shaping rather than reflecting social behavior. For these romances exerted a tremendous imaginative pull on courtly society, helping to mold through the ideals they portrayed the social milieu in which they were generated and read (Boulton 5).

Perhaps the most significant, and certainly the most famous, dimension of the courtly code concerns the cult of the lady, which shall receive additional treatment in Chapters Nine and Ten. For beyond the knight's duty to honor and protect women in general, there developed first in the Provençal lyric poetry of the troubadours and shortly thereafter in the courtly narratives of northern France an ethic that celebrated the ennobling effect of love for an idealized lady who became in the lover's imagination the external embodiment of his quest for perfection. Some scholars see a feudalisation of love in the relationship between the knight and his lady as he puts himself in her service and sets as his highest goal that of serving and pleasing her. His chivalric exploits, then, assume a new dimension as he seeks, at least theoretically, not so much to increase his own fame or that of his lord and his court but to perform deeds worthy of winning his lady's approval and ultimately her favors. Speaking of knights who "devote their hearts to loving par amour," Geoffroi de Charny observes: "And they are rightly to be praised and honored, as well as the excellent ladies who have so directed them and by whom they are formed. It is right to honor, serve, and love these excellent ladies" (qtd. in Miller, *Chaucer: Sources and Background* 208). Chaucer focuses his portrayal of the Squire in the "General Prologue" on the Squire's courtly and amatory qualities, describing him as "a lovyere and a lusty bacheler" (GP, l. 80) and detailing his proficiencies as a polished courtier:

> He koude songes make and wel endite,
> Juste and eek daunce, and weel purtreye and write.
> So hoote he lovede that by nyghtertale
> He sleep namoore than dooth a nyghtyngale.
> (GP, ll. 80, 95-98)

Desire to win the lady's notice and approval also played a significant role in the continuing popularity of tournaments, which unlike battlefields afforded an opportunity for spectators to enjoy the action. In his account of Arthur's court after the feasting at Whitsuntide, Geoffrey of Monmouth provides early testimony that tournaments attracted a female audience: "The knights planned an imitation battle, and competed together on horseback, while their womenfolk watched from the city walls and aroused them to passionate excitement by their flirtatious behavior" (*The History of the Kings of Britain* 230). Chretien de Troyes' *Lancelot* also provides a famous account of women patronizing tournaments and of the hero's willingness to perform the ultimate sacrifice of allowing himself to be disgraced before the assembly if so doing would please his lady. In "The Knight's Tale" Palamon and Arcite's dispute is resolved through a massive tournament under the watchful eyes of Emelye and other ladies. Through the tournament, Keen argues, "the force of sexual passion [was] sublimated into the quest for virtue" (*Chivalry* 101).

But the knight's obligation to please and serve his lady often led to conflicting loyalties within the chivalric code, as is evident in Chretien de Troyes' *Yvain*. Shortly after his pledge to make service to his lady his highest priority, the hero faces his friend Gawain's challenge to pursue glory on the tournament circuit; his attempt to mediate between these two commitments by accepting his lady's clearly defined time limit for his heroic exploits fails miserably when he becomes so caught up in the excitement of tournament glory that he completely forgets his promise to his lady and incurs her vehement rejection—thereby precipitating a severe identity crisis. In "The Knight's Tale" Chaucer portrays a similar conflict between the warrior's loyalty to his companion-in-arms and the lover's devotion to his lady. When both Palamon and Arcite fall in love at first sight with Emelye from their prison window, the bond that has linked them instantly dissolves, and they become bitter enemies. Palamon's reminder that Arcite, as his cousin and his brother-in-arms, should devote himself to advancing Palamon's interests elicits a quick retort from Arcite: "Love is a gretter lawe, by my pan,/Than may be yeve to any erthely man" (ll. 1165-66). An even more fundamental conflict lay at the heart of the courtly code: its rhetoric made the lady central in the lover's life and made obtaining her favor the goal of his existence, his *summum bonum*, usurping the place that in the Christian code ought to be reserved for God alone.

In *Sir Gawain and the Green Knight*, a romance by Chaucer's anonymous contemporary, we see a fusion of chivalry's heroic, religious, and courtly values. It provides an instructive contrast with *The Song of Roland* on the shifting emphases the chivalric code underwent between the early twelfth and the late fourteenth centuries. Though *Sir Gawain*'s central focus concerns a test for both Gawain and for Arthur's court, Gawain, unlike Roland, never approaches a battlefield. His testing begins when he has to prove his loyalty to his lord by accepting in Arthur's place the Green Knight's challenge to single confrontation. The blow Gawain delivers to his adversary evokes no resistance, but it puts him in the difficult position of having to prove his honor by first seeking out and then passively submitting himself to the Green Knight's return blow, trusting only his own virtue and God's protection to spare him.

But Gawain does not realize that his true test takes place in the bedchamber of his adversary's castle, where he must resist the lady's seductive advances while at the same time never lapsing from the most courteous and mannerly speech. Gawain negotiates his way through the code's multiple requirements: he preserves his chastity without resorting to bad manners and proves his courage by keeping his word to submit to the ax's blow. But his success is only partial: he places faith in a talisman rather than in the shield of his virtue and in the Virgin's protection, and he fails to keep his word to his host to exchange each day's winnings. His intense regret over his understandable impulse to save his life by seeking additional protection from the lady's magical belt highlights the exacting standard to which he is holding himself. But critical opinion remains divided on whether the Gawain-poet sees the fault as resting with Gawain or—considering its often conflicting, superhuman demands—with the chivalric code itself.

As mentioned earlier, the chivalric code, both in its religious and in its heroic aspects, continued to exert significant influence on fourteenth-century England's ruling class. Because of the hostility between England and France and because of the schism within the Church itself, Christian Europe could not mount a concerted and successful effort to overthrow Muslim domination of the Holy Land during the fourteenth century. Still, crusading retained a strong grip, both as a religious ideal and as a military reality on at least three fronts: Moorish Spain, the Saracen Middle East, and pagan eastern Europe (Hatton, "Chaucer's Crusading Knight" 80-83; Keen, "Chaucer's Knight" 48). Indeed as Robertson maintains, "Crusades were regarded with respect, and often with enthusiasm, by many European leaders, both lay and ecclesiastic, during the later years of the fourteenth century" ("The Probable Date and Purpose of Chaucer's 'Knight's Tale'" 428).

The Hundred Years' War, which had its origins in the complicated feudal ties that existed between the kings of France and England, provided another important arena for Englishmen to exercise chivalric prowess during this era. By the early fourteenth century the king of England controlled substantial parts of western France, especially the duchy of Aquitaine, but he held these lands in a feudal relationship to the king of France. The immediately precipitating factor for the war occurred when the young Edward III of England decided to press his claim to the French throne after the death of Charles V. As Charles's nephew, his claim had considerable validity, but because it derived from his mother's side—and also perhaps because of Edward's youth and Englishness—the French nobles ignored it and chose Philip VI instead (Allmand 7-10). Edward's insistence on pushing forth with his claim—either for its own sake or for strengthening his position with respect to other English territories in France—remained a dominant part of his national policy throughout his long and mostly successful reign.

In the early phases of the war England's two major victories against much larger French forces, first at Crécy in 1346 and later at Poitiers in 1356, did much to garner popular support for the war and to validate the chivalric ethic. Edward III's oldest son, Edward— the famous Black Prince—distinguished himself for valor in both of these engagements and became a popular national hero. Speaking of the battle at Crécy, the French chronicler Jean Froissart reports:

> King Edward, who had not put on his battle-helmet all that day, came down with his whole division to his son the Prince. He embraced him and said: "Dear son, God grant that you may long go on in this way. You are indeed my son, for you have done your duty most loyally this day. You have proved yourself worthy to rule a land." (*Chronicles* 93)

At Poitiers the Black Prince fought "like a raging lion under his battle-helmet and . . . revelled in the fighting and the rout of the enemy. . . ." (Froissart 141). Froissart also reports on the Black Prince's chivalrous behavior in treating a defeated adversary, King John II of France, who was taken captive after having shown himself to be a "brave knight and stout fighter" (Froissart 158). Speaking of those who observed his behavior, Froissart comments: "Their esteem for him increased and it was generally agreed that in him they would have a most chivalrous lord and master if he was granted life to go on in the same auspicious way"(144).

Battlefield successes and accounts of noteworthy deeds reinforced the chivalrous ethic in Edward's England and enabled him consciously to promote it to build national cohesiveness and commitment to his cause. By focusing public attention on chivalry's more colorful and dramatic aspects, the tournaments Edward sponsored became potent propaganda instruments as he sought to heighten the public's association between his reign and that of the legendary King Arthur (Barker 68-69). Edward's dedication to, and exploitation of, chivalric ideals culminated in his founding at Windsor Castle what became the most renowned of chivalric orders: the Order of the Garter.

But medieval warfare had its less noble and less savory aspects as well. For instance, a prominent part of French strategy consisted of avoiding confrontation with the English rather than engaging in dramatic pitched battles (Allmand 15). And while the desire for glory might send knights into battle, the opportunity to seize booty was a major inducement as well, since usually the expense of acquiring arms fell on the knights themselves. Looting and plundering were accepted concomitants of battle, reported matter-of-factly by Froissart: "The [Black] Prince's men plundered and carried off everything they found there [the castle of Romorantin] and in the town" (126). Indeed the Prince could be capable of merciless brutality, as in the sack of Limoges:

Then the Prince . . . with all the others and their men burst into the city, followed by pillagers on foot, all in a mood to wreak havoc and do murder, killing indiscriminately, for those were their orders. There were pitiful scenes. Men, women, and children flung themselves on their knees before the Prince, crying: "Have mercy on us, gentle sir!" But he was so inflamed with anger that he would not listen. Neither man nor woman was heeded, but all who could be found were put to the sword. . . . (Froissart 178)

The English also frequently engaged in *chevauchée*, violent raids through the unarmed countryside with much pillaging and looting, as a means of undermining the people's faith in the French king's power to protect them. The Black Prince's campaigns in France involved such excursions as well as the more notable battles (Allmand 15, 55).

By the 1370s English fortunes in the war had soured. The taxes needed to support it caused increasing resistance; the Black Prince was suffering from a debilitating disease that made further combat impossible for him; and Edward was aging. The Prince's death in 1376, followed by his father's a year later, led to the accession of the ten-year-old Richard II. If in Edward III's reign chivalry struck a sympathetic chord throughout most of English society, in Richard II's serious reservations about its ethos sounded a persistent note. In this climate interest in peace negotiations intensified.

During the 1380s and 1390s several extended truces, occasionally linked with marriage negotiations, fostered hopes of bringing hostilities between the two countries to an end. In France Philippe de Mézières spoke out against the bloodshed between Christian brothers, arguing that martial energies ought to focus on defeating pagan foes. In fact he addressed a letter to the young English king urging just such a program. He also founded the Order of the Passion of Jesus Christ, based on a vision he experienced in Jerusalem's Church of the Holy Sepulcher and dedicated to uniting Christian knights in a common fight against the Turks. Philippe devoted himself to renewing chivalry by creating "a chivalric utopia" (Middleton, "War by Other Means" 125). The Order of the Passion attracted considerable interest in both France and England, at one point garnering members or promises of support from more than 80 nobles from both countries, including several from Chaucer's circle of friends. Plans for crusades were seriously entertained and in a few cases, such as the siege of Nicopolis, actually undertaken. Unfortunately, by 1397 all these hopes for a united Christian front against the Turks had gone down to defeat (Robertson, "The Probable Date and

Purpose of Chaucer's 'Knight's Tale'" 419-27). And though the French and the English agreed to a truce in 1396, the fundamental issues between the two sides remained unresolved (Allmand 26).

Thus in spite of crusading rhetoric's continuing appeal during this period, crusading itself never really became a central aspect of national policy. People took it seriously, were sincere in their professed devotion to its ideals, and recognized their obligations to serve God in this active way. But though crusading continued to exercise a powerful hold on their imaginations, it did not occupy an important place in the formation of national agendas. Anne Middleton highlights this disparity:

> Whatever became of chivalry in the later Middle Ages—and there seems to be general agreement that there were changes, however one interprets them—had chiefly to do with the virtual absence of crusading as a fundamental objective from the center of national military enterprise, while it remained central to the self-rationalizing activities of warriors. ("War by Other Means" 120)

In addition to military enterprises undertaken in the observance of feudal or religious obligations, the fourteenth century also witnessed an increase in another kind of military service: that of the mercenary who put his martial skills at the disposal of whoever was prepared to pay, regardless of the cause. The ethos of knight errantry encouraged young men, especially younger sons of the landed aristocracy and members of the lesser nobility, to go off to search for opportunities to try their skills, gain renown—and fill their coffers. Frequently they found employment from princes who secured their services to gain an advantage over opponents who might well also have hired mercenaries.

Often without clear-cut leadership and without a stable source of income, these bands of armed horsemen, known as free companies, tended to degenerate into gangs, taking whatever they wanted, sending shock waves of terror throughout the land, and causing social and economic ravages equal to those caused by the plague (Keen, *Chivalry* 228). Pope Urban V (1362-70) provides a detailed list of the mercenaries' destructive activities in Italy:

> That multitude of villains of divers nations, associated in arms by avidity . . . unbridled in every kind of cruelty, extorting money; methodically devastating the country and the open towns, burning houses and barns, destroying trees and vines, obliging poor peasants to fly . . . torturing and maiming those from whom they expected to

obtain ransom, without regard to ecclesiastical dignity or sex or age; violating wives, virgins and nuns, and constraining even gentle-women to follow their camps, to do their pleasure and carry arms and baggage. (qtd. in Jones, *Chaucer's Knight* 87)

Problems were especially acute when the mercenaries were paid off and released from service because they remained armed while being leaderless and unrestrained; often their behavior in oppressing the defenseless stood in direct contrast to chivalric ideals. But these armed companies did not simply reject chivalric notions; one may argue, as Keen does, that chivalry itself, with its emphasis on glorifying martial behavior and its tolerance for taking booty as an appropriate reward for undertaking warfare's risks and expenses, was part of the problem (*Chivalry* 228-31).

Though Chaucer was not born into an aristocratic family, from his adolescence onward he spent much of his time serving some of England's most powerful nobles. He spent his impressionable youth close to Edward III's court and no doubt shared in the national mystique associated with the Black Prince. He fought, and was captured and ransomed, in one of the Hundred Years' War's campaigns. Throughout the vagaries of Richard's reign Chaucer served as a diplomat and negotiator. Thus he was in a position to observe the nobility and its chivalric ethos at very close range, while always retaining an outsider's viewpoint. Knightly figures appear in a number of contexts in Chaucer's works: the Man in Black in *The Book of the Duchess*, Troilus, the Squire, Januarie and Damyan in "The Merchant's Tale," and Arveragus and Aurelius in "The Franklin's Tale." But his portrayal of the Knight in the "General Prologue" and "The Knight's Tale" itself provide the primary loci for coming to grips with his treatment of the chivalric ethic.

A great deal of critical ink has been expended in assessing the precise nature of the Knight's portrait and the function of his tale in its primary position in the Canterbury collection. The preponderance of critical opinion has generally supported the view that the Knight is an idealized representative of his estate—"a verray, parfit, gentil knyght" (GP, l. 72)—who exhibits genuine religious devotion in his choice of campaigns and in his apparent haste to join the pilgrimage. Unlike the Squire, whose campaigns all relate to the political differences of the Hundred Years' War, the Knight engaged in religiously motivated campaigns. Indeed Thomas Hatton argues that Chaucer mentions the Knight's involvement in Moorish Spain to evoke Roland and Oliver's paradigmatic knighthood and that the Knight's idealized portrait is

"slanted" precisely to support crusading activity of the sort advocated
by Philippe de Mézières (81-87). Robertson concludes:

> There is little reason to doubt that Chaucer wished to convey a set
> of genuinely revered ideals, emphasizing the need for Christian
> harmony in a joint effort against pagan encroachments from the
> north of Europe to the Byzantine Empire, and beyond that to
> Jerusalem itself in the portrait of his Knight. ("The Probable Date
> and Purpose of Chaucer's 'Knight's Tale'" 439)

Allied with this assessment of the Knight is that which sees his tale—
with its balanced symmetry, its philosophical high-mindedness, its
ruler seeking to establish order and justice, its idealized treatment of
love, its detailed rendering of tournament pageantry—as a celebration of chivalric lifestyle and values. Charles Muscatine articulates
such a view in arguing that "the 'Knight's Tale' is essentially neither a
story, nor a static picture, but a poetic pageant, and . . . all its materials are organized and contributory to a complex design expressing
the nature of the noble life" ("Form, Texture, and Meaning in 'The
Knight's Tale'" 69).

But Terry Jones in his controversial *Chaucer's Knight: The Portrait of
a Medieval Mercenary* challenges this view, arguing instead that
Chaucer's apparently positive portrait of the Knight masks an ironic
depiction of a mercenary soldier who fought in some of the least
palatable engagements of his day. Turning upside down the argument
about the Knight's campaigns, he points out that the Knight was not
present at the battles—like Crécy, Poitiers, and Najera—that made the
reputations of English chivalry and that, at a time when there were
constant and diverse pressures on the English crown, no mention occurs of the Knight's ever serving his own sovereign or land (2).

Though Jones's insistence that Chaucer's audience would readily
have recognized the Knight as representing the mercenaries that
plagued fourteenth-century Europe is extreme, Chaucer's treatment of
the Knight and his tale is sufficiently ambivalent to suggest that the
poet himself may have been exploring chivalry's inadequacies and the
extent of its compatibility with Christianity. As Peggy Knapp argues,
Jones's book "opens up the question of whether a presentation of the
institution of Christian chivalry as it defined and defended itself might
also reveal its own contradictions" (17). For example, instead of assigning his Knight a crusader's tale or a heroic *chanson de geste*, Chaucer
chooses a tale that, though reflective of the values of the aristocratic
class, is set in a totally pagan context. Some critics have suggested that

this tale presents a vision of life that is limited to the natural order; V. A. Kolve, for instance, maintains that "Chaucer's subject is nothing less than the pagan past at its most noble and dignified, imagined from within" (*Chaucer and the Imagery of Narrative* 86). He points to such features as the narrator's explicitly denying knowledge about what happens to Arcite after death, the essentially pagan view of pilgrimage that emerges in old Egeus's consolatory words, and the fact that Theseus is a man functioning within the limited lights of natural reason (150-57).

Indeed the figure of Theseus, the tale's embodiment of the chivalric ruler, remains another critical knot. Some critics paint him as a noble ruler, doing his best to minimize violence, maintain order, and achieve justice tempered by mercy: he yields to the widows' pleas for help upon his triumphal return to Athens, accedes to the ladies' requests for mercy on Palamon and Arcite when their actions could merit a death sentence, and establishes rules that aim to minimize serious injuries and prevent deaths in the tournament. Another view stresses his limitations and failures when forces beyond his control, whose operations he cannot comprehend, undermine his attempts to command events. This line of thinking sees him as an essentially well-meaning man, striving to do his best according to his limited insights. The most negative assessment portrays him as a tyrant whose career is marked by violence and pride as he subdues the Amazons and wreaks havoc in Thebes and who subverts Palamon's love for Emelye into a cynical political marriage that will solidify his own rule. But whatever flaws readers may detect in the tale or its characters, "It is clear," Patterson maintains, "that the Knight himself intends it [the tale] to celebrate both Theseus as a model of rational governance and chivalry as a force for civilization" (*Chaucer and the Subject of History* 198). But does Chaucer? Winthrop Wetherbee argues that making the Knight the narrator of a tale so celebratory of chivalric values was an unusual stroke on Chaucer's part because normally chivalric romances are told by a narrator who remains somewhat distanced from the world he is depicting. The Knight, however, shares the values of his protagonists and tries to portray chivalry as the most desirable basis for achieving social order, succeeding only partially because of chivalry's inherent weaknesses:

> What confounds the Knight is ultimately the fundamentally flawed character of the code of values he seeks to affirm. . . . The chivalric code is shown incapable of dealing with its own inherent violence, or of assimilating the feminine as anything but an occasion for violence. The more or less hapless oscillation of the male characters

in the poem between the forces of love and war provide the basis for a powerful critique of chivalric culture, committed to pursuits that leave it at the mercy of its own inherent weaknesses. . . . ("Romance and Epic in Chaucer's 'Knight's Tale'" 306)

Kurt Olsson points to the Knight's spiritual failure. In spite of his reliance on Boethian passages to explore life's mysteries, the Knight has a false sense of security: "The Knight, however, does not recognize the extent of human weakness in himself or others, and he fails to express a need for grace. His choice is to seek external peace, and to that end he creates his easy rhetoric and morality"(152).

Thus with respect to the Knight and his tale's relationship to chivalry, recent critical discussion has centered not so much on whether the Knight is or is not an ideal representative of the chivalric order as on whether or not Chaucer found chivalry an adequate code for conduct—especially that of a ruling elite. In his exploration of "the crisis of chivalry" Patterson argues: "'The Knight's Tale' shows us the chivalric mind engaged in an act of self-legitimization that simultaneously and secretly undoes itself" (*Chaucer and the Subject of History* 169). Maintaining that "the chivalric life was its own goal" (175), Patterson says that chivalry's failure, as Chaucer saw it, rested on its own self-absorption and inability to recognize and respond to social change: "It was noble culture's inability to come to self-consciousness, to rewrite its own ideology in relation to socioeconomic change, that the 'Knight's Tale' records" (230).

For throughout the Middle Ages chivalric ideals had provided the theoretical underpinnings justifying the nobility's claim to the right to rule, its assumption of moral and social superiority that made its precedence of place a natural right. But in Chaucer's day that assumption was under serious assault as chivalry's inherent flaws and limitations placed it under intense scrutiny, both in the context of the seemingly endless conflict between France and England and in that of disastrous crusading expeditions, such as the one to Nicopolis. In its ambivalence "The Knight's Tale" reflects and participates in the culture's dialogue about the viability of chivalric values, inviting its audience to assess the validity of chivalry's self-justifying rhetoric in serving the common good, which Chaucer saw as the true goal of rulership.

The tales that Chaucer assigns to the pilgrim who represents himself—the only teller who actually narrates two stories—reinforce the impression that he had serious reservations about the chivalric ethic. "The Tale of Sir Thopas" is often read as a parody of chivalric romances; the long prose "Tale of Melibee," on the other hand, addresses the wisdom of avoiding violent redress for wrongs one has suffered. In that tale when youthful voices push for revenge, an old counselor rises up to remind the assembly of war's terrible consequences:

> "Lordynges," quod he, "ther is ful many a man that crieth 'Werre, werre!' that woot ful litel what werre amounteth. Werre at his big-ynnyng hath so greet an entryng and so large that every wight may entre whan hym liketh and lightly fynde werre; but certes what ende that shal thereof bifalle, it is nat light to knowe. For soothly, whan that werre is ones bigonne, ther is ful many a child unborn of his mooder that shal sterve yong by cause of thilke werre, or elles lyve in sorwe and dye in wrecchednesse." (*The Riverside Chaucer* 219)

Though conceding the impossibility of separating Chaucer's own at-titudes from those of his characters, R.F. Yeager argues that, among other factors, Chaucer's handling of the Chaucer-pilgrim's two tales supports the view that he came to favor pacifism:

> If we accept meaningful content for the *Thopas* its subject must in-clude the potential failure of military idealism to fulfill chivalry's promise of "peace through strength" and the honorable life. . . . it would seem that in the two tales Chaucer assigned his namesake Geoffrey he embarked in different directions, only to arrive at last in the same place. . . . Probably they do reveal the opposition of Chaucer the man to war in most, if not all, cases. . . . Chaucer's preference for peace seems permanent, if somewhat inchoate; im-plicitly apparent throughout his work is a ubiquitous skepticism about the claims of chivalry. . . . ("'Pax Poetica'" 116, 120-1)

The questions about the nature and value of chivalry that Chaucer and his audience struggled with remain vital. For chivalry is not truly dead: it lives on in the concept of "an officer and a gentleman," in the rhetoric of battle and the panoply of military parades, and in a system of etiquette, now honored mostly in the breach, governing the social behavior of "ladies and gentlemen." The debate that en-gaged late fourteenth-century society about military rhetoric as a suf-ficient guide to national policy continues to reverberate as we move into the new millenium.

CHAPTER SEVEN

The Cry of the Poor: Unrest and Rebellion among the Peasants

*T*he crisis in the ruling class's chivalric ideology discussed in Chapter Six and the new economic realities to be discussed in Chapter Eight challenged the medieval world's dominant social ideology: the estates ideal of a society in which each class willingly assumes its divinely ordained responsibilities toward the others. The three-estates conceptual framework—each having its proper societal role—emerged in the medieval West's formative phase. Estates theory maintains that society functions best when each class fulfills its proper function. For the third estate—the peasant, artisan, and merchant class to which nine out of ten people belonged (Fossier, *Peasant Life in the Medieval West* 7)—that role consists of performing the labor that sustains the other two estates: the clergy who pray and the aristocrats/warriors who protect and rule. Though this model assumes rigid barriers between each group, late medieval society experienced considerable social fluidity, as rapidly changing conditions gave people the opportunity to strive for improved social status. In such an atmosphere the ideal of social harmony that the estates model envisaged came under severe strain—if indeed it had ever reflected social reality. For the Late Middle Ages witnessed glimpses of the same revolutionary fervor Abbé Sièyes expressed when, in an eighteenth-century tract entitled *What Is the Third Estate?*, he insists that while the third estate has long been "nothing," it seeks to "become something" (51-52).

During Chaucer's lifetime the Peasants' Revolt of 1381 was the most explosive manifestation of England's social tension. Scholars have traditionally seen *The Canterbury Tales* as paying only glancing attention to this upheaval. But Chaucer could scarcely have been indifferent to events that struck so close to home: the rebels poured through Aldgate while the poet lived in the house above it, and they destroyed the Savoy, the nearby palace of John of Gaunt, his royal patron. Recently new interest has focused on Chaucer's views concerning this revolutionary event and, more broadly, on his overall social and political attitudes (Ganim, "Chaucer and the Noise of the People" 303). Disagreement remains, however, about whether the poet's loyalties lay mainly with his royal patrons or whether his ironic stance judiciously masks sympathetic understanding of the rebels' grievances. Exploring medieval social ideology, the realities of peasant life, and the immediate context of the Peasants' Revolt will provide a framework for exploring this question.

Since Christianity's inception its posture toward the poor and oppressed has been ambivalent. On one hand, its central message has revolutionary social implications. Simply by accepting slaves among its members Christianity had the potential for disrupting the social order. Many Gospel stories and sayings stress Jesus's alignment with the poor and the oppressed. Other New Testament texts, like Paul's Epistle to the Galatians, remind Christians of their fundamental unity (3: 28), erasing the ancient world's most deeply rooted stratifications. But on the other hand, by teaching that passively accepting earthly suffering yields a heavenly reward, Christianity preached acceptance of the status quo, even when that meant tolerating oppression, as can be seen in Paul's Epistle to the Ephesians: "Slaves be obedient to the men who are called your masters in this world, with deep respect and sincere loyalty, as you are obedient to Christ" (6: 5).

Indeed Christianity had little impact on slavery's continuation after the Roman Empire disintegrated. The Church did not try to end slavery, neither providing sanctuary for escaped slaves nor freeing its own. "As an institution," Pierre Bonnassie comments, "the Church never opposed slavery, but, on the contrary, both approved it in principle and practiced it" (*From Slavery to Feudalism* 25). During the early medieval period slaves continued to be considered subhuman; they were subject to beatings and mutilations and were treated like property. Eventually, though, this form of slavery faded away. Early medieval laborers, though very poor, strove to improve their lot: they pushed back the frontier by opening new lands to cultivation, perfected their tools, and introduced technical innovations like water mills and irrigation systems. By the end of the tenth century a number of factors—the weakening of the state structure, technological improvements in farming, the beginnings of a popular religion movement, and the need for a more mobile population to satisfy the demands of a growing agricultural economy—all worked together to bring about a collapse of slavery (Bonnassie 16-55).

But human bondage had two distinct phases during the Middle Ages: the first continued the ancient world's slave system; the second responded to new socio-economic conditions after the millennium (Evergates, *Feudal Society in the Bailliage of Troyes* 157). The peasantry of the High and Late Middle Ages derives from this second wave of bondage. Typically the medieval peasant has been portrayed as tied to the land, as living in abject poverty, as ignorant as well as illiterate, and as passively accepting his social position: "conservative, sedentary, placid and unwarlike" (Rosener, *Peasants in the Middle Ages* 13-14). But much contemporary scholarship yields a considerably more complex picture (Freedman, *The Origins of Peasant Servitude* 3).

Central to the peasants' status was their relationship to the land they cultivated, especially the nature and extent of their obligations to the landowner. At the millennium agricultural laborers usually fell into two categories: either they had some claim to free lands, called allods, or they were tenants farming another man's lands. But the two categories frequently overlapped: the former might seek to add to their income by working lands in addition to their own, while the latter might have claims on land other than that which they worked for someone else (Bonnassie 296). Another significant distinction was that between serfs and peasants: while the former were peasants, the latter were not necessarily serfs. Though not exactly slaves, serfs "tended to belong to their lord as a form of property and transmitted this subordination to their descendants" (Freedman 5); peasants, on the other hand, paid rent on their land and had restraints on their liberty but had some traditional claim to their land (Freedman 4-6). Here too there was considerable overlap between the two categories. Contrary trends operated throughout the medieval period: landholders exerted pressure to bring ever more free, or allodial, land under their jurisdiction—sometimes by force and sometimes in exchange for protection—while peasants sought to clear previously unfarmed lands, often not part of the seigniorial system (Lis and Soly, *Poverty and Capitalism in Pre-Industrial Europe* 2-5).

While the medieval peasantry was taking shape, significant changes were also occurring in domestic dwellings: individual houses were replacing large communal halls, as a tribal structure gave way to one centered on the family occupying and farming a plot of land. Especially significant was the shift to cooking in the house and to greater separation between humans and animals under the same roof. These developments fostered a greater sense of independence (Fossier 67-71). Between the twelfth and the end of the thirteenth century other significant changes occurred: the amount of cultivated land greatly expanded in response to population growth; better plows and the three-field system of crop rotation led to greater land use; and better building materials and more effective farming techniques produced more lasting settlements (Rosener 14-35).

While some forces worked for cultivators, others militated against them. Though they enjoyed a measure of freedom from proprietors, their condition was nevertheless precarious: many factors undermined their ability to control their lands. Every time something went wrong in their lives they had sell off or borrow on their property: "The result was always the same: the transformation of allods into tenures" (Bonnassie 297). The emergence of professional mounted warriors—the knightly class discussed in Chapter Six—accelerated the process by which cultivators lost their recently gained freedom. The armed, mounted warriors increasingly separated themselves from the rest of the population as the growing expense of conducting warfare excluded the peasantry from its pursuit. In contrast to earlier periods, the rural population then focused much more intensely on farming, leaving political and military activities to those who had the necessary resources (Rosener 12-13). The armed warriors' increasing violence denied peasants continued enjoyment of their greater freedom and increased productivity. The former ensconced themselves in strong fortifications, and the gap between the kinds of weapons to which each group had access increased, leaving the peasants vulnerable to attack (Bonnassie 304-6).

Estates theory developed during this second wave of bondage. The theological foundation for the era's organic view of society goes back to the Early Christian period. In the Epistle to the Romans, Paul, urging Christians to serve the community, draws an analogy between human society and the human body: "For just as in a single human body there are many limbs and organs, all with different functions, so we who are united with Christ, though many, form one body, and belong to one another as its limbs and organs" (12: 4-5). Social theorists subsequently adapted Paul's analogy for their own purposes, arguing that the whole body's health depends on each part's appropriately carrying out its function (Duby, *The Three Orders* 70). In the twelfth century John of Salisbury's *Policraticus* develops the idea at length, equating laborers with the body's feet: "The feet are the name of those who exercise the humbler duties, by whose service all the members of the republic may walk along the earth" (125).

But though social theorists stressed reciprocity and each group's responsibilities to the whole body politic, medieval estates theory has its roots in two dichotomies that reinforce social inequality: that between the rulers and the ruled and that between the clergy and the laity. Some give orders and others obey them; some have holiness and wisdom; and others benefit from their prayers and insights. Those who neither rule nor pray carry out society's work. After discussing the roles of the clergy and the nobility, Adalbero of Laon—an eleventh-century bishop who articulated the estates concept—describes the third class as "a miserable race which owns nothing that it does not get by its own labour" (qtd. in Hilton, *Bond Men Made Free* 54). Thus despite the ideal of a harmonious social order in which each group willingly plays its assigned part, estates theory rests on fundamental social inequality; it applies the ecclesiastical culture's hierarchical assumptions to society as a whole and makes an arbitrarily granted moral superiority the basis for social stratification (Duby, *The Three Orders* 57). The theory that links human sinfulness to bondage, holding that servitude results from permanent moral inferiority, justifies this inequality. Again a biblical passage—Genesis's link between hard labor and original sin (3:17-19)—plays an important role: "The value specific to the populace, to which was attributed a saving grace on a par with valor and purity, was the pain of the flesh, the suffering due to labor" (Duby, *The Three Orders* 158).

As the seigniorial class tightened its grip, two social patterns developed: the *manorial* system, in which the lord owns the land and peasants have the right to its use, under specified conditions, in exchange for their labor, and the *village* system, in which peasants pay rent to the lord for using his land. The manorial system tended to be more restrictive for peasants. The manor consisted of both the lord's house and its accompanying land—his demesne—as well as the lands his tenants farmed. The lord's income derived both from products the land yielded and from rent, some of it paid through labor, collected from his tenants (Postan, *The Medieval Economy and Society* 73-74). Manors gradually developed a variety of workshops, becoming self-sufficient entities while tightening the landlord's hold on his tenants. Less tangible developments also had a substantial impact on them. The lord gained legal immunities that enabled him to monopolize resources, and the line separating bonded peasants from freemen tended to blur, with the latter often no better off than the former (Rosener 14-21). Thus a central feature of the manorial system was that the tenants lived in some degree of bondage (Postan 74).

Gradually the village system almost completely overshadowed the manorial system. Under the former land was divided into three parts: one, the demesne, served the lord's purposes; the second was subdivided into plots the peasant families used; and the third, undeveloped land and forests, served the community at large. Even when peasants had no right to own land, the fields that their families subdivided for their own use created a strong sense of proprietorship (Hilton, *Bond Men Made Free* 38). This proprietary sense led to recurrent legal tussles over rights to the land and to violent outbreaks between lords and peasants. In addition to villages with clear ties to landlords, there were also "franchised communities" in which inhabitants enjoyed formal exemptions from monetary or personal obligations resulting from special grants made by lords to individual villages. Such grants in effect created new social categories (Evergates 41). The peasant-lord relationship had many permutations, occasionally virtually disappearing (Postan 79).

Thus medieval peasants were often considerably more mobile than their stereotype suggests. Zvi Razi's detailed study of Halesowen, an English medieval village, shows that even before the Black Death peasants enjoyed some mobility which that cataclasm only increased (*Life, Marriage and Death in a Medieval Parish* 30-31; 117-18). Though stressing the lords' ongoing efforts to assert their rights over peasants who had moved beyond their jurisdiction, Theodore Evergates observes: "There is no question about the fact of actual physical mobility of ordinary peasants at any time during the twelfth and thirteenth centuries; movement not only occurred, it was considered normal" (23). Still, relief from obligations to landlords was temporary at best (Evergates 41).

While peasants sought to limit restrictions and demands on them, lords strove to ensure an adequate labor supply, for its absence greatly diminished their lands' value. Most rules governing the peasantry served to preserve the lord's claim on peasant labor. Thus besides having to provide unpaid labor on the lord's demesne, peasants, at least theoretically, were forbidden to marry outside the lord's jurisdiction unless they had his permission; peasant families had to submit to his claiming part or all of their belongings at the time of death, thereby being reminded that they had no right to own property; they had to pay a yearly tax as a sign of their dependent status; they had to obtain the lord's permission to send their sons to school; and they had to use—and pay for the use of—the lord's facilities, like mills and ovens (Hilton, *Bond Men Made Free* 60). As Evergates sums up, "Ultimately, the conditions of tenants reflected the will or policy of their landlords, tempered by necessity" (59). For though the stereotype depicts peasants as resigned to their lot, they sometimes showed a substantial willingness to make sacrifices to secure greater personal freedom—though paying fees to secure that freedom severely strained a peasant family's budget and though bondage usually entailed many complicated entanglements that could chip away at the rights secured through payment (Jordan, *From Servitude to Freedom* 61-78).

Still, the conditions of peasant life did not particularly reward individual initiative (Fossier 30). Once peasants had met their obligations to their lords and provided the necessities for their own daily lives, little motivation remained to produce more or to accumulate goods. Most peasants' lifestyle followed a predictable pattern: people lived in villages, farmed the fields, and hunted and gathered in nearby forests (Cherubini, "The Peasant and Agriculture" 116). In good times such activities produced an adequate supply of life's necessities. As Chaucer's Clerk reports in his tale, Walter's villagers enjoy the fruits of their labor:

> Noght fer fro thilke paleys honurable,
> Where as this markys shoop his mariage,
> There stood a throop, of site delitable,
> In which that povre folk of that village
> Hadden hir beestes and hir herbergage,
> And of hire labour tooke hir sustenance,
> After that the erthe yaf hem habundance. (ll. 197-203)

But, as noted earlier, peasants constantly lived on the margin: any natural disaster or change in circumstance could lead to serious hardship (Fossier 113). However, despite these harsh conditions and despite the systemic lack of incentives for improving their lot, the peasantry did strive for advancement and status, which derived from owning one's own animals and having a strong claim to the land the family farmed (Hilton, *Bond Men Made Free* 33-34). The village system provided greater social mobility than the manorial system: it gave peasants more freedom and more opportunity for communal farming and village life. As we shall see in Chapter Eight, they could seek opportunities to sell their excess products in markets beyond their own village sphere (Rosener 53-54), thereby spurring the growth of trade and the market economy. Peasants could also increase their status by acquiring more land, which hired help would then work (Hilton, *Bond Men Made Free* 34).

But the peasants' involvement in the market seems to have been confined to "the products of the henhouse and the kitchen-garden: fruit, fresh and dried, cheese and milk, fruits, nuts, and mushrooms from the woods, and small handcrafted objects" (Cherubini 121). Landowners usually controlled the sale of items more central to the economy, such as grain and wine (121). Limited markets as well as technological constrictions on producing and distributing agricultural products prevented large-scale enterprises from developing, capping the possibilities for social mobility. Thus the peasantry rarely broke into even the nobility's lowest levels because stringent social barriers caused both nobles and gentry to see peasants "as different creatures from themselves, almost as a different race" (Hilton, *Bond Men Made Free* 35). The distance between the two major groupings of peasants related to the quantity rather than to the kinds of their possessions; their lifestyles had much in common with each other (35).

Grain production was the bedrock of the peasant economy, bread being the dietary staple for all classes, especially the lower ones. The kind of bread one ate even reflected social status (Cherubini 118). The Wife of Bath's smug willingness to let virgins "be breed of pured whete-seed" (WBP, l. 143), while she, a wife many times over, is content to be "barly-breed" (144), reflects Chaucer's awareness of the social stratification attached to differing kinds of bread; so does the fact that the poor widow in "The Nun's Priest's Tale" is well satisfied with "broun breed" (NPT, l. 2844).

The precariousness of medieval agriculture made the quest for a steady bread supply central to most peasant drives for greater political and economic independence. For the nobility relied on its exclusive control of such necessities as mills and baking ovens for much of its income (Cherubini 118-24). The local mill thus became one of the village's established communal gathering spots. Because it needed water and a sloped siting, the mill was usually distant from the village center. Both its location and its connection with the lord's hated authority provoked malaise, as did the miller who ran it (Fossier 66). "The Reeve's Tale" reflects these associations in its portrayal of John and Alayn, two Cambridge students who go to Symkyn's mill expecting both an attempted swindling and—because they are university students—a successful countermeasure on their part. Their initial failure to outmaneuver Symkyn leads to a night of sexual indulgence with his wife and daughter, the runaway horse serving as the emblem for the tale's uncontrolled sensuality (Kolve, *Chaucer and the Imagery of Narrative* 236-52). Robyn the Miller's portrayal in the "General Prologue" and in the prologue to his tale also suggests these connotations: his bagpipes are linked with potent sexuality, and his disorderly drunkenness points to his capacity for social disruption—a capacity he demonstrates when he undermines the social order by asserting his right to tell his tale out of turn.

Early in the fourteenth century the population growth that had been underway since the twelfth century reached its peak (Cherubini 114). But at that point signs of crisis began to appear in the peasant economy because lands under cultivation failed to keep pace with the expanding population, and meeting heavy feudal obligations became an increasing burden that eroded the peasantry's declining resources. For after the preceding centuries' economic prosperity, Europe experienced a period of decline: a significantly colder climate led to contracting arable lands, and the resulting inadequate food supplies led to famine (Ziegler 30-34). The poor nutrition debilitated peasants who were left ill-equipped to confront the ravaging epidemic of bubonic plague that hit at mid-century (Rosener 44). These conditions created an environment in which the plague could wreak maximum damage when it struck. As David Herlihy concludes: "There can be little doubt that the great mortalities of the plague were closely linked to the poor nutrition and bad health of substantial numbers of the population" (qtd. in Bowsky 61). The pestilence, as the disease was called at the time, killed about a third of Europe's population in its first and most deadly onslaught from 1347-1351 (Slack, "Responses to Plague in Early Modern Europe" 434). By 1385, when the disease had reappeared in several more cycles, the overall population decline ran as high as 40-50 percent (Russell, "Effects of Pestilence and Plague, 1315-1385" 470). After this rapid and dramatic decline, the population did not swing significantly upward for the next two centuries.

The postplague period, however, brought improvements to peasant living conditions because the high death toll created a labor shortage that led to wage increases as well as to greater physical and social mobility, thereby fostering rising expectations for a better life. Indeed some historians see the hundred years after the plague as "the golden age of the English peasant" (Patterson, *Chaucer and the Subject of History* 251); as we shall see in the next chapter, they argue that the countryside—rather than the cities with their rising middle class—initiated social change (Patterson, *Chaucer and the Subject of History* 252-53). For the peasants—characterized as having "an extremely active social conscience" (Fossier 44)—did not automatically accept the role that the dominant ideology imposed on them and drew on the Gospels to nourish their resistance: "Invoking the Gospels' inversion of worldly power and vainglory, a venerable current of opinion held that peasants would have less reason to fear heavenly judgment than other orders of society because of their humility and subjugation in this life" (Freedman 219).

Rather than developing under the influence of particular leaders or movements, the peasants' resistance emerged from a desire to counter both social and financial pressure from the ruling classes: they rejected their lords' attempts to increase labor requirements, to impose additional taxes, to limit access to cultivated and uncultivated lands, and to require the use of and payment for services like grinding corn. These issues spurred sporadic rebellion as early as the eleventh century, anticipating later efforts to cast off domination (Fossier 45-46). But while the peasants strove to cast off restrictions on their freedom, their lords clung tenaciously to old models (Jordan, *From Servitude to Freedom* 98-99). Pressure on the peasantry intensified in the thirteenth century when increased demands for monetary payments to replace traditional labor payments came from both the aristocracy and the monarchy, as both sought to increase their income (Hill, *The Manor, the Plowman, and the Shepherd* 26). "The peasant is thus caught in between, with old obligations to the estate and new responsibilities to the king," Ordelle Hill observes (26).

In late fourteenth-century England one of the most famous and most explosive signs of the tension resulting from the ruling class's determination to increase its revenues and secure its prerogatives and the peasants' rising expectations occurred: the Peasants' Revolt of 1381. The higher wages and greater mobility created by the plague's devastation led to increased awareness of injustice. When landowners attempted to recoup lost income by imposing new taxes that discriminated against those with low incomes, to limit their peasants' ability to add new land to their holdings, to enforce claims to free labor, and to restrict rising wages through legislation, the peasants' resentments crystallized into active revolt during June of 1381. A new poll tax provided a focal point for their anger (Ormrod, "The Peasants' Revolt" 1). Though short-lived and abortive in attaining its goals, the uprising wreaked havoc in London. The rebels destroyed such landmarks as John of Gaunt's Savoy Palace and killed several prominent citizens closely allied with the aristocracy and with the clerical hierarchy who, because of extensive landholdings, often functioned as feudal overlords. These events sent shock waves through the ruling class, underlining the ongoing struggle for control over labor and land.

The uprising started in London's outlying districts. The rebels, by no means drawn exclusively from the lowest social rung, included both farmers and artisans. London also contributed its share of participants: craftsmen, guildsmen, and day laborers joined in (Prescott, "London in the Peasants' Revolt" 132-33). They acted more from frustration than from desperation. As Hilton notes, "Those major social grievances acute enough to generate rebellious actions were not the ones that divided the poor from the middling and rich peasants, or the labourers from their employers, but rather those which divided the mass of the population from the lords, the lawyers and government officials" (*Bond Men Made Free* 184).

Among the artisans certainly involved were the millers: records show that several millers were hanged for their part in the revolt or played leadership roles in it. As suggested earlier, because they functioned as the lords' agents, their social role was ambiguous. But whether their legendary dishonesty was directed primarily at the peasants whose grains they ground or at the lords whose mills they worked remains uncertain (Patterson, *Chaucer and the Subject of History* 254-55). Significantly, as Patterson points out, "The peasants themselves seem to have seen the figure of the miller as capable of embodying both their grievances and their desire for an almost apocalyptic reckoning" (257).

The rebellion also attracted some clerics. While the entrenched wealth of the ecclesiastical hierarchy and of feudal monastics was a prime target for the rebels—the archbishop of Canterbury becoming one of their most prominent casualties—some lower clergymen allied themselves with the rebels' cause. Froissart's account, though written at a considerable remove from the events themselves and from an unabashedly royalist perspective, points to the important ideological and tactical roles some clergymen played in it. In many ways they too experienced oppression from the privileged: they were subject to taxation and wage restrictions; they had to subsist on low salaries; they often had their income depleted by monasteries that succeeded in incorporating them into their estates (Hilton, *Bond Men Made Free* 207-9).

But the lower clergy's involvement in the revolt probably had deeper roots than their own social and economic grievances: their access to biblical and patristic materials helped them articulate a radical Christianity. Froissart's account of the rebels' motives reflects the role of biblical images and ideas in their rhetoric:

> These bad people in the counties just mentioned began to rebel because, they said, they were held too much in subjection, and when the world began there had been no serfs and could not be, unless they had rebelled against their lord, as Lucifer did against God; but they were not of that stature, being neither angels nor spirits, but men formed in the image of their masters, and they were treated as

animals. This was a thing they could no longer endure, wishing rather to be all one and the same; and, if they worked for their masters, they wanted to have wages for it. (211-12)

The chronicler Walsingham attributes to John Ball, whom Froissart characterizes as "a crack-brained priest" (212), the rallying cry "Whan Adam dalf and Eve span, wo was thanne a gentilman" ["When Adam dug and Eve spun, who was then a gentleman"] (qtd. in Hilton, *Bond Men Made Free* 211). Also, Ball's letters, which achieved wide circulation, refer to millers in allegorical—and apocalyptic—overtones:

> Johan the Mullere hath ygrounde smal, smal, smal;
> The Kyngis sone of heuene shalle pay for alle.
> Be war or ye be wo. . . .
> Jakke Mylner asketh help to turne hys milne aright. He
> hath grounden smal smal; the kingis sone of heven he
> schal pay for alle.
> (qtd. in Patterson, *Chaucer and the Subject of History* 257)

Ball's fiery rhetoric helped fuel the rebellion:

> Good people, things cannot go right in England and never will, until goods are held in common and there are no more villeins and gentlefolk, but we are all one and the same. In what way are those whom we call lords greater than ourselves? . . . If we all spring from a single father and mother, Adam and Eve, how can they claim or prove that they are lords more than us, except by making us produce and grow the wealth which they spend? . . . They have shelter and ease in their fine manors, and we have hardship and toil, the wind and the rain in the fields. (qtd. in Froissart 212-13)

Though scholars have been hesitant to link the 1381 revolt too closely with the Lollard movement, which was then barely in its infancy as we have seen in Chapter Three, Hilton argues that Ball is a "proto-Lollard" with ideas typical of other dissenting movements on the Continent: doing away with monks and with the hierarchical Church structure, linking tithes to the moral probity of the clergy, and parceling out Church property among the laity (*Bond Men Made Free* 227).

The revolt was thus more than an inchoate eruption of rage and frustration. Its ideological roots stretched out in two directions: to the long-standing legal tensions between peasants and feudal over-lords about rights to land and labor and to the biblical tradition, which, while usually serving to reinforce the established hierarchical social order, nevertheless harbored images and ideas that had a socially subversive potential (229).

As previously mentioned, rebellion began in the outlying areas around London, such as Essex and Kent, when tax collectors, attempting to enforce an unpopular tax, met with resistance that quickly escalated into violence when officials tried to bring to justice those who had opposed and attacked the tax collectors. Another precipitating event occurred when one of the king's agents jailed a man, claiming him as a serf. Tempers rose quickly, and the peasants began to organize themselves for open revolt, their anger directed more at the king's advisers than at the young Richard II himself (137-39). Indeed the rebels believed that they had the king's tacit support; they saw themselves, no doubt falsely, as allied with the monarchy as distinct from the privileged classes, one of their slogans being "with King Richard and the true commons" (qtd. in Hilton, *Bond Men Made Free* 225). Because they saw the monarchy as transcending individuals and classes (225), when they experienced oppression they blamed those in the king's service rather than the king himself, in a time-honored medieval political pattern.

After creating disturbances in outlying areas for several weeks, the rebels—with Wat Tyler, Jack Straw, and John Ball emerging as their leaders—began to converge outside of London, looking for a meeting with the king to address their issues. When that meeting failed to materialize, the angry rebels joined others already in London, where sympathizers had aided their entry by insisting on the lowering of London Bridge. In the city the rebels, aided by townsmen, engaged in a destructive spree. Their anger focused on the persons and property of those whom they saw as the privileged class—on lawyers, clergymen, prominent civil servants. Another group to feel their wrath were the Flemings, a foreign minority. John of Gaunt, their most desired target, escaped by virtue of his absence from town, but his palace did not. Simon Sudbury, the archbishop of Canterbury, was not so lucky: he and others were beheaded at the Tower of London (Hilton, *Bond Men Made Free* 137-97).

When the king's attempts to negotiate with the rebels in London itself failed, on the following day he and his advisers met with them outside the city at Mile End to hear their grievances. Asked what they wanted from him, the rebels responded: "We want you to make us free forever and ever, we and our heirs and our lands, so that we shall never again be called serfs or bondmen" (qtd. in Froissart 221). Among their other demands was their insistence on the execution of those whom they called traitors and on free access to private game preserves (Hilton, *Bond Men Made Free* 230). Richard appeared to agree with these demands, telling the majority of the rebels to disperse while leaving behind several representatives from each village, to whom he would give letters carrying his seal. From that point on power shifted to the royalists: the rebels were appeased, and some began to drift away. On the next day, when the leaders met with the king to press their demands, the mayor of London killed Wat Tyler, the rebel leader, thereby unnerving the rebels and leaving the movement in disarray. The anger and frustration that had fomented for months, even years, dissolved as fear replaced the bravado with which the rebels had pressed their claims. The rebellion collapsed quickly after John Ball and Jack Straw were caught and executed, their heads displayed on London Bridge (Froissart 229).

The core motive spurring the rebels was the straightforward—and revolutionary—desire for freedom from bondage. The centrality of that goal helps to explain the intensity of the rebels' desire to destroy manorial records and their special wrath against lawyers; anger against official abuse, not frustration about food shortages, fueled this revolt (Hilton, *Bond Men Made Free* 156, 161, 226-27). Not just court records but literate culture itself seems to have been under attack. Susan Crane has argued that the uprising evidences the rebels' frustration at the encroachments that a spreading literate culture was making among those whose traditions were essentially oral. For literacy can become an instrument of control and oppression that leaves the illiterate both voiceless and powerless. Crane cites contemporary accounts of the uprising's events, which, because written from the perspective of the empowered, almost universally depict the rebels as a noisy, babbling mob incapable of planned, concerted action: "England's lower strata appear in written records as incoherent and irrational creatures or as models of submission and faith, variously constructed by various writers' own positions and preoccupations" ("The Writing Lesson of 1381" 201). In effect the chronicles erase the peasants' faces and mute their voices. The existing accounts almost entirely reflect the perspective of the literate, power-holding authorities who ultimately prevailed. Theirs is the story that survived. John Gower's *Vox Clamantis,* for instance, treats the revolt as "the image of primal chaos and reversal to bestiality which follows on the challenge to the established political order" (Pearsall, "Interpretive Models for the Peasants' Revolt" 65). Crane's argument helps to explain why, in addition to lawyers and government officials, the rebels targeted everyone who could write, as Walsingham's chronicle reports: "they . . . had it cried around the city that all lawyers, all the men of the Chancery and the Exchequer and everyone who could write a writ or a letter should be beheaded, wherever they could be found" (qtd. in Crane, "The Writing Lesson of 1381" 205).

Royalists like Froissart could take comfort that the rebellion had lasted only a few days before dissipating like a bad dream with the coming of daylight. But the fact remained: poorly armed and disorderly peasants had wreaked havoc against the king's representatives in the countryside, stormed London, and, however briefly, held it in thrall, forcing the king to meet with them and acknowledge their claims. Still more, the movement's ideological underpinnings derived from the Bible, medieval society's most revered text. Surely the privileged classes must have experienced a foreboding shiver as they thought about the implications of those few days' events. For among the most significant legacies of this and other medieval peasant movements is "the concept of the freeman, owing no obligation, not even deference to an overlord" (Hilton, *Bond Men Made Free* 235). Still, as Hilton notes, "Villeinage was never abolished; it withered away. It was in the fourteenth century that the withering process began, but it was an uneven process and in many areas it was long before the manorial lords faced up to the fact" (*The Decline of Serfdom in Medieval England* 33).

Chaucer would have been very familiar with agrarian changes during this period: his wardship of two manors in Kent, the seedbed of the revolt, and his roles as justice of the peace, clerk of the works, and especially customs officer would have heightened his awareness of contemporary issues relating to wages, taxes, and restrictions on labor (Hill, *The Manor, the Plowman and the Shepherd* 74). But assessing his response to the events associated with the rebellion and to its long-range implications is complicated. The rebellion hit so close to home he could hardly have maintained aloof indifference. In addition to having the rebels course under his very door, Chaucer, as one closely allied with the crown and with Gaunt, must have felt himself and must actually have been a potential target of the rebels' wrath. Yet only a brief reference in "The Nun's Priest's Tale" clearly relates to the 1381 events. When the fox is carrying Chaunticleer away to make a meal of him, the narrator describes the resulting barnyard furor in terms that specifically evoke the uprising:

> So hydous was the noyse—a, benedicitee!—
> Certes, he Jakke Straw and his meynee

Ne madde nevere shoutes half so shrille
Whan that they wolden any Flemyng kille,
As thilke day was maad upon the fox.
Of bras they broghten bemes, and of box,
Of horn, of boon, in whiche they blewe and powped,
And therwithal they shriked and they howped.
It semed as that hevene sholde falle. (ll. 3393-401)

Chaucer's linkage between the barnyard furor and the peasants' noisy clamor deflates and brings under control what must have been a frightening experience.

J. Stephen Russell has found another likely reference to the uprising in Book II of *The House of Fame* (ll. 935-49); the eagle's invitation for the narrator to gaze up at the Milky Way he finds to be "thick with allusions to the Peasants' Revolt and particularly to the catastrophic events of June 1381" ("Is London Burning?" 107). Specifically, he points to references to Watling Street and Al[d]gate as well as to Phaeton's difficulty in keeping his cart under control as highlighting central locations and events related to the peasants' rampage through London (108-9). Once again Chaucer's own responses to the experience are distanced and disguised.

Thus finding his attitude towards the societal tensions of which the Peasants' Revolt was only the most dramatic manifestation will require us to look further. For recent scholars have detected sympathetic allegiance to both his royalist patrons and to the rebels in his work. Alcuin Blamires, for instance, sees him as identifying with the establishment he served throughout his professional career ("The General Prologue as Covert History"). Lee Patterson, on the other hand, argues that Chaucer makes "a conscious and deliberate decision" to distance himself from "the forms and values of aristocratic culture" (*Chaucer and the Subject of History* 254). Paul Olson balances between the two positions, saying that while Chaucer satirizes the peasants' destructive bent, "he does not ignore the problems that have led to the demise of internal order in England" (84).

Chaucer's portrayal of peasants ranges between two extremes: peasants are a noisy rabble upsetting social order by their contentious behavior, or they are saintly by virtue of their uncomplaining acceptance of their lot in life. The above-cited passage from "The Nun's Priest's Tale" reflects the former view, as does the passage from *The Parliament of Fowls* in which the lower fowls' loud clamoring threatens to bring Dame Nature's parliament to chaotic dissolution. But Chaucer's portrait of the Plowman in the "General Prologue" reflects a new trend toward an idealized portrayal of peasants in the fourteenth century, resulting perhaps from the influence of such classical works as Virgil's *Georgics,* which Chaucer must have known (Hill, *The Manor, the Plowman and the Shepherd* 77). The Plowman also reveals the influence of *Piers Plowman,* a lengthy poem of social commentary in two versions by Chaucer's contemporary William Langland (Mann, *Chaucer and Medieval Estates Satire* 70-73). It presents the ideal conception of proper estates behavior: echoing the biblical injunction on attaining spiritual perfection, it epitomizes Christian *caritas,* a properly ordered love of God and neighbor:

> A trewe sywnkere and a good was he,
> Lvynge in pees and parfit charitee.
> God loved he best with al his hoole herte
> At alle tymes, thogh him gamed or smerte,
> And thanne his neighcbor right as hymselve.(ll. 531-35)

By uncomplainingly carting loads of dung and dutifully paying his Church tithes, the Plowman enacts his assigned social role, unlike the contemporary plowman who, by demanding greater wages and seeking better opportunities in other kinds of work, was often "a figure of discontent" (Hill, *The Manor, the Plowman and the Shepherd* 45).

That Chaucer makes the Plowman the blood brother of the equally idealized Parson highlights the proper relationship between their two functions (Mann, *Chaucer and Medieval Estates Satire* 67). The Plowman's ready willingness to tithe parallels the Parson's reluctance to exact payment from impoverished parishioners (67-68). By uncomplainingly accepting his life's material circumstances, the Plowman reinforces the ruling class's mystique of social harmony and of societal patterns based on a deeply ingrained natural order. His portrait presents a saintly figure who assumes the burden of heavy labor in a Christlike spirit, thereby encouraging the attitudes most beneficial to the ruling order. For what officialdom most sought was compliant manual labor. Indeed Blamires argues that by describing the Plowman in terms that specifically counter contemporary attacks on the behavior of actual peasants and by making his Plowman such an ideal figure, Chaucer masks his distaste for actual ones, thereby highlighting his identification with his royal patrons ("The General Prologue as Covert History").

The Widow who owns the barnyard over which the lordly Chaunticleer presides in "The Nun's Priest's Tale" provides another instance of abstemious living cheerfully undertaken. Perhaps as an implicit reproach to the aristocratic pretensions of the Prioress, the teller's religious superior, and certainly as a contrast to the barnyard creatures' colorful splendor, the Nun's Priest carefully details the Widow's simple life:

> This wydwe, of which I telle yow my tale. . . .
> In pacience ladde a ful symple lyf,
> For litel was hir catel and hir rente. . . .
> Ful sooty was hir bour and eek hir halle,
> In which she eet ful many a sklendre meel.
> Of poynaunt sauce hir neded never a deel.
> No deyntee morsel passed thurgh hir throte. . . .
> No wyn ne drank she, neither whit ne reed;
> Hir bord was served moost with whit and blak—
> milk and broun breed, in which she foond no lak;
>   (ll. 2824-45)

The Widow's lifestyle rivals a monastic ascetic's. As with the Plowman's portrait, hers reflects an uncomplaining acceptance of her life's allotted material circumstances; her virtue emanates, at least in part, from that acceptance.

"The Clerk's Tale" also presents subservient peasants willingly subjecting themselves to the lord's will: both Griselde and her father, Janicula, quickly yield when Walter claims her as his bride. Janicula's response to Walter's request for her hand would warm any aristocrat's heart:

> "Lord," quod he, "my willynge
> Is as ye wole, ne ayeynes youre likynge
> I wol no thyng, ye be my lord so deere;
> Right as yow lust, governeth this mateere."(ll. 319-22)

After the wedding Griselde subjects herself to her aristocratic husband's most tyrannical behavior, keeping her promise never to "grucche" and maintaining a composed demeanor in facing Walter's most outrageous actions. But Griselde's compliance, though tinged with faint reproach at Walter, strains our capacity to accept it as virtuous. Also, Janicula's comments when Walter ignominiously sends her back home reflect the ingrained peasant suspicion about the commitment behind an aristocrat's promises. Thus in this case Chaucer makes the model problematic by pressing it to extremes, by pointing to an allegorical reading to address Walter's autocratic excesses, and by drawing attention to the husband's cruelty through the narrator's remarks.

Another subtle commentary occurs in the fact that Griselde, elevated from her peasant-class background by Walter's willful assertion of his right to choose any bride he wants, proves herself a capable and judicious governor in Walter's absence:

> Nat oonly this Grisildis thurgh hir wit
> Koude al the feet of wyfly hoomlinesse,
> But eek, whan that the cas requireth it,
> The commune profit coude she redresse.
> Ther nas discord, rancour, ne hevynesse
> In al that land that she ne koude apese,
> And wisely brynge hem alle in reste and ese.
>
> Though that hire housbonde absent were anon. . . .
> So wyse and ripe wordes hadde she,
> And juggementz of so greet equitee,
> That she from hevene sent was, as men wende,
> Peple to save and every wrong t'amende. (ll. 428-41)

A change of dress and environment transforms the poorest peasant in Walter's realm into one whose capacity to rule rivals his own.

In "The Reeve's Tale," however, Chaucer seems to denigrate peasants' social aspirations by poking fun at Symkyn the Miller and his wife, the parson's daughter who had been raised in a nunnery:

> A wyf he hadde, ycomen of noble kyn;
> The person of the toun hir fader was.
> With hire he yaf ful many a panne of bras,
> For that Symkyn sholde in his blood allye.
> She was yfostred in a nonnerye;
> For Symkyn wolde no wyf, as he sayde,
> But she were wel ynorissed and a mayde,
> To saven his estaat of yomanrye.
> And she was proud, and peert as is a pye. (ll. 3942-50)

None of the other villagers dares call the wife anything but "dame," and no man ventures to tease or flirt with her for fear of reprisal. Symkyn's marriage reflects his aspirations for social status, which he hopes to keep improving through an advantageous alliance for his daughter; his social snobbery heightens the Cambridge clerk's revenge because the daughter's loss of virginity makes her a less attractive marriage prospect.

Thus Chaucer's response to peasants appears in conflicting images: the almost saintly Plowman, the virtuous Widow, and the sweet-tempered and honor-bound Griselde contrast with the smug anti-intellectualism of John the Carpenter in "The Miller's Tale," the cynical mean-spiritedness of the Reeve, and the greedy dishonesty of Symkyn the Miller in "The Reeve's Tale." But perhaps more significant than individual passages are various scholars' attempts to read the rebellion directly into the structure of *The Canterbury Tales*. For instance, Lee Patterson sees a peasant's revolt occurring within the frame of the Canterbury pilgrimage itself. The Miller's insistence on inserting himself into the tale-telling game on his own terms in direct response to the Knight's performance and in overt repudiation of Harry Bailly's deference to the Monk challenges official culture's claim to automatic precedence. As we have seen in the chroniclers, the prominent role that millers played in the actual uprising reinforces that view. "The Miller's Tale" itself can be seen as a witty deflation of both aristocratic and clerical pretensions. Its smooth artistry—ostensibly the drunken and churlish Miller's—and its privileging of nature's claims over artificial behavioral codes also contest official views.

Beyond simply challenging the right to precedence, the Miller asserts his right to interpret: through his tale he subverts the stories, both courtly and clerical, through which the ruling classes maintain their control. Arguing that in *The Canterbury Tales* "the pilgrimage 'Peasants' Revolt' comes about through generic and iconological attack" (75), Paul Olson observes:

> Chaucer obviously understood the extent to which groups in revolt displace their rulers' stories of saints and statesmen and mock their decorum, social and literary, in the process. To breathe fire into his revolt, John Ball, according to the chroniclers, altered the functions Augustine assigned Nimrod, Noah, and Canaan; and Robin does the same thing by altering the functions and meanings of the Knight's set of characters and his story. (77)

The Miller overturns the Knight's vision of a harmonious social order under the Duke's benevolent guidance by replacing Theseus with a dim-witted carpenter whose attempts to control his wife's sexuality expose him to communal ridicule. And he evokes clerical culture's most sacred story—that of Mary and her carpenter husband—and one of its most revered texts—the Song of Songs—to juxtapose his tale's overt with their repressed sexuality. Finally, through Nicholas's ready willingness to recast the biblical story of Noah and the Flood to serve his lechery, Chaucer points to "the role of medieval clerics in manipulating typology" (Prior 57).

Susan Crane's analysis points to another embedded reflection of the Peasants' Revolt's assault on the tyranny of the written word in "The Wife of Bath's Prologue": she sees Alisoun's direct attack on Jankyn's "book of wykked wyves," literate culture's instrument of social control, as parallel to the uprising's attack on clerical culture. Citing a contemporary account of events in Cambridge during the revolt, she draws our attention to a report that "a certain old woman named Margaret Starre scattered the heap of ashes to the wind, crying, 'Away with the knowledge of clerks, away with it'" (qtd. in "The Writing Lesson of 1381" 215). She links that report with the Wife of Bath's ripping out the pages from her fifth husband's antifeminist tract (215-16).

But beyond the sheer fact of the Wife's rebellion against clerical power is Chaucer's recognition of how the exclusive right to interpret hallowed texts becomes the basis for clerical control: the right to say what the culture's central texts mean underpins the right to rule. Both the Miller and the Wife of Bath—he implicitly, she explicitly—challenge that right and in so doing weaken the ideological foundations of medieval society. As Crane argues:

> In staging the impossibility of speaking against literate paradigms, Chaucer makes the voicelessness of suppressed groups a subject rather than an unconsidered condition of his writing. He returns us to Sieyes's revolutionary formulation of what the third estate has been, "nothing," and what it wants, "to become something." Insubstantial as that expression of desire may be—desire for a "something" as yet unexperienced and unarticulated—its inscription in writing is a first recognition that those outside literate culture may indeed have something to say. ("The Writing Lesson of 1381" 217)

By presenting the Plowman as an idealized and silent icon who embodies central Christian virtues, Chaucer may be pointing out the failings of actual peasants, but he also, like Langland, undercuts their long-standing portrayal as quarrelsome and subhuman. Furthermore, by giving voices to such usually silenced figures as the Miller and the Wife of Bath, by giving them equal time to articulate their views—no matter what pieties they challenge nor how outrageously they do so, Chaucer, perhaps unwittingly, charts new territory.

CHAPTER EIGHT

All That Glitters: Trade, Industry, and the Money Economy

*A*mong the many changes that undermined the dominant class's chivalric ideology in the late medieval world, those in the economic sphere had the greatest direct impact on people's everyday lives. Those changes had their roots in the eleventh and twelfth centuries as Europe moved from a subsistence, mainly agrarian economy in which wealth was hoarded and raided to one that generated surpluses for both local and international trade. In the gift-based or exchange economy characteristic of the early medieval period's warrior societies, goods that were not consumed were stockpiled rather than invested, leaving the economy to languish. The shift toward investment that took place in the eleventh century set the stage for a major transition (Cipolla, *Before the Industrial Revolution* 160-64).

This transformation—which Robert Lopez characterizes as "the commercial revolution" (*The Commercial Revolution of the Middle Ages 950-1350* vii)—witnessed the growth of towns and cities, the revival of trade, and an increased reliance on a money, and credit, economy. It also created opportunities for social mobility, as accumulated wealth derived from trade rather than land allowed people to improve their status. "Every sector of social and economic life was transformed," Carlo Cipolla maintains. "Sets of values, personal circumstances and relations, types of administration, education, production, and exchange, all underwent drastic transformation" (122). However, because the era's conceptual framework did not readily integrate the new economic realities, the shifts exacted a psychological cost. Negative attitudes about engaging in trade lingered for centuries, and people worried that accumulating wealth would negate their chances for salvation.

After reviewing the nature of this revolution and the reasons for the moral disquiet it fostered, we shall be better able to assess Chaucer's attitude toward the whole world of commerce and to explore its portrayal in *The Canterbury Tales*. Chaucer himself had roots firmly planted in the merchant class, and his own family history aptly illustrates the dramatic rise in fortune and status that the changing economic environment made possible: in three generations his family moved from prosperous trading to a prestigious court position. An involved participant in London's business scene, Chaucer's father was a wine merchant whose mercantile success provided the financial basis for the poet's education and advancement as a civil servant (Pearsall, *The Life of Geoffrey Chaucer* 12). Chaucer spent his career on the periphery of court circles serving three kings; his son Thomas, however, became speaker in Parliament and one of the richest knights in the country, securing for himself a solid place at court. And Thomas's daughter, Alice, married the duke of Norfolk, who reached the pinnacle of power before losing both his position and his life in a political reversal (Pearsall, *Life* 276-82). Though Chaucer's career placed him in aristocratic circles where he might be expected to absorb the mindset of his social superiors, his perspective, especially in *The Canterbury Tales*, reveals his awareness of commerce's importance in society. Indeed his Januslike social position—his mercantile origins versus his aristocratic milieu—gave him a special vantage point from which to view his world, one which may have made him particularly sensitive to class distinctions (Pearsall, *Life* 245).

By Chaucer's time the commercial revolution was well underway, but Italy—not England—had been its seedbed. Never as feudalized as northern Europe, the Italian peninsula retained a rudimentary town structure even after Rome's decline. Located propitiously near the Byzantine and Islamic worlds—both more economically and culturally developed than Europe during the early medieval period—it could take advantage of the trading opportunities that arose when the Crusades sparked increased contact with those worlds. Commercial centers like Venice, Genoa, and Florence, responding to supply and demand, began trading on an ongoing rather than sporadic basis (Gilchrist, *The Church and Economic Activity* 24). "Capitalism was born in such places," John Gilchrist notes. "Expressed simply, this consisted of bringing labour and capital together in a more convenient form than that provided by the existing feudal relationships" (24).

Even in the northern land-based economy, trade played a significant role because a given estate or region could readily produce only part of what it needed or wanted for comfortable living (Postan

105). In northern Europe fairs constituted a major mechanism for facilitating exchanges. St. Denis near Paris was the home of the oldest fair, and various locations in Flanders—Bruges, Lille, Ypres—also hosted important ones. By the fourteenth century Paris and Bruges had virtually ongoing fairs, thus establishing themselves as centers of commerce (Little, *Religious Poverty and the Profit Economy in Medieval Europe* 11-12). However, most fairs were held at irregular intervals and focused primarily on agricultural products. With the economy's expansion in the thirteenth century a need arose for merchants who were free to concentrate on trade and for more frequent and more regular markets (Bolton, *The Medieval English Economy* 119-20). As a result, local markets increased significantly, becoming permanent fixtures in the economy. The heightened interest in trade increased travel, as people engaged in buying and selling goods undertook journeys to accomplish their ends (Little 12-13). Chaucer's "The Shipman's Tale" unrolls in this commercial framework: a merchant leaves his home in St. Denis to make purchases in Bruges, for which he arranges a loan in Paris.

Growing trade also encouraged existing towns to expand and new ones to develop. Traditionally, scholars have seen towns and cities as progressive in contrast to the more conservative, more backward rural areas. Cipolla, for instance, characterizes towns as "a new and dynamic world where people felt they could break their ties with the past, where people hoped they would find opportunities for economic and social advancement, and where there would be ample reward for initiative, daring, and hard work" (119). In this view, change emanates from urban areas. But revisionist historians maintain that juxtaposing a progressive urban environment against a backward rural one is misleading. Catharina Lis and Hugo Soly point out: "The basic weakness of this dualist thesis of opposition between town and country is that it completely ignores the decisive importance of the rural economy. . . . The essential precondition [for the growth of towns] . . . was increased quantity and disposability in agrarian production" (9). Citing economic historians like Rodney Hilton and J. L. Bolton, Lee Patterson concludes that cities were not anomalies in the medieval economy and that their growth was an effect rather than a cause of economic developments (*Chaucer and the Subject of History* 326). Wherever the impetus originated, towns became increasingly important centers of commerce, seeking freedom from feudal ties through charters obtained from lords and through court actions that sought political ends through monetary means (Bolton, *The Medieval English Economy* 123-27).

The increased use and importance of money played an important role in the commercial revolution: "it marked the recognition and use of money as tool instead of as treasure, the release of new types and of vast quantities of specie into circulation, and the appearance of new techniques for the expeditious handling of money" (Little 18). The shift toward money increased flexibility and mobility in financial transactions; for money is long-lasting, easy to store, and capable of being exchanged by strangers, who can rely on its agreed-upon value (33). With money's increased prominence came a reliance on credit, a development that dates back to the commercial revolution's earliest phase (Cipolla 160). Credit was important because it too increased the flexibility of merchants' transactions: by leaving more of their capital available, credit allowed merchants to engage in multiple enterprises at one time and to defer payment from their own customers, thus increasing trade (Bolton, *The Medieval English Economy* 302-3). In addition, credit relieved the pressure of having inadequate money supplies: "There simply would not have been enough money available for all transactions to be conducted in cash," Bolton maintains (303). Thus by the late medieval period an active credit system facilitated trading, providing an essential link in the economy's overall vitality.

Expanding trade and credit extensions also brought the need for more efficient accounting. As transactions became more complicated, older methods of tracking what one had and what one owed—like the paragraph form and the single-entry system—proved inadequate. Double-entry bookkeeping, which developed in Italy well before it spread elsewhere, made possible a much clearer accounting of debits and credits (de Roover, *Business, Banking and Economic Thought* 165). For instance, as merchant-traders' businesses expanded, they tended to send others on long journeys, preferring to oversee their ventures from home. Their agents, however, needed clear-cut guidelines and accurate records for rendering their accounts; the double-entry system helped both merchants and their agents communicate clearly with each other concerning profits and losses. "The great achievement of the Italian merchants, roughly between 1250 and 1400," according to Raymond de Roover, was to create "an integrated system of classification in which the pigeonholes were called accounts and which rested on the principle of dual entries for all transactions" (122-23). Ultimately the system provided much more than accurate bookkeeping: it became "a tool of management or control" (123) and promoted a clear and constant awareness of profits and losses—of the bottom line.

Thus money, credit, and double-entry bookkeeping all speeded transactions and encouraged trade. As opportunities and inducements for trade escalated, merchants' activities increased in number and kind. Initially their task was to bring goods and purchasers into closer proximity, but the problems related to doing so, especially on an international scale, often prodded them toward many other activities. For instance, merchants tended to specialize in certain goods; to guarantee a steady supply of merchandise, they sometimes underwrote the production of the goods they later sold or made necessary goods or equipment available (Thrupp, *The Merchant Class* 7-10). But their activities could range far beyond direct involvement in supporting the trades from which they made their profits. As Sylvia Thrupp points out: "Wherever there was gain to be had, there were merchants to bid for it or intrigue for it" (*The Merchant Class* 12).

Interestingly, in England wealthy merchants oriented their wealth more toward consumption and land acquisition than toward expanding commercial investments. The merchant class did not try to carve out its own identity; rather it sought to imitate the aristocracy. Indeed one reason that merchant families often disappeared after a few generations was that, like the Chaucer family, their sons usually did not continue the family business but used the wealth it generated to acquire land or to establish themselves in a profession (Bolton, *The Medieval English Economy* 144, 285). Social advancement exerted a more powerful pull than acquiring greater wealth.

Merchants eager to improve their financial standing or their social status—or both—could use marriage to achieve their goals. Successful merchants who valued social status or youthful beauty more than greater wealth could negotiate to win their chosen bride. On the other hand, a man who achieved modest business success might, through a carefully planned marriage, significantly improve his financial base (Thrupp, *The Merchant Class* 29). So important were the consequences of marrying well that choosing a spouse wisely became a commercial venture: "The young man looked around carefully for a match, made business-like inquiries about his proposed bride's wealth and was willing to pay commission on her dowry to a marriage broker" (Bolton, *The Medieval English Economy* 284).

In mercantile marriages women often achieved de facto parity with their husbands. Patterson maintains that "it was within the bourgeois context that the companionate marriage developed most fully in the Middle Ages, a development that in turn placed spousal relations in question" (*Chaucer and the Subject of History* 344). Not only could women provide capital for their husbands' businesses, they were also important resources within the marriage. Wives were expected to be careful monitors of household goods, managing their resources efficiently and overseeing affairs in their husbands' absence. A fortuitously preserved correspondence between a fourteenth century Italian couple—Francesco Datini, and his wife, Margherita—gives us a good window into a mercantile marriage. Away from his home in Prato for long periods of time, Francesco wrote detailed instructions to his wife on managing his goods and household—instructions that she usually carried out, though not without expressing her own views. Responding to his complaints, Margherita retorts: "It grieves me that everything is not as fit for you there as here, but it is natural that if one looks for trouble, one will find it. And sometimes it is good to experience a little discomfort, even if chiefly of the spirit; for what seems discomfort to us, would seem ease to many" (qtd. in Origo, *The Merchant of Prato* 168).

Women could also play a role in the successful operation of their husbands' businesses or operate their own, either as married women or, in a small minority of cases, as independent entrepreneurs (Thrupp, *The Merchant Class* 170). *The Book of Margery Kempe* records Margery's attempts at business enterprise:

> she [Margery speaks of herself in the third person] took up brewing, and was one of the greatest brewers in the town of N. for three or four years until she lost a great deal of money, for she had never had any experience in that business. . . . But yet she did not entirely give up the world, for she now thought up a new enterprise for herself. She had a horse-mill. She got herself two good horses and a man to grind people's corn, and thus she was confident of making her living. (44)

Chaucer's Wife of Bath, the only lay female among the pilgrims, also operates her own business and prospers at it: "Of clooth-makyng she hadde swich an haunt/She passed hem of Ypres and of Gaunt" (ll. 447-48). Indeed D. W. Robertson, Jr., argues that the Wife probably owned a fulling mill—thereby explaining how she attracted her last two young husbands—and that Chaucer's audience would have recognized the cloth trade as the source of her wealth ("'And for my land thus hastow mordred me?'" 410-14).

The Wife's involvement in cloth making highlights the fact that in England raw wool and finished cloth were the center of commercial activity; first one and then the other became England's main entry into the international market. England's ready supply of high-quality wool made it an early leader in the lucrative cloth industry. But once Flanders established itself as a prime producer of luxury fabrics in the thirteenth century, England, with its steady stream of desirable wool, found greater profit from exporting raw materials rather than finished cloth. Thus though merchants from Italy and southwest France actively traded in London, England's economy was most closely intertwined with that of Flanders throughout the late medieval period (Llyod, *The English Wool Trade* 1-59).

So important was the wool trade to both countries' economies that their rulers tried, with varying degrees of success, to manipulate it for both political and financial purposes. For example, Edward III—whom T. H. Lloyd characterizes as "woolmonger extraordinary" (vii)—relied heavily on that trade to gain a sound fiscal base for his military exploits in France because it gave him readiest access to needed funds. After bankrupting his Florentine lenders, he turned to resources nearer at hand: the English merchants over whom his right to curtail trade gave him some leverage (Lloyd 99-174). Edward also tried to use Flanders' reliance on English wool to force its alliance with England rather than with France (Waugh, *England in the Reign of Edward III* 67). His manipulation of the wool trade produced mixed results for his own policies, but by the end of the fourteenth century the English cloth industry enjoyed an upsurge while that of Flanders went into decline (Llyod 315-17).

Throughout this period the English and Flemish economies had many opportunities for cooperation. But they also experienced frequent periods of tension, as each country attempted to use trade to jockey for political and economic advantage. Sometimes those tensions erupted into open conflict; as we have seen in the preceding chapter, the Flemings became targets of the rebels' wrath during the 1381 uprising. It signaled some of the tensions resulting from changing economic conditions. For though England has been characterized as an "economic backwater" (Noonan, *The Scholastic Analysis of Usury* 191), it participated fully—though somewhat belatedly in comparison to Italy and the Low Countries—in the commercial revolution. Indeed as A. R. Bridbury argues, England's wool exports show no real signs of decline in the 1350s, thereby indicating that its recovery from the plague's impact must have been remarkably rapid ("The Black Death" 588).

As suggested earlier, the broad societal changes the commercial revolution fostered came with psychological costs: people regretted the weakening personal bonds that were, at least theoretically, the center of feudal relationships. "Thus life in the new profit economy,"

Lester Little observes, "raised acute problems involving impersonalism, money, and moral uncertainty" (19). One major problem was that ethical guidelines did not reflect the changes taking place in people's economic lives, thus creating anxiety about a person's chances for salvation. At issue were the Church's attitudes toward trade, money, acquiring material goods, and, especially, toward charging interest on loans. As moral theologians sought to bring people's economic practices within the religious sphere, they worked within a conceptual model still based on production for consumption rather than for trade (Tawney, *Religion and the Rise of Capitalism* 30-31). Indeed estates theory had no ready place for the increasingly numerous people—merchants, notaries, bankers, lawyers—engaged in trade and in all the professions it spawns. The conceptual problem went even deeper: market values introduced a relativistic standard of worth to a society whose belief system was grounded on absolutes (Patterson, *Chaucer and the Subject of History* 352).

Though most moralists conceded trade's legitimacy, they nevertheless saw it as suspect, if not downright harmful, because it encouraged undue emphasis on acquisition for its own sake. Honorius of Autun (ca.1080-ca.1156), contrasting the honest simplicity of agricultural toil with the commercial activity of merchants, argues that the latter have little likelihood of being saved because what they have is obtained unfairly (Little 38). And Thomas Aquinas, after distinguishing between theory and practice, "came to the discouraging conclusion that trade could be free from sin, but that it rarely was in actual practice" (de Roover 337). Behind their thinking lay a fundamental assumption: "that the danger of economic interests increased in direct proportion to the prominence of the pecuniary motives associated with them" (Tawney 33). Thus from a rigorist's point of view, merchants and their trading/financial activities were highly suspect. The simple reality of seeking profit as an end in itself, rather than as a reward for labor or as a means of meeting one's needs, was problematic (35).

Money itself was capable of provoking deeply ambivalent reactions: it was attractive and desirable for the ease and plenty it made possible, but it also had strongly negative associations. In *Piers Plowman* William Langland expresses his intense convictions about money's corrupting power in his portrayal of Lady Meed. As Derek Pearsall observes in his introduction to the poem: "He [Langland] shows with minute particularity in the Lady Meed passus (II-IV) how money dissolves all bonds of nature between man and man, and twists every relationship to its own remorseless ethic" (14). Money's potential for spiritual destruction made it threatening and repugnant, "a filthy and disgusting waste" (Little 34). That repugnance is evident in images associating money with excrement, as in the margins of Gothic manuscripts showing apes and humans excreting coins (34) and in the portrayal of a man "defacating a ducat" on a house at Goslar (Le Goff, *Your Money or Your Life* 34). Francis of Assisi, whose devotion to poverty was at the heart of his religious commitment, found money profoundly disgusting: according to a thirteenth-century text he advised his followers to "measure with one price of love, dung and money" (qtd. in Cook and Herzman 301). When one of his friars handled money that had been left as an offering:

> the holy Father [Francis] reproved him. . . . and bade him lift the money from the window with his mouth and convey it without the hedge of the dwelling, and put it with his own mouth on the dung of an ass. And all they that did see and hear were filled with very great fear, and from that time forth did despise money more than the dung of an ass, and daily were they animated with new examples to contemn it altogether. (qtd. in Cook and Herzman 301)

The negative attitude toward money appeared in shifting emphases concerning what constitutes humanity's greatest weakness. Whereas pride had traditionally taken first place as the sin to which people are most prone, moralists' denunciations after the eleventh century show that avarice begins to rival pride in seriousness (Little 36). Peter Damian (1007-72) signals this shift by maintaining that "Avarice is the root of all evil" (qtd. in Little 36). Chaucer's corrupt Pardoner makes that saying—*radix malorum est cupiditas*—the basis for all his preaching, well understanding how to exploit his congregation's uneasiness about wealth for his own enrichment and priding himself on his ability to move his auditors away from the very sin of which he is guilty. Other manifestations of malaise about wealth appear in the Romanesque portal sculpture at Moissac, which tells the biblical story of Dives, the rich man, who ignores the beggar Lazarus's request for help; their roles are reversed in the afterlife, when Lazarus rests in Abraham's bosom while demons torment Dives in hell (Little 37). The twelfth century also witnessed a surge of interest in the *Life of Saint Alexis*, an account of how an early Christian saint gave up all his wealth to live in poverty (Little 40). Medieval fascination with that kind of commitment culminates in the intense reaction that Francis of Assisi's rejection of his mercantile patrimony and mission to the poor aroused.

But while moralists looked at both trading and acquiring wealth with a suspicious eye, what they attacked most vigorously was usury: making a loan with a prefixed increase at the time of repayment, regardless of the risks or other circumstances involved. So stringent was the ban on usury that the Third Lateran Council (1179) decreed excommunication and denial of Christian burial for those who engaged in it (Noonan 19). Nor was the Church's position on money-lending for interest divorced from popular sentiments. Its teaching was not "the pious rhetoric of professional moralists" (Tawney 37); rather, it gave shape to a broad societal consensus. For in a subsistence economy people had little opportunity to save their resources for emergencies. When they had to borrow, they did so out of real need—in short-term, small-scale transactions rather than in high-finance deals. Naturally they resented anyone who sought to profit from that need. "The Church," Tawney sums up, "accepts this popular sentiment, gives it a religious significance, and crystallizes it in a system, in which economic morality is preached from the pulpit, emphasized in the confessional, and enforced, in the last resource, in the courts" (39).

The scholastic moral theologians who developed and articulated the Church's official position grounded their usury teachings on a few Old Testament passages that attack taking advantage of one's neighbors or countrymen in need and from Luke 6:35, where Jesus enjoins people to "lend freely, hoping nothing thereby" (qtd. in Le Goff, *Your Money or Your Life* 20-23). But biblical injunctions against usury were less significant in the evolving dogma than were attacks by Church fathers and councils (Noonan 11), though those prohibitions were directed at clerics (Gilchrist 63). Ultimately, however, the arguments that the scholastics marshaled against usury rested on a philosophical basis related to natural law rather than on purely theological grounds (Noonan 3). Aristotle's views about trade played a substantial role in forming those arguments. For him, introducing money as an exchange mechanism creates an insatiable, and unnatural, desire to acquire more, just for the sake of having more. Uneasy about all kinds of trade, Aristotle attacks usury because it is "the unnatural breeding of money from money" (47). What was for the Greek philosopher a comprehensive distaste for commercial transactions was focused for scholastic thinkers like Albert the Great and Thomas Aquinas specifically on lending money for interest (47). Aquinas's position on usury may be summarized as follows: "when a lender sells both the substance of money and the use of money . . . he in fact either sells something that does not exist or sells the same thing twice.

Such a transaction . . . whichever way it is described, is manifestly contrary to natural justice" (180). A central argument against charging interest was that to do so was in effect to sell time that no one but God owns. Moralists also argued that the lender who charges interest seeks to profit without exerting the requisite labor--in effect getting something for nothing (Le Goff, *Your Money or Your Life* 39-42). An additional argument was that seeking profit from money is unnatural and illegitimate because money is by nature incapable of reproducing itself (Kirschner, "Raymond de Roover" 27-28).

Dante follows the scholastics in treating usury as gravely wrong, including it among the sins of violence punished inside the walls of Dis, the infernal city. In *Inferno* XI, responding to Dante's query about how usury offends God's goodness, Virgil explains its sinfulness by drawing on both Aristotle and the Bible (ll. 97-111). He argues that both God and Nature intend for humans to prosper in relation to the work they expend; resorting to usury is sinful because it circumvents the natural connection between labor and reward, promising something for nothing. When he reaches the burning plain in *Inferno* XVII Dante encounters some of his fellow Florentines among the usurers, their eyes fixated on the pouches hung around their necks; leaving them all nameless, he uses heraldic insignia to identify them as belonging to the city's most notable families (ll. 52-57).

In the fully developed teachings on usury a number of important features appear. First, requiring any interest on money lent was considered usury and therefore sinful. Second, usury was seen as a sin against justice rather than against charity because it violates a person's right to property, a right that—though it might not be desirable in an unfallen world—is necessary for maintaining a peaceful social order in a fallen one. Third, because usury violates justice, the usurer must make restitution to the person from whom he has taken unlawful interest if he wishes to have his sin forgiven. Fourth, intention plays an important role in the strictures against usury: even hoping for or desiring to profit from a loan is sinful. Finally, charging more for credit sales than for cash sales also constitutes usury. Usury, in short, is like theft that deprives people of their rightful property (Noonan 14-29).

But despite Christianity's uneasiness about trade, money, and interest-taking, both moral theory and social practice arrived at some accommodation with what was becoming a societal given. For as Jacques Le Goff points out, Christianity faced a challenge to its survival in the new economic environment—a nascent capitalism: "At stake was the legitimization of lawful profit, which had to be differentiated from unlawful usury" (*Your Money or Your Life* 10). Making a distinction between the two might not have posed such a problem if moralists had grasped what now passes for a truism: time is money (Gilchrist 68). Still, many people did charge interest in spite of threats of damnation (Little 179). Though their behavior did not conform to the ethical standards rigorists set before them, commercially active Christians paid little attention to the usury teachings in such areas as credit purchases, bank deposits, and bills of purchase; often, complicated transactions involving different currencies and variations in the rate of exchange disguised interest attached to loans. However, because the risk factor came to be one justification for charging interest, the prohibitions probably did limit Christians with tender consciences from making small loans and probably increased the number of people involved in risk-taking ventures (Noonan 195).

Besides the practical accommodations that tradespeople arrived at, some theoretical modifications also occurred. Gradually attitudes toward money became less emotionally charged as, with the help of Aristotle's theory of social utility, moral theologians began to recognize it as a tool rather than as the embodiment of evil. Even Aquinas could see money "as a measure of the price of things and as a medium of exchange" (Little 178). Nor were the scholastics opposed to profit in itself (Noonan 32). Moralists were willing to distinguish between honest merchants, those who profited from their activity only enough to sustain themselves and their families, and dishonest ones, whose gains were disproportionate to their efforts or their needs. Moralists also conceded the merchants' right to a reasonable return for their labor. They also justified some return for risks involved in loans made for speculative enterprises. However, they continued to stress the importance of intention, being unwilling to exonerate anyone whose purpose was to stockpile wealth for its own sake (Little 178-79). Charging no more than the just price was an important concept in the moralists' accommodation of trade, but ultimately the just price meant the fair market price—what the market will bear (177).

Scholastic moralists ultimately developed a rationale that allowed for five circumstances which justified taking interest. Among them was (1) a penalty for late payment on a loan and (2) a charge to compensate for the possibility of greater return on another investment. Another reason justifying a charge was that in effect it constituted (3) a salary for labor expended—or the moneylender's travel, his accounting efforts, his handling of money as well as for the labor originally expended to obtain the money he subsequently lent. Finally, moralists introduced the notion of risk, arguing that the lender was entitled to (4) some compensation for assuming possible loss either through the borrower's default or (5) through the uncertainty of the enterprise (Le Goff, *Your Money or Your Life* 73-74). While providing greater latitude for economic activity, allowing exceptions made the ban on usury difficult to apply (Gilchrist 68) and increased uncertainty about permissible and forbidden behavior.

Furthermore, those who charged interest did not necessarily face major punishment. Both popular opinion and ecclesiastical sanction fell lightly upon those who prospered from shrewd trading and complicated business transactions that often disguised interest-taking. The Church reserved the severest penalty of excommunication for those who openly sought clients for their moneylending, rather than applying it to all who benefited, or hoped to benefit, from a loan. As Noonan observes, "manifest usury, entailing excommunication and social disgrace, was charged only against those publicly setting themselves up to lend money at profit, who made moneylending their trade"(191). Those whose business activities masked profit-taking on loans enjoyed much more favorable public opinion than professional moneylenders, who incurred both social disgrace and strong religious sanctions (191).

Besides expanding the parameters of allowable interest-taking, moralists found escape hatches that would allow for the usurers' eventual salvation. The still-developing doctrine of purgatory, for instance, posited an intermediate state between immediate salvation and eternal damnation. Le Goff points out, "For the usurer who was ready for final contrition, Purgatory was the hope and, soon, the quasi-certainty of being saved, of being able to have both his money, here below, *and* his life, his eternal life beyond the grave" (*Your Money or Your Life* 92). A person engaged in commerce might find postponing immediate paradisal bliss an acceptable price for the benefits of enjoying his wealth here below.

A stumbling block for the person counting on a deathbed repentance was the requirement for restitution. That task fell to family and friends, who had to offer penance and prayers for the deceased; in addition they had to compensate those from whom the usurer had profited or make contributions to worthy causes in his name. After an appropriate period of punishment in purgatory, such a man might eventually be saved (Le Goff, *Your Money or Your Life* 80-84). Caesarius of Heisterbach (1180-1240) recounts the story of a usurer from Liège who was denied Christian burial and whose wife successfully pleaded his cause with the clerical authorities by arguing, "whatever shortcomings there may have been in my husband, I, who am part of his flesh, will most gladly make up for these and give satisfaction to God for his sins" (qtd. in Le Goff, *Your Money or Your Life* 79). The husband's apparitions to his wife made clear that her prayers were being heard (79). Also, the Scrovegni Chapel in Padua—better known as the Arena Chapel—was an offering made by a notorious usurer's son who hoped that it would turn the key to paradise for his father. Giotto captures this motif in one of the chapel's panels, which depicts the petitioning usurer, chapel in hand, kneeling before the heavenly hosts and seeking admittance to their midst.

The younger Scrovegni's underwriting the Arena Chapel points to a significant shift in thinking: instead of direct restitution to the injured party—with all of the difficulties and potential embarrassment such a course entailed—a substitute or alternative reparation was gaining acceptance. St. Louis rejected this approach as the devil's work: "he entices great usurers and great robbers into giving to charity what they should restore to their victims" (qtd. in Le Goff, *Your Money or Your Life* 45). But by the thirteenth century the wealthy who had accumulated their fortunes through prohibited means were already moving toward philanthropy (Little 212): "The merchant-bankers were well on their way to assuming their role as patrons of charity," Little comments (213).

Another sign of ameliorating attitudes toward those engaged in commerce was the moralists' emphasis on mercantile virtues rather than vices. San Bernadino of Siena, for instance, moved beyond castigating sinful avarice by focusing on the qualities needed in a good businessman. Among the virtues Bernardino emphasized were honesty, trustworthiness, and directness. But the only justification he would allow for profit-making was its benefit to society—to the common good (de Roover 343-44). The emergence of urban merchant saints also signaled more positive attitudes toward merchants. As early as 1199 Innocent III canonized Omobono of Cremona, a merchant who supported himself and his wife by engaging in profit-making activities while living a life of prayerful devotion and service to the needy. He became Cremona's patron saint, whose statue graced the main entrance to the cathedral, next to the Virgin and Child (Little 215). Sixty years later Federigo Visconti, the archbishop of Pisa, expounding in one of his sermons, claimed Francis of Assisi himself as a merchant saint: "How pleasing it must be for merchants to know that one of their cohorts, St. Francis, was a merchant and was also made a saint in our time. Oh, how much good hope there must be for merchants, who have such a merchant intermediary with God" (217). Ironically St. Francis, who had repudiated his father's mercantile wealth to embrace a life of poverty, was invoked as "the patron and protector of merchants" (217).

Over the course of the late medieval period, then, commercially active Christians continued their pursuits and acquired substantial wealth while remaining relatively comfortable with their consciences (Gilchrist 30). Yet the moralists' lack of clarity and unanimity about exactly where to draw the line between allowable and sinful profit-making could be troubling. In spite of softening attitudes, the merchant's position in society long remained anomalous and suspect. Furthermore, having issues related to profit-making and moneylending increasingly shift "from the external forum of canon law to the internal forum of conscience" (Gilchrist 62) did not necessarily lower the anxiety level, especially in times of crisis. When that anxiety turned outward, it resulted in making scapegoats of the most visible targets: Jews often bore the brunt of Christians' guilt over their involvement in interest-producing activities. Jews, for their part, could engage in moneylending with a clear conscience because their scriptural injunctions barred taking interest from their own people but not from others. Being outsiders in the Christian community, they were free to charge interest (Le Goff, *Your Money or Your Life* 35-36). Their doing so, however, made them lightning rods for Christian resentment. For though Jews—who lived mostly in cities where commercial activity was centered—were definitely a minority among those engaged in moneylending, their participation was disproportionate to their numbers (Little 56). As identifiable outsiders, they absorbed Christian society's displaced guilt and anxiety as it moved inexorably toward a trade-based economy: (54-56). "The Jews functioned as a scapegoat for Christian failure to adapt successfully to the profit economy," Little concludes (55).

Anxiety about commercial activities could also turn inward, especially as death approached. The court of one's own conscience does not necessarily render the most lenient judgments. The heightened interiority characteristic of late medieval spirituality only intensified the tension that those who engaged in trade experienced when they contemplated meeting their God. Francesco Datini opened his ledgers with the invocation, "In the name of God and of profit" (Origo 9). But years of exhortations—from his wife, from his good friend, and from preachers—to concern himself with the state of his soul proved sufficiently unsettling to move him to write to one of his partners, "You take no account of time . . . and do not remember that you must die. . . . I do otherwise: I give more thought to how matters will go after my death, than I do to those of this world" (235).

Datini's comments suggest how important the moment of death could become. If usurers who repented at that moment could be saved, it became a highly dramatic struggle (Le Goff, *Your Money or Your Life* 74-78). Hieronymus Bosch's *Death and the Miser,* a late fifteenth-century painting in Washington's National Gallery, captures such a moment: it depicts a gaunt and debilitated man, lying on his deathbed at the deciding moment. Death enters the door, his arrow poised to strike. A demon, striving to capture a soul, tantalizes the dying man with a moneybag, while an angel attempts to direct his vision toward the crucified Christ. At the foot of the bed we see the miser at a earlier time, stashing away coins in a sack held open by demon-like creatures. In the foreground lie a knight's helmet, glove, and sword, which the miser has set aside, preferring to pursue monetary gain and thus dramatizing the moral shift from the pride associated with the warrior class to the avarice linked with the merchant class. Ominously, the trussed-up drapery that lies in the dying man's line of vision if he is to focus on the cross repeats the shape of the money pouch with which the demon is tempting him. In this case, the outcome remains unresolved, but the signs pointing toward salvation are not propitious.

Uneasiness about trade and finance was especially intense in conservative areas like England (Noonan 191). Given the shifting, ill-defined attitudes and the persistent malaise about the moral validity of trade, what evidence can we find concerning Chaucer's overall response to the world of commerce? As mentioned earlier, his roots were deeply planted in commercial soil, but he was certainly well versed in the moralists' condemnations, and he spent his adult life in a courtly environment where trade would be denigrated. Did Chaucer, like his contemporary William Langland, react with repugnance, or was he at ease with commerce and the values it fostered? Did his mercantile origins provoke a Francislike rejection of his heritage, or did it promote sympathetic understanding? As usual with this elusive poet, answers are not easy to find.

His early poems—the dream visions—are a courtly genre, and his finished masterpiece, *Troilus and Criseyde,* though set in ancient Troy, also reflects a courtly world and courtly values. That is not the case with *The Canterbury Tales,* however. The world of "getting and spending" is very much alive both in the tales and in the frame. Right from the "General Prologue" we are immersed in the world of commerce. Though the "Prologue" opens with traditional images from courtly dream visions—springtime, flowers, singing birds—it quickly shifts to Harry Bailly's tavern, where the innkeeper's eye for business underpins the terms of the storytelling contest that becomes the work's substance: the contest's reward, after all, will bring all the pilgrims back to the Tabard for a meal, and the greatest winner will be Harry when he collects the price of their dinners.

In the "Prologue's" portraits of individual pilgrims—among the most original elements in the *Tales*—Chaucer includes a broad societal range, while excluding those from the highest and lowest strata. Though he draws on the three-estates concept for his portrayals, the broad middle range makes up the vast majority of pilgrims, and he includes several figures—like the Franklin and the Merchant—whose status is not clear-cut in the fluid fourteenth-century environment. Furthermore, Chaucer pays considerable attention to money and to how each pilgrim obtains and spends it (Eberle, "Commercial Language and the Commercial Outlook" 161-162). Some critics, like Ruth Nevo, see the monetary references as part of an ironic attack on avarice ("Motive and Mask" 1-9). But unlike the satiric literature that makes such references to draw attention to moral flaws, Chaucer's treatment leaves the condemnations unspoken. Indeed as Patricia Eberle argues, there may not be any condemnation: "In the 'General Prologue' Chaucer is assuming for both his narrator and his audience a lively interest in the world of getting and spending money, the world of commerce. As narrator, he is neither praising nor condemning that commercial outlook; he is simply taking it for granted" (163).

Besides the pervasive commercial terminology, the "General Prologue" also refers to the Wife of Bath's involvement in trade and includes a composite portrait of five guildsmen. Both the Wife's portrait and that of the guildsmen stress concern about attire, display, and social positioning. In addition, two substantial portrayals of merchants appear in the *Tales:* the merchant-pilgrim who recounts the tale of Januarie and May and one of the central figures in "The Shipman's Tale."

The Merchant in the "General Prologue" remains an ambiguous figure: the narrator describes his attire—his "mottelee," his "Flaundryssh bever hat," "his bootes clasped fair and fetisly" (ll. 270-73); he mentions his trade-related activities—his sea-going travel and his moneychanging ("wel koude he in eschaunge sheeldes selle" l. 278) and his involvement with profit-seeking ("sownynge alwey th'encrees of his wynnyng" l. 275). Twice he describes him as "worthy" (ll. 279, 283), and he observes that "ther wiste no wight that he was in dette" (l. 280). But the significance of those comments remains shrouded in the narrator's characteristic irony.

Clearly the Merchant is not one of the idealized pilgrims. But the extent to which Chaucer intends an attack on his values and activities remains an open issue. Some readers see a very negative person—not only materialistic but usurious and dishonest; others see a surprisingly neutral account of a figure whom moralists were apt to attack much more vigorously. Jill Mann points out that many details in the Merchant's portrait have roots in the satiric tradition that stereotypes merchants as guilty of greed and cunning, willing to exploit others, even the poor, for their own gain. But though a moralistic tradition lies behind much of the language Chaucer chooses to depict the Merchant, he does not exploit it in the usual manner, leaving out, for instance, any mention of a victim (Mann, *Chaucer and Medieval Estates Satire* 99-103). On the other hand, Paul Olson sees Chaucer's overall presentation of the Merchant and his world as a pervasive critique of commercial values: he argues that by associating the Merchant with the Wife of Bath and the Franklin, Chaucer links their tales with "growing controversies over the effects of commerce on the values of churchmen and laity" (39). He sees all three as belonging to a new "sect" of Epicureanism whose values center on an unabashed materialism, which leads to neglect of the common good, a development with serious spiritual consequences: "Where no one seeks anything behind the material surfaces, life loses its divine purpose" (275).

But aside from the overall negative aura that some moralists associated with any engagement with trade, one cannot easily prove the Merchant guilty of any prohibited activity when assessing his actions against contemporary business practices. Kenneth Cahn's study of the foreign exchange concludes by exonerating him of usury or moneylending: "It is certain that he was neither a usurer nor a speculator" ("Chaucer's Merchants and the Foreign Exchange" 91). Explaining that "in the Middle Ages to sell shields meant to borrow sterling" (82), Cahn connects the reference to the Merchant's engaging in such activity (l. 278) to his participating in the merchants' exchange—a legal activity: basically it meant that someone surrendered funds at one location and picked up their equivalent at another time and place. Because the value of the money differed at the two locations, due to shifts in the rate of exchange, such transactions often entailed gain for one person and loss for the other. Both parties, the seller and the buyer, faced a measure of risk, but generally the seller was at a disadvantage; what he gained was a safe transfer of funds and financial fluidity during the exchange. Chaucer's Merchant was an able dealer in this fluid medieval market (Cahn 83-115). Though Wight Martindale questions some aspects of Cahn's analysis, he concurs in seeing the Merchant as an upright participant in the commercial world and interprets his indebtedness—which some see as a sign of hypocrisy—as normal for one engaged in trade: "Chaucer's Merchant is honest, innovative, and successful in a very competitive business, doing what many other businessmen did, but perhaps a little better" ("Chaucer's Merchants" 314).

Turning to the merchant in "The Shipman's Tale," we again encounter someone engaged in complicated financial exchanges. Before leaving his home in Saint Denis to go to Bruges to purchase goods that he will later sell, he makes the precariousness of his business clear to his wife:

> For of us chapmen, also God me save,
> And by that lord that clepid is Seint Yve,
> Scarsly amonges twelve tweye shul thryve
> Continuelly, lastynge unto oure age. . . .
> And therfore have I greet necessitee
> Upon this queynte world t'avyse me,
> For everemoore we moote stonde in drede
> Of hap and fortune in oure chapmanhede.
> (ll. 226-29; 235-38)

In this deal he does encounter higher-than-expected prices, requiring him to arrange a loan in Paris. As Cahn observes, "The French merchant was quite wealthy and usually solvent, but at one particular instance (through an unexpected price rise) he had to borrow a sum of money which he subsequently and quickly paid" (118). In this transaction, however, he comes out a thousand francs ahead and goes home "murie as a papejay" (l. 339).

Some critics assess this merchant negatively, arguing that he is "a financial entrepreneur—not a money lender, not a banker, not a tradesman-merchant, but someone who derived a significant part of his income through the newly flourishing fourteenth-century money market" (Hahn, "Money, Sexuality, Wordplay, and Context" 238). In this view, the complicated business transactions in which the merchant engages become the means by which he disguises his usurious practices (239). But a number of recent critics present a much more positive view. Pearsall, for instance, stresses the merchant's virtues: "Indeed, the merchant, and the capitalist values for which he stands, are given an unprecedentedly measured and sympathetic treatment. . . . He is friendly without being obsequious, generous without being foolishly indulgent, careful without being mean" (*Life* 252). Patterson sees the tale as providing "a justification for the commercial life" (*Chaucer and the Subject of History* 352) and argues that it eschews blaming social ills on mercantile activity: "Specifically, it refuses to explain the economic order in terms of a culpable mercantilism whose motives and morals can then serve as the efficient cause of deplorable social effects" (356).

Chaucer also uses this tale, and other passages throughout the *Tales,* to explore the relationship between commerce, marriage, and sexuality. In "The Man of Law's Tale" Syrian merchants bring Custance's beauty and virtue to the attention of Alla, their Muslim lord. In "The Merchant's Tale" once Januarie has decided to marry, he shops for a bride in the market of his mind, mentally picking through possible candidates like so many pieces of meat; his wealth makes it possible, in effect, to buy for himself the young bride of his choice. Discussing this scene, Priscilla Martin notes that "the image of the mirror in the marketplace . . . conflating the imaginative and the commercial exposes the economic basis of romance which romantic conventions in their purest form conceal" (*Chaucer's Women* 104). For in societies that deny women economic power, marriage becomes a form of prostitution: sexuality is the only commodity that women can readily exploit: "A way for a woman to improve her economic position is therefore to sell her sexuality. She can play with the system by marrying. She can play against it by trying to increase her own independent power. Prostitution, an illegitimate inversion of approved sexual activity, neatly combines both methods" (Martin 82)

The clerical concept of the marriage debt (see Chapter Ten)— the term used to express each partner's responsibility to respond to the other's sexual needs and desires—provides a conceptual basis for applying a commercial framework to sexual relationships (Martin 96). The Wife of Bath—who in her first three marriages was in a situation similar to May's in "The Merchant's Tale"—exploits that interchangeability, making very explicit the commercial basis of her marriages: what she pays her old husbands in sexual terms she collects in financial ones:

> Namely abedde hadden they meschaunce:
> Ther wolde I chide and do hem no plesaunce;
> I wolde no lenger in the bed abyde,

If that I felte his arm over my syde,
Til he had maad his raunson unto me;
Thanne wolde I suffre hym do his nycetee.
And therfore every man this tale I telle,
Wynne whoso may, for al is for to selle;
With empty hand men may none haukes lure.
For wynnyng wolde I al his lust endure,
And make me a feyned appetit. (ll. 407-17)

By middle age the Wife seems to have been able to broker herself into a position of secure prosperity. "Her wealth comes from several sources," Martin points out. "She has gained money from her marriages, by the traditional male route of annexing the spouse's property and by the traditional female route of widowhood. . . . She is also running a business as a clothmaker" (92). By the time she married her fourth and fifth husbands she was in a financial position to command her choice. Robertson's exegetical analysis makes Chaucer's treatment of the Wife a means of attacking commercial values ("'And for my land thus' hastow mordred me?'" 416). Stewart Justman concurs, maintaining that Chaucer uses the Wife's outrageousness to express medieval society's negative attitudes toward trade: "In the Wife of Bath's plea for freedom to transact love and possess husbands . . . Chaucer burlesques the clamorous economic desires of men. So it is that the Wife's discourse on the suspect-but-reluctantly-tolerated institution of marriage evokes the also suspiciously permitted pursuit of profit. Sexual motives map onto economic ones" ("Trade as Pudendum" 347).

"The Shipman's Tale" also explores the link between sexuality and finance: the plot turns not so much upon the merchant's business transactions as on the way his wife is able to negotiate the commodity of her sexuality to profit all parties involved. She tells her husband's lecherous friend, Don John, the monk, that for a hundred francs she will satisfy his desires. The monk borrows that sum from the merchant, gives it to the wife, and receives her favors in exchange. Subsequently the monk informs the merchant that he has repaid the loan to the wife in the merchant's absence. Confirming that the monk has given her such a sum, the wife says she has spent it all, thinking it was an expression of gratitude for their frequent hospitality, not repayment for a loan. Noting her husband's discomfiture, however, she promises that she will compensate him in bed:

But sith I se I stonde in this disjoynt,
I wol answere yow shortly to the poynt.

> Ye han mo slakkere dettours than am I!
> For I wol paye yow wel and redily
> Fro day to day, and if so be I faille,
> I am youre wyf; score it upon my taille,
> And I shal paye as soone as evere I may. (ll. 411-17)

In this tale, William Woods maintains, the wife is the center of action, and she "embodies the conflicts inherent in a marriage assimilated to the mercantile imperative of buying and selling and 'quid pro quo'" ("A Professional Thyng" 139). As the plot evolves, the wife follows in the footsteps of her merchant-husband, besting him at his own game by turning her sexual favors into a commodity (Woods 142). She uses her sexuality to gain parity with her husband in a world that treated women like commodities and circumscribed their economic power, for "the hard truth remains that this merchant's wife is not authorized to spend on her own initiative" (148).

Other critics cast a more benign eye on the tale. According to Thomas Hahn, it establishes "a peculiar, yet significant and satisfying union of money and sexuality" ("Money, Sexuality, Wordplay, and Context" 235). Indeed Woods points out that the tale highlights that connection through the merchant's transformation from an inadequate sexual partner prior to his successful business venture to a vigorous one upon his return: "He proves his manhood by using his borrowed money as a plough" (145). In this commercially grounded world everybody profits: the monk satisfies his lust; the wife pays off her debt for some finery; and the merchant—though he is out a hundred francs that he can well afford to spare—enjoys a willing sexual partner. In short, as Patterson observes, "Somehow, by a process we can only with difficulty specify, the very fact of exchange has produced a surplus value: something has come of nothing" (*Chaucer and the Subject of History* 349).

Thus though critics of an exegetical bent see the tale as a cynical exposé of commercialism and sensuality, several recent critics come to more positive conclusions. Unlike Robertson and Justman, Woods and Patterson see Chaucer's linking of women, sexuality, and money as a way of expressing his perception that women are in some way societally liberating. Patterson also argues that the merchant's and Januarie's willingness to accept their wives' exculpatory accounts of their behavior reveals not so much reprehensible gullibility as the open-hearted trust necessary for successful commercial exchange (*Chaucer and the Subject of History* 358). In his biography of Chaucer,

Pearsall finds that the poet eschews the moralists' all-out condemnations of commercial activity:

> Chaucer views this world, of exchanges and equivalences, the London that he knew, with a remarkable acuteness and an equally remarkable lack of outrage. . . . On the contrary, Chaucer seems hardly to raise an eyebrow at economic practices which still incurred widespread ecclesiastical censure and public condemnation. (*Life* 250-51)

Given his background and his milieu, Chaucer would have encountered a wide range of attitudes toward the commercial revolution and its values. While critical opinion about his own views remains divided, a significant body of recent work sees him as ready and, if not to totally embrace, at least to recognize positive values in the commercial milieu that gave him birth.

IV.

GENDER AND SEXUALITY

CHAPTER NINE

The Face in the Mirror:
What Manner Woman?

*I*f, as we have seen in Chapter Seven, late medieval culture confronted pressures from a restive peasantry beginning to question the social theories that kept it subordinate, it also faced tension resulting from a pervasive malaise concerning women's proper role in Christian society. As Clarissa Atkinson comments, "The relationship of women to Christianity has never been simple, and it certainly was not simple in medieval times. The messages were loud and numerous, but not consistent" (*The Oldest Vocation* 6). The intense gender-related rhetoric of a centuries-old clerical tradition polarized medieval women into creatures of supreme virtue or extreme vice—with the emphasis usually falling firmly on the negative. Women were either virginal Marys—the embodiment of every perfection—or seductive Eves—the source of every evil and temptation. For though the twelfth-century Marian cult and the concomitant cult of the courtly lady counterbalanced the clerical tradition's negative thrust, they did not significantly undermine its deep-seated misogyny. Thus when a medieval woman sought her own features in her mind's mirror, she found reflected there a preexisting pattern that patriarchal culture had already shaped.

Retracing the roots of these polarizing attitudes and their impact on late medieval perceptions will prepare us to explore the problematic aspects of Chaucer's portrayal of women. Then we may ask ourselves whether he fully shared his culture's misogynistic attitudes or whether, to some extent, he transcended them. For by Chaucer's era patriarchal social structures were still very much in place, but, as with so many aspects of traditional medieval culture, a dialogue concerning their underpinnings was underway: an increasingly laicized Christianity struggled to reconcile women's conflicting images with the lived experience of both sexes. By the fifteenth century Christine de

Pizan—"one of the few true feminists before the modern era" (Gies, *Women in the Middle Ages* 10) and the first woman to earn income from a literary career—launched a counterattack on a famous misogynistic text: Jean de Meun's section of the *Roman de la rose*. She thereby ignited an intense cultural debate known as the *querelle de la Rose* ("dispute concerning the Rose"), which participated in the more intense and protracted *querelle des femmes* ("dispute concerning women").

Chaucer, who had extensive, long-lasting connections with powerful women at court, introduces into his work a *querrelle* of his own. He had an "apparently lifelong engagement with the woman question" (Hansen, *Chaucer and the Fictions of Gender* 10). To explore that question Chaucer was negotiating between two literary traditions: the Ovidian one deriving from the *Heroides*, which explores the suffering of women wronged by unfaithful men, and the antifeminist one, which stereotypically focuses on women's faults (Mann, "Chaucer and the 'Woman Question'" 174). In *The Canterbury Tales* "the woman question" is a pervasively interlaced thematic thread: the rivalry between the Wife of Bath's and the Clerk's views extends and deepens the combativeness evident in the Knight's and the Miller's competing class perspectives. Beneath the tensions in that rivalry two questions reverberate throughout Chaucer's poetry and throughout his age: the question the arrogant Roman official Almalchius poses to Saint Cecile in "The Second Nun's Tale"—"what maner womman artow?" (1. 424)—and the question the rapist Knight in "The Wife of Bath's Tale" must rightly answer to save his life—"what thyng is it that wommen moost desiren (?)" (l. 905). Indeed, as Lee Patterson suggests, "the ambivalence toward women is one aspect of a nexus of unresolved tensions endemic to medieval culture as a whole: between, for instance, history and apocalypse, character and vocation, nature and grace" ("'For the Wyves love of Bathe'" 659).

Central in shaping Christian society's attitudes toward women were Biblical images and concepts. The Genesis account of humanity's creation played a pivotal role, establishing the outline within which the feminine stereotype's more sharply defined features took shape. Significantly, Genesis presents two separate accounts of woman's coming into being. In the first—which R. Howard Bloch says has been subject to "cultural amnesia" (*Medieval Misogyny* 22)— God creates the two sexes concurrently (1: 27). The second account, however, firmly established itself in the Christian imagination. In it Eve is created from Adam's rib in response to his desire for a suitable companion. This account posits the male as primary, the female as ancillary: "For the woman of the Yahvist version . . . assumes, within the founding articulations of gender in the first centuries of Christianity, the burden of all that is inferior, debased, scandalous, and perverse" (Bloch 25). Following quickly upon the creation account, that of the temptation and fall makes woman the first to succumb to the serpent's seductive rhetoric; Adam's trespass responds to her initiative, thereby establishing another predominant trait in the traditional portrait: woman as the temptress/seductress who leads man astray from the godly obedience and devotion that would characterize his life were it not for her false allure. Augustine allegorized this version of the fall to represent the typical human yielding to sin: "Whenever Eve, or human appetite, perceives the apple, or the inherently beautiful object, the power of suggestion, or the serpent, may cause her to wish to possess it; having succumbed to suggestion, she may then corrupt Adam, or reason, so that a sin is committed" (Heinrichs, "Tropological Woman in Chaucer" 209). Chaucer's draws on this interpretation in "The Parson's Tale" to link Adam's primal sin with any mortal sin humans may commit (Heinrichs 209-10). Thus the exegetical tradition strongly associates women with carnal appetite.

Other scriptural women such as Job's wife, who after his final losses urges him to "curse God, and die" (Job 2: 9), and Delilah, who betrays the sleeping Samson to his enemies, reinforced the view of women as seductresses who lead men away from God or expose them to danger. So too did the story of Solomon, reputed for his wisdom, who incurred divine wrath because he succumbed in his old age to the temptations of foreign wives who "turned his heart to follow other gods" (1 Kings 11: 4). Also the Book of Proverbs, in its sharp dichotomizing between the faithful and the false woman, Wisdom and Folly, anticipates the Christian juxtaposition of Mary and Eve. Indeed scripture frequently portrays the Hebrew people's violations of their covenant with Yahweh, often involving worship of their neighbors' fertility goddesses, as sexual transgressions women instigated. In Proverbs the father's advice to his son warning him away from the seductive woman underscores the connection biblical writers established between sexual and religious infidelity:

> It [discretion] will save you from the adulteress,
> from the loose woman with her smooth words,
> who has forsaken the partner of her youth
> and forgotten the covenant of her God;
> for her house is the way down to death,
> and her course leads to the land of the dead. (2: 1618)

In the Christian era women remained equally problematical. A tantalizing passage from Paul holds out the vision of a world in which divisions and distinctions between the sexes are wiped out: "All baptized in Christ, you have all clothed yourselves in Christ, and there are no more distinctions between . . . male and female, but all of you are one in Christ Jesus" (Gal. 3: 28). Furthermore, women played important roles both in Jesus's public ministry and in the early Church (McNamara, *The New Song* 7-65). But as Barbara Newman comments, "Egalitarian praxis barely survived beyond the immediate circle of Jesus and his friends, except in a few fiercely repressed and marginalized groups" (*From Virile Woman to WomanChrist* 3-4). For the late antique period's intense otherworldliness and rejection of the flesh strongly influenced Christian attitudes toward women, fostering the cult of virginity that became strongly embedded in Christian thinking.

Striving to achieve spiritual perfection by denying their sexuality, celibate males projected onto women all their fears about their own weaknesses and the tensions resulting from their sexual repression. For instance, Athanasius's *The Life of Anthony*, an influential account of conversion to the ascetic life, records the saint's struggle with temptation as follows: "The beleaguered devil undertook one night to assume the form of a woman and to imitate her every gesture, solely that he might beguile Anthony" (34). Jerome, another influential ascetic voice, reports how, even in the midst of his desert regime, images of women tormented him: "Now, although in my fear of hell I had consigned myself to this prison, where I had no companions but scorpions and wild beasts, I often found myself surrounded by dancing girls!" (qtd. in Blamires, *Woman Defamed and Woman Defended* 74). Tertullian, an early third-century commentator, attacked women's corrupting ways in sweeping terms: "*You* are the devil's gateway . . . *you* are the first deserter of the divine law, *you* are she who persuaded him whom the devil was not valiant enough to attack. *You* destroyed so easily God's image, man. On account of *your* desert—that is, death—even the Son of God had to die" (qtd. in Rogers, *The Troublesome Helpmate* 15). The clerical tradition portrayed women as a threat to society, "an active negative force" (Farmer, "Persuasive Voices" 519). As "the devil's gateway"—their bodies a beautiful covering that disguises the spiritual putrification that lies within—women unleash the forces of chaos. Indeed many Church fathers projected onto women what they saw as the most threatening, problematic aspects of human nature. As Katharine Rogers comments, "Under the guidance of the Fathers, Christian literature became misogynistic to a degree unequaled in the Western world before or since" (21).

While patristic writers railed against women's sensuality, they also reduced women to purely sexual beings intended only for reproduction, which they denigrated as disgusting and dirty (Rogers 22). Women exist to reproduce—else another man would have been a better companion for Adam. Yet reproduction mires women in physicality, tying them to the material world from which Christianity promises deliverance. If body and soul comprise human beings, then the male absorbs the latter while the female is relegated to the former. In the patristic framework "the flesh becomes gendered as specifically feminine" (Bloch 46). Thus appears the standard medieval dichotomy between the rational male and the sensual/emotional female, one that underlies the hierarchical scheme that justifies subordinating one to the other, "for reason governs the senses and the soul governs the body" (Lucas, *Woman in the Middle Ages* 5).

Another target for the clerical attack on women was their purported interest in ornamentation, lavish dress, cosmetics—anything associated with altering nature and creating an attractive, but deceptive, exterior. For beneath that alluring exterior lies a disgusting carnality. A patristic writer in the Eastern Church, John Chrysostom, apparently forgetting that skin functions similarly for males, admonishes: "If men could see beneath the skin, the sight of women would make them nauseous. . . . Since we are loath to touch spittle or dung even with our fingertips, how can we desire to embrace such a sack of dung?" (qtd. in Dalarun, "The Clerical Gaze" 20).

Women's pleasing surface at once explains their seductiveness and underscores their superficiality. Thus eschewing ornamentation both prevents women from leading men into sin and punishes them for their sinfulness. Tertullian, for instance, advises women to downplay their attractiveness; among the practices he attacks are tinting clothes, dyeing hair, using cosmetics, and wearing jewelry (Lucas, *Woman in the Middle Ages* 21-22). Feminine ease at creating a deceptive surface makes it difficult to assess women accurately. Jerome, for instance, laments the problems of choosing a wife; reducing women to market commodities, he warns:

> Notice too that in the case of a wife you cannot pick and choose: you must take her as you find her. . . . Horses, asses, cattle, dogs, even slaves of the smallest worth, clothes, kettles, wooden seats, cups, and earthenware pitchers, are first tried and then bought: a wife is the only thing that is not shown before she is married for

fear she may not give satisfaction. (qtd. in Blamires, *Woman Defamed and Woman Defended* 70-71)

Clerical misogynists also linked women's seductiveness to their use of language, roundly and at great length attacking women for their talkativeness, as is evident in Tertullian's *Ad uxorem* ("To Wives"): "Their loquaciousness leads to the use of words offensive to modesty . . . and their prurient gossip is responsible for inciting others to engage in the lustful conduct which such talk exemplifies" (qtd. in Wilson and Makowski, *Wykked Wyves and the Woes of Marriage* 39). This passage suggests that women's speech is not merely prolific but enticing and seditious, once again recalling the original revolt against divine ordinance (Bloch 15).

Feminine rhetoric's seductiveness and the ease with which women lead and are led astray became prime justifications for denying them the right to teach or preach. Drawing on the First Epistle to Timothy, clerics insisted on controlling women by keeping them silent: "Their role is to learn, listening quietly and with due submission. . . . they should keep quiet. For Adam was formed first, then Eve" (2: 11-13). In 1 Corinthians Paul links this prohibition specifically to women's speech at public gatherings: "As in all congregations of God's people, women should keep silent at the meeting. They have no permission to talk, but should keep their place as the law directs. If there is something they want to know, they can ask their husbands at home. It is a shocking thing for a woman to talk at the meeting" (14: 34-36). Some thirteenth century Parisian theologians, however, tempered this negativism; they recognized that women led the era's heightened lay spirituality and that devout wives might well be able to have a positive influence on their husbands. For instance, Thomas of Chobham argues that women should use their persuasive skills, their sexual allure, and even their trickery to bring their avaricious husbands to a more generous frame of mind (Farmer 517).

Chaucer provides several accounts of women's exerting a positive moral influence through persuasive speech. For example, Cecile in "The Second Nun's Tale" assumes an evangelical role: she converts her husband, her brother-in-law, and numerous Roman officials, and she forthrightly challenges her judge's values. In "The Tale of Melibee" Prudence plays a didactic role: she lectures her husband at length about eschewing revenge and showing patience and mercy to his enemies, ultimately persuading him to accept the wisdom of her views. Even the long-suffering Griselde in "The Clerk's Tale" seizes the opportunity to advise her husband about treating his new wife more kindly than he has treated her. Of course, the Wife of Bath, claiming experience as her chief authority, most forcefully asserts her right to speak her mind. For a performance that radically modifies clerical teachings about human sexuality, she earns the Pardoner's ironic praise for being "a noble prechour" (WBP, l. 165). And the Hag in her tale actually functions in the way Thomas of Chobham envisioned: she uses the marital bed, though not yet her sexual allure, for her much-needed efforts to bring her recalcitrant and boorish husband to a proper appreciation of spiritual values. Her sermon on true "gentillesse" helps him finally to realize his aged spouse's inner worth, thereby paving the way for his winning a faithful *and* beautiful wife.

Despite some recognition that women could employ speech for positive moral purposes, clerical assessments of women's role were mostly negative. The misogynistic elements Christianity derived from biblical and patristic roots received substantial reinforcement from classical sources as well. Christian allegorists made Circe, the seductive enchantress who transforms Odysseus's men into swine, an apt counterpart to the biblical Eve, as a female capable of reducing men to their animal nature and depriving them of their reason. She became "a kind of Eve raised to a higher power, a demonic figure personifying the linkage between the feminine, the natural, and the deadly. . . . the figure of Circe fit in remarkably well with Christian doctrines concerning the nature of women and sexuality that the early church fathers promulgated during this period and passed on to the Middle Ages" (Yarnall, *Transformations of Circe* 79).

The Siren, another temptress from classical mythology, was also portrayed as seeking to ruin men. Marbod of Rennes, a twelfth-century commentator, warns: "Turbulent Charybdis, who sucks in and draws to its death everything near her, bears female form. The Siren is also like this: she entices fools by singing lovely melodies, draws them towards her once they are enticed, and when they are drawn in she plunges them into the annihilating abyss" (qtd. in Blamires, *Woman Defamed and Woman Defended* 102). Dante portrays the Siren in *Purgatorio* XIX when the pilgrim lets down his guard in a dream. She appears disgusting at first, but his gaze slowly transforms her into a creature of delight. Spurred by an unnamed lady, Virgil intervenes to reveal the Siren's true nature: "L'altra prendea, e dinanzi l'aprìa/fendendo i drappi, e mostravami 'l ventre:/quel mi svegliò col puzzo che n'uscìa." ["He seized the other and laid her bare in front, tearing her clothes, and showing me her belly. That awoke me with the stench that came from her."] (ll. 31-33). Thus both Circe and the Siren reinforce the medieval image of woman as seductress/temptress.

The classical philosophical tradition also fueled misogynistic attitudes. Kerstin Aspegren draws its rendering of women in bold strokes: "*Womanly* was used as a synonym for imperfect and evil, manly for perfect and good (*The Male Woman* 11). Aristotle's teachings, when they entered the mainstream of European philosophy in the thirteenth century, reinforced official misogyny's already strong current. He contrasts *form*—the active, defining principle in any entity—and *matter*—the passive element that form shapes, equating form with the male, matter with the female:

> An animal is a living body, a body with Soul in it. The female always provides the material, the male that which fashions the material into shape. . . .Thus the physical part, the body, comes from the female, and the Soul from the male, since the Soul is the essence of a particular body. . . . we should look upon the female state as being as it were a deformity, though one which occurs in the ordinary course of nature. (qtd. in Blamires, *Woman Defamed and Woman Defended* 40-41)

In discussing the relationship between a man and a woman, Aristotle maintains that their friendship resembles that between an aristocrat and his social inferior, thereby justifying the man's deriving greater benefit from the relationship to bring it into better balance (Aspegren 46-47). Not surprisingly, because friendship must exist between equals, he doubts the possibility of true friendship between marital partners (Wilson and Makowski 19). Deeply influenced by Aristotle, Thomas Aquinas advances parallel ideas; he contends, for instance, that a child owes the father greater love than the mother (Blamires, *Woman Defamed and Woman Defended* 47). Farmer sums up the relationship between Aristotle's and Aquinas's views on women as follows: "While Aquinas mitigated Aristotle's assessment of women as defective men, he nevertheless followed Aristotle in claiming that woman's rational capacities were inferior to man's and in suggesting that her inferior reason was the result of her more feeble body. Woman's weaker intelligence, Aquinas believed, affected her moral behavior and justified her subjection to men" (520).

The Stoic philosophical tradition, which emphasized the need for maintaining rational control at all times and for avoiding the distractions and emotional upheaval resulting from passionate involvement with women, also contributed to misogynistic attitudes. This tradition fostered the conviction that women, with their sexual blandishments and their domestic demands, distract the philosopher from higher and worthier pursuits, causing even the wisest to go astray. A thirteenth-century fabliau entitled *The Lay of Aristotle* highlights woman's ability to undermine reason: the great philosopher allows Phyllis to ride him like a horse—often a symbol of sensuality—to obtain her sexual favors. Depictions of this scene in secular art, showing the wise man on all fours, became very popular (Kolve, *Chaucer and the Imagery of Narrative* 246-47). Jehan Le Fevre's observations about this famous incident capture the opposition between women and wisdom that characterizes the medieval clerical tradition:

> For a woman surmounted all of these [philosophical works] in mounting him and conquered the master of logic. . . . The hussy used him as a horse and spurred him on like a female ass. She lifted her crotch far too high when she rode the male. The governor was governed and the roles of the sexes reversed, for she was active and he passive, willing to neigh under her. . . . Never had such a thing been seen before: the woman was the mounted knight and the man, with a halter under his hoary beard, was the horse that carried the burden. (qtd. in Blamires, *Woman Defamed and Woman Defended* 180-81)

Misogynistic attitudes shaped not just men's but women's attitudes; the letters of Héloïse, the twelfth-century abbess whose youthful love affair with the philosopher Abelard became legendary, reveal how, ironically, Héloïse paid for her privileged status as an educated woman by absorbing the clerical culture's pervasive misogyny. Lamenting the castration Abelard suffered because of her uncle's desire for vengeance even after their marriage, she cries out: "What misery for me—born as I was to be the cause of such a crime! Is it the general lot of women to bring total ruin on great men?" (*The Letters of Abelard and Héloïse* 130). She proceeds to conjure up the standard roll call of ruinous females so dear to the clerical misogynists—Eve, Delilah, Solomon's seductress, Job's wife—and concludes, "The cunning arch-tempter well knew from repeated experience that men are most easily brought to ruin through their wives. . . ." (131). Héloïse's self-condemnation dramatically highlights the power of cultural conditioning. A brilliant young woman— seduced by a man twice her age, a man who had been entrusted with the responsibility for her education, a man by whom she conceived and bore a child whom she had to leave in others' care, a man who manipulated her into a celibate life she did not want—casts herself stereotypically as the ruinous temptress.

Counter to this negative clerical rhetoric was another strand that focused on Mary—whose presence in the New Testament's canonical texts is minimal—as a pinnacle of earthly perfection (McNamara, *The New Song* 14). The roots of Marian devotion lie firmly in the cult of virginity, which took a strong grip in early Christianity. Indeed the emphasis on virginity most probably generated the cult of Mary rather than the reverse. McNamara theorizes that it had its roots in the ideals of Early Christian women who chose to pursue a celibate life and whose interests are reflected in the apocryphal rather than the canonical gospels (79). The emphasis on virginity led to singling out one woman's perfections in contrast to the supposed deficiencies of most others. Though the classical world had notions of parthenogenesis—spontaneous, sexless births—Christianity brought the virgin birth of Jesus and the desirability of virginity to the center of its self-definition (Warner, *Alone of All Her Sex* 34-49).

The importance that the ascetic Early Christian culture ascribed to virginity created a groundswell that eventually propelled Mary into a prominent position in Christian thinking and devotion, reaching its zenith during the late medieval period in the wake of the twelfth-century's Cistercian spirituality. Marian devotion, which focused on the Virgin as a mediatrix between humans and a more severe and judgmental deity, became central to late medieval piety. Indeed she was also thought to respond favorably to prayers on her own authority, requiring from her devotees not so much sinlessness as faithfulness (Atkinson, *The Oldest Vocation* 133).

Chaucer appears to have shared in the medieval attraction to Mary, though it may not have been central to his faith: his poetry makes only marginal use of Marian themes and materials. An early short poem, "An ABC," perhaps written in response to a request from Blanche of Lancaster, addresses Mary in terms familiar through centuries of Christian devotion (*Chaucer* 1076). Marian hymns also appear in the prologues to the tales of the Second Nun and the Prioress. There the stress lies primarily on Mary's perfections, her intercessory powers, her unique nature: she is addressed as "mayde and mooder," "daughter of thy Sone," "welle of mercy," "synful soules cure," "Virgine wemmelees." (SNT, ll. 36-49). Beverly Boyd points out that, through allusion and "collage"—a process by which the poet "layered borrowed passages in a complex of sources themselves borrowed, leaving the reader with echoes" (147)—

Chaucer wrote "some of the best lyric poetry of the time" (153). Thus both the spiritually immature Prioress, who focuses on her own childlike vulnerability, and her more spiritually advanced companion show strong reverence for Mary.

Central to Mary's importance in Christian devotion was her redefinition as a new or second Eve. Building on Paul's juxtaposition of Jesus with Adam, the former undoing the damage wrought by the latter's sin, Iranaeus and Justin Martyr applied a similar concept to Mary (Warner 59-60). Jerome makes the juxtaposition explicit: "Death came through Eve, but life has come through Mary. And thus the gift of virginity has been bestowed most richly upon women, seeing that it has had its beginning from a woman" (qtd. in Blamires, *Woman Defamed and Woman Defended* 76). Whereas the former brought sin and death into the world through her disobedience, whose punishment is manifest in the pain of childbirth, the latter, through her purity and obedience, gives life to the god-child untainted by sexuality and thus without pain, indeed without even destroying her physical wholeness (Warner 73-74).

Celebrating Mary's perfections did little to ameliorate the perception of women in general, largely because pursuing those ideals means denying central aspects of women's nature. The medieval cult of Mary had inherent contradictions and placed impossible demands on women (77). Bloch points to the paradoxes women confront because of the Christian stress on virginity:

> To urge a woman to chastity is to urge her in some profound sense to deny her femininity, since to transcend the body is to escape that which is gendered feminine. . . . The logic of virginity thus leads syllogistically to an even deeper paradox. . . . That is, if the feminine is elided to the side of the flesh such that the woman is the body of the man, and if renunciation of the flesh is the only means to equality, then woman is put in the position such that the only way she can be equal is to renounce the feminine or to be a man. (106-7)

Jerome makes this point very clearly: "As long as a woman is for birth and children, she is different from man as body is from soul. But when she wishes to serve Christ more than the world, then she will cease to be a woman, and will be called man" (qtd. in Warner 73). Thus there emerged in Early Christian monasticism an ideal that shaped religious women's aspirations for centuries: that of the virile woman—or virago (Newman, *From Virile Woman to WomanChrist* 4).

Drawing on the angelism that characterized monastic ideology (see Chapter Four), the female aspirant to perfection could parallel the male's attempts to reach spiritual heights through self-abnegation: "The 'virile woman' is a subset of the class 'embodied angel'" (Newman 4).

Among the earliest female martyrs, willingness to face cruel torture and death to preserve virginity was central in establishing sanctity. These virgin-martyrs—like Agatha, Eulalia, Lucy—became models for nuns throughout the medieval period: "Their model lives were to be kept before the eyes of the nuns to underline the reality that virginity entailed inordinate struggle, aggressive defense, but also ultimately great rewards," Jane Schulenburg comments. She maintains that the common expression "to cut off your nose to spite your face" originated in actions early medieval nuns took to preserve their virginity: when invading marauders threatened rape, some nuns—often at the instigation of their abbess—took this drastic action to make themselves repugnant to their attackers as we can see in the story of Saint Eusebia, an abbess near Marseille:

> The infidels burst into the monastery, and Eusebia urged the holy virgins, caring more for preserving their purity than their life, to cut off their noses in order to irritate by this bloody spectacle the rage of the barbarians and to extinguish their passions. With incredible zeal, she [Eusebia] and all of her companions accomplished this act; the barbarians massacred them in the number of forty, while they professed Christ with an admirable constancy. (qtd. in Schulenburg, "The Heroics of Virginity" 47)

So strong was the emphasis on virginity for women that some of the Church fathers like Jerome and Ambrose considered suicide a proper response when a woman's virginity was threatened (Schulenburg 34). Thus for women the only way to achieve heroic virtue was through a lifelong commitment to virginity. "The paradox central to Christian attitudes toward women," Warner points out, "is that it attempted to reinstate women by removing the conditions that stamped them as inferior and kept them in servitude: marriage and motherhood" (72).

Christianity harbored another paradoxical attitude toward women: its ethic valorizes the spiritual power of virtues like humility, meekness, and patience—qualities most frequently associated with women. Indeed McNamara argues that Jesus's female disciples influenced the way in which he was portrayed in the textual tradition:

"The sympathy and compassion of the literary Jesus validated a set of virtues which could be positively opposed to the traditional manliness so admired in the ancient world" (*The New Song* 27). Also, because women were regarded as the weaker sex, their virtuous behavior was deemed more noteworthy than that of males. When female mystics like Hildegard of Bingen wanted to validate their daring to criticize the male power structure, they bolstered their position with such arguments. Hildegard "developed a paradoxical self-image combining two different versions of the feminine: the 'weak woman' (whom God had chosen to shame strong men) and the exalted virgin" (Newman, *From Virile Woman to WomanChrist* 6). Thus within the religious framework, women encountered conflicting images of feminine perfection and mixed signals concerning their worth.

Alongside the clerical rhetoric that divided women into epitomes of virtue or vice medieval secular culture developed a discourse that also forced women into abstract molds: the courtly tradition's lyric and narrative poetry. In these texts woman appears as a physically desirable but difficult-to-attain goal for her refined though still unworthy lover, often her social inferior (Wilson and Makowski 68). The phenomenon of romantic love parallels the rise in women's power to dispose of property at a time when the Church made consent a central feature of marriage; it proved more effective than misogynistic discourse in keeping women societally constrained, as Bloch points out: "The invention of Western romantic love represented, above all, a usurping reappropriation of woman at the moment she became capable of appropriating what had traditionally constituted masculine modes of wealth" (196).

For while the literature that gave romantic love its defining features appears to overturn the clerical negatives, that appearance is deceptive. Superficially the beloved lady assumes a central position, becoming for her lover the embodiment of all virtue, the only source of true joy, the inspiration that drives his efforts, the sign of his true worth. But rather than expressing the lady's own values and desires, her unattainability often simply projects the lover's quest for perfection—her regard and favors to be won as the reward for his persistent devotion and/or for his extraordinary exploits. The male poet also concentrates on the lady's effect on him, as Elizabeth Petroff notes: "It is this exploration of female power, of the effect (often chaos-producing) on an articulate man of an apparently passive and powerless beloved object, that creates the supposedly inverted hierarchy in courtly poetry" (31). Thus the lady of the troubadours, of romance—even the *donna angelicata* of Guido Guinizelli and Dante—embodies her poet-lover's aspiration to transcendence rather than functions as an autonomous person. As feminist scholars have recognized, the courtly tradition's idealized lady but thinly disguises medieval culture's ongoing marginalization of women: it too sets before women a dehumanizing ideal. Bloch summarizes the misogynistic thrust of romantic love behind its surface appearance of feminine empowerment: "Misogyny and courtly love are coconspiring abstractions of the feminine" (196). Thus whether medieval women turned to religious or secular models, they saw themselves portrayed in impersonal abstractions—stereotypes, both positive and negative, that remained at several removes from their own experience. Because women were, for the most part, cut off from literate culture and thus from engaging actively in the learned dialogue, these stereotypes dominated public discourse, if not always the much-more-difficult-to-trace oral tradition.

Against this long tradition of polarizing rhetoric, both clerical and courtly, how are we to locate Chaucer's views about women? Clearly he was no twentieth-century feminist. But for a fourteenth-century male, well acquainted with misogynistic discourse, he appears to have had an unusual appreciation for women and for their social plight. Donald Howard holds that this special affinity results from Chaucer's close contact with several powerful and talented women early in his career and from the fact that he had "what may be called an androgynous personality. He lived in a man's world, achieved eminence as a public figure and a writer in a man's world, yet he had no difficulty at all seeing the world through women's eyes" (*Chaucer* 97). Though feminist assessments and responses to Chaucer's work cover a broad spectrum, many feminist critics disagree with that view. But Chaucer at least seems to have recognized that women cannot readily be contained within the frameworks that men create for them.

Several aspects of his work highlight the poet's unusual sensitivity to women. First, he recognizes women as subjects in their own right—with wishes, goals, preferences that often do not coincide with those of the males who seek to control their lives. In "The Knight's Tale," for instance, Emilye for the most part remains the prize for which two competing knights are contesting. Throughout the lengthy process of determining which of them better deserves her, no one thinks to ask her preference. But in the inner sanctum of Diana's temple where no one can hear her Emilye finds the voice to utter her wish not to marry at all:

Chaste goddesse, wel wostow that I
Desire to ben a mayden al my lyf,
Ne nevere wol I be no love ne wyf.
I am, thow woost, yet of thy compaignye,
A mayde, and love huntynge and venerye,
And for to walken in the wodes wilde,
And noght to ben a wyf and be with childe.
Noght wol I knowe compaignye of man.
Now help me, lady, sith ye may and kan,
Fro tho thre formes that thou hast in thee. (ll. 2304-13)

Though her prayer proves futile, her momentary independence shows Chaucer's awareness of her subjective identity.

In "The Merchant's Tale" May appears to have little choice about marrying old Januarie, who epitomizes men's tendency to make women the instruments of their well-being. While the narrative focuses on his self-absorbed satisfaction of his own lust, occasional comments alert the reader that May's responses to his love-making differ from his own. On the wedding night, for instance, while Januarie delights in having May by his side, the narrator comments on their contrasting responses:

But God woot what that May thoughte in hir herte,
Whan she hym saugh up sittynge in his sherte,
In his nyght-cappe, and with his nekke lene;
She preyseth nat his pleyyng worth a bene. (ll. 1851-54)

The tale's events reveal a woman who, though lacking in moral integrity, nevertheless has a perspective separate from her husband's and the ability to act on her own initiative. Far from being the simple wax that Januarie had hoped to mold to his specifications, May shows her ability to make wax serve her own ends when she uses it to make a key to allow her lover to gain admittance to the garden in which her husband seeks to confine her.

In *The Parliament of Fowls* the formel eagle exercises the autonomy denied to Emelye and May in choosing a spouse. The assemblage of birds—all eager to select their mates and get on with Nature's procreative work—waits impatiently as the three aristocratic eagles argue over which one has the better claim to the formel's affections. When all the arguments have been heard, Dame Nature forcefully establishes that the choice belongs to the formel despite all the rhetoric about which suitor has the best claim to her:

> But fynally, this is my conclusioun,
> That she hireself shal han hir eleccioun
> Of whom hire lest; whoso be wroth or blythe,
> Hym that she cheest, he shal han hire as swithe.
> (ll. 620-23)

Granted this opportunity, the formel quickly puts off all her suitors:

> Almyghty queen, unto this yer be don,
> I axe respit for to avise me,
> And after that to have my choys al fre.
> This al and som that I wol speke and seye;
> Ye gete no more, although ye do me deye! (ll. 647-51)

She leaves them dangling for a year, while requesting a completely free choice when the time for a decision arrives. Still, like Emelye, she appears constrained ultimately to marry.

In addition to recognizing women's independent subjectivity, Chaucer almost always chooses women as his most virtuous and vulnerable characters; he appears to have been unusually sensitive to women's capacity for patient endurance and aware of women's suffering as caused by male oppression and deceitfulness. In "The Man of Law's Tale," for instance, Custance, as her name suggests, maintains her faith and her virtue through a series of hardships that stretch over many years and follow her across continents. Though her two jealous mothers-in-law initiate her sharpest trials, her plight results from her father's decision to send her off to a foreign country to marry a man she has never met. When sorrow and resignation mark the day of her departure (ll. 264-66), the narrator comments first sympathetically, then ironically on her reaction:

> Allas, what wonder is it thogh she wepte,
> That shal be sent to strange nacioun
> Fro freendes that so tendrely hire kepte,
> And to be bounden under subjeccioun
> Of oon, she knoweth nat his condiccioun?
> Housbondes been alle goode, and han ben yoore;
> That knowen wyves; I dar sey yow na moore. (ll. 267-73)

As if explicitly rebutting the comment about all husbands being good, the narrator in "The Clerk's Tale" observes, "But wedded men ne knowe no mesure/Whan that they finde a pacient creature" (ll.

622-23). For in retelling one of the fourteenth century's favorite stories, that of an aristocratic husband's protracted and cruel trials to test his wife's fidelity to her word, Chaucer heightens the pathos of Griselde's separation from her children and reproves Walter's inhuman behavior both in her gentle chiding before her return to her father's home and in the narrator's critical comments about Walter. Most telling is that Griselde prevails—for all her patient, uncomplaining obedience. Walter cracks in the face of her perseverance; no longer able to face his own inhumanity, he is the one who cries "ynogh!" (l. 1051), thereby proving that—in the words of "The Franklin's Tale's" narrator—"pacience is an heigh vertu, certeyn/For it venquysseth, as thise clerkes seyn,/Thynges that rigour sholde nevere atteyne" (ll. 773-75). As Elaine Tuttle Hansen observes, Chaucer here investigates "the implications of Griselda's paradoxical position as a woman: the fact that she attains certain kinds of power by embracing powerlessness; the fact that she is strong . . . because she is so perfectly weak" ("The Powers of Silence" 232).

Another facet of Chaucer's views on women appears in his attitude toward male infidelity to vows made to women. In a study of minor female characters who are betrayed, Richard Firth Green argues that Chaucer rejects Continental cynicism and deserves special plaudits "for his recognition of the double standard by which the sworn word between man and man might be regarded as absolutely binding, whereas in affairs of the heart it became merely an expedient device to gain one's end" ("Chaucer's Victimized Women" 18). In *The Legend of Good Women*, a story collection that he abandons unfinished, the poet explicitly assumes the task of telling virtuous women's stories. He takes up this charge after suffering the God of Love's ire for having translated the *Roman de la rose*—"That is an heresye ageyns my lawe" (G, l. 256)—and for having told the story of Criseyde's faithlessness—"Hast thow nat mad in Englysh ek the bok/How that Crisseyde Troylus forsok,/In shewynge how that wemen han don mis?" (G, ll. 264-66). Interceding on the poet's behalf, Queen Alceste promises that

> He shal no more agilten in this wyse,
> But he shal maken, as ye wol devyse,
> Of women trewe in lovynge al here lyve,
> Wherso ye wol, of mayden or of wyve,
> And fortheren yow [the God of Love] as muche as he mysseyde
> Or in the Rose or elles in Crisseyde. (G, ll. 426-31)

The narrator proceeds with a catalogue of stories from classical antiquity, all told to put women in the most positive light. Male behavior, on the other hand, he casts much more negatively than what appears in long-standing tradition. Alistair Minnis draws attention to the fact that Chaucer adapts this approach from Ovid: "Chaucer has taken the fundamental strategy of the *Heroides*, where women's voices rise in protest against their unworthy lovers, and augmented it with considerable skill and a degree of daring. In his poem women have in effect taken over the position of moral superiority supposedly enjoyed by men" ("Repainting the Lion" 167).

In effect Chaucer responds to the challenge the Wife of Bath raises when, in her prologue, she wonders what would happen to the misogynists' catalogue of women's vices if women rather than men got to tell the stories: "Who peyntede the leon, tel me who?" (1. 692), she asks, suggesting that the lion's story would sound very different from the hunter's. In the *Legend* "Chaucer was pleasurably engaged in the exciting literary experiment of repainting the lion" (Minnis, "Repainting the Lion" 158). Within the framework of his patriarchal society, he creates a temporary space within which entrenched interpretive patterns are thrown into question; by so doing he disturbs, if not repudiates, the basis on which they rest (168-69). But the mission, whether self-imposed or mandated by his female patrons, of freeing women from the criticism that an entrenched clerical tradition directed at them resulted in portrayals that some readers find monotonous and one-dimensional. Not so with Criseyde and the Wife of Bath, of all Chaucer's women the most complex and most controversial.

In retelling the tale of Criseyde's betrayal of Troilus's love Chaucer's narrator stresses her vulnerability and her fearfulness and withholds judgment when he must report her infidelity. But determining Criseyde's status as unknowing victim of Pandarus's and Troilus's schemes or as a complicitous partner who seeks the sexual encounters she pretends to avoid remains one of the poem's interpretive cruxes: deciding the degree of her culpability highlights the difficulty of determining how Chaucer fares on the feminist litmus test. For either reading allows for both positive and negative assessments of Chaucer's underlying attitudes toward women.

No section of Chaucer's poem makes us more aware of Criseyde's complexity than the remarkable Book II. There Chaucer takes the reader not only into Criseyde's palace chamber but also into her mind's chamber as she debates the pros and cons of accepting Troilus as her lover. In her first solitary reflection on her new status as Troilus's beloved, Criseyde specifically recognizes her right to choose: "For man may love, of possibilite,/A womman so, his herte may tobreste,/And she naught love ayein, but if hire leste" (ll. 607-9). However, Troilus's unexpected appearance beneath her window, in all his military splendor, awakens her own sensuality and undermines that strong statement of independence: "Criseÿda gan al his chere aspien,/And leet it so softe in hire herte synke,/That to hireself she seyde, 'Who yaf me drynke?'" (II, ll. 649-51).

Further reflection leads her to conflicting conclusions about which course best supports her freedom. She recognizes that she has no husband to cry "Check mat!" (l. 754) as she pursues her inclinations and that her widowed status imposes no barriers to the love affair: "I am myn owene womman, wel at ese—" (l. 750). But she shrinks from jeopardizing the very liberty that allows her to explore her options: "Allas! Syn I am free,/Sholde I now love, and put in jupartie/ My sikernesse, and thrallen libertee?" (ll. 771-73). Her niece Antigone's fortuitously timed song praising love appeals to Criseyde's emotions and further compromises her efforts to rationally balance alternatives. What the reader sees in her delicate waverings is neither cold calculation nor rapturous longing but desire blending with keen appreciation of her social vulnerability.

Criseyde thus emerges as a complex, multidimensional figure whose intricacies of character have yet to exhaust the scholarly community. Exegetical critics like D. W. Robertson, Jr., see Criseyde as illustrating feminine weakness and deceptiveness and castigate Troilus for his lust and spiritual blindness. Other male critics like E. Talbot Donaldson, who explicitly places himself among those who love Criseyde (*Speaking of Chaucer* 71), seem to be themselves taken by her beauty and fragility, finding in her the epitome of feminine perfection; they are as loathe to fault her as is the Chaucerian narrator.

Feminist readings range across a spectrum. Some downplay Criseyde's infidelity and focus on her as a survivor who calculatedly sizes up her situation and makes choices based on a pragmatic assessment of what is best for her. Others stress the lies and plots to which Pandarus and Troilus subject her to excuse her behavior. David Aers's new historicist analysis points to the contradiction between aristocratic love conventions and social reality, maintaining that the poet seeks "to explore the tension between the place women occupied in society and the various self-images presented to them" ("Criseyde: Woman in Medieval Society" 180). He stresses the social/cultural constraints that impede both Criseyde's freedom of action and her ability to develop full personhood, laying the blame for the psychic collapse of both lovers firmly on a society that treats human beings like commodities (183-91). Gretchen Mieszkowski's reading discusses the extent to which Chaucer, clearly altering Boccaccio's *Filostrato,* decreases Criseyde's independent action and autonomous exercise of her own will. Arguing that Troilus loves neither Criseyde's qualities nor her character, Mieszkowski holds that Criseyde well illustrates Simone de Beauvoir's thesis that woman exists as "the second sex that reinforces the male experience of himself as a consciousness who controls his world. . . . Criseyde mirrors the men around her. She reflects them and echoes them so directly that their purposes, values, and way of seeing the world seem to be hers as well as theirs" ("Chaucer's Much Loved Criseyde" 121). This mirroring becomes most evident in Criseyde's language: while both Troilus and Pandarus speak in their own idiom, Criseyde adapts hers to that of her interlocutor (Mieszkowski 121-23). In this reading Chaucer's portrayal of Criseyde's mirroring nature signals his critique of the romantic ideal's fundamentally defective conception of woman. Deprived of true autonomy, Criseyde cannot but fail to be capable of genuine love and thus must inevitably fall short of Troilus's expectations: "Criseyde comes to stand not only for Eve and man's original betrayal but also for the flaw in the poem's ideal of woman and of romantic love . . . Criseyde must betray Troilus because a mirror must reflect whatever is in front of it" (Mieszkowski 130).

No female figure more memorably addresses the issues women posed in late medieval culture than does the Wife of Bath. She is an explosive presence in *The Canterbury Tales.* Like the Miller's putting off of the Monk in order to "quit" the Knight, her performance forestalls the Parson's humorless moralizing and introduces a celebratory defense of sensuality that challenges clerical asceticism. Her account of her first three marriages to old husbands captures the misogynists' most nightmarish visions about women, as she unabashedly relates the ways in which she controlled her husbands. By appropriating the standard attacks against women and by using her sexual favors as currency, she overcomes the vulnerability into which her youthful marriages placed her—making the best defense a good offense.

But her fifth marriage to Jankyn, a young clerk, ignites the most intense response from her. Tormented by hours of Jankyn's reading to her from his "book of wykked wyves," a compendium of just the kind of antifeminist rhetoric discussed earlier in this chapter, she assails the clerks' blanket condemnations of women:

> For trusteth wel, it is an impossible
> That any clerk wol speke good of wyves,

But if it be of hooly seintes lyves,
Ne of noon oother womman never the mo. (ll. 688-91)

Then she makes a point worthy of a contemporary feminist: as mentioned above, she raises the question of who is telling the story:

Who peyntede the leon, tel me who?
By God, if wommen hadde writen stories,
As clerkes han withinne hire oratories,
They wolde han writen of men moore wikkednesse
Than al the mark of Adam may redresse. (ll. 692-96)

Seeing no respite from Jankyn's cataloguing of the ills women cause, Alisoun's rancor turns physical as she grabs the book and tears three pages from it:

And whan I saugh he wolde nevere fyne
To reden on this cursed book al nyght,
Al sodeynly thre leves have I plyght
Out of his book, right as he radde. . . . (ll. 788-91)

Her revolt, which precipitates a battle between her and her husband, ultimately yields a truce, a space within which they can carve out a mutually respectful relationship. The issues set in motion at the end of the prologue carry over into her tale, where the Knight, the reluctant husband of a poor, ugly, and aged wife, responds positively to the opportunity to transcend stereotypical male thinking about women by yielding to his wife the right to decide between his having an old, ugly, but faithful wife and a young, beautiful, but possibly faithless one.

Critical opinion about the Wife of Bath's relationship to the antifeminist textual tradition—out of which she is in large measure constructed—varies greatly. Exegetical critics see her as the antitype of biblical women like the *mulier fortis* ("virtuous woman") in Proverbs and the Samaritan woman at the well, who also had five husbands. Feminists are by no means united in their ideas about what she reveals about the poet who created her. Elaine Tuttle Hansen, for instance, rejects the view, including her own earlier reading, of a humane, tolerant Chaucer who had a special empathy for women and who achieves "aesthetic or moral transcendence" (*Chaucer and the Fictions of Gender* 36). Instead she comments, "I hear not a swelling chorus of female voices entering the text and speaking for and about themselves, but something of a monotone making known both feminine absence and masculine anxiety . . . his poetry explores the consequent difficulty that men face in securing masculine identity and dominance" (12-13). Characterizing the Wife of Bath as "a feminine monstrosity who is the product of the masculine imagination against which she ineffectively and only superficially rebels" (35), Hansen stresses Alisoun's "powerlessness, self-destructiveness, and silencing" (27).

On the other hand, Carolyn Dinshaw sees the Wife of Bath as Chaucer's "favorite character" (*Chaucer's Sexual Poetics* 116). She holds that, "Through the Wife, Chaucer imagines the possibility of a masculine reading that is not antifeminist, that does acknowledge, in good faith, feminine desire; and further, he represents the struggle and violence to the feminine that accompany the articulation of this fantasy" (117). For Dinshaw, Chaucer's accomplishment in creating the Wife consists essentially of the fact that "he has imagined patriarchy from the Other's point of view and has duly reckoned the costs of clerkly discourse in terms of the feminine body" (130). Lynne Dickson argues from a similar perspective: "Chaucer is perhaps the best example that the medieval period offers of a man invested in revising and resisting antifeminist discourse" ("Deflection in the Mirror" 70-71). She concludes that both the Wife's prologue and her tale challenge traditional patriarchal misogyny in two ways: first, they invite readers to eschew simplistic masculinist responses and to react rather "as complex sexual beings" (62); second, they vividly portray Alisoun's difficulties in escaping the accumulated pressure of this tradition (which we might remember from Héloïse's internalization of the texts' misogyny) and provide brief glimpses of an alternative: "a feminine community of readers and speakers" (62). In her prologue this community manifests itself in the Wife's references to "wise wyves" (l. 225), in her confiding in her "gossib" (l. 530) rather than in her parish priest, and in her including several other female confidantes in her circle (Dickson 83-84). The Wife's tale goes even further in presenting an authoritative female community by investing a group of women with the power to determine the fate of the rapist knight (63). However, Dickson maintains, "Feminine discourse remains a possibility that the text is willing to admit, but only in imaginary terms; feminine speech is ultimately left unaffirmed, imagined but not actualized" (63).

The problem for medieval women—and for a poet like Chaucer, who may well have been sympathetic to them—was finding a way of imaging and imagining women not colored by absolutizing discourse. Jill Mann sums up the dilemma as follows:

The problem confronting Chaucer when he began to write was thus not simply how woman was to be represented—as good or bad—but rather how she was to be represented in terms that broke free of these traditional polarities, and even more important, how she was to be represented *for herself,* rather than endlessly evaluated from the male standpoint that is equally evident whether she is portrayed as shrew or as patient helpmeet. (*Geoffrey Chaucer* 3)

Encountering the Wife of Bath, in all her vibrant vitality, one suspects that she took hold of her creator's imagination in a way he could not have predicted when he initially conceived of her. That he changed his mind about which tale to assign her—moving from the straightforward bawdiness and commercialism of the fabliau ultimately assigned to the Shipman to the wish-fulfilling romance in which the Wife unconsciously reveals herself—suggests that his conception underwent transformation through the creative process's alchemy. Her confessional prologue consists almost entirely of amalgamated antifeminist texts like those contained in Jankyn's "book of wikked wyves." But as Chaucer imagines the Wife appropriating those texts, she becomes a whole much greater than the sum of its parts; she balloons into an independent self, generating energy that her creator can scarcely control. Edward Nolan, commenting on that transformative process, notes "the gradual generation of an autonomous center of energy that somehow renders credible the idea that a real woman is speaking this language" (*Now Through a Glass Darkly* 202); he continues:

She functions as a mirror of our own pilgrimage of intellect, memory, and will as she suffers into truth. The question is not whether there is a real woman here. The question is how does Chaucer manipulate those antifeminist clichés so that the illusion of a real woman rises up so credibly before our eyes and hearts. (202)

Several times Chaucer uses the mirror image to highlight male appropriation of woman's features. In "The Merchant's Tale" Januarie—having decided to seek a wife in his old age—turns his mind into a mirror and sees in it a procession of candidates to serve his physical needs and sexual appetites. Troilus does much the same when he retires to his chamber after having been struck to the core by Criseyde's beauty: "Thus gan he make a mirour of his mynde/In which he saugh al holly hire figure," (I, ll. 365-66). And early in Book II Pandarus gazes fixedly at Criseyde, pondering just how and when to begin his proxy seduction for Troilus and attempting to discern her likely response. As he stares into her face—so intently that she asks if he is seeing her for the first time—what he sees is a mirror:

> And with that word he gan right inwardly
> Byholden hire and loken on hire face,
> And seyde, "On swich a mirour goode grace!"(ll. 264-66)

Januarie's, Troilus's, and Pandarus's mirrors are those created by the patriarchy: they reflect images of women who serve men's needs— for sexual fulfillment, for nurturing, for feeling superior. Chaucer seems to have recognized the distortions in those mirrors and, if one agrees with Dickson, to have recognized, if only fleetingly, the need for a mirror that could give women a more accurate, more complex image of themselves, one that would help them imagine new roles and new powers for themselves. But protean and fluid as was Chaucer's imagination, he could not completely escape the boundaries of his time and gender.

Still new seeds were being softly sown. In a quiet anchorhold Chaucer's contemporary, the mystic Julian of Norwich, was wrestling to articulate insights that cast another light on human physicality and sensuality—one ultimately more attuned to the centrality of the Incarnation in Christian theology. Recorded in *The Revelations of Divine Love*, Julian's intense mystical "showings" became the basis for lifetime contemplation. Though she saw herself as the Church's faithful daughter and consciously molded her will to its teachings, she pertinaciously clung to the insights gained from her mystic experiences. Her visions brought her to the certainty that the divine resides not just in spirit but in sensuality as well:

> I saw with absolute certainty that our substance is in God, and, moreover, that he is in our sensuality too. The moment that our soul was made sensual, at that moment was it destined from all eternity to be in the City of God. . . . Our substance and our sensuality together are rightly named our soul because they are united by God. That wonderful city, the seat of our Lord Jesus, is our sensuality in which he is enclosed, just as the substance of our nature is enclosed in him as with his blessed soul he sits at rest in the Godhead. (159-61)

By reclaiming human sensuality—and the feminine with which a long tradition linked it—and associating it with the divine, Julian was able to cross a threshold that Chaucer appears to have approached, but without ever being able to fully commit himself to reaching the other side. Perhaps that holding back accounts for the palinode at the end of *Troilus and Criseyde* and the "Retraction" at the end of *The Canterbury Tales*. And perhaps for that reason the female faces in the mirrors he creates are never totally free of the features the patriarchy had sketched.

CHAPTER TEN

Till Death Us Depart: Love, Marriage, and Sexuality

A church ceremony with clergy and other witnesses, an exchange of vows with each spouse consenting to love and support the other in a lasting and affectionate union, a belief that this loving union is a divinely blessed sacrament that reflects God's love and contributes to the couple's spiritual well-being—all these elements now considered integrally associated with Christian marriage developed slowly and did not merge until the late medieval period. Indeed the most positive articulations about marriage's spiritual dimension and its contribution to the couple's well-being—though they made scattered appearances among various commentators across the centuries—had to await the twentieth century. Christian love did not center on the marital relationship, which at best was thought to distract one's attention from God or at worst to plunge one into sinful sensuality. For clerical culture fostered a misogamous tradition closely linked to the misogynistic tradition discussed in the previous chapter. While the Church ultimately had much to say about marital standards and practices, for many centuries its distaste for sexuality made it remain aloof to marriage.

Throughout the medieval period both secular and religious forces shaped the evolving process by which Christian Europe arrived at a commonly shared view of what comprised a societally and ecclesiastically sanctioned marriage. Attitudes and views from widely differing cultures and value systems needed to fuse. As Christopher Brooke notes: "Medieval marriage was a piquant mixture of notions and customs deriving from the ancient world, from the inheritance of Judaism and the early Church, from Rome and the barbarians" (*The Medieval Idea of Marriage* 39). Furthermore, in the twelfth century a literary tradition that celebrated human love as a highly desirable goal deeply influenced the relationship between the sexes both outside of marriage and within it.

By the late fourteenth century the values associated with love and marriage remained a lively concern, certainly in Chaucer's circle, which has been credited with promoting Valentine's Day as a special day for lovers (Kelly, *Chaucer and Cult of Saint Valentine* xi-xix). The *Parliament of Fowls*, with its annual gathering of birds to choose a mate under Nature's benevolent oversight, is clearly a Valentine's Day poem, and Chaucer's contemporaries thought of him as a love poet. Much of his early poetry deals with that subject, and certainly *The Canterbury Tales* paints many shades of the relationship between the sexes, especially the marital one. His extensive, open-ended treatment of love and marriage reflects and invites participation in the cultural dialogue concerning their nature and relationship. In *Troilus and Criseyde* Chaucer assumes the stance of one who, but for his ineptitude, would join the ranks of lovers; his "unlykliness," however, reduces him to reporting his observations from the sidelines. This stance permits him to retain a perspective at once involved and distanced, enabling him to convey the many-faceted nature of this most desired, and most vexing, of relationships. To appreciate the dimensions of the cultural dialogue we need to explore the separate strands that were coming together in a still unfinished pattern during the late medieval period. We will first consider marriage in its secular framework and the influence that twelfth-century vernacular love literature exerted on it; then we will explore the religious and clerical views that increasingly shaped marital ideas and practices.

Because Roman culture provided the overarching matrix within which Christianity developed, its influence on medieval ideas about marriage was pervasive and long-lasting. Essentially marriage in Roman society consisted of a relatively informal agreement between the spouses and/or their families (Brooke 39-40). Neither cohabitation nor sexual consummation was necessary to constitute a marriage if marital affection was present, but the spouses' free consent was essential (Brundage, *Law, Sex, and Christian Society in Medieval Europe* 35-36). Rome also developed a form of marriage that allowed a woman to retain membership in her own family rather than being absorbed into her husband's, thereby retaining her inheritance rights. The Roman consent requirement gave women a measure of autonomy lacking in other ancient societies (Gies, *Marriage and the Family in the Middle Ages* 21) and had far-reaching implications for medieval ideas about marriage. Another area of Roman thought that influenced evolving Christian attitudes toward marriage and sexuality was Stoicism, which appealed primarily to the intellectual elite. Sexual activity for the Stoics was highly suspect because it involves losing rational control and giving way to passion; the wise person, therefore, limits its practice to a bare minimum.

Germanic culture also shaped medieval marriage concepts; among the Germanic tribes familial considerations, especially those of the extended kinship group or clan, dominated marriage practices (Gies, *Marriage and the Family in the Middle Ages* 33). Marriage was "a social fact" rather than "a legal status," and men with high status might have several wives, with promiscuity after marriage tolerated for men but not for women (Brundage 128). Germanic marital attitudes centered on the conviction that consummation was its defining feature; marital affection had no significant role. A man could acquire a wife by purchasing her, by abducting her, or by obtaining her consent. Purchase—the preferred form of marriage—entailed having the two families reach an agreement concerning what the man's family would pay the woman's family to compensate for her removal to his sphere of influence. If a man lacked the resources or the will to pay the bride-price, he could secure a wife by abduction—which was frowned upon—or by obtaining her consent, though in that case the woman's family retained legal control over her (Brundage 128-35).

As the landed aristocracy, with its practices rooted in Germanic traditions, attempted to solidify its position in the tenth and eleventh centuries, it wanted marriage to consolidate and expand landholdings as well as to guarantee a male heir with the appropriate qualities to inherit those holdings: "The purpose of marriage was to unite a valiant progenitor to a wife in such a manner that his legitimate son, bearer of the blood and name of a valorous ancestor, should be able to bring that ancestor to life again in his own person" (Duby, *The Knight, the Lady and the Priest* 37). Another important purpose marriage served in aristocratic circles was to secure peace between warring factions or families (Klapisch-Zuber, "Women and the Family" 287). Thus marriage met pragmatic societal needs; personal considerations were not a factor.

Precisely in these aristocratic circles, however, there arose in the twelfth century an elaborate literary artifice—most commonly but controversially known as courtly love—which reflected the inner life's claims and celebrated love between the sexes as the prime means of individual, especially male, fulfillment and ennoblement. Scholars have long debated the extent to which this phenomenon reflected social realities rather than purely literary ones. Indeed this body of literature—troubadour poetry, chivalric romances, dream visions—may well have preceded and contributed to a significant shift in social reality. Stephen Jaeger, for instance, argues that the romances educated a warrior class eager to respond to an idealized code of conduct that placed a high premium on refined feelings and genteel manners (236-54). Toril Moi pushes the argument further, maintaining that adherence to courtly values helped to empower the ruling class: "Signaling their cultural superiority, the effeminisation of the aristocracy paradoxically enough comes to signify their 'natural' right to power" ("Desire in Language" 19).

The origins of courtly love have proven difficult to pinpoint. Some scholars see it as a carryover of the feudal bond between a lord and his vassal into male-female relationships, with the man assuming the role of vassal and the lady that of lord. Others link the emergence of the phenomenon to the Marian cult's rising popularity in the twelfth century—except that it has been difficult to determine which came first. Still others link it to Neoplatonism or to the Cathar heresy (Boase, *The Origin and Meaning of Courtly Love* 27-93). In *The Allegory of Love* C. S. Lewis argues that courtly love, emerging in the specific cultural conditions of twelfth-century southern France, was a new and unique phenomenon in human experience (11-13). Peter Dronke, on the other hand, finds similar feelings expressed in the poetry of many cultures and denies that anything unusual happened in the twelfth century (*Medieval Latin and the Rise of the European Love Lyric* 46). Exegetical critics like D. W. Robertson, Jr., maintain that the whole concept of courtly love is a scholarly invention, having nothing to do with any medieval reality (*A Preface to Chaucer* 392). But a view that has considerable credence is that which ties it to Arabic love poetry. As Roger Boase observes, "The cultural supremacy of the Islamic world in the period immediately preceding the rise of the troubadour lyric is indisputable. . . . More important still, poetry was an art in which the Arabs, according to their own estimate, excelled" (63). Whatever its origins, in the Christian West romantic love motifs appeared first in the troubadours' vernacular poetry in southern France and spread quickly to the chivalric romances and dream visions more characteristic of northern France. Courtly love—or *fin' amors* as it was called in Provençal poetry—casts women as beautiful, distant objects whom their lovers must win by heroic exploits and refined character. The new sensibility significantly affected the era's courting patterns: "Ravishment was giving way to seduction as the preferred method of capturing an heiress against her family's wishes. This change in courting patterns is reflected not only in poetic praise of *fin' amors*, but also in canon law" (Brundage 210).

Among the most salient beliefs associated with courtly love was that experiencing love is in itself a sign of gentility—"love runs soonest in a gentle heart." Thus love at first sight is central to the convention. It strikes swiftly, the dominant image being that of Cupid's arrow piercing the lover's eye and then penetrating his heart. The experience of love ennobles the lover: he becomes braver in battle, eager to perform any service that will highlight his devotion to his lady, and humble about his unworthiness. Equally important was the belief that love could induce a serious malady—called *amor heroes*—whose symptoms include sleeplessness, lack of appetite, lethargy, and bodily wasting. "The disease of love," Mary Wack says, "according to medieval physicians, is a disorder of the mind and body, closely related to melancholia, and potentially fatal if not treated. In their view, however, lovesickess did not afflict everyone alike: the sufferer was typically thought to be a noble man" (xi). Wack's *Lovesickness in the Middle Ages* discusses this phenomenon in detail, focusing on Constantine the African's revival of classical concepts about lovesickness simultaneously with the emergence of vernacular courtly love poetry (xiii). Through Constantine's *Viaticum* the West acquired both "a theoretical framework and a technical vocabulary with which to discuss passionate love" (Wack 32). Because leaving the disease untreated was considered dangerous, the work devotes considerable attention to cures: among them are drinking wine, taking baths, engaging in pleasurable activities like music, poetry, conversation—and intercourse (41-48). The literary tradition makes the lover's lady—through her sympathetic response to his plight and ultimately through yielding to his desires—the best, perhaps the only, physician.

Several Chaucerian lovers suffer from lovesickness: Troilus has the most intense case, while that of "The Knight's Tale's" Arcite provides the most detailed description of its symptoms:

> His slep, his mete, his drynke, is hym biraft,
> That lene he wex and drye as is a shaft;
> His eyen holwe and grisly to biholde,
> His hewe falow and pale as asshen colde,
> And solitarie he was and evere allone,
> And waillynge al the nyght, makynge his mone. . . .
> So feble eek were his spiritz, and so lowe,
> And chaunged so, that no man koude knowe
> His speche nor his voys, though men it herde.
> (ll. 1361-71)

Damyan in "The Merchant's Tale" and Aurelius in "The Franklin's Tale" also suffer from the disease, as do both Nicholas and Absoloum in "The Miller's Tale." In the latter instance, however, Absoloum's disgust at kissing Alisoun's "nether ye" initiates his cure (Williams, "Radical Therapy" 227-55).

Romantic conventions seem to make the knight/lover subordinate to the lady as he strives to make himself worthy of her. But though the courtly code stresses the lover's ennoblement through love, it frequently masks motives much more pragmatic and self-focused: the sought-after lady becomes simply an object of male desire—in effect, a projection of the male's most idealized image of himself (Ferrante, *Woman as Image in Medieval Literature* 66-67). Summing up, Jaeger observes that the courtly code is "at the same time an ethical code, an instrument of ambition, and a mask for self-interest, always practiced with an element of dissimulation" (254). The courtly code makes love a means of validating the male power structure as David Aers observes in discussing *Troilus and Criseyde*: "The passages describing how Troilus's 'love' makes him a class paragon are intelligible precisely and only because the woman represents the masculine self-image and class ideal. To 'love' is to become fused with the most revered values in the community where the male's identity emerges" (*Community, Gender, and Individual Identity* 124).

In aristocratic circles idealized portrayals of noble and ennobling love coexisted with expedient, arranged marriages. Chaucer's "The Knight's Tale" offers a good example of this duality. Palamon and Arcite, from their prison tower, are struck in conventional fashion by Emelye's beauty and immediately fall in love with her, thereby dissolving their sworn bond of brotherhood. After many years of silent suffering and despair about ever winning Emelye's love, after the elaborate tournament that Theseus orchestrates to decide which one deserves her, after Arcite's shocking death and years of mourning his loss, Palamon and Emelye's wedding occurs at Theseus's instigation to achieve his political ends. Throughout all the turmoil that surrounds her fate, Emelye remains a silent icon: no one asks her what her wishes are, and she never publicly articulates them. Even as she expresses her desire not to marry in the inner sanctum of Diana's temple, she recognizes its futility and quickly modifies her prayer, asking that she be married to the man who loves her most. By the tale's end Emelye no longer exerts power over male behavior; she has been absorbed into Theseus's grand scheme, serving to bring hostilities to an end.

In aristocratic/courtly arenas marriage continued to serve familial and political goals, leaving the couple's interests and preferences, especially those of the woman, as unimportant considerations. But alongside this pragmatic approach to marriage, the idealized code that made winning a beautiful, distant woman the ultimate badge of the male lover's worth provided a competing ideology for the relationship between the sexes; the values associated with this code, which the aristocracy embraced as an instrument of its own refinement and thus as a justification for its position of power, continued to interweave themselves with evolving conceptions about the nature of marriage throughout the late medieval period.

Among the peasantry marriage also served to advance the family's economic and/or social interests. When familial land or money was at stake, young people had little to say about choosing a spouse; when neither was involved, they had much more freedom (Hanawalt, *The Ties That Bound* 200-1). But though pragmatic considerations played a central role in peasant marriages, recent studies suggest that they involved considerable mutuality, both economic and emotional, and that stereotypes about the woman's totally subordinate position are inaccurate. "Partnership is the most appropriate term to describe marriage in medieval peasant society," Barbara Hanawalt maintains (219).

So far our discussion of marriage has focused on its secular side. But religious conceptions about marriage played an increasingly important role in medieval society, cross-pollinating those in the secular arena. In the canonical reforms of the eleventh through the thirteenth centuries the Church increasingly asserted its interest and authority in the marital relationship. Gradually the canonists arrived at some consensus about Christian marriage's essential features, and the Church set up ecclesiastical courts to adjudicate disputes and to set penalties for transgressions. More importantly, the late medieval period witnessed the gradual merging of romantic love's intense emotion with marital affection between spouses—affirmed by some clerical commentators; the Church officially recognized marriage both as a model of Christ's love for the Church and as a grace-giving sacrament. Chaucer's Parson, ever the rigid cleric, acknowledges marriage's sacramental status and its imaging of the relationship between Christ and the Church, but he focuses on its role as a remedy against lechery (Pars T, ll. 911-38).

The reasons for the Church's ambivalence about marriage go back to Christianity's formative phase and are rooted in scripture itself. Genesis 1:20 enjoins God's creatures to go forth and multiply, and Genesis 2:24 supports the marital bond's value by urging that for the sake of one's spouse one should leave parents behind, placing the new attachment above the old. While Jesus's comments on marriage in the Gospels are not extensive, they accept existing Jewish marital practices and support monogamous and indissoluble union, except in the case of adultery (Matt. 19:6-9), thereby treating sexuality and marriage as God-ordained goods, part of the divine plan for human life. On the other hand, the Hebraic scriptures, though supportive of marriage and procreation, often associate sexuality with sinfulness by imaging the Hebrew people's violation of their covenant with Yahweh as sexual infidelities and insisting on purification rites after intercourse (Brundage 51-53). Perhaps most influential in shaping medieval attitudes is Paul's teaching in 1 Cor. (7:7-9), which establishes a hierarchy of values by placing celibacy and widowhood above the married state. His views grew out of his belief in an imminent apocalypse: at such a time spousal distractions detract from full service to God.

Another important dimension of Paul's teachings on marriage relates to the sexual rights of each spouse—what came to be known as paying the conjugal debt: "The husband must give the wife what is due her, and equally the wife must give the husband his due. The wife cannot claim her body as her own; it is her husband's. Equally the husband cannot claim his body as his own; it is his wife's" (1 Cor. 7: 3-5). Later canonists upheld Paul's position, recognizing the right to marital sex as a serious responsibility; for instance, because Norman wives demanded their sexual rights, William the Conqueror had to release his soldiers from their military obligations just when he wanted to consolidate his victories (Brundage 198). If one spouse in a marriage subsequently decided to enter the religious life, he or she had to obtain the other's consent for the loss of conjugal rights (Makowski, "The Conjugal Debt" 137). And though the Church praised chastity in marriage, both parties had to agree to forgo sexual relations. *The Book of Margery Kempe,* for instance, records Margery's struggle—after having borne fourteen children and then having undergone an intense religious experience—to persuade her husband to yield his conjugal rights:

> And after this time she never had any desire to have sexual intercourse with her husband, for paying the debt of matrimony was so abominable to her that she would rather, she thought, have eaten and drunk the ooze and muck in the gutter than consent to intercourse, except out of obedience. And so she said to her husband,

"I may not deny you my body, but all the love and affection of my heart is withdrawn from all earthly creatures and set on God alone." But he would have his will with her, and she obeyed with much weeping and sorrowing because she could not live in chastity. (46)

Margery's husband finally agreed to a chaste marriage—though not without setting some conditions—telling her, "May your body be as freely available to God as it has been to me" (60).

With respect to the conjugal debt Paul stresses the spouses' equal responsibility and equal rights. But in a famous passage from the Epistle to the Ephesians he establishes a hierarchical model for marital relationships, one that had a long and contentious history: "Wives, be subject to your husbands as though to the Lord; for the man is the head of the woman, just as Christ is head of the church. Christ is, indeed, the savior of that body; but just as the church is subject to Christ, so must women be subject to their husbands in everything" (5: 22-24). While insisting on the wife's subordination, this passage encompasses the most positive aspect of Paul's teaching about marriage because he makes it image the relationship between Christ and the Church. That concept underpins the emergence of the doctrine that marriage is fully and truly a sacrament, an outward sign capable of giving grace. Paul's views were especially instrumental in forming Christianity's theology of marriage. Brundage summarizes his position as follows:

St. Paul . . . considered sex a serious hindrance to spiritual perfection. Paul adamantly opposed sexual licentiousness and pleasure-seeking, particularly outside of marriage. Within marriage Paul felt that couples should keep their sexual passions under firm control. Still Paul considered marital sex sacred, a central feature of the bonding of husband and wife, a paradigm of the spiritual union of Christ with the Church. (74)

Thus Pauline teaching captures the ambivalence that was to characterize much of the Church's evolving doctrine on marriage and sexuality; but the balance in some of his statements dipped toward the negative in later commentators' interpretations.

Over the next few centuries the increasing asceticism in many quarters of the Roman world undoubtedly shaped the Church's views on marriage and sexuality. The patristic period, which coincided with the monastic movement's formative phase, helped shape the

Church's views on virginity and celibacy. Virginity, as we have seen in Chapter Four, was considered similar to angelic life, anticipating heaven's sexless existence. Saint Jerome, the fourth-century ascetic, observes: "What others are going to be in heaven, virgins have already begun to be on this earth. If we are promised the likeness of angels (who are not distinguished into sexes), either we shall lack sex, like the angels, or, what is clearly proved to be the case, we shall arise in our own sex, but not perform the offices of sex" (qtd. in Kolve and Olson 338). "Hali Meidhad," a thirteenth-century treatise written for women, shows the continuity between patristic and later medieval views: "Angel and maiden are equal in virtue through the power of virginity. . . . This virtue is the only one that in this mortal life foreshadows in itself a state of the immortal bliss in that blessed land where bride does not take groom nor bridegroom bride; and teaches here on earth by its way of life the way of life in heaven" (Millett and Wogan-Browne, *Medieval English Prose for Women* 11).

The early Church's fixation on virginity contributed to the emergence of spiritual marriage, "a legally binding marriage in which sexual relations have been remitted by the consent of both parties for reasons of piety" (Elliott, *Spiritual Marriage* 3). The chaste marriage of Mary and Joseph, though its circumstances were admittedly unique, set the standard for ideal Christian marriage (176-83). As with Margery Kempe, women often took the lead in pushing for spiritual marriage: it could give them increased autonomy within the framework of an overwhelmingly patriarchal institution. For that very reason, Church authorities tempered their support with injunctions on the necessity of paying the marriage debt when either partner claimed it. Spiritual marriages provide some of the most positive treatments of the marital relationship in early medieval literature (53-73).

Chaucer portrays such a marriage in "The Second Nun's Tale," which recounts the story of Saint Cecile, adapted from *The Golden Legend,* a popular collection of saints' lives. Prior to her marriage Cecile prays to God to preserve her virginity:

> O Lord, my soule and eek my body gye
> Unwemmed, lest that I confounded be. (ll. 136-37)

On her wedding night she persuades her husband to refrain from sexual relations by revealing that an angel guards her purity (ll. 152-54). Cecile's virginity becomes the starting point for her active and spiritually fertile life as she preaches and converts others to Christianity. She dies not for trying to preserve her virginity but for refusing to yield to secular authority. Her story—quite possibly a "pious fiction" (Elliott 64)—presents the classic elements in a virginal marriage: "reluctance to marry, conversion of the spouse on the wedding night, and a secret resolve to preserve virginity" (65). In contrast, in "The Physician's Tale" virginity functions as an end in itself as a father lops off his innocent daughter's head to preserve her from a corrupt judge's lechery. In its literal-minded extremism the tale invites the audience to reflect upon—and perhaps to question—the value of virginity for its own sake.

The ascetic tendency to celebrate virginity as an absolute value led to a denigration of marriage. Though Christianity rejected the sharp dualism of sects like the Gnostics and the Manichees, who saw the spiritual and the material as diametrically opposed, it too saw sexuality as highly suspect and marriage as a grudging concession to human frailty and to the necessity for perpetuating the species. Thus marriage, though never rejected as an option for Christians, became a second-best lifestyle, and a whole corpus of misogamous literature vigorously advanced that view. For instance, Saint Jerome wrote a much-circulated treatise, *Adversus Joviniam,* in which he roundly attacked Jovinian's view that virginity was no more virtuous than marriage. Rejecting Jovinian's analysis of Paul, Jerome painstakingly argues:

> Let us go back to the beginning of the quotation: "It is better for a man not to touch a woman." Now if it is good not to touch a woman, it is bad to do so, for the only opposite to "good" is "bad". . . . It is as though one were to say, It is good to be fed on the purest wheat and to eat the finest bread, but in case anyone is forced by starvation to eat cow-dung I concede the eating of barley bread." Now does wheat lose its purity if barley is to be preferred to cow-dung? That thing is good by nature which does not have to be compared with evil, and which is not overshadowed by merely being preferred to something else. (qtd. in Kolve and Olson 330-31)

Elsewhere Jerome links marriage to gluttony and suggests that remarriage is like a dog returning to its own vomit (Wilson and Makowski 50). Jerome's negative attitude toward marriage led him to argue that producing more virgins for the Church is its only justification (Clark, "'Adam's Only Companion'" 18).

Though Jerome's views were much quoted, Augustine of Hippo's were ultimately more influential. His long struggle, recorded in his *Confessions,* to tame his own sexual urges significantly shaped those views. Long after his intellectual conversion to Christianity, he resisted embracing chastity, tying his full conversion to the moment when he gave up his marriage plans and accepted continence as a way of life. Augustine articulated the framework within which much of the Church's teaching on marriage and sexuality developed. As Brundage observes: "Augustine's underlying belief in the intrinsic sinfulness of carnal desire and the sensual delight that accompanied sexual union became a standard premise of Western beliefs about sexuality during the Middle Ages and beyond" (80). Yet like Paul, Augustine's teaching was more balanced than one might expect: though his polemical treatises treat marriage and sexuality negatively, his work as a whole conveys more positive views. For instance, in *De boni conjugali* ("On the Good of Marriage") he maintains that marriage functions as a sacrament, and he recognizes marital friendship as a benefit of marriage: "It [marriage] does not seem to me to be good only because of the procreation of children, but also because of the natural companionship between the sexes" (qtd. in Lawler, *Marriage and Sacrament* 58).

Framing his thinking against the Manichaeans and Pelagians, Augustine arrived at the posture that became medieval orthodoxy. Against the former—who saw marriage and procreation as evil because they perpetuate the spirit's imprisonment in the material world—he maintains that marriage and sexuality come from God and are essentially good. Against the latter—who had a positive view of human nature—he holds that in the postlapsarian state sexual intercourse almost inevitably involves sinfulness, even in marriage (Clark 15). Stressing the impact of original sin on human nature, he argues that sexual desire is "the most pervasive manifestation of man's disobedience to God's designs" (Brundage 80). In the prelapsarian state human beings could exercise rational control over their sexuality, but—as a consequence of sin—they can no longer control their sexual impulses (84). They experience concupiscence, most notably a predisposition toward the sinful—because irrational— pleasure that sex entails. Because of the human will's weakened condition, an essentially good sexuality can serve sinful ends, specifically when sexual pleasure becomes its own goal, unrelated to procreation, which is its primary justification. Thus Augustine reverses the Manichaean antimarriage and antiprocreation stance. But his negative attitude toward sexual pleasure for its own sake and his insistence on procreation as its essential justification became hallmarks of Christianity's views on marriage and sexuality.

Augustine did recognize additional valid reasons for marital sexual activity: satisfying the needs of one's partner—the Pauline concept of "paying the marriage debt"—and avoiding fornication. The latter, essentially a concession to human frailty, reflected biblical attacks on sexual activity outside marriage. In general though, most medieval clerics thought that marital partners should engage in as little sexual intercourse as possible. The English Dominican John Bromyard, for instance, saw marriage as "a life-long curbing of desire punctuated occasionally by serious and solemn attempts to conceive a child" (Brundage 503). Indeed throughout the medieval period many clerical commentators maintained that engaging in sex for pleasure alone was sinful even in marriage, and some, like Peter Damian, held that any sexual activity, even for the right reasons, entailed at least venial sin (197). Chaucer's Parson, in his lengthy penitential sermon, conveys the standard clerical views about marital sexuality:

> Thanne shal men understonde that for thre thynges a man and his wyf flesshly mowen assemble. The firste is in entente of engendrure of children to the service of God, for certes that is the cause final of matrimoyne. Another cause is to yelden everych of hem to oother the dette of hir bodies, for neither of hem hath power of his owene body. The thridde is for to eschewe leccherye and vileynye. (936-38)

He further explains that in the first and second instances sexual activity is meritorious; in the third it is slightly sinful. But he strongly attacks sex pursued simply for pleasure, even among the married:

> The fourthe manere is for to understonde, as if they assemble oonly for amorous love and for noon of the foreseyde causes, but for to accomplice thilke brennynge delit, they rekke nevere how ofte. Soothly it is deedly synne; and yet, with sorwe, somme folk wol peynen hem moore to doon than to hire appetit suffiseth. (942-43)

Another significant clerical teaching on marriage had to do with establishing required periods of abstinence from sex even within a marriage. The Church's negative attitude toward sexual pleasure and its belief that engaging in it involved impurity that needed to be cleansed before one participated in religious activity led to two kinds of prohibitions on marital sexual activity: those relating to the ecclesiastical calendar and those based on the woman's menstrual cycle. Though these kinds of strictures appear in patristic writings (Brundage 91-92), their fuller elaboration came in the penitential manuals that appeared in the early medieval period. Depending on the commentator one consulted, there were rules against marital sex during Advent and Lent, on feast days, on the vigil of feast days, on Sunday, on Friday, before receiving communion as well as during menstruation, pregnancy, lactation, and so on. Couples were also urged to postpone sexual relations from one to three or more days after their marriage and to spend that time in prayer and penance (154-64). Brundage concludes: "The mandatory periods of sexual abstinence prescribed in varying combinations by virtually all penitentials had the result for those who obeyed them scrupulously of reducing the frequency of marital intercourse to remarkably low levels" (159). In "The Miller's Tale" Nicholas exploits his clerical knowledge of such prohibitions when he alludes to them to convince old John to stow himself in a separate tub from Alisoun so that no sin will take place between them as they await the coming of a second flood, thereby clearing the way for his own amatory exploits.

Negative attitudes toward sexuality continued to appear in the works of traditional theologians well into the late medieval period and beyond. Bonaventure, a thirteenth-century Franciscan, held that, "The sexual act itself is diseased, for it cannot be performed without disorder" (qtd. in Brundage 424); he also taught that those who engage too frequently in sexual intercourse shorten their lives. Similarly, Aquinas held that sexual activity has debilitating effects and that military commanders should discourage their warriors from dissipating their strength by engaging in sex (424-25); the vestiges of this attitude appear in coaches' banning sex for athletes before important sporting events. Only a few clerical commentators recognized the marriage partners' mutual consolation and support as a valid reason for having sexual relations (197). As Brundage comments, "A happy marriage, some decretists thought, should be a source of love and emotional support as well as a remedy for lust" (278).

In spite of significant clerical interest in prescribing, circumscribing, and proscribing marital activities the laity continued for many centuries to follow its own practices in these areas: families arranged marriages for unwilling spouses when economic interests were at stake; men repudiated wives and took new, or additional, ones when it suited their fancy; couples started living together without any prior public ceremony. But gradually the Church established its authority over both the form and the substance of Christian marriage. From the eleventh to the thirteenth centuries reform-minded canonists pushed for greater consistency and uniformity in the Church's position on marriage, while simultaneously striving to enforce celibacy on the secular clergy. The consensus view among reformers saw marriage as having several defining features: it is monogamous, exogamous, and indissoluble; it rests firmly on the spouses' free consent; it provides the only legitimate sphere for sexual activity, which, in any case, should be subject to rigid controls; and it falls under ecclesiastical jurisdiction (183). Like Augustine, the reformers strenuously objected to sexual pleasure for its own sake, adopting an essentially Stoic approach that placed a high premium on maintaining rational control and on keeping sexual activity to a minimum for purely procreative purposes (281-83). Concomitantly—and perhaps in reaction to the canonists' stark view—the vernacular poets celebrated passionate love's beneficent impact on the lovers (184-85).

One unresolved ecclesiastical issue about marriage was whether consent or consummation constituted its defining feature. One school of thought—the French model deriving from Roman tradition—made marital consent alone the determining factor; the other—the Italian model going back to Germanic roots—maintained the necessity of coitus for a true marriage (Bloch 184-85). The principle for which the Church stood most firmly was the need for consent between the partners to create a valid union. This emphasis on free choice paralleled a broader societal movement that recognized the importance of individualism, one that appears both in the secular love poetry discussed earlier and in the thinking of twelfth-century clerics. Pope Alexander III's (1159-81) rulings on marriage all tended to increase individual choice and thus to highlight marriage's personal dimension. Both the poets' romantic love and Alexander's decretals "reflected a dawning consciousness of the importance of individual choice, coupled with a new awareness of marriage as a personal relationship—sentiments that a few decades earlier had seemed heretical" (Brundage 333). Thus the growing appreciation for the claims of the inner life manifested itself in the eventual, but by no means uniform, merging of secular and ecclesiastical values about love and marriage (227-28).

Increasing willingness to recognize the inner life's claims heightened the importance of the Church's insistence on consent between the partners. So strong was this stress that the Church recognized clandestine marriages at which only the two partners witnessed their mutual vows. "This principle had extraordinary social consequences," David Herlihy comments; he points out that the Church's insistence on the each individual's right to choose a spouse undermined familial attempts to use marriage to advance economic interests, lords' control over their subordinates, and indeed even the

Church's desire to play a central role in sanctioning marriage. For couples who did not follow the Church's prescriptions were considered to have illicit but valid marriages (*Medieval Households* 81). The Church's insistence on marital consent prevented Western Europe from ever developing into a full-blown patriarchy because it allowed individuals to thwart the designs of families intent on alliances that disregarded the partners' wishes (Brundage 265). Indeed Alan Macfarlane's study of love and marriage in England, though focused on the later medieval period and beyond, stresses the extent to which marriage in England always had an unusual emphasis on young people's right to decide on a marriage partner and the Church's support for that position (*Marriage and Love in England: Modes of Reproduction 1300–1840* 119-47): "If possible, a trial of strength should be avoided. Yet the Church was ultimately on the side of the couple" (145). Still, marriage had too many economic and social implications for families to give up their influence in this area without considerable resistance; they continued to exert pressure on the individual's choice of a spouse long after the Church's requirement for free consent had been clearly articulated (Brundage 437-38).

Several of Chaucer's tales bear on the consent issue. The Wife of Bath's marriages to her first three husbands, initially at the age of twelve, and Januarie's marriage to May in "The Merchant's Tale" suggest that, though these marriages take place with clerical oversight, the Church's consent requirement might not carry much weight when a wealthy old man set his eye on a desirable young woman. In "The Clerk's Tale" Walter and Griselde's nuptials lack a clerical presence, but Walter goes through the motions of obtaining consent from both Griselde and her father, a formality that he subsequently uses to justify abusing his wife. But "The Franklin's Tale"—still for many critics Chaucer's treatment of an ideal marriage—makes a "powerful statement of the necessity for absolute freedom in marriage—a total independence of choice," as David Raybin has recently argued ("'Wommen, Of Kynde, Desiren Libertee'" 65). Focusing on Dorigen, he maintains that in this tale "Chaucer explores the 'trouthe' that is uncovered when a wife gains the unconstrained choice that makes her something more than a rose in a flowering garden, and her husband something more than her gardener" (78-79).

The Church's firm insistence on the necessity for consent bolstered the growing acceptance of marriage's sacramental nature. As we have seen, the view that the marital bond reflects Christ's relationship with the Church goes back to Paul and Augustine. As the outward sign of a spiritual reality, marriage was considered a sacrament, but clerical culture long resisted recognizing it as capable of giving grace. Twelfth-century theologians did not reach consensus on this issue (Brundage 254). Lawler explains, "The early scholastics did not doubt that marriage was a sign of grace, but they did doubt that it was a cause of grace. They hesitated, therefore, to include it among the sacraments of the Church" (61). In 1215 the Fourth Lateran Council did recognize marriage's sacramental nature and set forth guidelines for marriage ceremonies, but the faithful often ignored these for some time to come. The Dominicans, especially Albert the Great and Thomas Aquinas, affirmed marriage's sacramental status and led an educational process that gradually produced a shift in attitudes (Lawler 61-62).

In succeeding centuries the Church sought—not without much resistance but with increasing success—to impose its understanding of marriage on the laity and to bring disputes about it into Church courts. Gradually the Church presided over rituals that coalesced into the traditional marriage ceremony: "the exchange of gifts, the exchange of promises, the blessing of a priest, the nuptial mass, the benediction of the marriage chamber" (Brooke, *The Medieval Idea of Marriage* 139). Usually the marriage ceremony occurred at the church door rather than inside the church proper (139). The spouses' marital vows, publicly proclaimed, reflected the ecclesiastical view of marriage and assumed the form that has remained remarkably consistent over the centuries. The woman's vows, quoted below, parallel the man's, though they are more explicit about her sexual obligations: "I take thee N. to be my wedded housbonde, to have and to holde, fro this day forwarde, for better or wors, for richer for pourer, in sicknesse and in hele, to be bonere and boxom, in bedde and atte bord, tyll dethe vs departhe, if holy chirche it wol ordeyne and thereto I plight thee my trouthe" (qtd. in Hanawalt, *The Ties That Bound* 203).

Ironically, of the several tales that depict or allude to marriage ceremonies in *The Canterbury Tales* "The Merchant's Tale" portrays one that receives the Church's full blessing, though it deals with the marriage between an aged bachelor seeking to legitimize his lechery and a beautiful but shallow young woman who finds him repugnant: Januarie and May are wedded with all solemnity as the priest comes forth to bless their union:

> But finally ycomen is the day
> That to the chirche bothe be they went
> For to receyve the hooly sacrement.

> Forth comth the preest, with stole aboute his nekke. . . .
> And seyde his orisons, as is usage,
> And croucheth hem, and bad God sholde hem blesse,
> And made al siker ynogh with hoolynesse.
>   (ll. 1700-3; 1706-8)

In spite of Januarie's external compliance with the clergy's requirements, he misappropriates clerical discourse for his own lascivious
purposes, entering into marriage to legalize his lechery: "A man may
do no synne with his wyf,/Ne hurte hymselven with his owene knyf"
(ll. 1839-40). While he rhapsodizes about the joys of marriage, he totally ignores the clerical teaching that sexual activity even in marriage is sinful if pursued for the sake of pleasure alone. As Peggy
Knapp points out:

> There is a pervasive sense that January is trying to outsmart God:
> by submitting to the sacrament of marriage late in life, he will
> somehow avoid the consequences of his earlier libertinism, and by
> celebrating sex within marriage, he will avoid his ongoing sin of
> selfish, exploitative sensuality (which, even when enacted with
> one's spouse) is licentious, even idolatrous. (108)

Januarie's selfish sensuality, thinly disguised in the language of the
Song of Songs' mystic spirituality, underscores the potential for self-
delusion that lies not far beneath the surface of romantic love,
whether it exists within or outside of marriage.

Chaucer's most extensive, and most searching, treatment of love's
joys and pitfalls occurs not in *The Canterbury Tales* but in *Troilus and
Criseyde*, where the lovers never enter into a formal marriage, unless it
be a clandestine one (Kelly, "Clandestine Marriage" 446-50). Here the
poet explores the process by which the lover moves from arrogant self-
sufficiency to enraptured dependency to disillusioned hopelessness.
Troilus suffers all of the pangs and exhibits all of the foolishness—and
sometimes the selfishness—of the stereotypical courtly lover. He responds instantaneously and irrevocably to Criseyde's beauty, languishes
in despair over the impossibility of ever winning her love without daring to even approach her, participates willingly in Pandarus's plotting
and submits to his indignities to gain access to her, and finally suffers
intensely when he must admit that she has betrayed him.

Critics have argued endlessly about how Chaucer expects his
readers to assess this love. Complicating the issue is the fact that a
Christian narrator is recounting a story that takes place in a pre-

Christian world. In the palinode the narrator directly addresses his readers, advising them to eschew human love in favor of divine love, which can never fail them:

> O yonge, fresshe folkes, he or she,
> In which that love up groweth with youre age,
> Repeyreth hom fro worldly vanyte. . . .
> And loveth hym the which that right for love
> Upon a crois, oure soules for to beye,
> First starf, and roos, and sit in hevene above;
> For he nyl falsen no wight, dar I seye,
> That wol his herte al holly on hym leye.
>   (ll. 1835-37; 1842-46)

Exegetical critics see this palinode as governing the meaning of the entire poem. At the other end are critics who read this passage as purely formulaic, a concession to conventional piety. Many intermediate positions have also been advanced.

Without attempting to resolve these disparate views, we can note a few additional points. First, as Derek Brewer observes, "not only Troilus himself but also Chaucer treats the love between Troilus and Criseyde as in accordance with the divine ordering of the world, and as entirely honorable" (23). Indeed at the end of Book III, after Troilus and Criseyde have consummated their love, Troilus sings a Neoplatonic hymn, adapted from Boethius's *Consolation,* celebrating love's harmonious ordering of the universe:

> Love, that of erthe and se hath governaunce. . . .
> Love, that with an holsom alliaunce
> Halt peples joyned, as hym lest hem gye,
> Love, that knetteth lawe of compaignie,
> And couples doth in vertu for to dwelle,
> Bynd this acord, that I have told and telle. (ll. 1744-50)

Also significant is the fact that Troilus's initial arrogant self-sufficiency dissolves as he experiences a lover's humbling uncertainty and that, even after facing the undeniable evidence of Criseyde's rejection, he cannot bring himself to stop loving her. Elizabeth Kirby has gone so far as to compare Troilus's unconditional love to that of "the suffering God incarnate" ("'Paradis Stood Formed in Hire Yen'" 271). She points out that the poem forces the reader to confront competing claims:

> The reader must grope his way through the characters' experience
> as he does through his own. The conflict between story and "epi-
> logue," between divine and human values, is only the last and most
> overt of the conflicts that run through the entire poem. Every as-
> pect of the story is presented so as to render as devastating as pos-
> sible the conflict of good with good, motive with motive, reality
> with reality, and, above all, love with love. (273)

Thus, the fact that, after his death, Troilus can look down from the
eighth sphere and laugh at his former woes does not negate the experiential value of his love for Criseyde; only after he has lived through
the painful, joyous, messy events linked with human love does he—
can he—achieve the divine perspective's amused detachment.

Perhaps the love-and-marriage-related issue in Chaucer's work
which has attracted most critical commentary is that of "maistrie," the
question of which partner should control the relationship. Of course,
clerical teaching, drawing on Paul's hierarchical model, was unequivo-
cal on this matter: the husband ought to rule the wife as the head
rules the body. In courtly literature, however, the lady was often cast in
the position of a feudal lord: she was the one to whom her lover owed
his highest allegiance and the one whose slightest wish he ought to
obey. Reconciling the two perspectives, in both life and literature, provided a basis for lively discussion. In the early twentieth century
George Lyman Kittredge formulated his theory that Chaucer explored this issue from a variety of perspectives in a group of dramatically interconnected tales called "the Marriage Group" (185-211). He
sees the Wife of Bath as setting a debate in motion by arguing that
marriages are happy when husbands relinquish control to their wives.
The Clerk responds with a tale about an inordinately submissive wife
but deflects the terms of his argument by coyly maintaining that it applies to divine-human relationships rather than to marital ones. The
Merchant, in what some critics have interpreted as his unconscious
revelation of disgust at his own duping, tells a tale about a wife who appears submissive but who is actually aggressively pursuing her own desires. Finally, "The Franklin's Tale" resolves the issue by portraying a
relationship in which each partner treats the other as an equal.

The opening section of "The Franklin's Tale" clearly portrays the
opposition between a woman's role as beloved lady and as wife.
Arveragus, who has successfully wooed Dorigen in courtly fashion,
persuades her to marry him: she agrees "to take hym for hir housbonde and hir lord" (l. 742). But Arveragus eschews the authoritari-
anism implicit in that phrase:

And for to lede the moore in blisse hir lyves,
Of his free wyl he swoor hire as a knyght
That nevere in al his lyf he, day ne nyght,
Ne sholde upon hym take no maistrie
Agayn hir wyl, ne kithe hire jalousie,
But hire obeye, and folwe hir wyl in al,
As any lovere to his lady shal. (ll. 744-50)

Dorigen for her part vows to be his "humble trewe wyf" (l. 758).
Their promise of mutuality highlights their determination to avoid
the hierarchical model in marriage. But their personal relationship
exists in a social matrix that requires Arveragus to retain the appearance of sovereignty, thus compromising their promise for the sake of
social expediency. By the end of the tale Dorigen has lost much of
her autonomy; she too has become just an instrument by which
three males can support their claim to noble behavior. The focus
shifts away from Dorigen when the narrator leaves the audience with
a question that centers on the males' behavior and omits her completely: "Lordynges, this question, thanne, wol I aske now,/Which
was the mooste fre, as thynketh yow?" (ll. 1621-22). The mutual accommodation that Arveragus and Dorigen arrive at in the early
phase of their marriage strikes Kittredge and other critics as
Chaucer's solution to the problem of "maistrye." The exegetical critics, however, reject this view, finding Arveragus guilty of culpably ab-
dicating a husband's rightful authority and thus depriving Dorigen
of needed guidance. Feminist critics, on the other hand, see Arveragus's concession of power as more apparent than real: in her crisis
Dorigen essentially reverts to the position of subservient wife, doing,
however reluctantly, what her husband commands.

The pilgrim who advances the most extensive and provocative
commentary about marital relationships is the Wife of Bath. Having
absorbed and transformed clerical discourse, she cites the Genesis
passage on procreation: "God bad us for to wexe and multiplye" (l.
28) and then recalls the Pauline teachings on the desirability, but
not the necessity, for celibacy:

Poul dorste nat comanden, atte leeste,
A thyng of which his maister yaf noon heeste.
The dart is set up for virginitee;
Cacche whoso may, who renneth best lat see.
But this word is nat taken of every wight. . . .
Al nys but conseil to virginitee. (ll. 73-77; 82)

Conceding that virginity constitutes the more spiritually perfect way of life, the Wife cheerfully admits that she does not aspire to perfection and, overturning Jerome's argument, that she is perfectly content to be barley rather than white bread, to be an earthen vessel rather than a golden bowl in the Lord's household:

> For wel ye knowe, a lord in his houshold,
> He nath nat every vessel al of gold;
> Somme been of tree, and doon hir lord servyse.
> (ll. 99-101)

On the subject of the marriage debt the Wife of Bath assumes a more aggressive stance, expressing her determination to demand full payment:

> An housbonde I wol have—I wol nat lette—
> Which shal be bothe my dettour and my thral,
> And have his tribulacion withal
> Upon his flessh, whil that I am his wyf.
> I have the power durynge al my lyf
> Upon his propre body, and noght he. (ll. 154-59)

Scholars disagree on the nature and implications of the Wife's activity as an exegete. D. W. Robertson, Jr., sees her as "hopelessly carnal and literal" (*A Preface to Chaucer* 317), her attitudes deeply embedded in the perspectives of the Old Law; she hears only the language of the flesh and remains deaf to that of the spirit (322-29). He argues that the first section of her prologue highlights her failure as an exegete, and he ultimately deprives her of individuality, making her the embodiment of a particular mindset—"carnal understanding": "Alisoun of Bath is not a 'character' in the modern sense at all, but an elaborate iconographic figure designed to show the manifold implications of an attitude" (330).

While Robertson and others see the Wife's views on sexuality and marriage as outrageous, Donald Howard maintains that "it is hard to fault her theology" because she accepts the premise that fallen human nature makes the attainment of Christian perfection impossible for everyone (*The Idea of The Canterbury Tales* 250). Her views remain essentially within the bounds of orthodoxy, though she undoubtedly accentuates differently than do the clerics. Whatever the Wife's precise degree of orthodoxy, the very fact that she functions like a biblical commentator, arrogating to herself a jealously guarded clerical prerogative, is highly significant. Peter Brown and Andrew Butcher see the Wife's performance, both prologue and tale, rather than "The Franklin's Tale" as Chaucer's most considered response to late fourteenth century societal attitudes about marriage: "Chaucer was concerned to show that sexuality, rather than being condemned to the status of a divisive force, belonged within marriage. At the same time he attempted to demonstrate that marriage is a spiritual as well as a material bond" (45). Citing the devastating impact of plague, they argue that marriage was the core of late medieval survival and renewal efforts and that the Wife's performance underscores those concerns (44).

In the official culture women remained very economically circumscribed because their access to resources and profit-making opportunities were very limited. As discussed in Chapter Eight, market values governed marriage as well as commerce, with women often serving as commodities. To combat the constrictions of the male-dominated official world, women resorted to more informal social structures, like neighborhoods or extended families, as avenues for self-expression (Brown and Butcher 27-44). This mostly oral culture, which Alisoun draws on in the prologue to her tale, gave women the freedom to express "ideas contradictory to or subversive of exclusive male dominance" (28). This culture provides the Wife with a community in which to develop and express her views. In her first three marriages to rich, old husbands Alisoun of Bath fulfills the worst nightmares of a long misogamous tradition by turning the table on her husbands, exploiting them both sexually and financially. Not only does she collect the marriage debt—she charges for it, wearing out her husbands' physical reserves. In her fifth marriage, however, she confronts the weight of clerical authority head-on, definitively rejecting it by tearing out pages from Jankyn's collection of misogynistic authorities. The marriage of mutuality that Alisoun and Jankyn achieve after their donnybrook necessitates rejecting clerical influence outright, as Brown and Butcher explain:

> Only when the book is burned, and the noxious influence of church-sanctioned authority removed, can man and wife enter into a state which is truly a marriage between equal individuals, in which freedom, not restraint, is the predominant atmosphere. . . . There is a sense of discovery, of a genuine breakthrough at this point in the prologue. The Wife, the reader, and not least Jankyn, who has renounced his position of dominance and put himself under female control, have arrived at an important moment of realization. He denies male mastery and so liberates them both. (49-50)

The issues that appear at the end of the prologue carry over into the tale where the Knight—the reluctant husband of a poor, ugly, and aged wife—has the opportunity to transcend stereotypical male thinking about women. Doing so enables both the Knight and his wife to achieve the kind of marriage each seeks. Brown and Butcher see Chaucer as reaching back to a radical Christian tradition—one that contemporary Church practices and attitudes blurred beyond recognition—by setting forth in the sermon on "gentilesse" an opposition between purely material values based on externals and the inner spiritual reality to which Christians should be faithful (51-52).

Chaucer's works portray an almost encyclopedic array of amorous and marital attitudes and practices. Indeed such relationships constitute one of the major recurring themes in *The Canterbury Tales*. Notable also is that its most heroic and/or virtuous women, like Custance, Griselde and Dorigen, achieve their status within the framework of marriage and motherhood, not—as we have seen in Chapter Nine—by overcoming their femininity and becoming pseudomales. For Chaucer love and marriage afford opportunities for self-delusion, for economic exploitation, for selfishness, for autocratic domination—but also for self-transcendence, for personal growth, for mutual support. As Christopher Brooke sums up, "Chaucer is profoundly elusive. What is clear is that he had a capacious view of love and sexuality" (227). As the late medieval Christian world struggled to resolve the confusingly varied perspectives on love, sexuality, and marriage it had inherited from multiple traditions, the laity's experience and the testimony of poets like Chaucer played an increasingly insistent role in the cultural dialogue that ultimately yielded a much more affirmative view of love and marriage's role in securing human happiness.

V.

CONCLUSION

Chapter Eleven

A Zone of Freedom: Carnival as the Emblem of an Age

One of the features of medieval culture that people today find most puzzling is the way in which piety and laughter, even irreverence and obscenity, coexist. Taught to think of the medieval era as one of faith, devotion, and respect for hierarchical authority—one in which the Church successfully enforced ascetic values—we expect to find in its art and literature polite reticence about bodily functions, reverent piety about sacred matters, and respectful deference toward those who embody cultural ideals. Instead we sometimes encounter bawdy frankness, parodic inversions of sacred motifs, and satiric jibes directed at officials, especially clerics, portrayed as exploitative and licentious. Indeed we are invited to laugh at just what the official culture holds most sacred.

Chaucer's *Canterbury Tales* provides a compelling instance of the medieval tendency to blur the line between the holy and the profane. Far from being idiosyncratic or gratuitously shocking, the irreverence and bawdiness in tales like that of the Miller link it to characteristic features of medieval life. As we have seen, the spiritually serious purpose of pilgrimage provides the basic framework for the story collection; it orients the enterprise toward the saint's shrine, emblematic of humanity's heavenly goal, and it calls the pilgrims to the penitential attitude and behavior that will assure attainment of that goal. But once Harry Bailly makes his proposal for a tale-telling contest as a pleasant pastime, the focus shifts from the journey's end, with its emphasis on individual salvation, to the communal celebration involved in the journey-in-progress. Play and laughter become governing features as the pilgrims enter the world of game, as Gabriel Josipovici stresses: "At the centre of *The Canterbury Tales* stands a game, mirroring that other game, which poet and reader have agreed to play. Both games take place within a context of real life, but, because they are games, the participants are answerable to none of the laws which govern real life, but only to those rules which they have agreed upon beforehand" ("Fiction and Game in *The Canterbury Tales*" 189-90). In effect, the ludic element in the *Tales* moves it outside the realm of ordinary living and into the borderline world of festive celebration.

To gain a better understanding of the comic, festive, burlesque element in medieval culture, we need to turn our attention away from the official world of literacy and high culture to the oral world of folk customs and beliefs briefly discussed in the previous chapter. In Chapter One we traced the broad framework of medieval thought rooted in sacred scripture and in the Neoplatonic/Aristotelian philosophical tradition, one preserved and passed on by an educated, Latinate clergy. Though much of what we know about the medieval world derives from the written records that reflect the official culture, the picture remains incomplete if we fail to recognize that a vibrant, tenacious, usually oral tradition of popular culture coexisted with the elite culture in complex, sometimes paradoxical relationships. "We cannot understand the spiritual society adequately," Aaron Gurevich insists, "without the mythopoetic and folkloric tradition, the heritage of the common people which was only partially absorbed by the 'official' culture" (xviii).

Though we are making a distinction between learned and popular culture—associating the former with the literate minority and the latter with the illiterate majority—the boundary between the two was very permeable. Indeed several commentators have observed that the medieval period frequently blurs the line between these two worlds (Erickson 10). Jean-Claude Schmitt sees "the opposition of these two cultures" as "one of the most important features of feudal society. Their relationship was a complex one, shifting between mutual incomprehension and overt hostility, but without there ever being a complete cessation of the exchanges that such conflicts sometimes fostered" (*The Holy Greyhound* 1). Furthermore, the learned did not simply share popular views: those beliefs were central to the overall culture (Gurevich 176).

Popular culture embraces many areas of medieval life, but we will focus on those related to the comic and/or celebratory because that aspect is central to *The Canterbury Tales*. Scholars have long recognized that the comic impulse's roots lie deep in the human race's desire to assure its survival against constant threats to its own and the land's fertility. At critical periods in the agricultural cycle peasants shared a communal concern about assuring the success of their crops, a concern expressed in village rituals at seasons subsequently related to the rhythms of Christian spiritual life (Chambers, *The Medieval Stage* 109-10). An integral element of such rituals was some kind of sacrifice—vegetable, animal, or human. When human sacrifice was involved, the victim was often the community's leader or king, who had taken the lead role in the sacrificial act in the previous year, thereby absorbing the fertility spirit's power. With the depletion of that power at year's end the leader was replaced by another, who would then be sacrificed the following year. Gradually substitutes, both human and animal, took the leader's place. Out of such bloody beginnings came the practice of selecting a temporary authority figure (130-45).

Strangely enough, then, the practice of having a master of ceremonies has its origins in rites associated with making the community's leader a sacrificial victim. But how did the comic spirit make its way into such serious and violent events? One answer lies in the necessity of involving the entire community in the sacrificial rites; the daily toilsome routine came to a standstill. It was, as Chambers succinctly points out, "a holiday as well as a holy day" (147). Far from being a peripheral or inconsequential element in human society, play lies at the center of communal life. In *Homo Ludens: A Study of the Play Element in Culture* Johan Huizinga sets forth several characteristics of play: freedom, distinctness from the pragmatic purposes of quotidian life, separateness in time and space. Play is closely related to the sacred, and that relationship manifests itself in ritual (Huizinga 8-27). Closely allied to the playful, the comic has important societal functions: it helps assert control over that which is fearsome and overpowering. At least temporarily, laughter fends off terror by deflating the power that threatens destruction: when we laugh at what we fear, we undermine its power over us. As Laura Kendrick argues in *Chaucerian Play*, "Laughter is man's way of asserting his superiority or mastery in difficult situations. . . . Laughter denies the reality or seriousness of whatever threatens to immobilize man's mind or body" (1).

But official culture in the Middle Ages, basing itself on scriptural attacks and on the fact that scripture records no instance of Jesus laughing, was suspicious of laughter. "The Christian God," V. A. Kolve comments, "was never credited with a sense of humor. . . . Rather, a powerful case was established and reiterated throughout the Middle Ages that laughter and frivolity, the temporary abstention from involvement in all that is serious in the human condition, was an offense against God, a negation of the example of Christ, and a peril to men's souls" (*The Play Called Corpus Christi* 126). Still, as we have seen in Chapter Two, even the official culture recognized recreation's role, and hence that of play and laughter, in sustaining physical and spiritual health. Folk culture, for its part, clung tenaciously to its traditional festivities. At best the Church could absorb and transform, rather than stamp out, folk practices it found offensive. Its willingness to celebrate the most sacred religious feasts, Christmas and Easter, in the time frames associated with the most important popular celebrations highlights its willingness to accommodate and incorporate, thereby virtually assuring the survival of elements from those festivities alongside its own sacred rites.

A number of the folk practices associated with those feasts involved temporarily overturning existing hierarchical structures, parodying sacred practices or language, and reversing roles between men and women, humans and animals. For instance, the practice of instituting a boy-bishop was linked to the Feast of the Holy Innocents, the children slaughtered on King Herod's orders to destroy a potential competitor. One young boy from among those associated with a church became a mock bishop, temporarily assuming authority over the others. Ceremonial books like the one at Rouen provide some insight into what went on: the boy-bishop donned episcopal attire and accoutrements; a procession to the altar of the Holy Innocents took place; the boy-bishop gave his blessing, and the other boys deferred to him with reverential behavior; sometimes the bishop delivered a sermon, though not necessarily one he had written himself (Chambers 344-52). This practice had a scriptural basis: "The feast grew from an important biblical text—'He hath put down the mighty from their seat, and hath exalted the humble'—and it was conceived as a reverent celebration of this Christian truth" (Kolve, *The Play Called Corpus Christi* 137). But beneath the scriptural sanction for this practice lay the deeply rooted folk practice of instituting a temporary ruler who leads the community in festive, even riotous, celebrations. Thus though the boy-bishop ceremony had ecclesiastical approval and was usually manageable because of the boys' subjection to authority, it could get out of hand: injunctions against mockery of church services and leaders as well as complaints about harm done to church property suggest that the resulting festive atmosphere engendered behavior that officialdom was not always successful in keeping within acceptable bounds (Chambers 363-66).

Another kind of festivity, the written evidence for which comes primarily from France, was known as the Feast of Fools, or alternatively the Feast of Asses or the Feast of Subdeacons; it was usually celebrated on January 1, the Feast of the Circumcision. In this case, one of the subdeacons, among the lowliest of clerics, took charge, wielding a symbol of authority. This festival, in an ecclesiastical setting, reveals many features originally linked with popular festivities: role reversals, processions, songs and dances, food and drink, ball games, grotesque masks, and ritualized assaults like ducking and whipping. In some cases an ass was brought into the church, and responses to the prayers of the Mass were made by brays. The person taking the place of the priest ended Mass by braying three times, or he intoned the prayers in unusual pitches or with strange sounds (Chambers 275-90). V. A. Kolve comments, "The result was often a full-scale burlesque of sacred ceremony" (*The Play Called Corpus Christi* 135). A letter from 1445, from the University of Paris's dean of theology to the French clergy, gives some insight into the flavor of these feasts:

> Priests and clerks may be seen wearing masks and monstrous visages at the hours of office. They dance in the choir dressed as women, panders, or minstrels. They sing wanton songs. They eat black puddings at the horn of the altar while the celebrant is saying mass. They play at dice there. They cense with stinking smoke from the soles of old shoes. They run and leap through the church, without a blush at their shame. Finally they drive about the town and its theatres in shabby traps and carts; and rouse the laughter of their fellows and the bystanders in infamous performances, with indecent gestures and verses scurrilous and unchaste. (qtd. in Chambers 294)

The letter evidences clear clerical distaste for such goings-on, but the festivities were very popular and died out only gradually or continued in an altered form (Chambers 300).

In the visual arts the festive or comic impulse asserts itself literally on the margins or undersides of official representations. The marginalia on medieval manuscripts frequently introduce grotesques—all kinds of marvelous creatures and monstrous hybrids—to wean the eye away from the sacred images that dominate the page. In churches, misericords—the folding seats in choir stalls that aged or infirm clerics could lean back on to relieve weary limbs during prolonged religious offices—provided anonymous sculptors an opportunity for imaginative play. The stalls themselves were beautifully decorated in intricate and delicate patterns worthy of the sacred space they occupied. But the misericords provide a glimpse of another dimension to the sculptors' imagination. Sometimes—as in portrayals of the Green Man, with his bushy hair and flowing beard—they capture figures still alive in the folk imagination. In other instances they depict the role reversals associated with popular festivities: two misericords now housed at the Cluny Museum in Paris portray a pig playing a musical instrument and a pig family at dinner. Male/female reversals appear in depictions of shrewish wives beating their husbands or pulling their beards. Misericords also provide an avenue for subtle satiric thrusts: in the chapel at the Chateau of Castelnau-Bretenoux one misericord shows a stocky woman—her head hunched up against her shoulders, her nose directly beneath the spot which would support the monkly posterior, and her arms and legs widely spread apart as if straining to hold up the clerical buttocks. This rendering of the "sniffing the bottom" motif may reflect its anonymous sculptor's sense of oppression or sense of humor—or perhaps a mixture of both. In short, a playful, often mocking spirit asserts itself in these hidden-away spots.

The resurgence of a vernacular dramatic tradition in the late medieval world provided another opportunity for popular celebration and for satiric jabs at authority figures. By the Late Middle Ages the great mystery cycles, linked to the Feast of Corpus Christi in early summer, had moved out of ecclesiastical settings into town centers and drew their audiences from all societal levels (Kolve, *The Play Called Corpus Christi* 6). These dramas drew the entire community together, both as actors in a sacred drama and as audience. The shift in venue brought with it a shift in mood, as Kolve explains:

> When drama moved into the streets and the market place, into a milieu already the home of men's playing and games, it was redefined *as* a game and allowed to exploit fully its nonearnest, gratuitous nature at the same time as its range of subject and its cast of sacred personae grew. It was a special kind of game, of course. . . . It is the kind of game in which a peasant is made a king or knight, and after it is over becomes once again a peasant. (19)

Drama brought the events of sacred history into the people's quotidian life: reenacting those events in broad daylight with little separation between actors and audience created a framework that was both timeless and here-and-now (101-4). The typological approach discussed in Chapter One created a sacred time that obliterated the historical distance between events. But while this feature helped people confront the meaning of the sacred events they were witnessing for their own lives, the communal and celebratory atmosphere in which the performances took place supported the emergence of festive features—comic action, parody, and social reversals.

Indeed these dramas' most original elements are "almost exclusively comic actions" (143). For instance, the Noah plays introduce the comic figure of Noah's wife, for whom there is no biblical basis except the mere fact that she existed. Also, the plays depicting the Adoration of the Shepherds often include some sort of verbal or physical struggle (or both). In the Chester cycle, for instance, one young, recalcitrant shepherd refuses to join the others in paying respect to the infant Jesus and complains about the quality of their food. He challenges them all to a wrestling match in which he overcomes three shepherds who are his seniors and who exercise authority over him (155-56). This apparently extraneous element again relates to the essential Christian theme of the Lord putting down the mighty and exalting the humble. "The truth enshrined in that custom," Kolve maintains, "was felt to be a part of the deepest significance of the Incarnation" (156). But if these practices highlighted religious truths, their inversions of established hierarchies also created opportunities for parody and social critique. They brought some explosive concepts out of the realm of beneath-the-breath mutterings and marginalized tomfoolery into a societally sanctioned, albeit temporary, arena.

By the late medieval period festivities that encompassed all social classes—which Lindahl characterizes as "mixed-class entertainments"—had a number of distinctive features: autocratic rulers enforced rigid rules and presided over the festivities; the events had a formal and processional as well as a competitive element; some kind of hierarchical structure was enforced; the sacred and the profane coexisted; and the line between observer and participant blurred because the same people functioned as both audience and performers. The closeness of the audience/performer interaction highlights the fact that festival art is acutely sensitive to its audience's needs and requirements (Lindahl, "The Festive Form of the *Canterbury Tales*" 534-40). These characteristics of medieval festivals appear in *The Canterbury Tales*, as Carl Lindahl argues:

> Chaucer shaped his poem to simulate the structure of the medieval festival, fitting the patterns of action in the frame and links to a model of oral group performance thoroughly familiar to his contemporaries. . . . Chaucer reshapes literature into festival, crafting a frozen representation of a lively play form never before (or since) rendered into writing, a play world fully consonant in its

rules and interactions with celebrations the poet's contemporaries witnessed and enacted. (533)

Though scholars of drama and anthropology have long been aware of folk festival practices, the work of the Russian critic Mikhail Bakhtin has yielded new insights that have a potential for illuminating Chaucer's poetry. He uses the concept of the "carnivalesque" to describe a whole range of attitudes and behaviors that characterize folk or popular culture (*Rabelais and His World* 4). Lent—beginning with Ash Wednesday's somber *memento mori*, which fixes attention on one's preparedness to face judgment—ushers in a period of fasting, self-denial, prayer, and penance, a time when clerical voices reiterate and enforce ascetic, often guilt-inducing, regulations and prohibitions. Carnival, on the other hand, is a time of release, of self-indulgence, of excess—and of burlesque inversions that reject normal societal constraints. In the Late Middle Ages carnival activities, though they culminated on Mardi Gras, could last as long as three months and could involve a wide range of activities (Andreas, "'New Science' from 'Olde Bokes'" 139). Indeed as Anthony Gash notes, "The term *Christmas* was frequently applied to the whole season from Christmas Day to Shrove Tuesday" ("Carnival Against Lent" 83). Thus a substantial portion of the year was given over to celebratory activities that proceeded from a value system at odds with otherworldly asceticism.

The carnivalesque is closely linked to the deeply rooted human attempt to create a zone of freedom beyond the strictures imposed by the reigning orthodoxies and power structures, be they secular or religious. "Carnival is the people's second life, organized on the basis of laughter," Bahktin maintains. "It is a festive life. Festivity is a peculiar feature of all comic rituals and spectacles of the Middle Ages" (*Rabelais and His World* 8). Besides having universal appeal, carnival is also totally engrossing and functions only on its own terms (7). Carnival asserts the unquenchable spirit of freedom, of hostility toward all that controls and constrains: "It marked the suspension of all hierarchical rank, privileges, norms, and prohibitions. Carnival was the true feast of time, the feast of becoming, change, and renewal. It rejected all that was immortalized and completed" (10).

The carnivalesque in medieval culture has a close relationship to the grotesque: there is a strong link between folk humor and "grotesque realism" (Bahktin 18). While clerical culture exalts the spirit, the grotesque celebrates the body: "The essential principle of grotesque realism is degradation, that is, the lowering of all that is high, spiritual, ideal, abstract; it is a transfer to the material level, to the sphere of earth and body in their indissoluble unity" (19-20). The grotesque emphasizes becoming or process rather than classic perfection, focusing on the body at its points of greatest transformation—soon after birth or approaching death—not in its classic maturity. Also, it highlights those parts of the body that put the inside into contact with the outside—mouth, nose, belly, sexual organs, anus—and it celebrates eating, defecating, copulating, birthing—often with abusive or scatological language (21-27).

As suggested earlier, a number of characteristics associated with folk festivals and with the grotesque are inherent in Christianity itself: the elevation of the lowly and the wisdom of apparent folly are important scriptural motifs. Jesus praises the publican who sees himself as a sinner and prays from the back of the temple, rather than the Pharisee who places himself in a prominent position at the front of the temple (Luke 18: 9-14) The beatitudes are built on the concept of reversal: "blessed are the poor," "blessed are the meek." Even more fundamentally, of course, the idea of a man/God who submits himself to ignominious crucifixion involves an inversion of customary ideas about power and requires a faith that appears foolish: "Make no mistake about it: if any one of you thinks of himself as wise, in the ordinary sense of the word, then he must learn to be a fool before he really can be wise. Why? Because the wisdom of this world is foolishness to God." (1 Cor. 3:18). Aaron Gurevich sums up the link between basic Christian motifs and the medieval grotesque as follows: "The synthesis of extreme seriousness and tragedy, on the one hand, and of the tendency to maximum lowering, on the other, was in essence part of Christian dogma, in which the concept of the Incarnation united the divine and the human in their extreme manifestation" (181).

We might argue, then, that the mindset associated with carnival brought to the fore aspects of Christian belief that medieval society tended to submerge. The traditional view is that official culture sanctioned, or at least condoned, festive irreverence because it provided a safe, containable, time-and-space-bound framework for releasing pent-up hostilities that might otherwise erupt more dangerously. Chambers, for instance, notes that despite some official attempts by religious leaders like Robert Grosseteste and Jean Gerson to curb the most outrageous festival practices, the Church not only tolerated but actually supported the village festivals (93). More recently, Lindahl comments on the role of festive inversions as a cultural safety valve: "Such inversions were not only desirable but necessary for the lower classes. The festival presented their only opportunity for sanctioned social ascent. The subservience of the churls at all other times made them not only relish but demand exalted treatment on holidays" (553). Though Lindahl sees the social inversions associated with festivals as reinforcing existing hierarchical structures, he recognizes their potential for unsettling the status quo (553).

Other recent scholars, especially those of a new historicist persuasion, build on Bakhtin's belief that carnival affords the opportunity to create the world anew (*Rabelais* 34); they see seeds of revolution in the carnival atmosphere. Arguing from the highly interactive relationship between performers and audience and the limited and clerically controlled written record, Anthony Gash, for instance, challenges V. A. Kolve's view that medieval drama communicated uniform dogma to a receptive, passively accepting populace (94). The loosening of cultural constraints that carnival fosters could lead to rebellious action, as did happen in fifteenth-century Norwich, when discontented artisans used the symbolic contrast between Christmas and Lent for political purposes: "The winter festivities provided not only an opportunity for sedition, but also a symbolism for protest" (Gash 85). In the fluid, dynamic atmosphere of popular celebration no one group or person could control what meanings words and actions communicated: winks, gestures, facial expressions, intonations—all are capable of undermining officially sanctioned interpretations and carefully buttressed power structures. As Gash concludes: "Thus winter holidays became . . . the site of a game of equivocation and interpretation, which . . . could become extremely serious"(94).

The central issue boils down to the following question: are the reversals and irreverences—and the laughter they generate—that are so integral to folk festivities essentially functioning like a safety valve on a pressure cooker, letting off steam in a periodic and controlled way so as to permit society to continue unchanged, or is the license and rebelliousness that breaks forth in them more like the beginning of an uncontrolled chain reaction that forebodes an explosion? In *The Name of the Rose* Umberto Eco, with twentieth-century hindsight, explores this issue through his blind old monk Jorge, who, recognizing the seditious seeds in laughter, exerts all his remaining energy to preventing its infectious spirit from gaining a societal foothold. For him laughter is allowable only when it stays on society's periphery: "But laughter is weakness, corruption, the foolishness of the flesh. It is the peasant's entertainment, the drunkard's license; even the church in her wisdom has granted the moment of feast, carnival, fair, this diurnal pollution that releases humors and distracts from other desires and other ambitions" (474). He is willing, however, to take extreme measures to prevent Aristotle's lost treatise on comedy from resurfacing, fearing that the Philosopher's prestige would legitimate laughter and give it a weight capable of undermining the very bases of medieval society: "But this book could teach that freeing oneself of the fear of the Devil is wisdom . . . on the day when the Philosopher's word would justify the marginal jests of the debauched imagination, or when what has been marginal would leap to the center, every trace of the center would be lost" (474-75).

Though carnivalesque elements are interwoven throughout Chaucer's work, our discussion will focus on three characters— Harry Bailly, the Miller, and the Wife of Bath—and on the fabliau genre that creates a world that functions on carnivalesque values. As suggested earlier, Harry Bailly shifts the focus of the pilgrimage, directing it toward the world of play, game, and festive competition. His role as innkeeper signals a move into an arena where carnival values reign. Quickly becoming the master of ceremonies, he enjoys the status of temporary ruler granted the privilege of autocratic governance within an agreed-upon framework:

> And for to make yow the moore mury,
> I wol myselven goodly with yow ryde,
> Right at myn owene cost, and be youre gyde;
> And whoso wole my juggement withseye
> Shal paye al that we spenden by the weye.
> And if ye vouche sauf that it be so,
> Tel me anon, withouten wordes mo,
> And I wol erly shape me therfore. (GP, ll. 802-9)

The wide disparity between the offense—opposing Harry's rule— and the penalty—assuming financial responsibility for all the pilgrims' expenses on the journey—suggests that the pilgrims have moved outside the realm of ordinary reckonings. Once they enter the world of game, they can unquestioningly accept Harry's right to set rules and establish penalties for violations, however shaky he proves in maintaining the authority he has seized. But throughout the links to the tales Harry frequently tries to restore order and defers to the "gentils," an attitude that signals his willingness to enforce social distinctions and privileges, which carnival values suspend, if not erase. Even that deference has its place among festival values, as John Ganim points out: "Despite his sense of amusement and recreation, he bristles at and seeks to control the very sorts of anarchic explosions that his stress on festivity almost by nature releases. His restraint may be more than burgher-like respectability: popular rituals, even when filled with festive qualities, are often performed with a certain dignified awareness" (*Chaucerian Theatricality* 37).

The Miller is pure carnival. His portrait in the "General Prologue" highlights his uncompromising physicality: "a stout carl for the nones;/Ful byg he was of brawn, and eek of bones. . . . He was shortsholdred, brood, a thikke knarre" (ll. 545-49). His description focuses on the body parts particularly associated with the carnivalesque—not the eyes, foreheads, and cheeks of romance but a prominent nose and mouth: "Upon the cop right of his nose he hade/A werte, and thereon stood a toft of herys/Reed as the brustles of a sowys erys" (ll. 554-56) and "His mouth as greet was as a greet forneys" (l. 559). Indeed that mouth has been linked iconographically with the gaping hell-mouths on dragonlike figures who swallow the damned. The Miller's bagpipes also link him to the carnivalesque: besides their boisterous noise making, their shape evokes male genitalia (Block, "Chaucer's Millers and Their Bagpipes" 239-43).

Aspects of the carnivalesque also emerge in the Miller's actions and attitudes in the prologue to his tale. Harry, the authority figure, encounters the first major challenge to his authority from the Miller, who in his drunkenness pushes himself forward and insists upon telling his tale out of turn:

> He nolde avalen neither hood ne hat,
> Ne abyde no man for his curteisie,
> But in Pilates voys he gan to crie,
> And swoor, "By armes, and by blood and bones,
> I kan a noble tale, for the nones,
> With which I wol now quite the Knyghtes tale."
> (Mil P, ll. 3122-27)

The Miller's intrusion brings a new dimension to the contest. No longer does the competitive element await deliberations based on criteria—"sentence and solaas"—from the clerkly sphere. Rather, the festival principles of one-upmanship and direct appeals to the audience govern. Significantly, the reference to "Pilates voys"— which refers to the exaggerated blustering exhibited by the tyrannical villains in the Christian story of salvation—evokes the popular genre of the mystery plays. The Miller's behavior operates within the realm of festival values:

His rebellion is in harmony with the great annual revolution
Chaucer has described in the opening lines of the General Prologue. . . . The Miller in pushing himself to the fore is, therefore,
claiming no more than the privilege of the Boy Bishop, the master
of the Feast of Fools, and the Lord of Misrule. By challenging the
Knight, the figure of authority, he follows the pattern of medieval
comedy. (David 93-94)

The Wife of Bath is another festive, carnivalesque figure. Her celebratory attitude toward her own sexuality, her willingness to associate herself with the earthy and the physical, her delight in seizing the
clerical prerogative of assigning meaning to authoritative texts, her
pride in having mastered her first three husbands—all reflect carnival values. We have seen that role reversals and overturnings, specifically of the weak over the strong, were an important part of the
festival atmosphere. Jean Klene reminds us that the motif of "the
world upside-down" goes back at least as far as ancient Sumerian and
Egyptian art ("Chaucer's Contribution to a Popular Topos" 322);
though she does not see social protest in this motif, she notes that it
involves a temporary or imaginary victory by those usually deprived
of power (326-27). Women's struggles to wrest control from men, as
in "the quarrel over the breeches" (327), was a significant feature of
these reversals. Because, as we have seen, the carnival world, unlike
the official world, celebrated the body over the spirit, it tended to be
much more hospitable toward women (Bahktin 240).

In addition, women could become the instruments of social critique—perhaps safer ones because they were excluded from political
and religious authority. As mentioned earlier, the mystery plays introduced the comic figure of Noah's wife and portrayed her as a
shrew who bitterly resists getting on the ark. The official gloss holds
that her behavior depicts humanity's resistance to God's salvific efforts or that it shows typically feminine recalcitrance and irrational-
ity that needs to be curbed by strong masculine action (Kolve, *The
Play Called Corpus Christi* 146-50). But Anthony Gash sees her as serving as an outlet for societal unrest:

She must have answered some deep social and expressive needs
for late medieval communities since her rebellious and anarchic
behaviour is unauthorized by the Bible. . . . Rather than describing
Noah's wife as a type of Eve, we might conjecture that one source
of her appeal was that by rebelling but not being punished, and by
being both independent and a wife (like Chaucer's Wife of Bath),

she eludes the polarized roles assigned to women in the Bible and
in medieval patriarchy. (79)

The Wife of Bath's struggle for and, in the case of her first three
marriages, her achievement of dominance over her husbands signal
her link to the reversals characteristic of the carnivalesque. Her vibrant physical energy and her exuberant language roll over her su-
perannuated mates, leaving them defenseless against her
onslaughts:

> For thogh the pope hadde seten hem biside,
> I wolde not spare hem at hire owene bord,
> For, by my trouthe, I quitte hem word for word.
> (WBP, ll. 420-22)

Despite Jesus's counsel to perfection and despite the Pauline advice
about treating widowhood as an opportunity to turn toward matters
spiritual, the Wife, though willing to acknowledge celibacy as an
ideal, frankly celebrates her own sexuality and expresses her intention to continue acting upon it:

> He [Christ] spak to hem that wolde lyve parfitly;
> And lordynges, by youre leve, that am nat I.
> I wol bistowe the flour of al myn age
> In the actes and in fruyt of mariage. (WBP, ll. 111-14)

Though many of the Wife's images—like that of the earthen vessel—
for her discussion of marriage have a biblical provenance, they also
derive from ancient mythic origins, thereby strengthening her ties to
the celebratory world (Ganim, *Chaucerian Theatricality* 54).

Her struggle with the young clerk Jankyn encompasses her challenge to the very foundations of official culture—its asserted right to
determine and enforce the meaning of the sacred texts that under-
pin the society's power structures. Calling into question the very
idea of universally applicable laws, she underscores the relativity and
subjectivity of interpretation, as John Ganim points out:

> In her insistence on the relativism of apparently official ideology . . .
> the Wife is . . . embodying the very mode of popular culture and of
> carnivalized literature: the privileging of the individual and idiosyn-
> cratic over the official, the representation of authority as partial and
> self-serving rather than objective, the appeal to interests rather than

to logic, and the sense of fixed positions—even naturally ordained ones such as sexuality—as reversible (rather than as negated). (*Chaucerian Theatricality* 53-54)

In *The Canterbury Tales* the carnivalesque reaches beyond isolated individual figures: Chaucer makes the juxtaposition of genres a part of the cultural conversation in which he engages his audience. By placing the fabliau genre—whose ethic Charles Muscatine has characterized as "hedonistic materialism" (*The Old French Fabliaux* 73)—at the Miller's disposal Chaucer challenges the order of the Knight's world of epic and romance. For whether the fabliau has aristocratic or bourgeois origins, its characteristic attitudes and language clearly invert the proprieties of official culture and associate it with the carnival world. Its practitioners are aware of courtly romance conventions, but they introduce them by means of parody (Berger, "Sex in the Literature of the Middle Ages" 163). In "The Miller's Tale," for instance, the successful lover's direct action and the woman's eager responsiveness replace the men's protracted posturing and the lady's ethereal indifference in "The Knight's Tale." The idealized vision of sexual relationships with which the courts amused themselves gives way to the spontaneous self-gratification of people acting on impulse.

Equally important, by making unabashed sexuality rather than ascetic self-denial an accepted guideline for human behavior, the fabliau overturns clerical perspectives. As numerous critics have noted, Alisoun—whose physical description emphasizes her youthful sensuality and who responds to her sexual instincts simply by yielding to them—is the only character who suffers no punishment in the tale's comic denouement. David underscores this point in the light of festive values: "Sex is frankly presented as the *summum bonum* because it is the supreme *physical* pleasure, a natural satisfaction like food and drink, the highest expression of the joy of life. . . . The tale thus gives its blessing to any form of sexual indulgence that is simple and natural" (96-97).

Besides rejecting asceticism, the tale also spoofs clerical learning. Nicholas's astrological lore, which becomes the butt of old John's anti-intellectual ridicule, does not help him penetrate divine mysteries; it simply provides an elaborate artifice for satisfying his sexual impulses. And Absoloum's mastering the language of mystical love serves his physical passion rather than his contemplative quest. Both the Oxford student and the parish clerk summarily abandon their pretensions to intellectual or spiritual pursuits as they yield to instinctual lust—and later to disgust and pain. Furthermore, the tale's typological references, to Noah and to Mary and Joseph, are highly parodic: "the fabliau opposes itself to the tendency of the medieval mind to see physical objects and everyday events as invisible signs of an invisible reality—the exegetical impulse. In the fabliau attempts to get to the bottom of the mysteries of life usually backfire" (David 99). Thus against "The Knight's Tale's" efforts—as in Theseus's Prime Mover speech—to understand the universal order in the face of personal disaster, "The Miller's Tale" immerses us in an amoral world of immediate gratification (David 103-4).

The fabliaux harbor another important feature associated with the carnivalesque: they use scatalogical or abusive situations and language. Thomas's "gift" to the Friar in "The Summoner's Tale" presents a classic instance of carnivalesque lowering. The long-suffering layman, whose name recalls the doubting apostle who had to see and touch the resurrected Jesus for himself, brings down the hypocritical and avaricious friar, who pretends to exist on a spiritual plane. Tired of being dunned for contributions, Thomas tells the friar to rummage for a gift near his buttocks, then lets loose an insulting fart. He compounds the insult by his prior success in getting the friar to promise that he would share his gift equally with the other brothers in his friary. The tale is replete with carnivalesque elements that James Andreas details as follows:

> its demystified, comic perspective on hell and damnation, the hypocritical *sermon joyeux* of the friar, the gross parodies of apostolic motifs from the New Testament and of sacred Christian ceremonies such as Pentecost and Whitsunday, the lambasting of the new scholastic and scientific learning, the pervasive anal character of the tale and its teller, and finally, the comic scapegoating of a figure of clerical authority. (139)

Through figures like the Miller and the Wife of Bath, as well as through raising a genre like the fabliau to new artistic heights, Chaucer may have tapped unsuspected wellsprings of poetic energy in himself. For in *The Canterbury Tales* he does not simply incorporate many elements of the carnival world *into* his fictive world but makes the carnivalesque the principle *of* the world he creates. In the narrator's profession of freedom from moral blame in recording the Miller's bawdy tale, in the expenditure of his best artistic resources on that tale, and in the explosive exuberance of the Wife's appropriation of clerical texts, Chaucer himself moves into the carnivalesque. Comparing the tendency of festive license to move beyond established bounds to what happens when Chaucer writes "The Miller's Prologue and Tale," David argues:

> The true Lord of Misrule is the artist himself, and the writing of fiction becomes a holiday during which the sanctions of everyday are suspended. . . . *The Canterbury Tales* is Chaucer's personal holiday from the business of being a noble philosophical court poet, and like all good holidays it gets out of hand. It will occupy him for the rest of his life. . . . The result is a new kind of fiction, a representation of life with a Shakespearean fullness. (106-7)

By incorporating festive elements into his work and by making the festive a central element of his art, Chaucer introduces into it an inherent imbalance of perspective. The tales and their links jostle the "gentils" and the "churls" against each other; the perceptions and assumptions of each are constantly being overturned, creating a permanent instability of meaning. John Ganim stresses how "the fiction of performance" goes to the core of Chaucer's achievement:

> The context serves to disturb rather than place the meaning of a story. By constantly contesting the settled character of its own written existence, *The Canterbury Tales* also insures its own permanence, the need for its constant reinterpretation. It appropriates the subversiveness of popular culture as a condition of its own survival. (*Chaucerian Theatricality* 29)

The Canterbury Tales confronts us directly with the issue of deciding whether the carnivalesque reinforces hierarchy, by signaling the temporary and provisionary character of its license, or whether it sets in motion the kind of disequilibrium that Eco's Jorge fears will threaten the whole social fabric. In returning his pilgrims, and his pilgrimage, to the orthodoxies and apocalyptic framework of "The Parson's Tale," Chaucer may be repeating his culture's characteristic reinforcement of entrenched hierarchies after the temporary license of a festive interlude. As Michael Camille argues with respect to the marginal aspects of medieval visual representations: "The centre is . . . dependent upon the margins for its continued existence" (*Image on the Edge* 10).

But when millers tell stories whose artistic merits compete with those of knights, when women challenge the interpretive authority of clerics—indeed when the comic and burlesque moves from society's fringes to its center, in the writings of a poet closely linked with official culture—then an explosive force is at large. The zone of freedom in Chaucer's fictional world—the boundaries it transgresses, the laughter it generates—creates an imaginative space in which seditious seeds can flourish. The carnivalesque no longer remains on the margins but has become a part of the encompassing frame.

In *The Name of the Rose* Eco makes the collapse of the jealously guarded library the symbol of the old order's collapse; living through that collapse Chaucer intuits it and embodies that explosive intuition in the openness he introduces into his conceptual framework. For the linear pilgrimage from the Tabard Inn to Canterbury Cathedral with tales strung out "like beads on a string" (Leyerle, "Thematic Interlace" 108-9) is deceptive. In the thematic interweavings and open-endedness of his stories and links, Chaucer has created what Eco characterizes as a rhizome labyrinth: "one which is so constructed that every path can be connected with every other one. It has no center, no periphery, no exit, because it is potentially infinite" (*Postscript to the Name of the Rose 57*). The rhizome image captures contemporary art's lack of closure: "in it an ordered world based on universally acknowledged laws is being replaced by a world based on ambiguity, both in the negative sense that directional centers are missing and in a positive sense, because values and dogma are constantly being placed in question" (Eco, *The Role of the Reader* 54). In open works the artist strives to prevent finality through "suggestiveness," which leaves apertures for the interpreter (53); such open works are "works in movement . . . [which] characteristically consist of unplanned or physically incomplete structural units" (56).

Eco's discussion of contemporary aesthetics illuminates Chaucer's work as well: *The Canterbury Tales's* loosely connected groupings, its thematic recursivity, its violation of the boundaries between frame and tales, its disregard of its own articulated plan—all give it an intrinsically fluid quality. Clearly *The Canterbury Tales* is unfinished. But we can justifiably wonder about the extent to which its incompletion is accidental rather than integral to the poet's vision. Was Chaucer simply untimely cut off, or was resisting closure central to his response to the confusing, conflicted times in which he lived? James Dean observes, "The failure of Chaucer's pilgrims to reach the shrine harmonizes with Chaucer's inability, or unwillingness, to finish *The Canterbury Tales.* Chaucer, at last, stresses process rather than product. Finally, it is the way, viage, that achieves prominence" ("Dismantling the Canterbury Book" 746). Reacting to the dissolving certainties of the ordered, hierarchic medieval intellectual universe, Chaucer wandered into a rhizome universe; he instinctively rendered his insight into the significance of that dissolution by redefining one of his culture's most central metaphors. The pilgrimage to a sacred destination that remains forever out of reach and the storytelling contest that gives equal time to the culture's silenced and marginalized voices brilliantly capture the shifting sands in Chaucer's world. Through the multiple narrative frames that allow him to revisit issues from a variety of perspectives, he conveys the complexity of his vision. As readers of *The Canterbury Tales* we inhabit a true textual internet, a potentially infinite space in which each point may connect with every other point in a vast web of interlocking but often conflicting meanings. In *The Canterbury Tales*—to adapt a phrase from Yeats—it is the frame that will not hold. Responding to the increasingly wobbly medieval conceptual framework, Chaucer gave carnivalesque elements a heightened role in his work and reoriented the fundamental medieval symbol of pilgrimage.

Bibliography

Abelard, Peter, and Héloïse. *The Letters of Abelard and Héloïse*. Trans. Betty Radice. New York: Penguin, 1974.

Aers, David, ed. *Medieval Literature: Criticism, Ideology, and History.* New York: St. Martin's, 1986.

———. *Community, Gender, and Individual Identity: English Writing 1360-1430*. London and New York: Routledge, 1988.

———. "Criseyde: Woman in Medieval Society." *Chaucer Review* 13 (1979): 177-200.

Alighieri, Dante. *On World-Government (De Monarchia)*. Trans. Herbert W. Schneider. New York: Macmillan, 1957.

Alighieri, Dante. *The Divine Comedy: Inferno. Purgatorio. Paradiso.* Trans. John D. Sinclair. New York: Oxford UP, 1939.

Allen, Judson Boyce. *The Ethical Poetic of the Later Middle Ages: A Decorum of Convenient Distinction*. Toronto: U of Toronto P, 1982.

Allen, Prudence, R.S.M. *The Concept of Woman: The Aristotelian Revolution, 750 BC-AD 1250*. Montreal: Eden, 1985.

Allmand, Christopher. *The Hundred Years' War: England and France at War c.1300-c.1450*. Cambridge: Cambridge UP, 1988.

Ames, Ruth. "Prototype and Parody in Chaucerian Exegesis." *The Fourteenth Century, Acta* 4 (1978): 87-105.

Andreas, James. "'Newe Science' from 'Olde Bokes': A Bakhtinian Approach to the 'Summoner's Tale.'" *Chaucer Review* 25.2 (1990): 138-51.

Anson, John. "The Female Transvestite in Early Monasticism: The Origin and Development of a Motif." *Viator* 5 (1974): 1-32.

Aspegren, Kerstin. *The Male Woman: A Feminine Ideal in the Early Church.* Ed. Rene Kieffer. Uppsala: Almquist and Wiksell, 1995.

Astell, Ann W. "Chaucer's 'Literature Group' and the Medieval Causes of Books." *ELH* 59.2 (1992): 269-87.

———. "The Translatio of Chaucer's Pardoner." *Exemplaria* 4.2 (1992): 411-29.

Aston, Margaret. "Corpus Christi and Corpus Regni: Heresy and the Peasants' Revolt." *Past and Present* 143 (May 1994): 3-47.

———. *Lollards and Reformers: Images and Literacy in Late Medieval Religion*. London: Hambledon, 1984.

———. "Lollard Women Priests?" *Journal of Ecclesiastical History* 31 (1980): 445-51.

———. "Wyclif and the Vernacular." *Studies in Church History* 5 (1986): 281-330.

Athanasius. *The Life of Anthony and the Letter to Marcellinus.* Trans. Robert C. Gregg. Classics in Western Spirituality. New York: Paulist P, 1980.

Atkinson, Clarissa W. *Mystic and Pilgrim: The Book and the World of Margery Kempe.* Ithaca and London: Cornell UP, 1983.

———. *The Oldest Vocation: Christian Motherhood in the Middle Ages.* Ithaca and London: Cornell UP, 1991.

____. "'Precious Balsam in a Fragile Glass': The Ideology of Virginity in the Later Middle Ages." *Journal of Family History* 8 (1983): 131-43.

Auerbach, Erich. *Mimesis: The Representation of Reality in Western Literature.* Trans. Willard Trask. Garden City, NY: Doubleday, 1957.

Augustine. *The City of God.* Trans. Henry Bettenson. 1972. London and New York: Penguin, 1984.

Augustine. *Confessions.* Trans. R. S. Pine-Coffin. New York: Penguin, 1961.

Augustine. *On Christian Doctrine.* Trans. D. W. Robertson, Jr. New York: Liberal Arts P, 1958.

Bakhtin, Mikhail. *The Dialogic Imagination: Four Essays.* Ed. Michael Holquist. Trans. Caryl Emerson and Michael Holquist. Austin: U of Texas P, 1981.

———. *Rabelais and His World.* Trans. Helene Iswolsky. Bloomington: Indiana UP, 1984.

Baldwin, Ralph. *The Unity of the Canterbury Tales.* Anglistica 5. Copenhagen: Rosenkilde and Bagger, 1955.

Barlow, Frank. *Thomas Becket.* Berkeley: U of California P, 1986.

Barber, Richard W. *The Knight and Chivalry.* Rev. ed. Rochester, NY: Boydell P, 1995.

Barker, Juliet R. V. *The Tournament in England 1100-1400.* Woodbridge, Suffolk: Boydell P, 1986.

Barraclough, Geoffrey. *The Medieval Papacy.* New York: Harcourt, Brace & World, 1968.

Bayard, Tania, trans. and ed. *A Medieval Home Companion: Housekeeping in the Fourteenth Century.* New York: HarperCollins, 1991.

Beer, Frances. *Women and Mystical Experience in the Middle Ages.* Rochester, NY: Boydell P, 1992.

Beidler, Peter G. "The Plague and Chaucer's Pardoner." *Chaucer Review* 16 (1982): 257-69.

Benedict. *The Rule of St. Benedict.* Trans. Basilius Steidle and Urban J. Schnitzhofer. Germany: Beuroner Kunstverlag, 1952.

Benkov, Edith Joyce. "Language and Women: From Silence to Speech." *Sign, Sentence, Discourse: Language in Medieval Thought and Literature.* Eds. Julian N. Wasserman and Lois Roney. Syracuse: Syracuse UP, 1989. 245-65.

Bennett, Judith M. "The Tie That Binds: Peasant Marriages and Families in Late Medieval England." *Journal of Interdisciplinary History* 15. 1 (1984): 111-29.

Benson, C. David. "Chaucer as Revolutionary." *Selected Essays: International Conference on Representing Revolution 1989.* Ed. John Michael Crafton. Carrollton: West Georgia College, 1991.

————. "Chaucer's Pardoner: His Sexuality and Modern Critics." *Medievalia* 8 (1985 for 1982): 337-49.

————. "Their Telling Difference: Chaucer the Pilgrim and His Two Contrasting Tales." *Chaucer Review* 18.1 (1983-84): 61-76.

Benson, Larry D., and John Leyerle, eds. *Chivalric Literature: Essays on Relations between Literature and Life in the Later Middle Ages.* Toronto: U of Toronto P, 1980.

Berger, Sidney E. "Sex in the Literature of the Middle Ages: The Fabliaux." *Sexual Practices and the Medieval Church.* Eds. Vern L Bullough and James Brundage. Buffalo: Prometheus, 1982. 162-76.

Bernardo, Aldo. "The Plague as the Key to Meaning in Boccaccio's *Decameron.*" *The Black Death: The Impact of the Fourteenth Century Plague.* Ed. Daniel Williman. Binghamton, NY: Center for Medieval and Renaissance Studies, 1982. 39-64.

Berndt, David E. "Monastic Acedia and Chaucer's Characterization of Daun Piers." *Studies in Philology* 68 (1971): 435-50.

Berry, Craig A. "The King's Business: Negotiating Chivalry in *Troilus and Criseyde.*" *Chaucer Review* 26.3 (1992): 236-65.

Besserman, Lawrence. "'Glosynge is a Glorious Thyng': Chaucer's Biblical Exegesis." Jeffrey, *Chaucer and the Scriptural Tradition.* 65-73.

Bisson, Lillian M. "In the Labyrinth: Reading *The Canterbury Tales* through *The Name of the Rose*" *Medieval Perspectives* 7 (1992): 19-33.

Bisson, Thomas N. "Medieval Lordship." *Speculum* 70 (1995): 743-59.

Blamires, Alcuin. *The Canterbury Tales: An Introduction to the Variety of Criticism.* Atlantic Highlands, New Jersey: Humanities Press International, 1987.

————. Lecture. "The 'General Prologue' as Covert History." Washington: Georgetown University, 17 March 1994.

————. "The Wife of Bath and Lollardy." *Medium Aevum* 58 (1989): 224-42.

————. ed. *Woman Defamed and Woman Defended: An Anthology of Medieval Texts.* Oxford: Clarendon, 1992.

Bloch, R. Howard. *Medieval Misogyny and the Invention of Western Romantic Love.* Chicago and London: U of Chicago P, 1991.

Block, Edward A. "Chaucer's Millers and Their Bagpipes." *Speculum* 29 (1954): 239-43.

Boase, Roger. *The Origin and Meaning of Courtly Love: A Critical Study of Scholarship.* Totawa, NJ: Rowman and Littlefield, 1977.

Boccaccio, Giovanni. *Boccaccio on Poetry: Being the Preface and the Fourteenth and Fifteenth Books of Boccaccio's Genealogia Deorum Gentiles.* Trans. Charles E. Osgood. 1930. Indianapolis and New York: Bobbs-Merrill, 1956.

Boccaccio, Giovanni. *Decameron.* Trans. G. H. McWilliam. New York: Penguin, 1972.

Boethius. *The Consolation of Philosophy.* Trans. V. E. Watts. New York: Penguin, 1969.

Boitani, Piero. "'My Tale Is of a Cock': The Problem of Literal Interpretation." *Literature and Religion in the Later Middle Ages: Philological Studies in Honor of Siegfried Wenzel.* Eds. Richard G. Neuhaus and John A. Alford. Binghamton, NY: Medieval and Renaissance Texts and Studies, 1995. 11-25.

Bolton, Brenda. *The Medieval Reformation.* New York: Holmes and Meier, 1983.

———. "Mulieres Sanctae." *Women in Medieval Society.* Ed. Susan Mosher Stuard. Philsdelphia: U of Pennslyvania P, 1976. 141-58.

Bolton, J. L. *The Medieval English Economy 1150-1500.* Totowa, NJ: Rowman and Littlefield, 1980.

Bonaventure. *The Soul's Journey into God. The Tree of Life. The Life of St. Francis.* Trans. Ewert Cousins. New York: Paulist P, 1978.

Bonnassie, Pierre. *From Slavery to Feudalism in South-Western Europe.* Trans. Jean Birrell. Cambridge: Cambridge UP, 1991.

Boughton, Bradford B. *Dictionary of Medieval Knighthood and Chivalry: Concepts and Terms.* Westport, CT: Greenwood, 1986.

Boulton, D'Arcy Jonathan Dacre. *The Knights of the Crown: The Monarchical Orders of Knighthood in Later Medieval Europe 1325-1520.* Woodbridge, Suffolk: Boydell, 1987.

Bridbury, A. R. "The Black Death." *The Economic History Review.* 2nd series. 26 (1973): 577-92.

Bowsky, William M., ed. *The Black Death: A Turning Point in History?* New York: Holt, Rinehart and Winston, 1971.

Boyd, Beverly. "Our Lady According to Geoffrey Chaucer: Translation and Collage." *Florilegium* 9. Carleton University Annual Papers on Late Antiquity and the Middle Ages, 1987.

Brewer, Derek. *Tradition and Innovation in Chaucer.* London: Macmillan, 1982.

Brooke, Christopher. *The Medieval Idea of Marriage.* Oxford and New York: Oxford UP, 1991.

Brooke, Rosalind and Charles. *Popular Religion in the Middle Ages: Western Europe 1000-1300.* London: Thames and Hudson, 1984.

Brown, Peter. *The Body and Society: Men, Women, and Sexual Renunciation in Early Christianity.* New York: Columbia UP, 1988.

———. *Chaucer at Work: The Making of the Canterbury Tales.* London and New York: Longman, 1994.

———. *The Cult of the Saints: Its Rise and Function in Latin Christianity.* Chicago: U of Chicago P, 1981.

Brown, Peter, and Andrew Butcher. *The Age of Saturn: Literature and History in the Canterbury Tales.* Cambridge, MA: Basil Blackwell, 1991.

Brundage, James. *Law, Sex, and Christian Society in Medieval Europe.* Chicago and London: U of Chicago P, 1987.

Bugge, John. *Virginitas: An Essay in the History of a Medieval Ideal.* The Hague: Martinus Nijhoff, 1975.

Bullough, Vern. *The Subordinate Sex: A History of Attitudes towards Women.* Urbana: U of Illinois P, 1973; Athens: U of Georgia P, 1988.

Bullough, Vern L., and James Brundage. *Sexual Practices and the Medieval Church.* Buffalo: Prometheus, 1982.

Bumke, Joachim. *Courtly Culture: Literature and Society in the High Middle Ages.* Trans. Thomas Dunlap. Berkeley: U of California P, 1991.

Burke, Peter. *Popular Culture in Early Modern Europe.* New York: Harper and Row, 1978.

Burrow, John. *Ricardian Poetry: Chaucer, Gower, Langland, and the Gawain Poet.* London: Routledge and Kegan Paul, 1971.

Burton, Janet. *Monastic and Religious Orders in Britain, 1000-1300.* Cambridge: Cambridge UP, 1994.

Butler, John. *The Quest for Becket's Bones: The Mystery of the Relics of St. Thomas of Canterbury.* New Haven and London: Yale UP, 1995.

Bynum, Caroline Walker. *Jesus as Mother: Studies in the Spirituality of the High Middle Ages.* Berkeley: U of California P, 1982.

Bynum, Caroline Walker, Steven Harrell, and Paula Rickman, eds. *Gender and Religion: On the Complexity of Symbols.* Boston: Beacon, 1986.

Cahn, Kenneth S. "Chaucer's Merchants and the Foreign Exchange: An Introduction to Medieval Finance." *Studies in the Age of Chaucer* 2 (1980): 81-119.

Camille, Michael. *Image on the Edge: The Margins of Medieval Art.* Cambridge: Harvard UP, 1992.

Campbell, Josie., ed. *Popular Culture in the Middle Ages.* Bowling Green, OH: Bowling Green U Popular P, 1986.

Carruthers, Mary, and Elizabeth Kirk, eds. *Acts of Interpretation: The Text in Its Context 700-1600.* Norman, OK: Pilgrim, 1982.

Castelli, Elizabeth. "Virginity and Its Meaning for Women's Sexuality in Early Christianity." *Journal of Feminist Studies in Religion.* 2 (1986): 61-88.

Cespedes, Frank V. "Chaucer's Pardoner and Preaching." *ELH* 44 (1977): 1-18.

Chambers, E. K. *The Medieval Stage.* 2 vols. London: Oxford UP, 1903.

Chaucer, Geoffrey. *The Riverside Chaucer.* Ed. Larry D. Benson. 3rd ed. Boston: Houghton Mifflin, 1987.

Cherubini, Giovanni. "The Peasant and Agriculture." Le Goff, *Medieval Callings* 113-39.

Christie-Murray, David. *A History of Heresy.* New York: Oxford UP, 1989.

Chrysostom, John. *A Comparison Between a King and a Monk/Against the Opponents of the Monastic Life.* Trans. David G. Hunter. Studies in the Bible and Early Christianity. Lewiston, NY: Edwin Mellen P, 1988.

Cipolla, Carlo M. *Before the Industrial Revolution: European Society and Economy 1000-1700.* 3rd ed. New York: Norton, 1993.

Clark, Elizabeth. "'Adam's Only Companion': Augustine and the Early Christian Debate on Marriage." Edwards and Spector 15-21.

Clein, Wendy. *Concepts of Chivalry in Sir Gawain and the Green Knight.* Norman, OK: Pilgrim, 1987.

Coleman, Edward. "Nasty Habits: Satire and the Medieval Monk." *History Today* (June 1993): 36-42.

Collette, Carolyn P. "A Closer Look at Seinte Cecile's Special Vision." *Chaucer Review* 10 (1976): 337-49.

Constable, Giles. "Opposition to Pilgrimage in the Middle Ages." *Studia Gratiana* 19 (1976): 125-46.

Coogan, Robert, trans. *Babylon on the Rhône: A Translation of Letters by Dante, Petrarch, and Catherine of Siena.* Potomac, MD: Studia Humanitas, 1983.

Cook, Jon. "Carnival and *The Canterbury Tales:* 'Only Equals May Laugh' (Herzen)." Aers, *Medieval Literature* 169-92.

Cook, William R., and Ronald B. Herzman. *The Medieval World View.* New York: Oxford UP, 1983.

Cooper, Helen. *The Structure of the Canterbury Tales.* London: Duckworth, 1983.

Cowen, Painton. *Rose Windows.* London: Thames and Hudson, 1979.

Cowgill, Bruce Kent. "'The Knight's Tale' and the Hundred Years' War." *Philological Quarterly* 54 (1975): 670-79.

Cox, Catherinne S. "'Grope wel bihynde': The Subversive Erotics of Chaucer's Summoner." *Exemplaria* 7.1 (1995): 145-77.

Cramer, Patricia. "Lordship, Bondage and the Erotic: The Psychological Bases of Chaucer's 'Clerk's Tale.'" *Journal of English and Germanic Philology* 89.4 (1990): 491-511.

Crane, Susan. *Gender and Romance in Chaucer's Canterbury Tales.* Princeton: Princeton UP, 1994.

Crane, Susan. "The Writing Lesson of 1381." Hanawalt 201-23.

Crow, Martin M., and Clair C. Olson, eds. *Chaucer Life-Records.* Oxford: Clarendon, 1966.

Curtius, Ernst Robert. *European Literature and the Latin Middle Ages.* Trans. Willard R. Trask. New York and Evanston: Harper and Row, 1953.

Daichman, Graciela A. *Wayward Nuns in Medieval Literature.* Syracuse: Syracuse UP, 1986.

Dalarun, Jacques. "The Clerical Gaze." Trans. Arthur Goldhammer. Klapisch-Zuber 15-42.

David, Alfred. *The Strumpet Muse: Art and Morals in Chaucer's Poetry.* Bloomington and London: Indiana UP, 1976.

Davidson, Linda Kay, and Maryjane Dunn-Wood. *Pilgrimage in the Middle Ages: A Research Guide.* Garland Medieval Bibliographies 16. New York and London: Garland, 1993.

Davis, Adam Brooke. "The Ends of Fiction: Narrative Boundaries and Chaucer's Attitude Toward Courtly Love." *Chaucer Review* 28.1 (1993): 54-66.

Dean, James. "Chaucer's Repentance: A Likely Story." *Chaucer Review.* 24. 1 (1989): 64-76.

———. "Dismantling the Canterbury Book." *PMLA* 100.5 (1985): 746-62.

Dean, James, and Christian Zacher, eds. *The Idea of Medieval Literature: New Essays on Chaucer and Medieval Culture in Honor of Donald R. Howard.* Newark: U of Delaware P, 1992.

Delaney, Sheila. "Difference and the Difference It Makes." *Florilegium* 10 (1988-1991): 83-92.

———. "Rewriting Women Good: Gender and the Anxiety of Influence in Two Late Medieval Texts." Wasserman and Blanch 75-92.

Delasanta, Rodney. "Penance and Poetry in the *Canterbury Tales.*" *PMLA* 93 (1978): 240-47.

Demaray, John. *Dante and the Book of the Cosmos.* Transactions of the American Philosophical Society. Vol. 77. Philadelphia: American Philosophical Society, 1987.

de Roover, Raymond. *Business, Banking and Economic Thought in Late Medieval and Early Modern Europe: Selected Studies of Raymond de Roover.* Ed. Julius Kirshner. Chicago and London: U of Chicago P, 1974.

Diamond, Arlyn. "Chaucer's Women, and Women's Chaucer." *The Authority of Experience: Essays in Feminist Criticism.* Eds. Lee R. Edwards and Arlyn Diamond. Amherst: U of Massachusetts P, 1977.

Dickson, Lynne. "Deflection in the Mirror: Feminine Discourse in 'The Wife of Bath's Prologue and Tale.'" *Studies in the Age of Chaucer.* Vol. 15. Ed. Lisa J. Kiser. Columbus, OH: New Chaucer Society, 1993. 61-90.

Dinshaw, Carolyn. *Chaucer's Sexual Poetics.* Madison: U of Wisconsin P, 1989.

Dobson, R. B. *The Peasants' Revolt of 1381.* 2nd ed. London: Macmillan, 1983.

Donaldson, E. Talbot. *Speaking of Chaucer.* New York: Norton, 1970.

Dor, Juliette, ed. *A Wyf Ther Was: Essays in Honor of Paule Mertens-Fonck.* Liège: U of Liège, 1992.

Dronke, Peter. *Dante and Medieval Latin Traditions*. Cambridge: Cambridge UP, 1986.

———. *Medieval Latin and the Rise of the European Love Lyric*. 2 vols. Oxford: Clarendon, 1968.

Duby, Georges. *The Age of the Cathedrals: Art and Society 980-1420*. Trans. Eleanor Levieux and Barbara Thompson. Chicago: U of Chicago P, 1981.

———. *The Chivalrous Society*. Trans. Cynthia Postan. Berkeley and Los Angeles: U of California P, 1977.

———. *The Knight, the Lady and the Priest: The Making of Modern Marriage in Medieval France*. Trans. Barbara Bray. New York: Pantheon, 1983.

———. *The Three Orders: Feudal Society Imagined*. Trans. Arthur Goldhammer. Chicago and London: U of Chicago P, 1980.

———. *William Marshall: The Flower of Chivalry*. Trans. Richard Howard. New York: Pantheon, 1985.

Dyer, Christopher. *Standards of Living in the Later Middle Ages: Social Change in England c. 1200-1520*. Cambridge: Cambridge UP, 1989.

Eberle, Patricia J. "Commercial Language and the Commercial Outlook in the 'General Prologue.'" *Chaucer Review* 18.2 (1983): 161-74.

Eco, Umberto. *The Name of the Rose*. Trans. William Weaver. San Diego: Harcourt Brace Jovanovich, 1983.

———. *Postscript to the Name of the Rose*. Trans. William Weaver. San Diego: Harcourt Brace Jovanovich, 1984.

———. *The Role of the Reader: Explorations in the Semiotics of Texts*. Bloomington: Indiana UP, 1979.

Edwards, Robert R., and Stephen Spector, eds. *The Olde Daunce: Love, Friendship, Sex and Marriage in the Medieval World*. Albany: State University of New York P, 1991.

Elliott, Dyan. *Spiritual Marriage: Sexual Abstinence in Medieval Wedlock*. Princeton: Princeton UP, 1993.

Ellis, Deborah S. "The Merchant's Wife's Tale: Language, Sex, and Commerce in Margery Kempe and Chaucer." *Exemplaria* 2.2 (October 1990): 595-626.

Erickson, Carolly. *The Medieval Vision: Essays in History and Perception*. New York: Oxford UP, 1976.

Evergates, Theodore. *Feudal Society in the Bailliage of Troyes under the Counts of Champagne, 1152-1284*. Baltimore and London: Johns Hopkins UP, 1975.

Farmer, Sharon. "Persuasive Voices: Clerical Images of Medieval Women." *Speculum* 61.3 (1986): 517-43.

Fein, Susanna Greer, David Raybin, and Peter Braeger, eds. *Rebels and Rivals: The Contestive Spirit in the Canterbury Tales*. Kalamazoo: Western Michigan U, 1991.

Ferrante, Joan. "Male Fantasy and Female Reality in Courtly Literature." *Women's Studies* 11 (1984): 67-97.

――――. *Woman as Image in Medieval Literature from the Twelfth Century to Dante.* New York: Columbia UP, 1975.

Finke, Laurie. "Mystical Bodies and the Dialogics of Vision" Wiethaus, 28-45.

Finucane, Ronald. *Miracles and Pilgrims: Popular Beliefs in Medieval England.* 1977. New York: St. Martin's, 1995.

Fiore, Silvestro. "The Medieval Pilgrimage: From the Legacy of Greco-Oriental Antiquity to the Threshold of Greco-Occidental Humanism." *Revue de Littérature Comparée.* 40 (1966): 5-22.

Fleming, John V. "Chaucer and Erasmus on the Pilgrimage to Canterbury: An Iconographical Speculation." *The Popular Literature of Medieval England.* Ed. Thomas J. Heffernan. Tennessee Studies in Literature 28. Knoxville: U of Tennessee P, 1985. 148-66.

Fletcher, Alan J. "The Topical Hypocrisy of Chaucer's Pardoner." *Chaucer Review* 25 (1990): 110-26.

Fossier, Robert. *Peasant Life in the Medieval West.* Trans. Juliet Vale. Oxford: Basil Blackwell, 1988.

Freedman, Paul. *The Origins of Peasant Servitude in Medieval Catalonia.* Cambridge Iberian and Latin American Studies. Cambridge: Cambridge UP, 1991.

Freinkel, Lisa. "*Inferno* and the Poetics of Usura." *Modern Language Notes* 107 (1992): 1-17.

Frese, Dolores Warwick. "'The Nun's Priest's Tale': Chaucer's Identified Masterpiece?" *Chaucer Review* 16 (1982): 330-43.

Froissart, Jean. *Chronicles.* Trans. and ed. Geoffrey Brereton. New York: Penguin, 1968.

Ganim, John. "Chaucer and the Noise of the People." *Exemplaria* 2.1 (1990). 303-28.

――――. *Chaucerian Theatricality.* Princeton: Princeton UP, 1990.

Gash, Anthony. "Carnival Against Lent: The Ambivalence of Medieval Drama." *Medieval Literature* Aers, 74-98.

Gaylord, Alan. "'Sentence' and 'Solaas' in Fragment VII of the *Canterbury Tales:* Harry Bailly as Horseback Editor." *PMLA* 82 (1967): 226-35.

――――. "Uncle Pandarus as Lady Philosophy." *Papers of the Michigan Academy of Science, Arts, and Letters* 46 (1961): 571-95.

Geary, Patrick. *Furta Sacra: The Theft of Sacred Relics in the Central Middle Ages.* 1978. Rev. ed. Princeton: Princeton UP, 1990.

Gellrich, Jesse M. *The Idea of the Book in the Middle Ages: Language Theory, Mythology, and Fiction.* Ithaca and London: Cornell UP, 1985.

Geoffrey of Monmouth. *The History of the Kings of Britain.* Trans. Lewis Thorpe. New York: Penguin, 1966.

Geoffrey of Vinsauf. *Poetria nova.* Trans. Margaret F. Nims. Toronto: Pontifical Institute of Medieval Studies, 1967.

Georgiana, Linda. "Lords, Churls, and Friars: The Return to Social Order in the Summoner's Tale." Fein, Raybin, and Braeger. 149-72.

Gies, Frances. *The Knight in History.* New York: Harper & Row, 1984.

Gies, Frances and Joseph. *Marriage and the Family in the Middle Ages.* New York: Harper & Row, 1987.

———. *Women in the Middle Ages.* New York: Harper and Row, 1980.

Gilchrist, John. *The Church and Economic Activity in the Middle Ages.* New York: St. Martin's, 1969.

Gold, Penelope Schine. *The Lady and the Virgin: Image, Attitude, and Experience in Twelfth-Century France.* Chicago and London: U of Chicago P, 1985.

Goodman, Jennifer R. "Chaucer's 'Squire's Tale' and the Rise of Chivalry." *Studies in the Age of Chaucer.* Vol. 5. Ed. Thomas J. Heffernan. Knoxville: New Chaucer Society, 1983. 127-36.

Green, Richard Firth. "Chaucer's Victimized Women." *Studies in the Age of Chaucer.* Vol. 10. Ed. Thomas J. Heffernan. Knoxville: New Chaucer Society, 1988. 3-25.

———. "The Pardoner's Pants (and Why They Matter)." *Studies in the Age of Chaucer.* Vol. 15. Ed. Lisa Kiser. Columbus, OH: New Chaucer Society, 1993. 131-45.

———. *Poets and Princepleasers: Literature and the English Court in the Late Middle Ages.* Toronto: U of Toronto P, 1980.

———. "The Sexual Normality of Chaucer's Pardoner." *Medievalia.* 8 (1985 for 1982): 351-58.

Green, Richard Hamilton. "Dante's 'Allegory of Poets' and the Medieval Theory of Poetry." *Comparative Literature* 9 (1957): 118-28.

Gregory the Great. *Morals on the Book of Job.* Trans. Anonymous. 3 vols. Oxford: John Henry Parker, 1844.

Grudin, Michaela Paasche. "Chaucer's 'Manciple's Tale' and the Poetics of Guile." *Chaucer Review* 25 (1991): 329-42.

———. "Discourse and the Problem of Closure in the *Canterbury Tales.*" *PMLA* 107.5 (1992): 1157-67.

Gurevich, Aaron. *Medieval Popular Culture: Problems of Belief and Perception.* Trans. Janos M. Bok and Paul A. Hollingsworth. Cambridge: Cambridge UP, 1988.

Haahr, Joan G. "Chaucer's 'Marriage Group' Revisited: The Wife of Bath and the Merchant in Debate." *Homo Carnalis, Acta* 14 (1987): 105-20.

Hahn, Thomas. "Money, Sexuality, Wordplay, and Context in the Shipman's Tale." Wasserman and Blanch. 235-49.

————. "Teaching the Resistant Woman: The Wife of Bath and the Academy." *Exemplaria* 4.2 (Fall 1992): 431-40.

Hahn, Thomas, and Richard W. Kaeuper. "Text and Context: Chaucer's Friar's Tale." *Studies in the Age of Chaucer.* Vol. 5. Ed. Thomas Heffernan. Knoxville: New Chaucer Society, 1983. 67-103.

Hall, Donald. *English Medieval Pilgrimage.* London: Routledge and Keegan Paul, 1965.

Hall, Louis Brewer. *The Perilous Vision of John Wyclif.* Chicago: Nelson-Hall, 1983.

Hamilton, Bernard. "The Impact of Crusader Jerusalem on Western Christendom." *Catholic Historical Review* 80 (1994): 695-713.

————. *The Medieval Inquisition.* London: Edward Arnold, 1981.

————. *Monastic Reform, Catharism, and the Crusades, 900-1300.* London: Variorum Reprints, 1979.

Hanawalt, Barbara A., ed. *Chaucer's England: Literature in Historical Context.* Medieval Studies at Minnesota. Vol. 4. Minneapolis: U of Minnesota P, 1992.

————. *The Ties That Bound: Peasant Families in Medieval England.* New York: Oxford UP, 1986.

Hanning, Robert W. "Chaucer and the Dangers of Poetry." *CEA Critic* 46 (1984): 17-26.

Hansen, Elaine Tuttle. *Chaucer and the Fictions of Gender.* Berkeley: U of California P, 1992.

————. "The Powers of Silence: The Case of the Clerk's Griselda." *Women and Power in the Middle Ages.* Eds. Mary Erler and Maryanne Kowaleski. Athens and London: U of Georgia P, 1988. 230-49.

Hardison, O. B., Jr. "Medieval Literary Criticism: General Introduction." *Classical and Medieval Literary Criticism: Translations and Interpretations.* Eds. Alex Preminger, Leon Golden, O. B. Hardison, Jr., and Kevin Kerrane. New York: Ungar, 1974.

Haskell, Ann S. "The Portrayal of Women by Chaucer and His Age." *What Manner of Woman.* Ed. Malvern Springer. New York: New York UP, 1977. 1-14.

Hatton, Thomas J. "Chaucer's Crusading Knight, A Slanted Ideal." *Chaucer Review* 3 (1968): 77-87.

Heffernan, Carol. "Chaucer's *Troilus and Criseyde:* The Disease of Love and Courtly Love." *Neophilologus* 74.2 (1990): 294-309.

Heinrichs, Katherine. "Tropological Woman in Chaucer: Literary Elaborations of an Exegetical Tradition." *English Studies* 76.3 (1995): 209-14.

Herlihy, David. *Medieval Households.* Cambridge and London: Harvard UP, 1985.

Hill, John M. *Chaucerian Belief: The Poetics of Reverence and Delight*. New Haven and London: Yale UP, 1991.

Hill, Ordelle G. *The Manor, the Plowman, and the Shepherd: Agrarian Themes and Imagery in Late Medieval and Early Renaissance English Literature*. Selinsgrove, PA: Susquehanna UP, 1993.

Hilton, Rodney. *Bond Men Made Free: Medieval Peasant Movements and the English Rising of 1381*. New York: Viking, 1973.

———. *The Decline of Serfdom in Medieval England*. Studies in Economic History. Ed. M.W. Flinn. London: Macmillan, 1969.

———. *The English Peasantry and the Later Middle Ages: The Ford Lectures for 1973 and Related Studies*. Oxford: Clarendon, 1975.

Hilton, Rodney, and T. H. Aston, eds. *The English Rising of 1381*. Cambridge: Cambridge UP, 1984.

Hoffman, Arthur W. "Chaucer's Prologue to Pilgrimage: The Two Voices." *Chaucer: Modern Essays in Criticism*. Ed. Edward Wagenknecht. London: Oxford UP, 1959. 30-46.

Holloway, Julia Bolton. *The Pilgrim and the Book: A Study of Dante, Langland and Chaucer*. New York: Peter Lang, 1987.

Holloway, Julia Bolton, Joan Bechtold, and Constance S. Wright, eds. *Equally in God's Image: Women in the Middle Ages*. New York: Peter Lang, 1990.

Holmes, J. Derek, and Bernard W. Bickers. *A Short History of the Catholic Church*. New York: Paulist, 1983.

Horace. *The Art of Poetry*. Trans. Burton Raffel. Albany: State U of New York P, 1974.

Horrox, Rosemary, trans. and ed. *The Black Death*. Manchester and New York: Manchester UP, 1994.

Howard, Donald R. *Chaucer: His Life, His Works, His World*. New York: Dutton, 1987.

———. "Fiction and Religion in Boccaccio and Chaucer." *Journal of the American Academy of Religion* 47 (1979): 307-28.

———. *The Idea of The Canterbury Tales*. Berkeley: U of California P, 1976.

———. *Writers and Pilgrims: Medieval Pilgrimage Narratives and Their Posterity*. Berkeley: U of California P, 1980.

Hudson, Anne. *The Premature Reformation: Wycliffite Texts and Lollard History*. Oxford: Clarendon, 1988.

———. "Wyclif and the English Language." *Wyclif in His Times*. Ed. Anthony Kenny. Oxford: Clarendon, 1986. 85-105.

Huizinga, Johan. *Homo Ludens: A Study of the Play Element in Human Culture*. Trans. Anonymous. Boston: Beacon, 1950.

————. *The Waning of the Middle Ages: A Study of the Forms of Life, Thought and Art in France and the Netherlands in the Dawn of the Renaissance in the XIVth and XVth Centuries*. Garden City, NY: Doubleday, 1954.

Huppé, Bernard. *A Reading of the Canterbury Tales*. Albany: State U of New York P, 1964.

Jacobs, Kathryn. "Rewriting the Marital Contract: Adultery in the *Canterbury Tales*." *Chaucer Review* 29.4 (1995): 337-47.

Jaeger, C. Stephen. *The Origins of Courtliness: Civilizing Trends and the Formation of Courtly Ideals 939-1210*. Philadelphia: U of Pennsylvania P, 1985.

Jeffrey, David Lyle, ed. *Chaucer and the Scriptural Tradition*. Ottawa: U of Ottawa P, 1984.

————. "Chaucer and Wyclif: Biblical Hermeneutic and Literary Theory in the Fourteenth Century." Jeffrey, 109-40.

————. trans. and ed. *The Law of Love: English Spirituality in the Age of Wyclif*. Grand Rapids, MI: Eerdmans, 1988.

John of Salisbury. *Policraticus: Of the Frivolities of Courtiers and the Footprints of Philosophers*. Ed. and trans. Cary J. Nederman. Cambridge: Cambridge UP, 1990.

Jonassen, Frederick B. "Carnival Food Imagery in Chaucer's Description of the Franklin." *Studies in the Age of Chaucer*. Ed. Lisa J. Kiser. Vol. 16. Columbus: Ohio State U, 1994. 99-117.

————. "The Inn, the Cathedral, and the Pilgrim of *The Canterbury Tales*." Fein, Raybin, and Braeger 1-35.

Jones, Terry. *Chaucer's Knight: The Portrait of a Medieval Mercenary*. London: Methuen, 1984.

Jordan, G. J. *The Inner History of the Great Schism: A Problem in Church Unity*. 1930. New York: Burt Franklin, 1972.

Jordan, Robert M. *Chaucer and the Shape of Creation: The Aesthetic Possibilities of Inorganic Structure*. Cambridge: Harvard UP, 1967.

————. *Chaucer's Poetics and the Modern Reader*. Berkeley: U of California P, 1987.

Jordan, William Chester. *From Servitude to Freedom: Manumission in the Senonais in the Thirteenth Century*. Philadelphia: U of Pennsylvania P, 1986.

Joseph, Gerhard. "Chaucer's Coinage: Foreign Exchange and the Puns of the 'Shipman's Tale.'" *Chaucer Review* 17 (1983): 341-57.

Josipovici, G.D. "Fiction and Game in *The Canterbury Tales*." *Critical Quarterly* 7 (1965): 185-97.

Julian of Norwich. *Revelations of Divine Love*. Trans. Clifton Wolters. New York: Penguin, 1966.

Justman, Stewart. "Trade as Pudendum: Chaucer's Wife of Bath." *Chaucer Review* 28 (1994): 344-52.

Kaske, Carol V. "Getting Around the Parson's Tale: An Alternative to Allegory and Irony." *Chaucer at Albany.* Ed. Rossell Hope Robbins. New York: Franklin, 1975. 147-78.

Kamowski, William. "'Coillons,' Relics, Skepticism and Faith on Chaucer's Road to Canterbury." *English Language Notes* 28 (1991): 1-8.

Kavanaugh, Aidan, O.S.B. "Eastern Influences on the Rule of Saint Benedict." Verdon, 29-53.

Keen, Maurice. "Chaucer's Knight, the English Aristocracy and the Crusade." *English Court Culture in the Later Middle Ages.* Eds. V. J. Scattergood and J. W. Sherborne. New York: St. Martin's, 1983.

———. *Chivalry.* New Haven and London: Yale UP, 1984.

———. "Wyclif, the Bible, and Transubstantiation." Kenny 11-17.

Keenan, Hugh T., ed. *Typology and English Medieval Literature.* Georgia State U Series 7. New York: AMS, 1992.

Kellogg, Judith L. "'Large and Fre': The Influence of Middle English Romance on Chaucer's Chivalric Language." *Allegorica* 9 (1987/88): 221-48.

Kelly, Henry Ansgar. *Chaucer and the Cult of Saint Valentine.* Davis Medieval Texts and Studies. Vol. 5. Leiden: Brill, 1986.

———. "Clandestine Marriage and Chaucer's 'Troilus.'" *Viator* 4 (1973): 439-57.

Kempe, Margery. *The Book of Margery Kempe.* Trans. B. A. Windeatt. New York: Penguin, 1985.

Kendrick, Laura. *Chaucerian Play: Comedy and Control in the Canterbury Tales.* Berkeley: U of California P, 1988.

Kenny, Anthony, ed. *Wyclif in His Times.* Oxford: Clarendon, 1986.

Kermode, Frank. *The Genesis of Secrecy: On the Interpretation of Narrative.* Cambridge and London: Harvard UP, 1979.

Kieckhefer, Richard. *Unquiet Souls: Fourteenth Century Saints and Their Religious Milieu.* Chicago and London: U of Chicago P, 1984.

Kirby, Elizabeth D. "'Paradis Stood Formed in Hire Yen': Courtly Love and Chaucer's Re-Vision of Dante." Carruthers and Kirk 257-77.

Kirshner, Julius. "Raymond de Roover on Scholastic Economic Thought." De Roover 15-36.

Kiser, Lisa J. *Truth and Textuality in Chaucer's Poetry.* Hanover and London: UP of New England, 1991.

Kittredge, George Lyman. *Chaucer and His Poetry.* 1915. Cambridge: Harvard UP, 1970.

Klapisch-Zuber, Christiane, ed. *A History of Women in the West: Silences of the Middle Ages.* Cambridge and London: Belknap, 1992.

———. "Women and the Family." Le Goff, *Medieval Callings* 285-313.

Klene, Jean, C.S.C. "Chaucer's Contribution to a Popular Topos: The World Up-side-Down." *Viator* 11 (1980): 321-34.

Knapp, Daniel. "The Relyk of a Saint: A Gloss on Chaucer's Pilgrimage." *ELH* 39 (1972): 1-26.

Knapp, Peggy. *Chaucer and the Social Contest*. New York and London: Routledge, 1990.

Knowles, David. *Christian Monasticism*. London: World University Library, 1969.

———. *The Evolution of Medieval Thought*. New York: Vintage, 1964.

Kolve, V. A. *Chaucer and the Imagery of Narrative: The First Five Canterbury Tales*. Stanford: Stanford UP, 1984.

———. *The Play Called Corpus Christi*. Stanford: Stanford UP, 1966.

Kolve, V.A., and Glending Olson, eds. *The Canterbury Tales: Nine Tales and the General Prologue*. New York and London: Norton, 1989.

Kugel, James L, ed. *Poetry and Prophecy: The Beginnings of a Literary Tradition*. Ithaca and London: Cornell UP, 1990.

Labarge, Margaret Wade. *A Small Sound of the Trumpet: Women in Medieval Life*. Boston: Beacon, 1986.

Lambdin, Laura C. and Robert T., eds. *Chaucer's Pilgrims: An Historical Guide to the Pilgrims in The Canterbury Tales*. Westport, CT and London: Greenwood P, 1996.

Lambert, Malcolm. *Medieval Heresy: Popular Movements from the Gregorian Reform to the Reformation*. 2nd ed. Oxford, UK and Cambridge, USA: Blackwell, 1992.

Langland, William. *Piers Plowman: An Edition of the C-Text*. Ed. Derek Pearsall. Berkeley and Los Angeles: U of California P, 1978.

Lawler, Michael G. *Marriage and Sacrament: A Theology of Christian Marriage*. Collegeville, MN: Liturgical P, 1993.

Lawrence, C.H. *Medieval Monasticism: Forms of Religious Life in Western Europe in the Middle Ages*. 2nd ed. London and New York: Longman, 1989.

Lawton, David. "Chaucer's Two Ways: The Pilgrimage Frame of *The Canterbury Tales.*" *Studies in the Age of Chaucer*. Ed. Thomas J. Heffernan. Vol. 9. Knoxville: New Chaucer Society, 1987. 3-41.

Le Goff, Jacques. *The Birth of Purgatory*. Trans. Arthur Goldhammer. Chicago: U of Chicago P, 1984.

———. ed. *Medieval Callings*. Trans. Lydia Cochrane. Chicago: U of Chicago P, 1990.

———. *Your Money or Your Life: Economy and Religion in the Middle Ages*. New York: Zone Books, 1988.

Lea, Henry Charles. *A History of Auricular Confession and Indulgences in the Latin Church*. 3 vols. New York: Greenwood, 1968.

Leclercq, Jean, O.S.B. *The Love of Learning and the Desire for God: A Study of Monastic Culture.* Trans. Catharine Misrahi. New York: Fordham UP, 1982.

———. "Otium Monasticum as a Context for Artistic Creativity." Verdon 63-81.

Lee, Anne Thompson. "'A Woman True and Fair': Chaucer's Portrayal of Dorigen in the 'Franklin's Tale.'" *Chaucer Review* 19.2 (1984): 169-78.

Leff, Gordon. *Heresy in the Later Middle Ages: The Relation of Heterodoxy to Dissent c. 1250-c. 1450.* Vol. 2. New York: Barnes and Noble, 1967.

Leicester, H. Marshall, Jr. "Of Fire in the Dark: Public and Private Feminism in 'The Wife of Bath's Tale.'" *Women's Studies* 11 (1984): 157-78.

Lesnick, Daniel. *Preaching in Medieval Florence: The Social World of Franciscan and Dominican Spirituality.* Athens and London: U of Georgia P, 1989.

Lester, G. A. "Chaucer's Knight and the Medieval Tournament." *Neophilologus* 66 (1982): 460-68.

Levitan, Alan. "The Parody of Pentecost in Chaucer's *Summoner's Tale.*" *University of Toronto Quarterly* 40 (1970-71): 236-46.

Levy, Bernard. "Biblical Parody in the *Summoner's Tale.*" *TSL* 11 (1966): 45-60.

———. "The Quaint World of 'The Shipman's Tale.'" *Studies in Short Fiction* 4 (1967): 112-18.

Lewis, C. S. *The Allegory of Love: A Study in Medieval Tradition.* London and New York: Oxford UP, 1971.

———. *The Discarded Image: An Introduction to Medieval and Renaissance Literature.* Cambridge: Cambridge UP, 1964.

Leyerle, John. "Thematic Interlace in *The Canterbury Tales.*" *Essays and Studies.* Ed. E. Talbot Donaldson. Atlantic Highlands, NJ: Humanities P, 1976. 107-21.

Lindahl, Carl. *Earnest Games: Folkloric Patterns in the Canterbury Tales.* Bloomington and Indianapolis: Indiana UP, 1987.

———. "The Festive Form of the *Canterbury Tales.*" *ELH* 52 (1985): 531-74.

Lis, Catharina, and Hugo Soly. *Poverty and Capitalism in Pre-Industrial Europe.* Atlantic Highlands, NJ: Humanities P, 1979.

Little, Lester K. *Religious Poverty and the Profit Economy in Medieval Europe.* Ithaca: Cornell UP, 1978.

Lloyd, T. H. *The English Wool Trade in the Middle Ages.* Cambridge: Cambridge UP, 1977.

Logan, F. Donald. *Excommunication and the Secular Arm in Medieval England: A Study in Legal Procedure from the Thirteenth to the Fourteenth Century.* Toronto: Pontifical Institute of Medieval Studies, 1968.

Lopez, Robert S. *The Commercial Revolution of the Middle Ages, 950-1350.* Cambridge: Cambridge UP, 1976.

Loxton, Howard. *Pilgrimage to Canterbury.* London and Vancouver: David and Charles, 1978.

Lucas, Angela M. *Women in the Middle Ages: Religion, Marriage, Letters.* New York: St. Martin's, 1983.

Lucas, Angela M. and Peter J. "The Presentation of Marriage and Love in Chaucer's 'Franklin's Tale.'" *English Studies* 72.6 (December 1991): 501-12.

Macfarlane, Alan. *Marriage and Love in England: Modes of Reproduction 1300-1840.* New York: Basil Blackwell, 1986.

Makowski, Elizabeth. "The Conjugal Debt and Medieval Canon Law." Holloway, Wright, and Bechtold 129-44.

Mâle, Emile. *The Gothic Image: Religious Art in France of the Thirteenth Century.* Trans. Dora Nussey. New York: Harper & Row, 1958.

Mann, Jill. "Chaucer and the 'Woman Question.'" *This Noble Craft: Proceedings of the Xth Research Symposium of the Dutch and Belgian University Teachers of Old and Middle English and Historical Linguistics, Utrecht, 19-20 January 1989.* Ed. Erik Kooper. Amsterdam and Atlanta: Rodopi, 1991. 173-89.

———. *Chaucer and Medieval Estates Satire: The Literature of the Social Classes and the General Prologue to the Canterbury Tales.* Cambridge: Cambridge UP, 1973.

———. *Geoffrey Chaucer.* Atlantic Highlands, NJ: Humanities P International, 1991.

Mansfield, Mary C. *The Humiliation of Sinners: Public Penance in Thirteenth Century France.* Ithaca and London: Cornell UP, 1993.

Martin, Priscilla. *Chaucer's Women: Nuns, Wives and Amazons.* Iowa City: U of Iowa P, 1990.

Martindale, Wight, Jr. "Chaucer's Merchants: A Trade-Based Speculation on Their Activities." *Chaucer Review* 26 (1992): 309-16.

Mazzotta, Guiseppe. *Dante's Vision and the Circle of Knowledge.* Princeton: Princeton UP, 1993.

———. *The World at Play in Boccaccio's Decameron.* Princeton: Princeton UP, 1986.

McAlpine, Monica. "The Pardoner's Homosexuality and How It Matters." *PMLA* 95 (1980): 8-22.

McCall, John. "The Five-Book Structure in Chaucer's *Troilus.*" *Modern Language Quarterly* 23 (1962): 297-308.

McColly, William. "Why Chaucer's Knight Has No Coat of Arms." *English Language Notes* 21. 3 (1984): 1-6.

McFarlane, K. B. *John Wycliffe and the Beginnings of English Nonconformity.* New York: Macmillan, 1953.

McLaughlin, Eleanor Como. "Equality of Souls, Inequality of Sexes: Women in Medieval Theology." *Religion and Sexism: Images of Women in the Jewish and Christian Traditions.* Ed. Rosemary R. Reuther. New York: Simon & Schuster, 1974.

McLeod, Glenda. *Virtue and Venom: Catalogs of Women from Antiquity to the Renaissance.* Ann Arbor: U of Michigan P, 1991.

McNamara, Jo Ann. *The New Song: Celibate Women in the First Three Christian Centuries.* New York: Haworth, 1983.

———. "Sexual Equality and the Cult of Virginity in Early Christian Thought." *Feminist Studies* 3 (1976): 145-48.

McNeil, John T., and Helena M. Gamer, eds. *Medieval Handbooks of Penance.* Records of Civilization: Sources and Studies 29. New York: Columbia UP, 1938.

Medcalf, Stephen, ed. *The Later Middle Ages.* New York: Holmes and Meier, 1981.

Menocal, Maria Rosa. *The Arabic Tradition in Medieval Literary History: A Forgotten Heritage.* Philadelphia: U of Pennsylvania P, 1987.

Middleton, Anne. "The Idea of Public Poetry in the Reign of Richard II." *Speculum* 53 (1978): 94-114.

———. "War by Other Means: Marriage and Chivalry in Chaucer." *Studies in the Age of Chaucer.* Vol. 3. Ed. Thomas J. Heffernan. Knoxville: U of Tennessee, 1985. 119-33.

Mieszkowski, Gretchen. "Chaucer's Much Loved Criseyde." *Chaucer Review* 26. 2 (1991): 109-32.

Milis, Ludo J. R. *Angelic Monks and Earthly Men: Monasticism and Its Meaning to Medieval Society.* Woodbridge: Boydell, 1992.

Miller, Robert P., ed. *Chaucer: Sources and Backgrounds.* New York: Oxford UP, 1977.

———. "Chaucer's Pardoner, the Scriptural Eunuch, and the Pardoner's Tale." *Speculum* 30 (1955): 180-99.

Millett, Bella, and Jocelyn Wogan-Browne, eds. *Medieval English Prose for Women: Selections from the Katherine Group and Ancrene Wisse.* Oxford: Clarendon, 1990.

Minnis, A. J. *Medieval Theory of Authorship.* 2nd ed. Philadelphia: U of Pennsylvania P, 1988.

Minnis, Alastair. "Repainting the Lion: Chaucer's Profeminist Narratives." *Contexts of Pre-Novel Narrative: The European Tradition.* Ed. Roy Eriksen. Berlin: Mouton de Gruelter, 1994.

Moi, Toril. "Desire in Language: Andreas Capellanus and the Controversy of Courtly Love." Aers, *Medieval Literature* 11-33.

Moir, A. L. *The World Map in Hereford Cathedral Circa 1300.* 8th ed. Hereford: Friends of Hereford Cathedral, 1979.

Moore, Robert I. *The Formation of a Persecuting Society: Power and Deviance in Western Europe, 950-1250.* New York: Basil Blackwell, 1987.

———. *The Origins of European Dissent.* New York: St. Martin's, 1977.

Morrall, John B. *Political Thought in Medieval Times.* Toronto: U of Toronto P, 1980.

Morris, Colin. *The Papal Monarchy: The Western Church from 1050-1250.* Oxford: Clarendon, 1989.

Mullett, Michael. *Popular Culture and Popular Protest in Late Medieval and Early Modern Europe.* London, New York, and Sydney: Croom Helm, 1987.

Munro, John H. A. *Wool, Cloth, and Gold: The Struggle for Bullion in Anglo-Burgundian Trade 1340-1478.* Toronto: U of Toronto P, 1972.

Muscatine, Charles. *Chaucer and the French Tradition: A Study in Style and Meaning.* Berkeley: U of California P, 1964.

———. "Form, Texture and Meaning in Chaucer's 'Knight's Tale.'" *Chaucer: Modern Essays in Criticism.* Ed. Edward Wagenknecht. New York: Oxford UP, 1959. 60-82.

———. *The Old French Fabliaux.* New Haven and London: Yale UP, 1986.

———. *Poetry and Crisis in the Age of Chaucer.* Notre Dame and London: U of Notre Dame P, 1972.

Nevo, Ruth. "Motive and Mask in the 'General Prologue.'" *Modern Language Review* 58 (1963): 1-9.

Newman, Barbara. *From Virile Woman to WomanChrist: Studies in Medieval Religion and Literature.* Philadelphia: U of Pennsylvania P, 1995.

———. *Sister of Wisdom: St. Hildegard's Theology of the Feminine.* Berkeley and Los Angeles: U of California P, 1987.

Newman, F. X., ed. *The Meaning of Courtly Love.* Albany: State U of New York, 1968.

Nolan, Edward Peter. *Now Through a Glass Darkly: Specular Images of Being and Knowing from Virgil to Chaucer.* Ann Arbor: U of Michigan P, 1990.

Noonan, John T. *The Scholastic Analysis of Usury.* Cambridge: Harvard UP, 1957.

North, John David. *Chaucer's Universe.* New York: Oxford UP, 1988.

O'Brien, Timothy. "Troubling Waters: The Feminine and the Wife of Bath's Performance." *Modern Language Quarterly* 53.4 (1992): 377-91.

Olmert, Michael. "The Parson's Ludic Formula for Winning on the Road [to Canterbury]." *Chaucer Review* 20.2 (1985): 158-68.

Olson, Glending. "Chaucer's Idea of a Canterbury Game." *The Idea of Medieval Literature: New Essays on Chaucer and Medieval Culture in Honor of Donald R. Howard.* Eds. James M. Dean and Christian K. Zacher. Newark: U of Delaware, 1992. 72-90.

———. *Literature as Recreation in the Later Middle Ages.* Ithaca and London: Cornell UP, 1982.

———. "Making and Poetry in the Age of Chaucer." *Comparative Literature* 31 (1979): 272-90.

————. "The Marital Dilemma in the Wife of Bath's Tale: An Unnoticed Analogue and Its Chaucerian Court Context." *English Language Notes* 33. 1 (1995): 1-7.

Olson, Paul. *The Canterbury Tales and the Good Society*. Princeton: Princeton UP, 1986.

Olsson, Kurt. "'Securitas' and Chaucer's Knight." *Studies in the Age of Chaucer*. Vol. 9. Ed. Thomas J. Heffernan. Knoxville: U of Tennessee, 1987. 123-55.

Origo, Iris. *The Merchant of Prato*. New York: Penguin, 1963.

Ormrod, W. M. "The Peasants' Revolt and the Government of England." *Journal of British Studies* 29 (1990): 1-30.

————. *The Reign of Edward III: Crown and Political Society in England 1327-1377*. New Haven and London: Yale UP, 1990.

Otto of Freising. *The Two Cities: A Chronicle of Universal History to the Year 1146 A.D.* Eds. Austin P. Evans and Charles Knapp. Trans. Charles C. Mierow. New York: Columbia UP, 1928.

Owen, Charles A. *Pilgrimage and Storytelling in the Canterbury Tales: The Dialectic of "Ernest" and "Game."* Norman, OK: U of Oklahoma P, 1977.

Ozment, Stephen. *The Age of Reform (1250-1550): An Intellectual and Religious History of Late Medieval and Reformation Europe*. New Haven: Yale UP, 1980.

Paden, William, ed. *The Future of the Middle Ages: Medieval Literature in the 1990s*. Gainesville: UP of Florida, 1994.

Pagels, Elaine H. *Adam, Eve, and the Serpent*. New York: Random, 1988.

Panofsky, Erwin. *Gothic Architecture and Scholasticism*. Cleveland and New York: World, 1957.

Pantin, W. A. *The English Church in the Fourteenth Century*. 1955. Toronto: U of Toronto P, 1980.

Partner, Nancy F., ed. *Studying Medieval Women: Sex, Gender, Feminism*. Cambridge, MA: Medieval Academy, 1993.

Patterson, Lee. *Chaucer and the Subject of History*. Madison: U of Wisconsin P, 1991.

————. "'For the Wyves love of Bathe': Feminine Rhetoric and Poetic Resolution in the *Roman de la Rose* and the *Canterbury Tales*." *Speculum* 58 (1983): 656-95.

————. *Negotiating the Past: The Historical Understanding of Medieval Literature*. Madison: U of Wisconsin P, 1987.

————. "'No Man His Reson Herde': Peasant Consciousness, Chaucer's Miller, and the Structure of the *Canterbury Tales*." *Literary Practice and Social Change in Britain 1380-1530*. Ed. Lee Patterson. Berkeley and Los Angeles: U of California P, 1990. 111-55.

————. "'What Man Artow?': Authorial Self-Definition in 'The Tale of Sir Thopas' and 'The Tale of Melibee.'" *Studies in the Age of Chaucer*. Vol. 11. Ed. Thomas J. Heffernan. Knoxville: U of Tennessee, 1989. 117-76.

Payne, Robert O. *The Key of Remembrance: A Study of Chaucer's Poetics.* New Haven and London: Yale UP, 1963.

Pearsall, Derek. "Interpretative Models for the Peasants' Revolt." *Hermeneutics and Medieval Culture.* Eds. Patrick Gallacher and Helen Damico. Albany: State U of New York P, 1989. 63-71.

———. *The Life of Geoffrey Chaucer: A Critical Biography.* Oxford: Basil Blackwell, 1992.

Peck, Russell. "Biblical Interpretation: St. Paul and *The Canterbury Tales.*" Jeffrey. *Chaucer and the Scriptural Tradition* 144-70.

———. "Public Dreams and Private Myths: Perspectives in Middle English Literature." *PMLA* 90 (1975): 461-68.

Petrarch, Francesco. *Book Without a Name: A Translation of the Liber sine nomine.* Trans. Norman P. Zacour. Toronto: Pontifical Institute of Medieval Studies, 1973.

———. *Letters from Petrarch.* Trans. Morris Bishop. Bloomington and London: Indiana UP, 1966.

Petroff, Elizabeth Alvilda. *Body and Soul: Essays on Medieval Women and Mysticism.* New York and Oxford: Oxford UP, 1994.

Pichaske, David. *The Movement of the Canterbury Tales: Chaucer's Literary Pilgrimage.* Norwood, PA: Norwood Editions, 1977.

Portnoy, Phyllis. "Beyond the Gothic Cathedral: Post-Modern Reflections in *The Canterbury Tales.*" *Chaucer Review* 28. 3 (1994): 279-92.

Postan, M. M. *The Medieval Economy and Society: An Economic History of Britain in the Middle Ages.* London: Weidenfeld and Nicolson, 1972.

Prescott, Andrew. "London in the Peasants' Revolt: A Portrait Gallery." *The London Journal* 7 (1981): 125-43.

Prior, Sandra Pierson. "Parodying Typology and the Mystery Plays in the Miller's Tale." *Journal of Medieval and Renaissance Studies* 16 (1986): 57-73.

Purdon, Liam O., and Cindy L. Vitto, eds. *The Rusted Hauberk: Feudal Ideals of Order and Their Decline.* Gainesville: UP of Florida, 1994.

Ramsey, Lee C. *Chivalric Romances: Popular Literature in Medieval England.* Bloomington: Indiana UP, 1983.

Raybin, David. "'Wommen, Of Kynde, Desiren Libertee': Rereading Dorigen, Rereading Marriage." *Chaucer Review* 27.1 (1992): 65-86.

Razi, Zvi. *Life, Marriage and Death in a Medieval Parish: Economy, Society and Demography in Halesowen 1270-1400.* Cambridge: Cambridge UP, 1980.

Reeves, Marjorie, and Stephen Medcalf. "The Ideal, the Real, and the Quest for Perfection." Medcalf 56-107.

Reiss, Edmund. "Biblical Parody: Chaucer's 'Distortions' of Scripture." Jeffrey. *Chaucer and the Scriptural Tradition* 47-65.

——. "The Pilgrimage Narrative and *The Canterbury Tales.*" *Studies in Philology* 67 (1970): 295-305.

Rigby, S.H. *Chaucer in Context: Society, Allegory, and Gender.* Manchester and New York: Manchester UP, 1996.

Riley-Smith, Jonathan. "Crusading as an Act of Love." *History* (1980): 177-92.

Robertson, D. W., Jr. "'And for my land thus hastow mordred me?': Land Tenure, the Cloth Industry and the Wife of Bath." *Chaucer Review* 14 (1980): 403-20.

——. "Chaucer and Christian Tradition." Jeffrey. *Chaucer and the Scriptural Tradition* 3-32.

——. *A Preface to Chaucer: Studies in Medieval Perspectives.* Princeton: Princeton UP, 1962.

——. "The Probable Date and Purpose of Chaucer's 'Knight's Tale.'" *Studies in Philology* 84 (1987): 418-39.

Rogers, Katharine M. *The Troublesome Helpmate: A History of Misogyny in Literature.* Seattle and London: U of Washington P, 1966.

Rogers, William E. *Upon the Ways: The Structure of The Canterbury Tales.* English Literary Studies 36. Victoria, BC: U of Victoria, 1986.

Rosener, Werner. *Peasants in the Middle Ages.* Trans. Alexander Stutzer. Urbana and Chicago: U of Illinois P, 1992.

Rosenthal, Joel T., ed. *Medieval Women and the Sources of Medieval History.* Athens and London: U of Georgia P, 1990.

Rosenwein, Barbara H. *Rhinoceros Bound: Cluny in the Tenth Century.* Philadelphia: U of Pennsylvania P, 1982.

Ross, James Bruce, and Mary Martin McLaughlin, eds. *The Portable Medieval Reader.* New York: Penguin, 1977.

Ross, Lawrence J. "Symbol and Structure in the *Secunda Pastorum.*" *English Medieval Drama: Essays Critical and Contextual.* Eds. Jerome Taylor and Alan H. Nelson. Chicago and London: U of Chicago P, 1972. 177-212.

Russell, J. Stephen. "Is London Burning? A Chaucerian Allusion to the Rising of 1381." *Chaucer Review* 30.1 (1995): 107-9.

Russell, Josiah C. "Effects of Pestilence and Plague, 1315-1385." *Comparative Studies in Society and History* 8 (1965-66): 464-73.

Sanders, Barry. "Lie It as It Plays: Chaucer Becomes an Author." *Literacy and Orality.* Eds. David R. Olson and Nancy Torrance. Cambridge: Cambridge UP, 1991. 111-27.

Sayers, Jane. "Violence in the Medieval Cloister." *Journal of Ecclesiastical History* 41 (1990): 533-42.

Scaglione, Aldo. *Knights at Court: Courtliness, Chivalry and Courtesy from Ottonian Germany to the Italian Renaissance.* Berkeley and Los Angeles: U of California P, 1991.

Scanlon, Larry. "The Authority of Fable: Allegory and Irony in the 'Nun's Priest's Tale.'" *Exemplaria* 1.1 (1989): 43-68.

Scheps, Walter. "Chaucer's Numismatic Pardoner and the Personification of Avarice." *The Fourteenth Century, Acta* 4 (1977): 107-23.

Schibanoff, Susan. "Taking the Gold out of Egypt: The Art of Reading as a Woman." *Gender and Reading: Essays on Readers, Texts, and Contexts.* Eds. Elizabeth A. Flynn and Patrocino P. Schweickart. Baltimore: John Hopkins UP, 1986. 83-106.

Schimmelpfennig, Bernhard. *The Papacy.* Trans. James Sievert. New York: Columbia UP, 1992.

Schmitt, Jean-Claude. *The Holy Greyhound: Guinefort, Healer of Children Since the Thirteenth Century.* Trans. Martin Thom. Cambridge: Cambridge UP, 1983.

Scholz, Bernard W. "Hildegard von Bingen on the Nature of Woman." *American Benedictine Review* 31 (1980): 361-83.

Schulenberg, Jane Tibbetts. "The Heroics of Virginity: Brides of Christ and Sacrificial Mutilation." *Women in the Middle Ages and the Renaissance: Literary and Historical Perspectives.* Ed. Mary Beth Rose. Syracuse: Syracuse UP, 1986. 29-73.

Seznec, Jean. *The Survival of the Pagan Gods: The Mythological Tradition and Its Place in Renaissance Humanism and Art.* Trans. Barbara F. Sessions. New York: Harper & Row, 1953.

Shaffern, Robert W. "Learned Discussion of Indulgences for the Dead in the Middle Ages." *Church History* 61 (1992): 367-81.

Shahar, Shulamith. *The Fourth Estate: A History of Women in the Middle Ages.* Trans. Chaya Galai. London and New York: Methuen, 1983.

Sheingorn, Pamela, trans. *The Book of Saint Foy.* Philadelphia: U of Pennsylvania P, 1995.

Sièyes, Emmanuel Joseph *What Is the Third Estate?* Trans. M. Blondel. Ed. S. E. Finer. London and Dunmow: Pall Mall P, 1963.

Silverman, Albert H. "Sex and Money in Chaucer's 'Shipman's Tale.'" *Philological Quarterly* 32 (1953): 329-36.

Sir Gawain and the Green Knight. Ed. J. A. Burrow. New Haven and London: Yale UP, 1972.

Slack, Paul. "Responses to Plague in Early Modern Europe: The Implications of Public Health." *Social Research* 55 (1988): 433-53.

The Song of Roland: An Analytical Edition: II. Oxford Text and English Translation. Ed. and trans. Gerard J. Brault. University Park and London: Pennsylvania UP, 1978.

Southern, R. W. *Western Society and the Church in the Middle Ages.* New York: Penguin, 1970.

Spearing, A. C. *Medieval to Renaissance in English Poetry.* Cambridge: Cambridge UP, 1985.

Steinberg, Diane Vanner. "'We Do Usen Here No Wommen for to Selle': Embodiment of Social Practices in *Troilus and Criseyde.*" *Chaucer Review* 29.3 (1995): 259-73.

Stock, Brian. *The Implications of Literacy: Written Language and Models of Interpretation in the Eleventh and Twelfth Centuries.* Princeton: Princeton UP, 1983.

————. *Listening for the Text: On the Uses of the Past.* Baltimore and London: The Johns Hopkins UP, 1990.

Stopford, J. "Some Approaches to the Archaeology of Christian Pilgrimage." *World Archaeology* 26.1 (1994): 57-72.

Straus, Barrie Ruth. "'Truth' and 'Woman' in Chaucer's Franklin's Tale." *Exemplaria* 4. 1 (1992): 135-68.

Strohm, Paul. *Hochon's Arrow: The Social Imagination of Fourteenth-Century Texts.* Princeton: Princeton UP, 1992.

————. "Politics and Poetics: Usk and Chaucer in the 1380s." *Literary Practice and Social Change in Britain, 1380-1530.* Ed. Lee Patterson. Berkeley and Los Angeles: U of California P, 1990. 83-112.

————. *Social Chaucer.* Cambridge and London: Harvard UP, 1989.

Sumption, Jonathan. *Pilgrimage: An Image of Medieval Religion.* Totowa, NJ: Rowman and Littlefield, 1975.

Swanson, Robert N. *Universities, Academics and the Great Schism.* Cambridge: Cambridge UP, 1979.

Sypher, Wylie. *Four Stages of Renaissance Style: Transformations in Art and Literature 1400-1700.* Garden City, NY: Doubleday, 1955.

Szittya, Penn R. *The Antifraternal Tradition in Medieval Literature.* Princeton: Princeton UP, 1986.

Tawney, R. H. *Religion and the Rise of Capitalism: A Historical Study.* Gloucester, MA: Peter Smith, 1962.

Taylor, Paul Beekman. "The Uncourteous Knights of *The Canterbury Tales.*" *English Studies* 3 (1991): 209-19.

Theilmann, John M. "Medieval Pilgrimage and the Origins of Tourism." *Journal of Popular Culture* 20.4 (1986): 93-102.

Thomas of Celano. *Saint Francis of Assisi: First and Second Life of St. Francis with Selections from The Treatise on the Miracles of Blessed Francis.* Trans. Placid Hermann, O.F.M. Chicago: Franciscan Herald P, 1988.

Thompson, Sally. *Women Religious: The Founding of English Nunneries After the Norman Conquest.* Oxford: Clarendon, 1991.

Thormann, Janet. "The Circulation of Desire in the 'Shipman's Tale.'" *Literature and Psychology* 39. 3 (1993): 1-15.

Thrupp, Sylvia L. *Change in Medieval Society: Europe North of the Alps 1050-1500.* Toronto: U of Toronto P, 1988.

———. *The Merchant Class of Medieval London 1300-1500*. Ann Arbor: U of Michigan P, 1948.

Tillotson, J. H. "Peasant Unrest in the England of Richard III: Some Evidence from the Royal Records." *Historical Studies* 16 (1974): 1-16.

Travis, Peter W. "Chaucer's Trivial Fox Chase and the Peasants' Revolt of 1381." *Journal of Medieval and Renaissance Studies* 18. 2 (1988): 195-220.

Turner, Victor and Edith. *Image and Pilgrimage in Christian Culture*. New York: Columbia UP, 1978.

Tyerman, Christopher. *England and the Crusades, 1095-1588*. Chicago: Chicago UP, 1988.

Uitti, Karl. "Remarks on Medieval 'Courtoisie': Poetry and Grace." *Modern Philology* 92 (1994): 199-210.

Ullmann, Walter. *The Origins of the Great Schism: A Study in Fourteenth Century Ecclesiastical History*. Hamden, CT: Archon, 1972.

Vale, Juliet. *Edward III and Chivalry: Chivalric Society and Its Context*. Woodbridge, Suffolk: Boydell, 1982.

Vale, Malcolm. *War and Chivalry: Warfare and Aristocratic Culture in England, France, and Burgundy at the End of the Middle Ages*. Athens: U of Georgia P, 1981.

Van, Thomas A. "False Texts and Disappearing Women in the 'Wife of Bath's Prologue and Tale.'" *Chaucer Review* 29.2 (1994): 179-93.

Vance, Eugene. "Chaucer's Pardoner: Relics, Discourse and Frames of Propriety." *Literary History* 20 (1989): 723-45.

van Oort, Johannes. *Jerusalem and Babylon: A Study into Augustine's City of God and the Source of His Doctrine of the Two Cities*. Leiden: Brill, 1991.

Vauchez, André. *The Laity in the Middle Ages: Religious Beliefs and Devotional Practices*. Ed. Daniel E. Bornstein. Trans. Margery J. Schneider. Notre Dame and London: U of Notre Dame P, 1993.

Verdon, Timothy Gregory, ed. *Monasticism and the Arts*. Syracuse: Syracuse UP, 1984.

Von Simson, Otto. *The Gothic Cathedral: Origin of Gothic Form and the Medieval Concept of Order*. New York: Pantheon, 1962.

Wack, Mary Frances. *Lovesickness in the Middle Ages: The Viaticum and Its Commentaries*. Philadelphia: U of Pennsylvania, 1990.

Wagner, David, ed. *The Seven Liberal Arts in the Middle Ages*. Bloomington: Indiana UP, 1983.

Wakefield, Walter, and Austin P. Evans, eds. *Heresies of the High Middle Ages*. New York and London: Columbia UP, 1969.

Ward, Benedicta. *Miracles and the Medieval Mind: Theory, Record, and Event 1000-1215*. Rev. ed. Philadelphia: U of Pennsylvania P, 1987.

Ward, Jennifer C. *English Noblewomen in the Later Middle Ages*. London and New York: 1992.

Warner, Marina. *Alone of All Her Sex: The Myth and the Cult of the Virgin Mary*. New York: Random House, 1976.

Wasserman, Julian N., and Lois Roney, eds. *Sign, Sentence, Discourse: Language in Medieval Thought and Literature*. Syracuse: Syracuse UP, 1989.

Wasserman, Julian N., and Robert J. Blanch, eds. *Chaucer in the Eighties*. Syracuse: Syracuse UP, 1986.

Watts, D. G. "Popular Disorder in Southern England, 1250-1450." *Conflict and Community in Southern England: Essays in the Social History of Rural and Urban Labour from Medieval to Modern Times*. Ed. Barry Stapleton. New York: St. Martin's, 1992. 1-16.

Waugh, Scott L. *England in the Reign of Edward III*. Cambridge: Cambridge UP, 1991.

Wenzel, Siegfried. "Chaucer's Pardoner and His Relics." *Studies in the Age of Chaucer*. Vol. 11. Ed. Thomas J. Heffernan. Knoxville: New Chaucer Society, 1989. 37-43.

———. "The Pilgrimage of Life as a Late Medieval Genre." *Medieval Studies* 35 (1973): 370-88.

Wetherbee, Winthrop. *Chaucer and the Poets: An Essay on Troilus and Criseyde*. Ithaca and London: Cornell UP, 1984.

———. "Romance and Epic in Chaucer's Knight's Tale." *Exemplaria* 2 (1990): 303-28.

Wiethaus, Ulrike, ed. *Maps of Flesh and Light: The Religious Experience of Medieval Women Mystics*. Syracuse: Syracuse UP, 1993.

Williams, Arnold. "Chaucer and the Friars." *Speculum* 28 (1953): 499-513.

Williams, David. *The Canterbury Tales: A Literary Pilgrimage*. Boston: Twayne, 1987.

———. "Radical Therapy in the 'Miller's Tale.'" *Chaucer Review* 15 (1981): 227-55.

Williman, Daniel, ed. *The Black Death: The Impact of the Fourteenth Century Plague*. Binghamton, NY: Center for Medieval and Renaissance Studies, 1982.

Wilson, Katharina M., and Elizabeth M. Makowski. *Wykked Wyves and the Woes of Marriage: Misogamous Literature from Juvenal to Chaucer*. Albany: State U of New York P, 1990.

Wilson, Stephen, ed. *Saints and Their Cults: Studies in Religious Sociology, Folklore, and History*. Cambridge: Cambridge UP, 1983.

Wimsatt, James I. *Chaucer and His French Contemporaries: Natural Music in the Fourteenth Century*. Toronto: U of Toronto P, 1991.

Wood, Chauncey. "Artistic Intention and Chaucer's Uses of Scriptural Allusion." *Chaucer and the Scriptural Tradition*. Jeffrey 35-47.

Woodcock, Brian L. *Medieval Ecclesiastical Courts in the Diocese of Canterbury.* London: Oxford UP, 1952.

Woods, William F. "Chivalry and Nature in 'The Knight's Tale.'" *Philological Quarterly* 66 (1987): 287-301.

———. "A Professional Thyng: The Wife as Merchant's Apprentice in the 'Shipman's Tale.'" *Chaucer Review* 24 (1989): 139-49.

———. "'My Sweete Foo': Emelye's Role in 'The Knight's Tale'." *Studies in Philology* 88 (1991): 276-306.

Workman, Herbert B. *John Wyclif: A Study of the English Medieval Church.* Vol. 2. Oxford: Clarendon, 1926.

Yarnall, Judith. *Transformations of Circe: The History of an Enchantress.* Urbana and Chicago: U of Illinois P, 1994.

Yeager, R. F. "'Pax Poetica': On the Pacifism of Chaucer and Gower." *Studies in the Age of Chaucer.* Vol. 9. Ed. Thomas J. Heffernan. Columbus: New Chaucer Society, 1987. 97-121.

Zacher, Christian. *Curiosity and Pilgrimage: The Literature of Discovery in Fourteenth Century England.* Baltimore and London: The Johns Hopkins UP, 1976.

Ziegler, Philip. *The Black Death.* New York: Harper & Row, 1969.

Index

Printed in the United States
43107LVS00003B/1-9

9 780312 224660